Sparks

Refugee Life in the Confederacy

Refugee Life
in
the Confederacy

MARY ELIZABETH MASSEY

LOUISIANA STATE UNIVERSITY PRESS

Baton Rouge 1964

Manufactured in the United States of America by
Vail-Ballou Press, Inc., Binghamton, N. Y.

Library of Congress Catalog Card Number: 64-13639

Designed by William Nicoll

Published with the assistance
of a Ford Foundation grant

To Walter D. Smith

who gave me the time for writing this book
and to my fellow historians
at Winthrop College

Preface

The Civil War has inspired a greater number of books than any other war in United States history. Its causes and effects have been analyzed, innumerable issues debated, conclusions drawn, and theses advanced, criticized, and defended. Its battles, leaders, rookies, heroes, spies, and traitors have been accorded a significant place in history, and practically every aspect of the struggle has been subjected to interpretation and reinterpretation. It has excited the imagination, aroused the emotions, and appealed to the intellect and reason of both the amateur and professional historian. It would seem that there is little, if anything, left to tell, and yet much remains to be told about the Confederate homefront.

The most distinctive feature of the Civil War, as compared to those in which our country has more recently engaged, is that it was fought on American soil. Because the South was the battlefield, its citizens were the unwilling participants when the enemy came to their doors. Taken by surprise, the civilians were unprepared to meet the foe, unrealistic and ignorant of their responsibilities, and uninstructed as to what they should do. The problems, importance, and experiences of the Southern noncombatants merit further study, for their role in the war was important. Many historians have suggested that homefront conditions contributed to the South's defeat, but very few facets of the problem have been thoroughly investigated.

My purpose in writing this book is to present only one segment of the South's population, the refugees. Never before or since have so many Americans had to decide whether or not to abandon their homes in the face of an enemy invasion, and for this reason the tens of thousands of displaced Southerners have a unique place in our history. My original intention was to include all groups uprooted by the war—Confederate and Union sympathizers, Negroes, Indians, and whites, and those who left the South as well as those who tried to remain within Confederate lines. It soon became apparent that the inclusion of all refugees would necessitate a multivolumed study, and, advised by several authorities, whose opinions I value and respect, I decided to confine myself to the Confederate sympathizers who spent the war years trying to stay within the contracting Confederacy. All other displaced people are brought into the story only when they touch Confederate refugees in some way.

The problems incurred in writing this volume are similar to those encountered by anyone working in social history. I realized that it would take years to locate and investigate the manuscript materials, but I had no conception of the tediousness of the task. Although the records of those who refugeed afforded much information which was relatively easy to compile, it was necessary to carefully peruse thousands of letters and diaries which contained little or no mention of the displaced people. Traveling over a broad area from the Library of Congress to the University of Texas, I have tried to include refugees from all areas and from all social classes. That this study is heavily weighted in favor of the better educated groups I cannot deny, but these were the people who wrote during the war and who preserved their records. Because displaced people were more apt to lose or discard their personal papers than were those who stayed at home, much of the information has been gleaned from the writings of others and the newspapers of the period. I make no claim to having exhausted all sources, nor do I believe that anyone could. When I started the research I was naïve enough to think that I might do so, and it was during a hot summer at the University of Texas that Frank Wardlaw encouraged me by saying that no one could aspire to such a feat and I should content myself with something less. His statement gave me courage to continue, and now that the study is published I find that I did not use half of the material I collected; yet I have tried to present the story of a cross section of the Confederate refugees.

Organizing the book has been another major problem, and I now understand, as never before, what is meant by "bringing order out of chaos." The refugees were both individualistic and disorganized, and corralling them has been a challenge. I am sure that some readers will not approve of my organization, but after changing the plan several times, I have concluded this to be the most logical arrangement.

It is impossible to pay tribute to all who have assisted me with this book, but I want to mention those without whose help this volume could never have been written. To the many courteous, cooperative librarians and archivists who assisted me, I wish to say that I consider them to be the historian's best friend. Those who were compelled to endure my presence for extended periods merit special mention— James Patton, Anna Brooke Allan, and Carolyn Wallace of the Southern Historical Collection of the University of North Carolina; Mattie Russell of the Duke University Manuscript Divison; Llerena Friend of the University of Texas Barker Collection; V. L. Bedsole and his efficient staff of the Department of Archives and Manuscripts of Louisiana State University; and Ted Worley, recently of the Arkansas Historical Commission. Nor will I ever forget the services rendered by Gladys Smith, Annette Shinn, Susie McKeown, and Thelma Mayer of the Winthrop College Library.

I am deeply indebted to Bell I. Wiley and John K. Bettersworth for reading and criticizing all of the first draft of the manuscript, and to Dorothy Jones and William E. Rooney who read parts of it. It was Fletcher Green who gave me the idea for this study and who, with Mrs. Green, has encouraged all of my research projects for more years than any woman cares to admit. Stell and T. Harry Williams not only made valuable suggestions for the book but also made my summer of research in Baton Rouge the most pleasant I have ever known. Appreciated also is the encouragement given me by F. Jay Taylor, A. Elizabeth Taylor, David Donald, and Eleanor and Rembert Patrick. I am indebted to Donald Ellegood for the interest shown in the study long before it was completed and to Linda Long who has seen the book through press. A grant from the Southern Fellowship Fund made my first full summer of research in the refugee materials possible.

My long-suffering, cooperative colleagues at Winthrop merit special mention, for they have endured more than the public may realize. Mildred Beckwith and Alvin Duckett have listened to problems encountered in this project since the research first started, and their assistance and understanding are greatly appreciated. I am grateful for the interest shown by Charles S. Davis, and for the suggestions of John Moore, whose publishing experience has been invaluable to me. Ann Parks, Kathryn Davis Rawls, and Peggy Herron have deciphered, typed, retyped, and proofed the manuscript without once evidencing impatience with the author. When the galleys arrived during the Christmas season, Harry Brown graciously offered suggestions and made corrections which have greatly improved the book. I am very grateful for his assistance. I am also indebted to all of my friends who have understood the problems encountered when one tries to write amid other pressing academic duties.

All illustrations in this book were reproduced by the photographic department of the Henry E. Huntington Library, San Marino, California. The staff's cooperation, efficiency, and interest in the project merit this expression of appreciation.

I hope that the assistance given by so many people will not be regretted and their confidence in the subject and the author will not be shaken with the book's publication. Any defects or errors in the account are mine. Whether or not I have succeeded in portraying Confederate refugee life, I feel as though I have traveled the road with my "forgotten people."

M. E. M.

Contents

Illustrations

Following page 82

The citizens of Atlanta, ordered from the city by
General Sherman, load their household
effects on U.S. Army wagons.

Women refugees encamped near Vicksburg during the siege.

Georgia refugees in flight before Sherman's army
during its March to the Sea.

Flight of the Charleston citizens during the bombardment, 1863.

The flight of civilians from Savannah in December,
1861, when attack appeared imminent.

Southern refugees moving north from
Arkansas and southern Missouri.

Refugees moving south from Atlanta, 1864.

Registered enemies in New Orleans taking the oath of allegiance
to the United States in order to avoid banishment
by Federal authorities, 1863.

Refugees in Kingston, Georgia, 1864.

Unionist refugees in the swamps of Louisiana.

Refugee Life in the Confederacy

... *brought to their own doorsteps*

On a warm, sunny morning in May, 1861, pensive Judith Brockenbrough McGuire sat at a window of her Alexandria, Virginia, home. Gazing across the placid Potomac she could see the Capitol Dome in the distance. She could hear the drums beating in Washington, but an ominous stillness surrounded her in Alexandria. Her children had been sent to places of safety, most of her neighbors had left the vulnerable area, and the Episcopal High School, where her husband was principal, was closed. Mrs. McGuire confided to her diary that loneliness engulfed her and the talk of war made her nervous, but she had chosen to remain with John McGuire in their home while praying that conflict might be averted and that family and friends soon might be reunited.[1]

Judith McGuire had spent the tense days since mid-April sewing and cooking for the Virginia troops encamped nearby, attending services in the half-empty church and tending her plants as lovingly as if she were sure of gathering the flowers. But she sensed that this would not be her good fortune, and, preparing for any eventuality, she had buried the family silver and packed personal belongings that would be stored or taken with her should war come. Mrs. McGuire realized that Alexandria's proximity to Washington and her husband's strong secessionist sympathies would make it necessary for the couple to flee when the day of invasion arrived. That day dawned on May 25. As soon as John McGuire heard that Federal troops had occupied the town, he and his wife decided that they must leave their home immediately and seek refuge with friends. They hoped their displacement would be temporary and, like most refugees, expected that they soon would be home again. Such was not to be their fate, for at that moment they were beginning four hard years of refugee life. The McGuires were among the first of the Civil War refugees, but they would soon have plenty of company in their camp.

It was from the environs of Washington that the first mass exodus of Southern sympathizers began. A few miles up the Potomac from the McGuire home was the gracious mansion of Mary Custis Lee, who was now in her fifties and suffering from arthritis. In April she had said farewell to her husband and sent him to Richmond to assume command of the Virginia troops, but no sooner had he gone than he began urging his wife to leave "Arlington" with all possible speed. This Mrs. Lee found difficult to do, for the stately home held cherished memories and heirlooms, many of which were associated with her great-grandmother, Martha Washington. Realizing that General Robert E. Lee was right in insisting that she leave, she busied herself trying to decide which of the family possessions should be stored on the estate and which should be sent elsewhere for safe keeping. On May 14, she left her home, destined never again to live there.[2]

Thus began a movement that was to grow and spread during the Civil War, a movement which would eventually involve tens of thousands of Southern people and create a new social class, the refugees. A young North Carolinian, writing his wife a few hours after the First Battle of Manassas, surveyed the plight of civilians in northern Virginia and sadly mused that a people never realize "the horrors of war" until it is "brought to their own doorsteps."[3] The truth of his statement was to become glaringly evident before and long after he became a war casualty. As the conflict swept over the South and battles raged on the "doorsteps" in every state of the Confederacy, uprooted civilians became homeless wanderers. They created problems for themselves, other civilians, and for civil and military authorities. As battles were fought, as cities fell, as areas were endangered by skirmishes, forays, and lawlessness, the residents took safety in flight. Although the war's movements were erratic, affecting first one area and then another, refugees were created somewhere during every year. Once uprooted, a person was apt to retain his homeless status for the duration of the struggle, and the chances were that he would find himself in flight not once but many times, tossed about like a straw in the wind, his condition worsening with each passing year.

Some military events were more responsible for the mass exodus of civilians than others, but each had its effect. When one views the broad, general sweep of the war, year by year, he can better understand the movement of the people as it coincided with the military activities. In 1861, there were comparatively few refugees, and these came from the fringes of the Confederacy—northern and western Virginia, Kentucky, Missouri, and the coastal areas. The fall of Hatteras, Ship Island, and Port Royal caused many of their residents to move inland, and Confederate sympathizers in Kentucky and Missouri fled southward as Unionists went into the Federal-held areas of both states. In western and southern Missouri there was widespread guerrilla activity that made many homeless, a situation prevailing before the war but growing worse after it began.

In 1862, the situation changed rapidly, making it the year of greatest panic over the widest area, although most of the more spectacular mass evacuations by military authorities did not take place this early. The real meaning of the war dawned on the people in the late winter and spring as thousands left their homes and fled before the advancing Federal armies. Many who did not run when the enemy first approached were caught within Federal lines, but if life in the occupied zone became unbearable, or if the authorities considered them dangerous or obnoxious, these people then joined their neighbors as refugees. This was the year of the Peninsular Campaign, the fall of Norfolk, and the beginning of widespread activity in the Shenandoah Valley. Thousands of Virginians were driven from their homes, and in the area now designated as West Virginia the Southern sympathizers were leaving as the Unionists were arriving. Late in 1862, one of the most pathetic mass movements experienced by Virginians took place when the citizens of Fredericksburg were ordered to leave the city on the eve of battle, and rich and poor alike were cast out in the cold of winter with no place to go.

It was also in 1862 that the Federals penetrated the coastal areas of Georgia, Florida, and the Carolinas. Roanoke Island and New Bern fell, Fort Pulaski was captured, and for the first time, Charleston was seriously threatened. Along the Gulf Coast, there was great activity, and in April one of the first major shocks of the war occurred when New Orleans fell. David G. Farragut then began his ascent of the Mississippi and by June his gunboats had passed Vicksburg, a maneuver which sent the planters scurrying into the interior of Louisiana, Mississippi, and Arkansas. Although the fall of New Orleans had come so suddenly that relatively few of the residents left before the appearance of the Federals, many did move out in the summer and fall when the policies of General Benjamin F. Butler created an unfavorable climate for those of strong Confederate views. As soon as

New Orleans capitulated, Baton Rouge was seized with terror, and many who could do so left the city. It was also in 1862 that hundreds of citizens from southern and eastern Louisiana began their trek to Texas, a movement which was to continue throughout the war. Elsewhere along the Gulf other important events transpired, including the Confederate evacuation of Pensacola, Florida, and the fall of Galveston, but by the time the Texas island-city came under the control of the Union Army, most of its residents had already left for the mainland. After Galveston was retaken by the Confederates in 1863, the military authorities discouraged the refugees' returning home.

In other areas of the Confederacy, the Federals were executing their anaconda policy with spectacular success, and Southerners were swept ahead of the retreating Confederates. In February the capture of Fort Henry on the Tennessee River and Fort Donelson on the Cumberland opened these rivers to further penetration by the foe. Before the end of the month Nashville had fallen, but the residents were notified of this probability in time for many to leave the city. The days immediately preceding the entrance of the Federals were chaotic and confusing ones as the civilians rushed about making frantic preparations for flight. By March 1, U. S. Grant's army had entrenched itself at Pittsburg Landing on the Tennessee River and was preparing to battle the Confederates. In April the battle was fought at Shiloh, and later the same month General Henry W. Halleck besieged Corinth, which the Confederate forces evacuated in May. While these events were taking place Federal gunboats were moving down the Mississippi to join Farragut, and in June, Fort Pillow fell, and Memphis two days after it. As the Union forces moved down the Mississippi and up its tributaries, many of the inhabitants along the banks left their farms and plantations. With the Mississippi patrolled by Federal gunboats and most of Tennessee and the northern third of Arkansas controlled by Federal forces, the Confederate-held territory had contracted alarmingly by the end of 1862.

The year 1863 witnessed momentous developments. The change was less rapid as the war of attrition developed, but the total number of refugees increased during these months. In Virginia, much of the area previously fought over was still a battlefield, and citizens from the northern and western portions of the state continued to swell the ranks of the homeless. Along the coast of North Carolina there was military activity, but no deep penetration. In South Carolina, Charleston was experiencing bombardment and her citizens were encouraged to leave the city, but she was held by the Confederates throughout 1863 and

1864. Meanwhile, refugees from widespread areas of the South were flocking into the Piedmont and mountain districts of the Carolinas, for here was to be found maximum security in the period of growing insecurity. Savannah, like Charleston, was threatened but continued to hold out against enemy attack as she, too, absorbed incoming refugees, most of whom were from the Sea Islands and Florida.

Along the Gulf Coast in 1863, there was virtually a stalemate in military activity but not in the creation of refugees. Mobile was endangered but held, as she would be until 1865, but the city was becoming dangerously overcrowded with an influx of exiles banished from New Orleans by General N. P. Banks. Military and civil authorities, alarmed by the heavy concentration of noncombatants in this vital coastal city, urged that those who were not necessary to the defense of Mobile withdraw to interior sections of the state. Hundreds of civilians obeyed and joined the ranks of the refugees. Brownsville and Corpus Christi, on the Texas coast, were captured, and many Texans were similarly displaced. In the Mississippi Valley the movements were slow but decisive in 1863. The siege of Vicksburg contributed an interesting and thrilling chapter to refugee life as many of the people caught in this maneuver moved into caves during the shelling of the town. When Jackson and Vicksburg fell in the summer of 1863, hundreds of Mississippians moved eastward into Confederate territory. In this same year, Little Rock was captured and a part of its citizenry fled to southern Arkansas and Texas. Late in 1863, the battles in and around Chattanooga swept additional persons southward and eastward into Georgia and the Carolinas.

By 1864 the Confederacy was crumbling but the movement of refugees was being accelerated and expanded as additional civilians either chose to move or were forced to do so by military command. For a great many people, these displacements were not their first. Some were already refugees when they were again compelled to seek safety, but the areas promising security were more limited now than ever before. As the homeless pressed into them, living conditions became deplorable. In the East, only interior Georgia, the Carolinas, southern Virginia, and parts of Alabama and Florida were as yet uninvaded, and they could not be expected to accommodate adequately the hordes who arrived in the last year of the war. The fifteen months preceding Appomattox were the darkest the South had ever known. When 1864 dawned, the Confederacy was facing probable defeat and her refugeeing citizenry was filled with despair and homesickness. The Federal forces under W. T. Sherman were beginning their slow penetration of north Georgia with their immediate destination Atlanta. Before autumn arrived this campaign had added appreciably to the refugee rolls as Southerners fled in advance of the enemy. When Atlanta was threatened during the summer, the city was crowded with homeless humanity that had taken refuge there in the belief that it was completely safe. Many of the noncombatants left when the battle for the city began, but others who could not or would not leave remained to face the Federals. After Atlanta was captured and occupied by Union forces, General Sherman created hundreds of refugees when he ordered a mass civilian evacuation. In so doing he secured for himself the unique distinction of having been responsible for the single largest forced evacuation of an entire city during the Civil War. Few acts of the enemy provoked more widespread criticism among the Confederates than did this order, and few events of the war were so filled with human interest and pathos. The March to the Sea in the fall of 1864 compounded the misery of the refugees who had settled in the path of the advancing army, and again Sherman's actions provoked civilians to flight.

In Virginia, Grant's Wilderness Campaign and his strategy of fighting along his famous "line" also converted home-loving people into refugees. Very few noncombatants living to the south and southwest of Richmond had left their homes during the war, and for four years a great many people living in this area had received the homeless from other parts of the Confederacy. In 1864–65, hosts and guests alike were uprooted as the battles reached their doors. Hundreds of Petersburg citizens fled when the siege commenced, and many who had nowhere to go were forced to live under the stars, in tents, or in crowded farmhouses and outbuildings that dotted the countryside. Others from the stricken areas flocked into Richmond, already so crowded with noncombatants that the Confederate officials were fearful that their presence would seriously impede its defense. By the last winter and spring of the war, the refugees had very few choices of a home within Confederate lines.

In addition to the major campaigns during the last months of the war, there were the inevitable skirmishes, raids, foraging expeditions, attacks, and counterattacks, all of which threw the people into a panic and, in many cases, aroused the residents who had settled down, determined to wait out the war and run no more. Both armies were in part responsible for these sporadic movements and for the depredations which resulted. In 1864, the Confederates raided wide areas under Federal control as Jubal Early, wearing the mantle of Jackson and

Stuart, rode through the Valley of Virginia meeting the attacks of Philip Sheridan and David Hunter. The civilian population living in their paths had cause enough to forget the meaning of "security." In Tennessee and northern Mississippi, Nathan Bedford Forrest was on the loose and his fellow in arms, the swashbuckling John Morgan, was making his last raids into Kentucky and eastern Tennessee. The crippled John Hood, who had lost Atlanta, added to the confusion by turning his defeated army back toward Tennessee and doing battle for Nashville in December, 1864. West of the Mississippi, Sterling Price proved himself to be a determined fighter when he invaded Missouri in the belief that he could yet win that state. He spent October contesting Federal authority by means of raids which endangered the lives and property of the people. Such activities as these by the Confederate forces were primarily death gasps and were more colorful and daring than effective. Not only were they destructive, they created panic and hysteria in civilian ranks and served to raise the hopes of a great many loyal Southerners who were ever-willing to mistake wishful thinking for reality. As they anxiously and hopefully watched these exploits, refugees often expressed the belief that such daring deeds as these would change the course of the war and permit them to return to their homes, which would soon be within Confederate lines. When their predictions failed to materialize they were left more despondent than before, and as their morale sagged and their hopes vanished, homesickness engulfed them.

By 1865, the refugees had been churned, tossed, and bruised as had no people in the history of the nation. Many had quit running, either because they no longer cared what happened or because they had no place to go. Most were as weary as the soldiers in the field. A few were still living in comparative peace, and among these were the Confederates and Unionists in the mountains of Virginia, North Carolina, and Tennessee, but in the last months of the war, even they were subjected to frequent raids. Inland areas of the Carolinas had remained relatively untouched by the war and had continuously absorbed thousands of refugees throughout the conflict. In early 1865 Columbia was as crowded as any city in the Confederacy, with the possible exception of Richmond. In December, 1864, hundreds from Savannah and Charleston fled to Columbia in an effort to avoid Sherman's forces, but no sooner had these refugees reached their destination than word was received that the Federals were headed straight for the South Carolina capitol. When this news was circulated wild preparations for flight ensued, and the experienced refugees, as well as those who had heretofore lived an undisturbed life in this "safe" town, were on the move jamming the railroads and the highways that led toward Charlotte and the upcountry. Not long after they fled the call came to evacuate Richmond, and the officials and plain folk from Virginia started South. The two groups met head on in North Carolina, creating bedlam and confusion reminiscent of some of the battles and routs of recent years. George Stoneman and his Federal forces rode down from the mountains, adding to the chaos which already prevailed. In the midst of all this, General Lee surrendered in Virginia, followed by Joseph E. Johnston in North Carolina and by Edmund Kirby Smith in Texas. The officials who had left Richmond with President Jefferson Davis in early April had scattered and were in flight toward various destinations to the South and West. The President was captured in Georgia in May. The war was over.

Four years had passed since Judith McGuire and Mary Custis Lee left their homes on the Potomac, but in these years thousands of people from all walks of life had followed their lead. Southern civilians had experienced "the horrors of war . . . brought to their own doorsteps," and because of this they had become refugees. The end of the conflict found many of them hundreds of miles from home. The guns were silent, peace had come, but the refugees faced yet another move. They must again gather together their personal effects and make their way back to places from which they had come. Like the soldiers, they would have stories to tell, for they, too, had been away "at war."

. . . to be or not to be a refugee

The invasion of the Confederacy forced thousands of Southerners to become refugees, but to explain the movement with this
simple generalization would be to overlook numerous individual reasons for flight. It was a distinctive combination of circumstances which displaced every person and, while specific broad explana-
tions may be given, the thinking, attitudes, and temperament of the
individual also determined his decision of whether "to be or not to be"
a refugee. The question of whether or not to leave home confronted
millions of people during the Civil War, and most did not find the
answer easy. Nor is it simple to analyze their reasoning in the matter,
for only a minority took the time to record their inner conflicts during
the period of indecision. Although some were specific as to their
doubts, fears, and reasons for flight, most refugees wrote in retrospect
and tended to treat superficially, if at all, the thoughts and misgivings
of that crucial period. Therefore it is more difficult to analyze specific factors which determined the people's displacement than it is to
describe their other experiences, but one fact stands out: it was never
a pleasant experience to leave one's home.

All people did not have time to ponder the question of fleeing or
remaining, for when the enemy appeared unexpectedly the problem
confronted them abruptly. Too often they fled without pausing to
reflect upon the consequences, usually assuming that their displacement would be temporary. This was especially true early in the war
when they viewed the situation unrealistically and overconfidently.
Southerners had not bargained for a war on their doorsteps and no
group evidenced this more than those who fled in haste and panic be-

fore the advancing foe. A Georgia refugee, describing her hysterical flight early in the war, pensively wrote that had she known her displacement would last for more than a few weeks she would never have left her home. Months and years had passed and she had not been able to return because the enemy was *"still* in possession" of the area.[1] Other refugees soon regretted their decisions, as did this Georgia lady, and very few of those who left their homes early in the war thought that it would be for the duration of the conflict.

The greatest displacement agent during the war was fear of the enemy. More Southerners fled from their homes in advance of an invasion than were expelled by military authorities, but mass expulsions by Federal officers were highly publicized and used effectively as propaganda designed to arouse anger and a fighting spirit within the Confederacy. These exiles, driven from their homes by the hundreds, attracted greater attention than did those who left voluntarily because they were afraid of what might happen to them when the enemy arrived. The period immediately preceding an attack was one filled with rumors and half-truths, a condition often created by refugees passing through the community. Usually they had left their homes because they had heard of enemy atrocities and not necessarily experienced them, and the stories were exaggerated with each telling. Refugees seemed dedicated to creating other refugees and their crusade was eminently successful. As they told tales of pillage, destruction, murder, and rape, many who listened determined also to seek safety in flight.

Although phlegmatic people were known to react irrationally during a preinvasion scare, they were not as likely to be swayed by rumors or moved by fear of what might happen. But when normally cautious people became hysterical and threw discretion to the wind, they had a decided effect on others. When Sherman's army approached Columbia a resident later recalled that "the need for getting out of town was communicated one to another. . . . Many who had not thought of leaving . . . caught the contagious panic."[2] A Virginia editor told of refugees rushing into Harrisonburg screaming, "The Yankees are just below the town." When he went to the door he saw "respectable gentlemen" terrorized and "running around madly making preparations to leave." Bankers, merchants, professional men, and postal employees were "packing up valuables . . . making all haste for . . . a speedy exit." He refused to be aroused, returned to his desk and, in this instance, enjoyed the "last laugh" because this turned out to be a false alarm.[3]

Very often an alarm proved to be false, and it was sometimes months or years before the enemy appeared in an area which had earlier been alerted. Yet fear electrified the atmosphere for miles around when his presence was made known, and civilians fled from their homes. The fall of Fort Hatteras in August, 1861, caused North Carolinians along the coast to move inland. Six months before New Bern fell many of its citizens left, and others who wanted to get away were frustrated by uncooperative railroad officials who refused to take them aboard with "their goods and chattels." These early refugees were more ridiculed than pitied and were referred to as "the laughing stock" of North Carolina, but by the time New Bern fell, displaced people in general were commanding greater sympathy, and those from eastern North Carolina were commended for preferring the life of a nomad "to living under . . . Yankee rule." [4] Premature or unnecessary flight usually provoked criticism, but when one community fell to the Federals it set off a chain reaction. People far removed from the area began their preparations to leave, and the fall of New Bern caused Raleigh citizens to start searching for a refuge. One woman wrote that the townspeople expected the enemy to march directly into their city, and for weeks "this was the sole topic of conversation." [5] Yet it was not until the end of the war that Federal forces occupied Raleigh.

A year before Galveston fell, the inhabitants were leaving "in a constant stream," and when it was taken, fear gripped Houston as its citizens prepared to leave.[6] When Port Royal was captured, hundreds of residents from the islands and coastal areas went to Charleston. Included in this group was an eighty-five-year-old woman who had not gone to Charleston for fourteen years "for fear the trip would kill her," but was now willing to tempt fate when the Yankees were abroad in the land.[7] The same day that she arrived in the city with her atrocity stories, a resident noted that there was "great panic particularly among the women in Charleston" and that men were busy removing their families inland.[8] This exodus was triggered by fear, and when the immediate danger had passed many of these first refugees returned.

Any mass exodus of an hysterical people from an urban community was spectacular, but some were especially exciting and colorful. When word reached Nashville on a Sunday morning that Fort Donelson had fallen and the Cumberland River was open to invasion, congregations unceremoniously departed the churches to confer with family and friends as to what should be done. Homes and streets were scenes of mass hysteria. One spectator wrote that Nashville "became perfectly paralyzed . . . panic-stricken," and she confessed that she was "nearly frantic." [9] A newspaper correspondent reported that the panic had "never been equalled since Bull Run. . . . All who could do so packed up and fled. . . ." He was obviously disgusted with those who accepted rumor for fact when he noted, "Grown up men would tell you the enemy would be in the city in two hours, when he was at least sixty or seventy miles distant." [10]

A Virginia lady described the mass hysteria in Richmond when McClellan's forces threatened the city in the spring of 1862. She had never seen anything to equal the "extravagant rumors" which were being circulated, and she noted that the public was ready "to receive anything, no matter how absurd." [11] It was much the same story in all parts of the Confederacy at some time during the war. Panic seized the citizens of Baton Rouge when they heard New Orleans had fallen and those in Memphis when Fort Pillow was lost. Hundreds left Savannah when Fort Pulaski was captured and Atlantans prepared for flight after the Battle of Kennesaw Mountain. It was in the urban areas that hysteria was created from the fear of many people in close contact with each other, but those living in rural areas, when given warning, were also cast adrift because they were afraid of what the enemy might do.

Southerners who refused to be swept along with the mob were often critical of those who joined the exodus. And those who were most caustic were often the ones who had not yet been faced with the dilemma of whether or not to become refugees. One in this group was Samuel Andrew Agnew, a Presbyterian minister in Tippah County, Mississippi. He spent the first two years of the war interviewing and criticizing displaced people who passed his home en route to places of refuge in Alabama, Georgia, and the Carolinas. He noted that most of these passersby had left their homes because they feared what might happen when the Federals came, and he thought this extremely foolish. When fear gripped his neighborhood in 1863, his aunt "got in a fizz about going" to South Carolina, a condition which disgusted her nephew, and when she left he drew a sigh of relief as he wrote, "I hope she will be contented now." Although Agnew briefly toyed with the idea of leaving his home, he decided to remain, but he continued to evidence an interest in all refugees who passed his door.[12]

It was not always fear that made noncombatants join the refugee ranks. Men in the service were concerned about their families' safety when the enemy moved toward their homes. If they were in a position to know that danger was imminent, they often wrote their wives and mothers to leave, but in some cases the women told them of impending disaster and sought their advice. This was a decision few women were prepared to make although many did when there was no time to seek advice. General Leonidas Polk alerted his wife to the possibility that she would have to leave Nashville should Fort Donelson fall, and when he heard it had fallen he wrote that she must depart immediately.[13] Mrs. Polk agreed to his demands, but other wives were not moved as easily. When John A. Benbury feared for the safety of his wife and infant daughter living on the family plantation near Edenton, North Carolina, he spent weeks urging her to move to the interior. But not until the Ambrose E. Burnside expedition appeared in the waters near Edenton did she consent to leave her home.[14]

Jeremy Francis Gilmer, a colonel at the time, experienced a complete breakdown of domestic discipline when he devoted nearly three months to his campaign to get his wife out of Savannah in 1862. During the period he expressed his fear that "the Lincolnites" would take the city and she might then be unable to leave. He issued order after order for her to leave at once, and when his letters went unheeded he telegraphed her to get out of the city. When this failed, he wired military authorities in Savannah to order her to leave. He warned her to *"be not deceived"* by the assurances of the Confederates that all was well, for "such statements" were meant only to "inspire confidence among soldiers." [15] Mrs. Gilmer was enjoying her life in Savannah and was determined to remain. His orders irritated her and she let it be known when she asked, "Would you have us flying like sheep all over the country?" She thought it foolish to "run from the Yankees," and she refused to hide "in some dark corner of the land from fear of them," but she promised that she would leave "before the Union flag was hoisted" in Savannah.[16]

When it was impossible or inadvisable for all members of a household to leave in advance of the foe, those thought to be in greatest danger were sometimes sent away. Parents were often afraid of the fate that might befall their daughters, especially late in the war, after stories of ravage and rape had spread through the South. Many young women were sent to places thought to be safe, usually to the homes of friends or relatives. When Sherman's forces neared the South Carolina line, one mother described her fears and those of many others when she wrote that she had sent her daughter to Chester because "it was thought safer for a young girl just grown up to be well out of the reach of Yankee soldiery." [17]

It was sometimes expedient for men to leave home when the enemy approached, especially if they were violent secessionists, leaders of the Confederacy, or soldiers on leave. Not only did they risk capture, imprisonment, mistreatment, and even death if they remained, but their presence might result in the enemy's retaliating against their families. Although men were usually reluctant to leave their wives and children to face the Federals alone, the women very often insisted that they go even when they risked being called cowards by their neighbors. Many of these refugees fled to nearby woods or some other secluded spot, but others went so far from home that they were cut off from their families for an extended period. After Hamilton Polk, son of General Leonidas Polk, was wounded early in the war, he joined his mother's refugee household in Asheville, North Carolina. During the last winter of the war rumors of raids were often circulated in the community, and when they appeared reliable his mother and sister, Katherine Polk Gale, insisted that he go to Flat Rock, twenty miles distant. There he would remain until the danger had passed.[18]

Pressures from without the family as well as from within engendered fear in the people and drove them from their homes. Although sometimes unintentionally, ministers sounded the alarm that started the flight of their congregations. Six weeks before the First Battle of Manassas, a clergyman in Orange, Virginia, "warned the people that in another month . . . [their] homes . . . [would] probably be in the possession of the enemy," and he suggested that it might be well for them to contemplate the consequences.[19] Many of those who pondered the minister's words and observed the steady stream of refugees coming through the village concluded that they should leave ahead of the enemy's arrival. But often more effective than a preacher's words was his own decision to become a refugee. This was most apt to happen after the Federals occupied the community and ordered him to refrain from praying for the Confederacy and Jefferson Davis, and to offer prayers for the Union and Abraham Lincoln. When he could neither obey nor evade the order, the minister either left voluntarily or was driven away. If he held violent secessionist views or was an outspoken defender of the Confederacy, it was wise for him to avoid the clutches of the enemy, but when a preacher fled, a part of his congregation was sure to follow. Reverend John Bachman, who had offered the prayer at the South Carolina Secession Convention, left Charleston when it was presumed that General Sherman was heading toward that city, and his move provoked others to flight.[20] Because a clergyman's departure was usually followed by that of a part of his flock, ministers were often compared with Moses because they led their "children" to a "Promised Land."

As important as the preacher's words and deeds in determining the course to be followed by his parishioners were acts of violence against his person. The people were shocked that any religious leader would be subjected to brutal treatment, and if this could happen to the clergy, the safety of his congregation was also jeopardized. Violent assaults of this kind were most apt to occur in areas where law enforcement had broken down, where the minister expressed the minority opinion, or where a sizable group resented his ideas and his power to influence others. Brutality was usually the weapon of ruffians who thought such extreme measures necessary if the opposition was to be silenced. It was not the system employed by military officials, but the people rarely understood this. Alarmed by the attacks on clergymen, they sought safety elsewhere. When George Eagleton, a Presbyterian minister in Knoxville, refused to abandon his Confederate views after being ordered to do so, a gang of rowdies dragged him from his bed "in the middle of the night," and whipped him until he "fell unconscious." Soon thereafter he went to Bristol, followed by members of his congregation.[21]

Newspapers also exerted a tremendous pressure on the Southern people. Their effect depended on local conditions and the editor's views, but the press often sought to create a fear so great that citizens would flee in terror from the community. When military necessity made it advisable for noncombatants to leave an area, newspapers used every means at their command to force people out of town. They warned of possible injury, death, humiliation, and, if the citizens refused to leave, possible loss of the city and even of the war. Dozens of editorials cited the tragic case of New Orleans which had been sacrificed in order to protect the women and children from the horrors of a bombardment. Readers were reminded that the same catastrophe could befall their community. The press also cautioned citizens that should they delay departure until the enemy attacked, they would find transportation facilities either commandeered by the army or inadequate to the demand. Traffic would be at a standstill because of the press of humanity in flight, and civilians would then be caught in the line of fire. Thousands were sure to be killed. No frontier preacher ever pictured the torments of hell more vividly than the journalists described what might happen in a mass evacuation of a city under attack.

Arguments of this type were the editors' way of supporting military authorities, and although they were never successful in removing all noncombatants from a threatened area, editorials were generally more successful than the mild, unenforced orders of Confederate officials. Charlestonians afford an extreme example of a people who were exceedingly reluctant to establish permanent headquarters elsewhere, but the local newspapers fought a three-year battle to convince them that this would be a wise move. They printed and editorialized on the military orders, publicized the free "refugee tickets" available to those who could not pay their travel expenses, and criticized those who had once uprooted themselves only to return. Many times they urged fathers to send away "their tender ones," while publishing glowing accounts from Charleston refugees who were happily situated elsewhere.[22] That this crusade was only partially successful is indicated in an editorial published in the *Courier* on January 18, 1865. With the end of the war less than three months distant, the editor asked that men remove their families "to places of safety," and then return to the city "to enter on the duties of war."

The relations between refugees and both armies will be discussed more fully elsewhere, but because military policies were often responsible for the peoples' displacement, cursory mention is made here. Commanders at various times ordered the evacuation of communities but the Confederates usually "advised," "exhorted," "requested," or "urged" civilians to leave. Rarely did they force them, at the point of a gun, to do so. Federal orders were more positively stated and more often enforced. The primary reasons for group or individual expulsion were to rid an occupied area of subversive elements, to prove by example that people must conform or be expelled, and to create economic and psychological problems within the already hard-pressed Confederacy. Many Southerners left Federal-held territory voluntarily when life became unbearable, when they wanted to be in contact with loved ones within Confederate lines, or when they had suffered such irreparable property damage that they were compelled to move for economic reasons. Whatever their reasons for leaving Federal areas, refugees who went into those under Confederate control told their tales of suffering and mistreatment, warning others not yet in contact with the enemy that they must never allow themselves to be caught in Federal lines.

Wartime privations contributed significantly to civilian displacement as the economically hard-pressed people moved into areas which promised them employment or relief. Chances for either or both were better in Federal-held cities if the refugees were willing to take the oath of allegiance to the United States. This condition posed no great problem for those who were lukewarm or indifferent toward the Confederacy, but those with deep-seated Southern views found the decision more difficult. Women left alone to care for their families were in a dilemma, and if circumstances permitted a woman asked her husband's advice. Many wrote of pathetic conditions, explaining that they saw no alternative to going into Federal lines where jobs, free food, or the assistance of friends and relatives awaited them. Confederate soldiers did not generally encourage the move although some realized that their families had no choice, but Colonel Louis A. Bringier was more unreasonable and unrelenting than most. The Bringier plantation had been overrun early in the war and Mrs. Bringier had already spent two miserable years as a refugee when she suggested to her husband that it would be in the children's best interest if the family accepted the invitation of friends in New Orleans. This Colonel Bringier forbade her to do and warned her that if she went contrary to his wishes in the matter she could "prepare for a divorce." He added, "*I will never associate with you again.*" [23] This threat caused Mrs. Bringier to abandon her plan, but it did not solve her problems.

As distasteful to many Southerners as taking the oath was having to accept public charity or friendly assistance. Yet economic circumstances compelled proud people to live off the hospitality of friends and relatives for extended periods or to accept charity distributed by relief organizations. Sarah Morgan was only one of many dedicated Confederates faced with the decision of whether or not to go into a Federal-held city where they could live with relatives. As a refugee from Baton Rouge she had spent months going from place to place in Louisiana, and during her wanderings she had suffered a painful back injury. Common sense dictated that she would be more secure in her brother's home, but the agony of the decision was reflected when she wrote, " 'To be or not to be; that is the question.' Whether 'tis nobler in the Confederacy to suffer the pangs of unappeasable hunger and never-ending trouble, or to take passage to a Yankee port, and there remaining, end them. Which is best? I am so near daft that I cannot pretend to say; I only know that I shudder at the thought of going to New Orleans." [24] But go she did, as did many others when it was their only escape from starvation.

Confederate cities also lured people from their homes. Some were attracted to urban areas after being set adrift, and others voluntarily abandoned their homes for the advantages offered by the larger towns. Here they were more likely to find employment, public or private assistance, the safety of numbers, and more adequate transportation and communication facilities. As thousands moved into the cities they created grave housing and supply problems for all, and as prices rose many residents in turn went into rural areas and smaller towns where the necessities were more abundant and therefore cheaper. But as long as the community remained outside the battle zone new arrivals far outnumbered those who left. When the city was later attacked it was often the poorer refugees who could not or would not leave when requested to do so by the authorities.

Conditions prevailing in many parts of the South pushed people out of their homes and sent them scurrying in all directions. From remote areas and areas where law enforcement had broken down came thousands of poor folk who drifted into communities which promised them protection and relief. From the mountains, swamps, frontier, and other remote regions they came to escape the depredations of guerrillas, jayhawkers, bushwhackers, army stragglers, and even their neighbors. It mattered little to most of these people whether they went into Federal or Confederate territory, for their primary concern was security. Some were dedicated to the Confederate cause and many were families of soldiers, but they lacked distant contacts and the financial means for relocating themselves. They were running away from intolerable conditions and most were without definite goals. Early in the war it was noted that the poor hillside farmers in southwestern Missouri were leaving their homes in such numbers that they provided "an exodus equal to that of the children of Israel." [25] On the frontiers of Texas patrols were provided from "Red River to the Rio Grande," in an effort to safeguard the settlers, but these were so ineffective that by 1862, entire counties had been abandoned and land that had sold for $10 an acre a decade before could now be bought for fifty cents.[26]

Another cause of displacement was the Confederate conscription policy which ironically increased the ranks of both the army and the refugees. Undoubtedly some men accused of dodging the draft were not guilty (though many were), and the public was eager to place any apparently healthy man in this category if he was not obviously in the service of the Confederacy. As the First Conscription Act was being debated in Congress, men were accused of leaving their homes in an effort to avoid what was sure to come. A New Orleans editor noted the number who were leaving the city "to evade the demands of the Government," and he urged immediate suspension of all passports and an immediate declaration of martial law to "prevent any citizen from leaving the city."[27] After the Confederacy adopted the conscription policy, both Federal and Confederate officials noted that many Southern men evaded the law by becoming refugees. In 1862, Federal Colonel Frank H. Peck reported that Pass Christian, Mississippi, was "deserted by nearly all of its population who, as from other towns . . . are flying by the boat loads to escape impressment. . . ."[28] During the same period Governor John Gill Shorter of Alabama wrote Secretary of War James Seddon, "Numbers are escaping from the operations of the conscript law and are making this coast, now under the control of the enemy, their refuge."[29]

Men who avoided the draft very often referred to themselves as refugees, but the communities into which they went rarely accepted the classification. Editors dealt with them harshly, at first reacting facetiously in an effort to shame the evaders, and later more caustically when the problem became more serious. The Athens (Tennessee) *Post,* on February 21, 1862, published one of the first editorials aimed at the men who left home rather than face their responsibilities. Entitled "Gitten," the account told of two of the town's citizens who had "packed their traps and gone kiting" to avoid service in the army. The editor hoped that they would continue their flight "to the mountains of Hesidam, where the lion roareth and the whang doodle mourneth," but he also cautioned, "He who don't fight but runs away, may live to run some other day."

Women who insisted on taking pleasure jaunts during the war were often converted into refugees when the battle lines were drawn between them and their homes, preventing their return. This happened many times to women who insisted on visiting husbands in service. Although civilians were discouraged from unnecessary travel which clogged the transportation facilities, the women gadded whenever they could. Their menfolk sometimes encouraged visits to camp, but more often they merely acquiesced when their wives pleaded that they be permitted to come for a brief time. If a man forbade his wife to make the trip, his sensitive spouse often construed this to mean that he did not want to see her, and as she sulked he weakened in an effort to preserve domestic tranquility. When a wife visited camp she often became a displacement, thereby creating another problem for the husband. He worried about her being in the war zone and about what would happen to her if he were transferred or if the army retreated. If he were a high ranking officer he might arrange for her to remain near him, and it was usually the wives of these men who trailed after their husbands. When the wives of officers of lesser rank or of the enlisted men were cut off from their homes, they usually had to look after themselves, but they were refugees all the same.

While not the only one, Mrs. Joseph E. Johnston affords an example of a wife who refused to be separated from her husband for most of the war. She stayed near him in Virginia and later in the North Georgia and Atlanta campaigns. When General Johnston was leading his "strategic retreat" from Chattanooga to Atlanta, Mrs. Johnston was first settled in Dalton and then in Atlanta, but she protested vehemently whenever she was forced to move her headquarters. After being sent to Atlanta she made several trips back to Dalton "for a visit," and when Atlanta was endangered she refused to leave that city until the attack forced her to flee to Macon. During the weeks that she insisted on remaining in Atlanta against her husband's wishes, a carriage was kept in readiness to whisk her out of town when the shells began to fall. Only a general's wife could expect this luxury. When Johnston was relieved of his command he joined his wife in Macon, but when Atlanta fell the couple hastened to Columbia where they found the cost of living above their means. "We can't remain here . . . much longer," wrote the general, "even with Sherman's consent." [30] But before he could obtain his adversary's "consent" he was reassigned to his command and Mrs. Johnston was sent to Lincolnton, North Carolina, where she spent several miserable weeks as a refugee. The general had belatedly decided that she did not belong in an army camp.

There are many other causes for the people's being uprooted, some of which would surely have resulted in temporary displacement had there been no war, but which resulted in permanent displacement because the damage was irreparable in time of war. Examples in this category were the catastrophic fire in Charleston in 1861, the major floods in the river valleys, drouths, and epidemics such as the yellow fever outbreak in Wilmington in 1862. Once people were displaced they tended to stay away, and this was especially true when they were financially unable to rebuild destroyed property. Important also were work stoppages which caused laborers to go elsewhere in search of employment, and the replacement of white workers with Negroes. When the Federals occupied Norfolk they assigned contrabands to many jobs previously held by the Irish day laborers. This latter group was generally too poor to go any great distance to find employment, and, unable to pay rent in the city, they moved into shanties along the canal and eked out "a precarious livelihood hunting and fishing." [31] When schools and colleges closed during the war the faculties were left without income and some found it necessary to leave their homes to live with others or go where they could utilize their talents. Provision was sometimes made for them to live in campus buildings, but they could be evicted if either army commandeered the property. This was the situation in Macon when the *Confederate*, on June 21, 1864, warned the military authorities that "No power, no law, no necessity, no military officer can, by force take the freeman's castle and throw him homeless into the streets." But many freemen were rendered homeless when living quarters were appropriated in this manner. Thousands of others were thrust onto the roads of the Confederacy when their homes were destroyed, regardless of the cause.

Many of the very same forces and agencies which made refugees of Southerners, at some time during the war discouraged their leaving home. This apparent inconsistency can best be explained as an example of "circumstances altering cases." Yet it also served to confuse the people who encountered the problem of whether "to be or not to be" a refugee. Newspapers took either or both stands as the war progressed. As has been noted, the tendency was to ridicule refugees early in the war, often referring to them as cowards, traitors, or fools. But as the Federals advanced and Southerners came to realize that they were caught in a war against civilians as well as armies, the press reflected a more sympathetic attitude toward the homeless people. When editors discouraged their leaving home late in the war, it was because the contracting Confederacy was already so overcrowded that it was to everyone's best interest that the people stay where they were even if it meant living within Federal lines. By this time refugees were looked upon as nuisances who endangered the economy of the area, and newspapers in the overcrowded centers pleaded with those displaced not to come into the community. Editors who had earlier praised those fleeing from Federal rule now assured them that it was in their best interest to remain in enemy lines rather than come into crowded, inflation-ridden Confederate areas. It was their patriotic duty late in the war to live with the foe. Editorials urging the people to "stay put" clearly reflected the hopelessness, apathy, demoralization, and crumbling economy within the Confederacy.

By the time that Atlanta appeared doomed, many Georgia communities were filled to overflowing with refugees. One of these was Athens, a town which had received the homeless throughout the war and which was asked to absorb many from Atlanta in the spring and summer of 1864. The local editor expressed the opinion of many in the community when he announced that Athens could no longer ac-

commodate displaced people, and to support his argument that Atlantans would be better off to stay at home, he reprinted an editorial
earlier published in the Atlanta *Confederacy*. Its caption read, "To
Be or Not To Be a Refugee," and its thesis was that Atlantans should
not leave their homes. If they insisted on doing so they would create
problems for themselves and injure the South's chances of victory.
They would congest transportation lines and would consume the food
"which the Army requires." Although expressing sympathy for the
noncombatants caught in the dilemma, the writer noted that in "nine
out of ten cases" those who had remained at home during the war "had
suffered less than the friendless refugee seeking hospitality among
strangers." In his opinion, the only civilians justified in leaving were
those who had private means of transportation and assurances of food
and housing from others who could afford to receive them. Yet even
these fortunate folk could avoid "anxiety . . . inconvenience and
. . . privation" if they would "exercise a little philosophy and reason." [32] When the Atlanta editor wrote these words, neither he nor the
Athens editor who reprinted them could foresee that General Sherman
would order the evacuation of the city. Nor did the Athens editor
realize that the very day he published the argument his Atlanta colleague was on his way to Columbus, a voluntary refugee. [33]

Throughout the war, and in almost all cases, newspapers condoned
the flight of women, children, and infirm men when an area was under
attack or threatened with a bombardment, but they condemned any
man's leaving who could help in its defense. Seldom, however, did an
editor as bluntly and crudely express his opinion as did the author of
the editorial in the Mobile *Advertiser and Register* for February 17,
1864. He urged that women and children be evacuated immediately
but reminded the men that it was their duty to remain, for "it's a poor
cock that won't crow on his own dunghill." When Milledgeville was
threatened, the local editor criticized men who had not defended their
homes but had run from danger instead. He suggested that had those
"dispossessed of their property . . . taken up arms against the invader
. . . our armies would have been swelled by tens of thousands." As
it was, many of these men were "ekeing out a miserable existence as
an exile. . . ." He urged those in Milledgeville to stay and fight for
their homes. Five months later, after the Federals had marched through
the town, the same editor reminded the citizens who had fled and then
returned after the danger had passed that the homes most severely
damaged were those from which "the owners both male and female
had left." In the cases where "citizens remained in their houses day
and night . . . but few acts of diabolism" were reported. [34]

Thousands of Southerners fled from their homes with little or no thought as to the safety of their property, but thousands also remained hoping to protect theirs. Every year of the war made it increasingly evident that abandoned property was especially vulnerable to seizure, pillage, and destruction. Therefore those who were not confronted with the problem of whether or not to be a refugee until late in the conflict were more likely to pause and consider the consequences of abandonment. Some of those who argued the question fled in terror, but the refugee movement was slowed down somewhat in the last year of the war when Southerners were more reluctant to leave their homes to the advancing Yankees.

Many people caught in enemy lines argued that they would have left the area had they known in time that an invasion was imminent. It is true that circumstances sometimes changed so abruptly that civilians were not alerted, but this was less often the case in towns and cities than in rural areas. Residents usually knew when they were in a danger zone, but many ignored the warning of the military authorities and the press, especially in areas where the alarm had been sounded for months or even years while the city stood. After Savannah fell, many caught in the city charged the Confederate officials with failing to notify them of the impending danger. Local newspapers had either ceased publication or were printed on halfsheets during December and they could not stress conditions as they might otherwise have done, but most residents refused to believe the city could be taken. There had been false alarms before. A minority of the inhabitants had left when they presumed the Federals might head for Savannah, but most refused to budge. When a Charleston newspaper carried an account of the fall of Savannah it included the statement, "Very few of the citizens left . . . because the realization of their condition came too late." [35] This was challenged by a refugee who had left Savannah. He defended the Confederate officials "who did nothing to conceal . . . the real position and intentions of the enemy," but he admitted that the civilian evacuation was handicapped because railroad lines had been cut and "the one road leading from the town could be reached only by a single ferry." [36] Similar situations had been described frequently in the Confederate press, and people had been warned that this might happen if they waited too long to leave. In most cases, when civilians said they would have left had they known a city was in danger, they were rationalizing.

Although military officials are generally associated with urging civilians to leave an endangered town, they just as often sought to keep the rural folk at home. Their primary purpose was to encourage their raising food, but they also reminded them that they could better protect their property if they remained. Federal commanders frequently commented on the problem of keeping their troops in line when abandoned property offered temptations. Some requested that citizens return to their homes despite their now being located in Federal lines. One of these, General Samuel Curtis, stated that "much of the havoc of war" could be avoided if the people in northern Arkansas would come back to their cabins and farms.[37] The people, however, were suspicious of the enemy even when he promised them protection. Once displaced by fear of him, they could rarely be enticed to return.

Any analysis of why Southerners left their homes or refused to do so must take into consideration the individuals involved. Their temperament, background, and outlook influenced their decisions, and the reasons some gave for remaining at home often afford insight to the person. One does not have to be told that Clara Soloman was naïve, emotional, and impractical when he notes her comment following the fall of her beloved New Orleans: "I would not desert my native city in this, her hour of trial. . . . It is the duty of every native to stand or fall with the fortunes of . . . Louisiana." [38] There can be little doubt as to Mrs. Aaron V. Brown's determination to enjoy the comforts of home during the war and avoid the trials of a refugee. Living in Nashville when the city was captured, Mrs. Brown chose to remain although many of her friends left before its fall and others were ordered out when they refused to take the oath. She lived in comparative quiet until late in the war when Colonel John G. Parkhurst, suspecting her of subversive activities, asked her to give cause why she should not be banished into Confederate lines. She responded that she was a close personal friend of General Sherman and General Daniel E. Sickles, had served the "sick, needy and wounded," and had taken into her home "twenty Union refugees . . . from Alabama, . . . clothed and fed them for a month, . . . and made an earnest appeal to the ladies of the North to assist the thousands of miserable refugees in Nashville—most of whom were families of Federal soldiers." [39] Mrs. Brown told Parkhurst that she had no intention of being "a miserable refugee" and, to insure herself against such a fate, a few weeks later she invited the Parkhursts to dine with her.[40]

People often remained at home or delayed their departure because they were afraid of the uncertainties that lay ahead. Cautious, practical persons who had nowhere to go or who lacked the essentials of travel were naturally reluctant to start out for the unknown without visible means of support. Others were physically unable to make the trip or had a dependent in the family who could not travel. The confusing passport system, breakdown of public transportation and lack of private conveyances, the wretched road conditions in certain areas at certain seasons, fear of both armies and especially of the Confederate impressment agents, and the lawless bands abroad in the land deterred many from becoming refugees. It often took more courage to run than to stay.

Just as many men pleaded with their wives to leave an endangered area, there were those who urged them to stay at home rather than risk the insecure life of a refugee. Men in the service who believed their wives' fears ungrounded would not consent to their going elsewhere. Joseph Benedict Semmes, a commissary agent in the Confederate Army, forbade his wife's leaving Memphis. Throughout the late winter and spring of 1862, Mrs. Semmes bombarded him with requests to let her take the children out of the city. She told him of the rumors that were afloat and of their friends who were moving from Memphis. Every letter carried lists of people and businesses that had gone, but Semmes either ignored her pleas or assured her that the military authorities were "determined to protect Memphis at any cost." [41] He thought her fears foolish ones and he asked her to settle down and "be not afraid." Not until June 1, did he become alarmed, and well he might, for six days later the Federals took the city. Then he urged her to leave "at the first opportunity," and this Mrs. Semmes was eager to do.[42] Had she gone earlier the chances are that she could have packed more carefully, and certainly she would have been able to have taken a larger supply of clothing and other essentials with her.

The war came to the doors of an unprepared citizenry, and with it came the question of whether "to be or not to be" a refugee. Conditions which provoked thousands to flight failed to convince others that such extreme measures were either necessary or advisable. Agencies and individuals advocating that Southerners leave home under one set of circumstances discouraged it under others. In the final analysis the decision was usually up to the people themselves, and that they were so often confused as to what they should do is understandable. Like any people caught unprepared in a situation they could not comprehend, many Southerners reacted irrationally and inconsistently. The Civil War refugees came from all classes of people with all kinds of problems. Their story is therefore filled with inconsistencies, but at no time is this more clearly evidenced than during the period in which they made their decision to leave home. Once they left their moorings, they were apt to stay adrift for the duration of the war.

. . . half the world is refugeeing

The Civil War had almost run its course when Eliza Frances Andrews concluded that "half the world is refugeeing," but anyone who witnessed the population displacement during the conflict might have made a similar observation. As in any movement involving tens of thousands of people, the refugee ranks were composed of all classes, ages, and types. To attempt a description of the individuals would sound like the children's counting game, "rich man, poor man, beggarman, thief . . . ," and perhaps that is what the Wilmington editor had in mind when he referred to them as "farmers, merchants, doctors, lawyers." [1]

The poorer, uneducated people composed the majority of those displaced, but less is known about this group because few left records of their experiences. They are mentioned, however, in military reports, newspapers, and personal accounts of the better educated, more articulate Southerners; their identity is usually lost when referred to collectively as a "swarm," "crowd," "horde," or "stream" of humanity seen trudging along the roads of the Confederacy or infiltrating a community. Although the plain people far outnumbered the upper class refugees, it must be noted that a smaller percentage of poorer folk sought safety in flight.

A larger percentage of the upper class fled before the approaching enemy because it had more to lose. Among these were the families of men who had urged secession, defended slavery, and who were active supporters of the Confederacy. They could expect little or no sympathy from the foe. Included were high ranking military officials, political leaders, and outspoken critics of all things "Yankee."

Caught in enemy lines, they were likely to be arrogant, uncompromising, subversive, and adamant in their refusal to take the oath of allegiance to the United States. Therefore they were the ones who were most often banished by Federal officials. Another reason for flight was their financial ability to move their families and transportable goods into safer areas, often to their other plantations or homes. They also had more widespread social contacts than did the poorer folk and, when necessary, could live with their more comfortably situated relatives and friends. It was this group who left their property in the hands of overseers, trusted slaves, or neighbors—confident that they would soon return, not dreaming they might never again live on this land. Early in the war many of the socially prominent people rode away as if on a pleasure jaunt, but before long they discovered that refugeeing and vacationing were not the same.

An overwhelming majority of the refugees were women, children, and aged, infirm men who had to stay behind when the younger men marched off to war. These were the citizens least able to protect themselves or defend the community from the enemy. They sought personal safety and economic security in flight as they moved into the homes of relatives and friends or pressed into areas which seemed to afford protection. Among the most pitiful refugees were the older people who hoped for peace and stability during their declining years, but who were ruthlessly uprooted from their lifelong homes and rudely transplanted in strange surroundings and in overcrowded, makeshift quarters. Many had reason enough to conclude, as had James L. Pettigrew when South Carolina seceded, that they had seen "the last happy day" of their lives. James Campbell, an octogenerian living in the hills of Tennessee, is an example of a Southerner dedicated to the Confederacy but expecting to live out the war unmolested in his modest home. This old soldier who had fought with Andrew Jackson in 1812 was denied his simple request when his Unionist neighbors drove him from his home and then burned it to the ground. "Disconsolate and care-worn," he had no choice but to be a refugee.[2]

The effects of displacement on the elderly people worried their families. A North Carolinian, shocked to hear that her mother had been compelled to leave her home in Petersburg and move into a small, overcrowded farmhouse, insisted that the old lady come to stay with her in Charlotte. When friends in Virginia wrote that the mother was not physically able to make the trip, this did nothing to ease the daughter's mind. "What an old person like Mama must suffer in being driven from her *home*," she wrote, "I wonder how she bears it." [3] Newpapers evidenced editors' concern with the problem and none more so than the Charleston *Courier* whose editorial of February 15, 1864, was only one of many on the subject. The writer noted that displaced senior citizens suffered as much as did the soldiers, for it was "almost impossible for them to find a healthy rooting in a new place." For this reason he urged that the public always consider them "objects of the tenderest . . . sympathy." As difficult as it was for older people to be turned out of their homes, they often complained less about their misfortunes than did the younger refugees.

Children were also a very important part of the refugee movement and they increased both the problems and pleasures of those responsible for them. Although very few not yet in their teens kept records, they did sometimes write letters which have been preserved. Recollections written many years after the war are more numerous but they must be viewed critically. Their reliability depends on many factors, including the age of the child when he was a refugee, for they often confused what they actually remembered with what had been told them by their elders. Matilda Lamb was not quite five when she and her mother left Elizabeth City, North Carolina, but the circumstances of their departure in the middle of the night made a lasting impression on the child; her reminiscences include episodes that only a child would be apt to remember.

Some of the most refreshing and illuminating accounts of refugee life are found in the personal records of girls in their teens. Rosella Kenner, daughter of Confederate Congressman Duncan Kenner of Louisiana, was only thirteen when she left her home in 1862, but her memories of the event were vivid. No girl reflected an uninhibited teen-ager's reaction to refugee life more perfectly than Louise Wigfall, daughter of Senator Louis Trezevant Wigfall of Texas. Fourteen at the beginning of the war, Louise was a refugee in Greensboro, North Carolina in 1862, and in Macon, Georgia in 1864. Her chatty letters to her mother, more than her later reminiscences, reveal the true feelings of the carefree, fun-loving girl. And no mother's letters to her daughter reflect greater concern over her child's ideas, attitudes, and activities than Mrs. Wigfall's to Louise. William Morrell Wadley's daughter Sarah was sixteen when she started keeping a diary of her war experiences. Although the Wadleys were refugees for only a week, her account of the months spent in preparation for flight and the seven days of their displacement is a classic. These girls and other young people included many details which older people ignored or forgot, and they reflected many attitudes and confessed many secrets which would have surprised and shocked their parents. But refugeeing was "everyone's" movement and the reactions of young people are important to the story.

Parents reflected concern for their children who were without roots in their formative years, and they worried about their sons and daughters having to assume adult responsibilities while missing so many of the normal pleasures of childhood. They grieved about sons' having to take the place of their fathers, about the deprivations and fears they encountered daily, about the effects of insecurity on their development and about the interruption of their education. Although these worries were general over the South, the refugees knew them all and were equally concerned about the effects of displacement on the young. Yet many mothers confronted with these problems and heavy responsibilities found in their children a source of inspiration and comfort. They seldom expressed irritation with them as they traveled about, and they often noted that only the children's presence made refugee life bearable.

Because of the heterogeneity of the refugees the only thing all had in common was displacement. While some found satisfactory homes and a sufficiency of the necessities, others were poorly housed, or not housed at all, and inadequately fed. None lived elegantly for long or felt absolutely secure, but even those in similar circumstances reacted in dissimilar ways. The refugee's ability to adjust to wartime conditions depended not so much on prewar social standing as on his character and attitude. Those accustomed to luxury and ease, who maintained a relatively high standard of living during the war, were often the most complaining. Nor did age or sex always determine a person's ability to adjust to wartime conditions. The way in which the refugees met the challenge depended not so much on who they were as on what they were.

Because most of the more prominent refugees kept records or were mentioned in the accounts of others, they can be more easily identified. Included in the group were planters, families of high ranking military and political leaders, and professional and business groups. Most were identified with more than one profession or interest, and Confederate officials represented a variety of prewar pursuits. General Lee had made the army his career, but Mrs. Lee had inherited their home. She was among the first to be displaced, and despite her social position and aristocratic background, she experienced many of the fears and inconveniences common to all refugees. Because of her husband's position, Mrs. Lee was the recipient of courtesies and favors not accorded others for, as Judith McGuire wrote, "All Virginia has open doors for the family of General Lee." [4] But she was often entirely dependent on the generosity of relatives and friends and was once caught in enemy lines. As she traveled around Virginia she had to adjust to wartime travel conditions, and the most comfortable means of transportation available to the arthritic Mary Lee was a boxcar "fitted up to suit an invalid." [5]

Unlike Mrs. Lee, Mrs. Jefferson Davis did not move as a refugee but twice during the war: in 1862 when the Federals threatened Richmond, and again in 1865 just before Lee's surrender. Mrs. Davis preferred to risk personal danger rather than leave her husband, and it was only at his insistence that she left Richmond on the two occasions. Never during the war did she return to their plantation in Mississippi, for she considered Richmond her home and did not think of herself as a refugee. But there is no doubt as to her being one in the spring of 1865, and her trek South was as heartbreaking as that of any refugee. When Mrs. Davis stopped briefly with Mary Boykin Chesnut near Chester, South Carolina, Mrs. Chesnut registered disgust and disappointment with those fair-weather friends of the Davises who had now "gone into hiding." [6] The refugee experiences of the President and his wife were of short duration, yet few Southerners carried a heavier burden. After all the inconveniences and fears the cruelest blow of all was inflicted on the couple when their hegira ended in the capture of the President.

Other members of the Davis family were refugees through most of the war, among them the President's older brother and benefactor, Joseph Davis, who was in his eighties. After leaving his Mississippi plantation in 1862, Joseph Davis with his wife and nineteen-year-old granddaughter edged by degrees across the state. During this period Mrs. Davis died, but her husband and granddaughter crossed into Alabama and made their home in Tuscaloosa for the duration of the war. Joseph Davis was to learn that his prewar prominence and wealth counted for little and, like others, the old man fled to woods on numerous occasions when the Federals raided the area. As a refugee he was required to travel in broken-down, makeshift conveyances, to sleep in woods and abandoned cabins, and to endure innumerable privations. During the war his plantation was seized and his mansion burned, and having no place to go after the war he continued his nomadic life, living at various places in Mississippi and Louisiana. [7] This was the fate of many other Southerners who, like Joseph Davis, had been numbered among the most affluent and prominent in the prewar South.

Among the officers in the Confederate Army were men who had been prominent in professional, business, and social circles and whose families voluntarily became refugees. General Leonidas Polk had been a planter and Episcopal Bishop of Louisiana before volunteering his services to the Confederacy. After leaving Nashville, Mrs. Polk and her unmarried daughters went to the home of friends in New Orleans and were there when the city fell. Obtaining a pass from the Federal authorities to go into Confederate lines, Mrs. Polk consulted with her husband as to where she and the girls should settle. General Polk wanted her to locate herself for the duration and not have to run again, and it was decided that Asheville, in the mountains of North Carolina, afforded as safe a place as any. Mrs. Polk rented a house there and was soon joined by a married daughter, Katherine Polk Gale, and her family. Mrs. Gale's husband served on General Polk's staff during the war, but prior to the conflict he had been a merchant in Nashville and a planter in Mississippi. The Gales had been driven from two homes in Mississippi before deciding that it was to their best interests to join Mrs. Polk in her mountain retreat. After Hamilton Polk was wounded, he and his family also went to Asheville, and although the Polks and Gales endured privations, they were an exceptionally congenial, adaptable family. Their worst wartime shock was General Polk's death in 1864.[8]

Less well known than the Polks was the family of Minor Meriwether, an engineer who joined the army as a captain and rose to the rank of colonel. He left his wife and two sons in Memphis. General Sherman and Elizabeth Meriwether came to dislike each other when he took command of the city, and as Mrs. Meriwether was not one to keep silent, she was banished into Confederate lines. With her two small sons she went to Mississippi where her husband was stationed. As the Confederates retreated, Mrs. Meriwether backed across the state, paused long enough in Columbus to give birth to her third son, and then fled to Tuscaloosa where she lived for the remainder of the war. Her problems were many, not the least of which was feeding her children, but Elizabeth Meriwether was as determined and resourceful as any woman in the Confederacy.[9]

Benedict Joseph Semmes was a Memphis whiskey dealer when he went into the service as a lieutenant in the Confederate Commissary Department. His wife Jorantha was a New Yorker by birth, but a Southern sympathizer. She and the children remained in Memphis until after its fall and then left to live with her husband's cousins in Mississippi. When the Federals advanced, both families moved to

Alabama where they were confronted with many inevitable wartime problems but were nevertheless in far better circumstances than most refugees. Yet Mrs. Semmes lacked the ability to adjust to the changed conditions, as her letters to her husband indicate, and she spent three miserable years in her temporary quarters.[10]

So numerous were the displaced families of Confederate officers that it is impossible to list all of those of even the high ranking officials. Among the more prominent was Mrs. Stonewall Jackson who was sent to North Carolina when Richmond was threatened in 1862. While staying in Charlotte with her sister, Mrs. D. H. Hill, the Jackson's only child was born.[11] General Edmund Kirby Smith's seventy-year-old mother was banished from Florida for refusing to take the oath, but because she was unable to cross the Mississippi, she could not join her son in Louisiana.[12] Among others who spent most of the war period as refugees were the families of Edward Porter Alexander, William Dorsey Pender, John Pemberton, John B. Gordon, Basil Wilson Duke, Benjamin Hardin Helm, Roger Pryor, and Albert Sidney Johnston. While most families of Confederate officers experienced displacement at some time, there were exceptions. One of these was Mrs. P. G. T. Beauregard who was too ill to leave New Orleans when others in the family fled. She died there in 1864.

Political officials and their families were as vulnerable to insult and injury from the Federals as were the families of military leaders. Vice-President Alexander H. Stephens was undisturbed by the invader until 1864, when raiders appeared near his Georgia home. He went to the wartime home of his friend, Charles L. Pettigrew, in South Carolina, and his host wrote of Stephens' narrow escape, and commented that had he been apprehended, "the Yankees would have gotten a prize." [13] Many political officials in Richmond were cut off from their homes, but most of them considered the capital their official residence. When Richmond was endangered, as it was during George B. McClellan's Peninsular Campaign, their families were usually sent away temporarily; officials who could not themselves qualify as refugees during most of the war were in flight before the enemy in the last weeks of the conflict. After Congress adjourned in March, 1865, its members and others who saw the handwriting on the wall left Richmond, and on April 2, President Davis led the final exodus of officials from the stricken city. Riding this most famous refugee train of the war were all members of the cabinet, excepting Secretary of War John Cabell Breckinridge, and others prominent in Confederate political circles.[14] Anna Holmes Trenholm, wife of the ailing Secretary of the Treasury, was the only woman passenger. Her account of the trip to their home in South Carolina vividly describes the anxiety and worry that enshrouded the train as it pulled out of Richmond. Anna Trenholm was most concerned about her husband who lay on an improvised bed as far as Greensboro, where they transferred to an ambulance. Breaking the trip whenever they could, it took eight weeks for the Trenholms to reach Columbia.[15]

Josiah Gorgas also rode this train out of Richmond, but his family was left behind to follow a few days later. For six weeks he had been trying to get "Mama," as he affectionately referred to his wife, and the children to leave Richmond, but Mrs. Gorgas had been a refugee in 1862, and refused to leave her husband a second time. After her earlier displacement she had said that she would never again leave the city "until the capital is moved further South." [16] Despite her protests, Gorgas had made arrangements for her to leave on April 3, and "Mama" had started packing. However, she was not ready to go when orders for the evacuation came on the second.

During the spring of 1865 Confederate leaders and their families, as well as other Southerners, were headed toward their homes, a port of embarkation, or Mexico. In the group was Senator Williamson Simpson Oldham who left Richmond in March for his home in Texas. On the long trip he had many experiences familiar to other refugees throughout the war. He had not been on the road for very long when he realized that "the mighty had fallen," and that even a Confederate Senator could be treated indifferently and rudely by citizens who were now unimpressed by his position. He traveled in the company of refugees from all walks of life, rode in all kinds of conveyances, slept in makeshift quarters, and barely escaped the grasp of the Federals on several occasions. He visited with friends, many of whom were as yet in their refugee homes; and in Newnan, Georgia, he and twelve other Confederate Congressmen were stranded because of inadequate transportation. Late to experience the trials of a refugee, he nevertheless encountered innumerable difficulties in the spring of 1865 and concluded that it seemed to matter little that he had been an official in the Confederate government.[17]

State leaders and their families were also displaced during the war. When an invasion was imminent, capitals were moved and the officials fled, taking with them the archives and other properties. A week before the fall of Nashville, Governor Isham Harris and members of the legislature went to Memphis. When Memphis was doomed the archives were sent to Chattanooga, and Harris sought refuge with the

Confederate forces in Mississippi. Governor Thomas Overton Moore fled from Baton Rouge when he heard that New Orleans had fallen, and the wartime capital of Louisiana was first Opelousas and later Shreveport. After Henry Watkins Allen was elected governor of the state, Moore joined other Louisiana refugees in Texas. In 1863, Arkansas officials moved themselves and the capital to Washington in the extreme southern part of the state, and the same year Jackson was evacuated and the Mississippi capital moved to Columbus and then Macon. Governor Joseph E. Brown and other political leaders left Milledgeville in 1864, and early the next year the South Carolina government was moved out of Columbia before Sherman arrived in the city. Governor William "Extra Billy" Smith supervised the removal of the Virginia archives from Richmond at the end of the war, and Zebulon Vance of North Carolina feared capture and made ready to leave Raleigh.

Former office holders and leaders also sought to evade the enemy, and one of these was the former Governor of Virginia, John Letcher, who had been a Unionist until Lincoln called for troops in April, 1861, after which he threw his support to the Confederacy and led Virginia out of the Union. When his term as governor expired he moved his family to Lexington where they were living when David Hunter and the Federals appeared. At his wife's insistence Letcher fled to Bedford County leaving his family in Lexington. Mrs. Letcher was compelled to house two Federal officers who repaid her by setting fire to her home, and although she and the children escaped the flames they were unable to save any of their possessions. Most of her neighbors were too afraid of the Federals to render assistance until after the withdrawal of troops from the town.[18] When Governor Letcher returned he found his family homeless and destitute, but friends in Richmond were so indignant and filled with pity when they heard of the family's plight that they raised money to buy them a home in the city. As Letcher expressed his gratitude and accepted the offer, he was obviously moved by their generosity and thoughtfulness.[19]

Employees of the Confederate and state governments were also displaced, sometimes individually and sometimes en masse. The question of whether or not to remove most of the government workers from Richmond was debated after the Federals threatened the city in 1862. The capital was overcrowded and the high prices worked a hardship on those employed in the offices at relatively low salaries. But little was done about transferring the agencies to other cities, because some officials feared that it would be construed as an evacuation which would give comfort to the enemy while lowering home-front morale. When more than one hundred women note signers in the Treasury Department were sent to Columbia, it created "a good deal of excitement" in Richmond and throughout the Confederacy.[20] This was not considered to be simply a transfer which workers might refuse in ordinary times, but an order which must be obeyed by those who had to have jobs if they were to live. The women were referred to as "refugees" and as "objects of pity." All along the route to Columbia wherever their train stopped, people served them refreshments, brought them gifts and expressed indignation that they were being sent where "everything is strange and everybody a stranger." [21] But many of these women were actually refugees in Richmond who had been drawn to the capital by the employment opportunities in the offices. The press in Columbia urged citizens to open their doors to the displaced women, and reminded the Columbians that they had come from Virginia where "the noblest people . . . have thrown open their doors to refugees from other States." [22]

Hundreds of professional people accustomed to serving all classes of Southerners were among the wartime refugees, and many continued to serve in their displacement according to their skills. Ministers were often called upon to attend to the spiritual needs of both soldiers and civilians. Those who went into the service often settled their families in temporary homes, and others who were refugees preached and taught as circumstances dictated. Many of these dedicated, selfless men were never identified in contemporary accounts other than as "refugee preachers," but there were many prominent ministers whose services and experiences were recorded. One of these was Henry C. Lay, Episcopal Bishop of Arkansas with headquarters in Fort Smith when the war commenced. He moved his family to the home of friends in Huntsville, Alabama, in 1861, returned to Arkansas and continued his duties until 1863, when he left Little Rock. For most of the war he was separated from his family who were refugees in Alabama, Virginia, and North Carolina, while he occupied pulpits in many cities. Bishop Lay was serving St. Luke's Episcopal Church in Atlanta when the city fell, and he conversed and dined with General Sherman who gave him a pass to visit an aged, sick friend in Union lines. He worried about his family throughout the war and only a few weeks before its end he was still trying to find them a satisfactory place of refuge. "I have never applied myself with greater diligence to anything," he wrote, "than I have to this matter of hunting up a home." [23]

Benjamin Palmer, the fiery, outspoken Presbyterian minister in New Orleans, had stirred Southerners before the war, and after the Federal occupation of the city he and the authorities found themselves at odds. He left New Orleans and spent the remainder of the war as a refugee, preaching in several cities before going to his native South Carolina. His last sermon in Chattanooga was finished amid falling shells, and while in Columbia he continued to deliver his powerful, provocative messages which were so eloquent that Mary Boykin Chesnut was "shaken to the depths" by them.[24] When the Federals approached the city, the Palmers were among the hundreds of residents who fled to North Carolina.

The Presbyterian missionary to the Indians in northwestern Arkansas, Robert McGill Loughbridge, was less well known than Bishop Lay or Reverend Palmer, but he was just as dedicated to his profession and to the Confederacy. The turbulent conditions in this remote area caused him to remove his family to Texas. Their trip was a difficult one, complicated by the wild, lawless region through which they traveled and by the lack of water, food, and fodder. Loughbridge was a poor man with few contacts along the way, and the struggles were almost too much to endure. But the minister relied heavily on quotes from the Revelation to see them through the ordeal, and the family arrived safely at their destination where they lived for the remainder of the war.[25]

Primary and secondary teachers and tutors were often among the first people to be displaced and they sometimes planned their exodus far in advance of an invasion. They inserted notices in newspapers announcing their willingness to serve in an area farther removed from the enemy, and as early as the first fall of the war Richmond papers carried announcements which evidenced teachers' nervousness at being so close to the Yankees. On September 3, 1861, the *Enquirer* told of a mother and daughter both of whom had "many years experience" in teaching and who now asked nothing more than a position "South of Richmond." As the war came to broader areas of the South similar stipulations were made, and by 1863 Virginians who were usually reluctant to leave the state were requesting jobs elsewhere. One young lady, who was prepared to teach "English, Mathematics, Drawing, Painting, French, Latin and Music," was seeking an appointment "South of Raleigh." [26] Men were more willing than women to take their chances at finding teaching positions in strange communities, but after arriving on the scene they found it to their advantage to announce themselves as "deserving refugees." An able-bodied citizen, who stated that he had been driven from his home and had come to town to teach the young, was viewed skeptically by the residents, not because they questioned his ability to teach but because they questioned his being out of uniform. But most communities were so desperately in need of teachers that editors very often urged parents to give the stranger a chance. A Georgia refugee who arrived in Austin, Texas, assured the townspeople that he was a college graduate prepared to offer "an improved course of instruction . . . with appropriate, improved apparatus." He apparently lacked credentials but the editor nevertheless gave him his support and blessing and urged that the other citizens do likewise.[27]

Julia and Virginia LeGrand were among the qualified women who had taught a select group of young ladies before the war and who hoped to teach after they became refugees. They left New Orleans rather than take the oath, expecting to go to their brother's home in Texas, but the forces of war prevented this and pushed them eastward instead. They were entirely dependent on friends who were also refugees, first in Newnan and later in Thomasville, Georgia. The sisters were embarrassed at having to live off the generosity of others, and when Julia was invited to tutor the children of a planter she was tempted to accept the offer. However it did not include Virginia, and in such hard times strangers could scarcely be expected to support two people when the services of only one was required. Therefore Julia regretted that she must decline but wrote that it "would kill" her and her sister to be separated so far from home.[28] There were many refugees like the LeGrands who were qualified to serve as tutors but could not find positions because the families who might have employed them before the war were financially unable to do so during the conflict.

Many college professors went into military service or found employment in laboratories and offices, but some were too old or without the necessary qualifications for military or civilian wartime positions. If they could stay at home, they could usually manage to provide for their families; but if their homes were commandeered or destroyed, they were then displaced. Very few college professors found positions in other institutions, for the tendency was for schools to close or manage with the teaching staffs they had. An exception was Edward S. Joynes who was on the faculty of William and Mary College when the Federals took Williamsburg and fire destroyed a part of the college. It closed, but Joynes almost immediately received an appointment to the Hollins faculty where he taught until 1867. It was during this period that he first advocated a teacher training program for Southern women, and the 1863–64 Hollins catalogue carried a provocative article by Joynes on the subject.

Among the more energetic and resourceful refugee professors was Francis S. Holmes of the College of Charleston. After the institution closed early in the war, Holmes took his family to Edgefield in up-country South Carolina, where he acted as custodian for books and other possessions of the college, served in the Nitre Bureau, and became a respected citizen of the community. He was said to have produced "the finest corn in the upcountry," and was described by an Edgefield resident as a "useful citizen, deservedly popular." [29] He was noted for his versatility and practical bent, as testified to by his friend, Joseph LeConte, who described him as "a curious mixture of hospitable planter, ardent sportsman and devoted naturalist." [30] But perhaps his most outstanding wartime accomplishment was winning the affection of the people among whom he lived as a refugee, for most displaced Charlestonians did not endear themselves to those in the upper part of the state.

Joseph LeConte was also appointed to the Confederate Nitre Bureau after South Carolina College closed, and he continued to live in Columbia. His experiences with refugeeing were exceptionally brief but exceedingly rugged. For three months he endured the hardships of a displaced person when he went to Georgia to bring his daughter and sister out of the path of Sherman's army. On his return trip he escorted twenty refugees to safety and, excepting a Negro servant, he was the only man in the group. Arriving back in Columbia, he found orders to pack and send all of the Nitre Bureau's laboratory equipment to Richmond. By February 14, he had it crated and ready to ship but because of the great quantity of "freight both public and private," he was unable to get it on an outgoing train until the following day, and then only after "entreaty and considerable threatening." As soon as this was accomplished he and his brother John, also a professor, decided to take the family's most valuable possessions to a place of safety, but they were delayed by the "crowds of panic-stricken . . . way-worn, travel stained refugees" on the roads leading out of Columbia. Before they could get more than a few miles the LeContes were overtaken by the Federals who looted their wagons while the brothers hid for three days in the woods. After this experience there was nothing for them to do but return home.[31] The laboratory equipment which Joseph LeConte had so carefully packed and sent on its way to Richmond got only as far as Greensboro and "was never heard from again." [32]

Editors were even more likely to become refugees than were educators. They were often the community's most articulate, influential defenders of the Confederate cause, and the most caustic critics of the Yankees. They had much to lose should they fall into the hands of the enemy, but they were determined to air their views through the pages of their journals. When they left home and could do so, they took their presses and published wherever they paused.[33] It was during the war that Henry Watterson first made a name for himself as a reporter on the staff of the refugeeing Chattanooga *Rebel*, organ of the Army of Tennessee. During the Atlanta Campaign he was affiliated with the *Southern Confederacy*, as was another refugee humorist, Charles H. Smith, better known to his readers as "Bill Arp." When George W. Adair and J. Henley Smith, publishers of the *Confederacy*, decided to move the paper to Columbus, Watterson announced that he was tired of refugeeing and had decided to become a scout for General Hood.[34]

Among the older and more pathetic displaced editors was William E. Woodruff who had gone into the Arkansas Territory and founded the Arkansas *Gazette* in 1819. Retiring in 1850, he expected to live for the remainder of his days in Little Rock, but the war changed that. He was still an alert man with a sharp tongue when the Federals occupied the city, and although Woodruff was sympathetic to the Confederacy he took the oath in order to collect rents on his extensive properties in Little Rock. However he made the mistake of criticizing the enemy with tongue and pen, and General Frederick Steele intercepted letters Woodruff wrote to friends within Confederate lines. On the basis of statements made in these letters the old editor, his four daughters, and minor son were banished and the family spent nearly two years as miserable refugees living off the generosity of friends. Returning to Little Rock after the war, Woodruff found his home in a "deplorably desolate condition" with no "furniture of any kind . . . on the premises." [35]

As might be expected, James Dunwoody Brownson DeBow and the Federal authorities in New Orleans could not dwell for long side by side. DeBow took his family and his *Review* out of the city, although he never abandoned the idea of publishing elsewhere. For most of the war his family was in South Carolina, and at one time he considered buying a home for them in Columbia, but the cost of living in the city was beyond his means and he sent them to Winnsboro, a village near Columbia.[36] When the Federals came through the town in 1865, a New York *Herald* correspondent mentioned that "the wife of the reviewer" was among the "wealthy refugees" in Winnsboro.[37] Nothing could have been farther from the truth, for the DeBows had economic problems throughout the war and as his family increased, the editor worried about providing for them.

Bankers who refugeed were burdened with grave responsibilities, especially if they served as custodians for the banks' assets. Some established their banks in new locations during the war and continued to carry on business as best they could. One of these was John Cheesborough who was assigned the task of removing specie and papers from the Bank of Charleston to temporary headquarters in Columbia. Because the transfer of bankers and their transportable properties was usually shrouded in secrecy at the time it was taking place, Cheesborough did not tell his wife, a refugee in Asheville, of the move until after he was settled in Columbia. He then wrote of the many problems he had encountered and told her that he was living over the bank and taking his meals in the hotel. He felt his responsibilities and preferred to be in the building day and night.[38] As Cheesborough was moving to Columbia, other banks in eastern South Carolina were sending away their specie to be stored in safer areas, and those not yet removing their place of business were notifying patrons that they could no longer assume responsibility for personal possessions left in their care. The people were urged to empty their safety deposit boxes and "claim packages of any kind" which had been left at the banks. Officials made it plain that they would do all in their power to safeguard the banks' assets, but the circumstances were such that they could promise nothing more.[39]

Southern bankers evidenced a dedication to their jobs, and some transported valuables great distances, as in the case of those in New Orleans who took their specie to Richmond. Others managed to conduct business in their customary location through most of the war but were always alert to the possibility that they might have to leave at any time. The Bank of Wilmington in Wilmington, North Carolina, was one that remained open until the fall of 1864 when it appeared that the city could not stand much longer. William Reston took the assets out of Wilmington, stopped to pick up those of the Bank of Fayetteville, and proceeded to Pittsboro where he deposited all except some of the gold and silver in the bank vaults there. The specie he took to his family's refugee home in Moore County and hid under boards in the attic. There it stayed until November, 1865, when it was turned over "to the proper authorities." [40]

The most peripatetic of the refugeeing bankers was James Gettys McGready Ramsey, president of the Knoxville branch of the Bank of Tennessee which was also a Confederate depository. In an effort to protect the valuables entrusted to him, he went to Abingdon, Virginia, and then to Atlanta, Augusta, Charlotte, Greensboro, and back to Augusta. On his trip back to Georgia in 1865, he left the Confederate specie at Abbeville, South Carolina; after arriving in Augusta, Ramsey called a Board meeting where it was decided to send the bank's specie to Texas. It never reached its destination and Ramsey later wrote that he had opposed the decision but was overruled.[41]

As Ramsey refugeed with his responsibilities, his family was left in eastern Tennessee. Mrs. Ramsey had thought of going elsewhere and had once attempted to leave but returned when her military escort disappeared. It was after her teen-aged daughter, Sue, was banished that she also decided to leave Knoxville. Sue was a vivacious, hot-headed Confederate sympathizer who flaunted her views in the Federal-held territory. She was accused of displaying the Confederate flag, exchanging greetings and socializing with known Southern sympathizers, changing her church membership when her pastor was banished, playing and singing "Dixie," declining the "attentions of U.S. officers in Knoxville," and refusing to walk under the Federal flag or take the oath of allegiance. If guilty on all counts, the amazing fact is that she was permitted to remain at home until 1864. She left Knoxville and went to an uncle's home near Liberty, Virginia, but it was not long before Federal raiders drove them away. Two months after Sue left, Mrs. Ramsey and the other children left Knoxville under a flag of truce. They traveled with other refugees in a boxcar and this inspired Ramsey to say that his family was "*boxed* out of Federal lines." They were cordially received in Virginia but the Bristol citizens were unsure as to whether to refer to them as "Pilgrims, Exiles, . . . [or] Refugees." [42]

A distinct category of displaced people were those from Maryland, Kentucky, and Missouri who left their homes to cast lots with the Confederacy. Whether they left voluntarily or involuntarily and whether they entered military service or retained their civilian status, they were regarded as "refugees." The Border States' citizens were usually welcomed early in the war and praised for their unselfish devotion to the South, but as communities became overcrowded and times more difficult, public opinion often changed to open hostility. Marylanders were more resented than the others, and this was especially true in Richmond where a great many settled. They gave the appearance of being in much better financial circumstances than other residents, and some did manage to retain limited contacts with relatives and friends in Maryland who provided them with luxuries as well as necessities. Others who had come ostensibly to enter Confederate service but went into business instead were the primary targets for attack. They were accused of shirking their duty, breaking their promise, and making fortunes off the hard-pressed, self-sacrificing, patriotic Southerners. As time passed and conditions grew worse, these refugees were indiscriminately accused of being spies, and newspapers warned the people to beware of all persons coming from outside the Confederacy. In the thinking of many Southerners, these refugees moved from the status of patriot to traitor.

Marylanders came by the thousands and as early as June, 1861, a Confederate general wrote his wife that his uncle's home near Fredericksburg accommodated as many as twenty a night who were en route to Richmond.[43] In this first summer of the war travelers on the Virginia roads noted the number of Marylanders moving toward the Confederate Capital. One woman told of being overtaken by a "strange looking carriage" piled high with luggage and driven at a rapid rate of speed by a Negro. She was asked directions by one of the passengers who explained that he and his wife had "escaped from Maryland" and from "Lincoln Tyranny" and had crossed the Potomac in a skiff the day before. They had spent the night with a friend who had loaned them the carriage and driver, but they did not know the way to the city.[44] Similar episodes were reported by others throughout the war.

Hardships were not unknown to the Maryland refugees, but because some left the impression of being wealthy or materialistic and others were apparently avoiding military service, all were vulnerable to criticism. Many men who had come to serve in the army wanted to enlist only in the cavalry, and when they were not accepted they refused to volunteer for any other branch of the service. They were no different from the Virginians, many of whom also preferred the cavalry, but the ranks were filled when the infantry was in need of men. Because the Marylanders were exempt from conscription they could stay out of the service; this irritated the people, and none more than the editors. One in Richmond shouted to the recalcitrant refugees, "Calvary! artillery! infantry! What matters it by what weapon the despot is slain!"[45] Another in Lynchburg sarcastically suggested that

Marylanders would undoubtedly be "found most efficient" in the walking branch of the service.[46] Regardless of the reason for Maryland men coming to Virginia, when they were seen idling away their time, enjoying the social life, and escorting the Southern belles whose friends were away at war, they were a source of irritation to many. After a bill was introduced in the Confederate Congress to draft the refugees, the attack became more fierce. A spokesman for the bill accused the Marylanders of having fled "from the Lincoln draft" and of "eating up everything" in Richmond while "doing nothing for the cause." He estimated that there were at least 2,500 men "called refugees" in Richmond, and that one could hear the strains of "Maryland, My Maryland" coming from their lips as they entered "into every sort of speculation." [47]

Those who enlisted in Confederate service did not escape censure, however. Trouble often erupted between Virginians and Marylanders in the army, and this Phoebe Yates Pember noted in her nursing duties at Chimborazo Hospital. So serious was the problem in wards shared by the two groups that Mrs. Pember interceded to get the Maryland men moved into a separate ward. She noted that Virginians were "not kind in their feelings and acts" toward Marylanders, with whom she obviously sympathized when she wrote, "My love of justice was aroused, and I have taken them all (I suppose I must not say to my bosom) under my protective wing." [48] That she endeared herself to the underdogs was evidenced by the letters of appreciation she later received from them. One wrote that Virginians seemed to forget that many Marylanders were in the Confederate Army when they condemned the whole because there were "a few . . . engaged in *trade*, [and] making money." [49]

Kentuckians and Missourians also had their critics in those areas which absorbed hundreds of them, but many refugees from these states were impoverished when they entered Confederate lines and therefore created an additional economic burden for the communities in which they settled. There were exceptions, some of whom were relatives of Confederate officers or members of proud, affluent families loyal to the South. Yet even these were not always cordially welcomed as Mrs. Basil Wilson Duke discovered in Abingdon, Virginia, where there was "very little sympathy felt" for Kentucky refugees.[50] But the Kentuckians seemed to find greater sympathy than did either Missourians or Marylanders. General Jeremy Gilmer, who had contact with refugees from all areas, preferred Kentuckians to either of the others.[51] Probably no Kentucky refugee had a more difficult time than Elodie Todd, sister-in-law of the President of the United States. The outbreak of the war found her visiting in Alabama and in love with a young lawyer from Dallas County who entered the Confederate service. She was left behind to face Selma society while he was away at war, and her letters to him indicate that she was miserable with her situation. After their marriage she was more cordially received, but never sufficiently so to make her feel at home. She once wrote her fiancé, "We Kentuckians think ourselves as much Southerners as anybody, but the inhabitants of this little town think that because Kentucky is *not* on a *Cotton Plantation* . . . there is no difference between me and a *Northerner*." [52]

The Unionists who fled from the Confederate Army and from their neighbors compose a separate category of wartime refugees not included in this account. Yet they cannot be completely ignored, for their problems were similar to those of other refugees; only the enemy was different. As they moved along the roads of the Confederacy or cowered in some remote area, they were the victims of a ruthless foe and vindictive neighbors. Their movements were frequently mentioned in military reports, newspapers, and in the accounts of private citizens. It was noted that they usually traveled in groups of several hundred and experienced grave hardships. A Federal soldier saw several hundred hiding in the rocky regions of Tennessee, Alabama, and Mississippi, and so pitiful was their plight that he wrote his wife that this was "one of the most distressing sights" he had seen since leaving home.[53] *Harper's Weekly* used the refugees as subject for several illustrations, but it is difficult for one to distinguish Unionist from Confederate refugees in these drawings.[54] Their political convictions were not written in their gaunt, dirty, weary faces, and all refugees looked much alike before the end of the war. The clue as to the sympathies of many was to be found in the direction they were traveling, but this was not an entirely reliable gauge during the wartime confusion.

The refugees represented all groups of people, and although personal accounts were written primarily by the upper classes and the story heavily weighted in their favor, it is well to remember that the Civil War was a great leveler of society. After the first months it was difficult to distinguish between the classes and backgrounds of those displaced. After a long, hot, dusty trip all refugees were tired, dirty, and probably irritable. If in flight before the enemy, they were scared. Seeing them hovered together in a Vicksburg cave or camped in any area, it was impossible to determine their prewar social status. Confederates and Unionists, Marylanders and Virginians, Protestants and Catholics, Baptists and Episcopalians, day laborers and professional men looked equally pathetic and miserable.

A Texas editor, sitting on the porch of an Alleyton hotel and watching a refugee train pass in review, described what could have been a similar movement of displaced people anywhere in the Confederacy. There were "officers in gay uniforms, clerks in broadcloth, . . . planters in homespun, . . . wagoners in their dirty shirt sleeves, . . . deserters," and there were families traveling together and individuals making their way alone. The editor noted that the caravan presented a "sight worthy" to be painted, and he "thought if Hogarth had been there, he might have added one more relic that would have embellished his illustrious memory." [55] There is no doubt that William Hogarth would have been the artist to paint a refugee train in motion, for all of the earthy qualities he loved were there. And such was bound to be the case when, as Eliza Frances Andrews expressed it, "half the world is refugeeing." [56]

... *clashing carriage wheels and conflicting interests*

No sooner had the people determined to leave their homes than a great many problems confronted them. They had to decide how they would get away, what they would take with them and, if time permitted, what was to be done with the cherished and valuable possessions they could not take. Very few Southerners realized at this crucial moment how many challenges they would face before reaching their destination, for long trips in the mid-nineteenth century were never relaxing, and those in wartime meant even greater inconvenience, insecurity, and privation. When numbers of people traveled together, as they often did, the trip was more pleasant if everyone adjusted to the group and if personal preferences were made secondary considerations. Good sportsmanship and cheerfulness were necessary but difficult to maintain for any length of time. Refugees became increasingly weary, tense, and peevish, and the longer the trip the more obvious were the "conflicting interests." Had Southerners understood the ordeal which lay ahead, most would have hesitated before permitting themselves to be displaced.

There were many local conditions which affected the people's departure. If the enemy approached and hysteria prevailed, the residents seemed to move in all directions at the same time, grabbing whatever possessions were at hand and dashing away in a frenzied, haphazard manner. If the atmosphere were calmer, as it might be when danger was not imminent, they prepared for their exodus more carefully and methodically. But in either situation, the reaction depended on the individual, for some refused to be rushed under any circumstances and others became hysterical when hearing the most fantastic rumors. Some were packed and ready to go long before the enemy appeared, but others procrastinated until he arrived on the scene. In time of crisis people could not be counted on to follow their natural behavior pattern, for very often the strong buckled under pressure, the weak rose manfully to the occasion, and the phlegmatic became highly emotional.

The transportation available to the refugees was also an important consideration and often a major problem at the time of their displacement. If they had private conveyances and sufficient time to gather together their possessions, they could follow their own schedules and take all that space permitted. If they managed to get accommodations on public carriers they were more regimented and the amount of baggage more limited, depending on the facilities and local conditions. But the thousands who were compelled to flee on foot faced the greatest difficulties, for the quantity of supplies which they could carry was greatly curtailed. When cities were hurriedly evacuated, many people who confidently expected to travel on public conveyances discovered that there were more potential passengers than there were accommodations, and this situation inevitably contributed to the mass hysteria. The type of transportation utilized by the refugees not only determined how they would travel but also the amount of baggage they could take and this, in turn, usually had a bearing on the privation they would later experience. However, displaced people often discovered too late that the number of possessions taken was not as important as a sensible selection of practical items, and those who left in haste rarely had time to consider which of their belongings would be of greatest value.

Most refugees prepared for flight more hurriedly than they had ever before planned a trip, but William Wadley's family affords an extreme example of one which took an interminable length of time to ready themselves for their journey. During the first two years of the war they opened their home near Monroe to dozens of Louisiana refugees, most of whom were en route to Texas. The Wadleys often discussed what they would do should they ever have to leave, and the only thing all agreed on was that they would not go to Texas. They made no plans until Vicksburg fell, and then decided to go to Georgia where they owned property. For eleven weeks they prepared for the trip and during this period Wadley packed and sent the family's most prized possessions, including Sarah's piano, to Texas. He and the Negroes spent the remainder of the time working on the wagons, making harnesses, and packing the tremendous quantity of articles they were to take. Time and time again they overloaded the wagons, then unloaded, repaired, and reloaded them. As the family was about to leave, Wadley's younger daughter developed diphtheria, and he thought of abandoning his plan to leave home, confessing that for the first time in his life he didn't know what to do. But in late September the family rolled away from "Oakland" on what was probably the most carefully prepared but shortest flight in the war. Encumbered with all kinds of paraphernalia—mattresses, carpets, tents, potted plants, huge quantities of clothing and food, a wagonload of kitchen equipment and another wagonload of lumber—they got only as far as the Mississippi when they were turned back by the Federals.[1]

Such methodical packing was the exception and not the rule, and many refugees dashed away with nothing more than they could carry in a sheet, tablecloth, or pillow case. Others had only the clothes they wore, and those with private conveyances often dumped quantities of possessions into their carriages, wagons, or buggies and fled in complete disarray. When Mrs. Polk heard that she must leave Nashville, she had one hour in which to get aboard the last civilian train out of the city. Duties she did not assume she delegated to her daughters, and they managed to collect an impressive quantity of baggage and even took time to cut the family portraits from their frames. The one thing they failed to do and later regretted was to pack the turkey dinner prepared for them but left uneaten. En route to New Orleans they went days without food and many times thought of that dinner.[2]

Excessive quantities of baggage often proved to be a liability rather than an asset, and women were usually the worst offenders. Jorantha Semmes wrote her husband that one of his cousins expected to get rail accommodations to Montgomery for herself and ten heavy pieces of luggage.[3] Refugee sisters from Orange, Virginia, went to an aunt's in Gordonsville and were given a room each, but one complained that they were too crowded for comfort because their trunks filled both rooms.[4] Women often carried not only the essentials but also items of sentimental value, some even transporting their pianos from place to place. They were neither concerned with the problem of overloaded conveyances nor realistic about getting their luggage moved on and off trains. Those who were aware of the problems usually ignored them and expected that someone would come along to help a lady in distress. A young Georgian realized that she was going to have difficulties on a forthcoming trip by train because she was traveling so "*heavily*-freighted," but this did not deter her from continuing her shopping sprees to buy huge quantities of articles she knew she could not purchase in her next refuge.[5]

The quantity and array of items taken by some refugees added a ridiculous note to the movement and provoked comment from those who witnessed the passage of a caravan. A group was seen going through northern Louisiana with all kinds of heavy, bulky furniture piled carelessly in the wagons.[6] And an Alabama refugee left Huntsville with eight wagons filled with household possessions.[7] Countless others insisted on taking everything they could haul, even the kitchen stoves, but their problems often increased in proportion to their tonnage. Wagons broke under the strain and bogged down in mud, sometimes having to be unloaded before they could be extricated. Heavy articles were discarded along the way in order to lighten the load, and a caravan of overloaded conveyances slowed the refugees to such an extent that some were overtaken by the enemy they had left home to evade. A member of President Davis' party believed that he was captured because Mrs. Davis had insisted on taking such a tremendous quantity of baggage. He said that the group "crawled along with two great army wagons and two ambulances . . . leaving a trail like an army corps." He told Mrs. Davis that she was "burdened with all that stuff," but others assured her that the party could not possibly be overtaken.[8]

Another problem confronting refugees was the question of what should be done with their animals. Those harnessed to the conveyances were necessary, but others were also valuable as replacements and as potential sources of food and clothing. It was always difficult and sometimes impossible to buy animals, and as many were taken on the flight as circumstances permitted. But the question of whether or not to take family pets was another matter. They could be nuisances and must be fed, but adults as well as children were not inclined to leave them behind. Among the pets often seen with a party of refugees were dogs, cats, birds, rabbits, lambs, and deer.[9] When Joseph LeConte was trying to get out of the path of the Federals he "met one of the Rhetts with an immense train of waggons [*sic*], his man servant and his maid servant, his ox and his ass and everything that was his, including a drove of about 40 hogs and a flock of at least 50 turkeys, fleeing . . . from the face of Sherman."[10] A sight such as this was not unusual but few observers had LeConte's flair for describing it.

Refugees who transported large numbers of slaves were to be pitied, for conveyances had to be provided for them and their shabby possessions, food had to be obtained, and the sick had to be attended. A few trusted servants were usually an asset, but large numbers were a problem; yet they represented an investment and planters felt they must be protected as property if for no other reason. They were sometimes moved to safer areas before the whites left home, but after the first months of the war they were more often moved with the family.

Many Southerners were possession-conscious and this was especially apparent when they showed greater concern for their personal belongings than for themselves. A Louisiana planter who was making plans to take his family to Texas within a few weeks heard that a neighbor was going the next day. He asked his friend if he would have room to take three trunks for his wife. She was afraid the Federals would get them, and as concerned as she was about the trunks, she was not afraid for herself.[11] When refugees lost their baggage some reacted as if they had nothing for which to live. A Columbia woman, who had "most unfortunately" lost hers, wrote her daughter that she wished she had remained in the city and endured the fire and occupation. She might then have been able to save her personal belongings, and without them all seemed lost.[12] It was a tragedy to lose anything which could not be replaced in wartime. As a Richmond nurse watched people leaving during the city's evacuation she noted the tremendous amount of property being hauled out of the city. With sympathy and understanding she wrote, "No one could afford to abandon any article of wearing apparel or household use when going where they knew that nothing could be replaced. Baggage was as valuable as life." [13]

Refugees leaving Federal areas usually had little choice as to what they could take with them. There were restrictions on the amount and kind, but the policy and enforcement depended primarily on the military officials who were often inconsistent. The poundage, monetary value, or number of pieces of luggage might be limited, and when the people were banished they could often take no more than the clothes they wore and carried in their arms. In all cases they and their baggage were liable to be searched and any prohibited articles were subject to seizure; this they resented. Many displaced people vehemently protested having any possession taken from them, and especially those which were not contraband. Mrs. Semmes was irritated with the Federals who searched her and her baggage as she was leaving Memphis, and she told her husband about many articles which the "Yankees" took." [14]

The innumerable problems encountered by the "heavily-freighted" refugees suggest that those who traveled with their worldly possessions in a sheet or pillow case might have been the more fortunate. There can be no doubt that their trip was in some ways made easier, but they started refugee life with a scanty stock of essentials, and wartime shortages usually prevented their later procuring a sufficiency of them. Some who traveled in this way were humiliated to be seen carrying makeshift luggage, and a Virginia refugee believed that it was because she had her belongings tied in a sheet that she failed to receive either the respect or attention she thought she merited.[15] However, women were more easily embarrassed early in the conflict than they were later. They usually lost or concealed their false pride after experiencing the war's leveling effects, and they realized that even those refugees who had left home in handsome carriages followed by wagons filled with expensive furnishings and bounteous supplies had experienced the ravages of time and war. It did not take long for all refugees to look alike as they traveled through the South. The description of a caravan passing through a Georgia town was typical of all as the refugees were seen riding "in every conceivable style of conveyance, drawn by horses, mules, oxen and even a single steer or cow."[16]

During most of the war, and always in areas being evacuated, "everything that had wheels was in demand and even a cart was deemed a prize."[17] Because of the shortage and increasing cost of conveyances, most refugees could not afford to buy or rent those available. A Louisiana refugee told of the family's renting a "four-horse hack" to take them a distance of four miles at a cost of $3,000.[18] When Jorantha Semmes and her relatives had to move from Mississippi to Gainesville, Alabama, in the summer of 1863, they wanted to purchase wagons but none were for sale. They rented several for $8.00 a day, and bought horses priced from $500 to $1,000 each, but even at these figures the refugees thought themselves fortunate to be able to get them.[19]

When people were caught in a mass movement they could expect transportation costs to be exorbitant. Thousands of New Orleans citizens banished by General Banks were taken as far as Pascagoula, Mississippi, where they were unceremoniously put ashore and told to get to Mobile in whatever way they could. Liverymen took advantage of the exiles' need and charged several hundred dollars each to take them to the city. When the Mobile citizens heard this, many sent their private carriages and wagons to bring the refugees to town and no charge was made for the service.[20] Few displaced people could expect generosity such as this, and most of them at some time had to pay extortioners' prices. In the last year of the war owners often required payments in specie rather than in the depreciated Confederate money, and it was said during the Richmond evacuation that anyone would have "to give his kingdom for a horse" and even then his chances of finding one were slim.[21] In the spring of 1865, Robert Toombs and a party of refugees traveled through Georgia in "a shabby little covered cart," at the rate "of two miles an hour" and at the cost of "one hundred dollars a mile." [22] The once affluent could not be choosers late in the war, and one of the most embarrassing predicaments in which proud women found themselves was having to ride in a wagon. A Charlestonian who traveled by train from Columbia to Camden, South Carolina, discovered that her only transportation to the country home of relatives was a wagon. She debated for some time as to whether or not she should ride in this fashion, but when she realized the only alternative was to walk, she seated herself on her trunk in the wagon and rode "through the streets of Camden" feeling "queer" and embarrassed.[23]

Throughout the war there were many refugees who had no conveyances. Men who traveled alone often rode horseback with their possessions in saddle bags or small valises. This mode of travel enabled them to make a quick getaway and cover the ground rapidly—primary considerations for many. But there were also thousands of displaced people who traveled by foot and took very few of their belongings. A woman told of her aunt and cousins who walked 150 miles through the Ozarks to get away from the Federals, but all who walked away from the enemy were not the poorer people in remote areas.[24] A South Carolina gentleman of proud heritage was reported to have walked eighty miles to the home of his daughter, there being no transportation available.[25] Among the most pitiful of the walking refugees were the mothers who had to carry their babies. One whose home was burned went on foot from Georgetown to Charleston, carrying her infant, Bible, and "the few articles of clothing" she had managed to save from the fire.[26] Those who had crude conveyances but no animals were sometimes their own beasts of burden. Among these were an old man, his daughter, and grandchildren who were driven from their home in Fredericksburg. He managed to build three rickety carts in which the family's baggage and the younger children were placed, and the man, his daughter, and the oldest grandchild pulled these to Richmond.[27]

Refugees traveling in animal-drawn vehicles realized their dependence on the creatures and were concerned for their welfare. Should one be lost the chances of replacing it were slight, and no one relished the idea of being stranded in flight. Perhaps it was because the animals assumed a new importance that refugees so often spoke of them with affection and gratitude. Mrs. Meriwether was sincerely devoted to the mule, Adrienne, which was with the refugees from the time they left Memphis until they returned after the war. By Mrs. Meriwether's own admission, Adrienne was "no ordinary mule" but more like "a member of the family." She worried about its fodder supply and shelter and was equally concerned about its becoming "confused" in its displacement.[28] Although many refugees were as devoted as Mrs. Meriwether to their faithful animals, none paid a more beautiful tribute to theirs than she did to Adrienne. Travelers encountered many unexpected problems as they tried to protect the beasts. Most had presumed they would graze along the way and fodder would be sufficient, but this was not the case in those areas ravaged by war, drouth, or flood. If they had money with which to buy feed, it was not always available at any price; when it was, the price was likely to be high. A refugee noted that it "cost between 20 & 30 dollars a day to get fodder for the horses and mules" when it could be bought, and when it could not the animals had to be fed "ground meal" from the family's supplies.[29]

When refugees traveled on public conveyances they were relieved of some of the problems others encountered in their own vehicles, but there were always problems. Stagecoach service was both expensive and erratic at best, and the number of passengers and quantity of baggage had to be limited. Some refugees traveling on stagecoaches sent their bulky possessions by other means, but no one liked to be separated from his belongings if it could be avoided. Many learned from experience that once apart the chances of getting together were remote in time of war.

Railroads accommodated a greater number of passengers and more baggage than did stagecoaches, and for this reason many possession-conscious refugees preferred this mode of transportation. But even those traveling on trains could easily be separated from their baggage unless it was taken on board with them. Even after having seen it loaded on the baggage car they could not relax, for it was often unloaded to lighten the weight and sometimes the entire car was left at the station. When owners rushed to get accommodations for themselves and left their baggage on the platform expecting it to be loaded, it was likely to remain where it had been deposited. The surest way to protect one's possessions was to keep them in his grasp, but this was impossible when tremendous quantities were taken.

Trains were always overloaded and overtaxed during the war but never more so than during a mass evacuation from an urban area. There are descriptions of such a scene in every major town from which hundreds or thousands were fleeing. When the Federals neared Jackson, Mississippi, the station was "crowded with crushing and elbowing human beings, swaying to and fro—baggage being thrown hither and thither." Those trying to get out of town were "seeking the Mobile cars—seeking the Vicksburg cars—seeking anything to bear them away from the threatened and fast depopulating town." [30] In this crowd were Katherine Polk Gale and her children who were "seeking the Mobile cars." Mrs. Gale never forgot "the excitement at the depot" that day in May, and she recalled that her husband had to load the family's baggage on the train because there was no one else to do it. This was not unusual during the war, and Mrs. Gale was more fortunate than most women to have her husband with her. When she entered the car she had difficulty finding a seat but eventually located one for herself, and the children sat on the large hamper of food which had been brought along to insure the family's eating.[31]

The preinvasion hysteria in Columbia in February, 1865, was even more hectic than that in Jackson. It seemed that everyone was trying to get away, and an observer described the scene in the station as "universal confusion . . . such as might be looked for in . . . a city from which thousands were preparing to fly without previous preparation for flight." The depot was "crowded with anxious waiters with a wilderness of baggage, millions perhaps in value, much of which was left . . . and lost. In numerous instances those who succeeded in getting away, did so at the cost of trunks and luggage." [32] This was the sight which greeted Joseph LeConte when he tried to get the Nitre Bureau equipment aboard, and it was almost more than he could endure to see "the surging, pleading mass" of women and children begging to be taken aboard the outgoing trains.[33] One of these "pleading women," with her baby and the baby's nurse, arrived at the station just as the car doors were shut. Her husband suggested that she slide through a window and he would hand the baby to her, but the Negro "Mammy's" proportions were such that she would never make it through the window, and the woman would not leave without her.[34] One of Mrs. Chesnut's friends who tried to enter in the same way got caught halfway in and the train left while she dangled from the window. After much pulling, she was "hauled in by main force," and while it is doubtful that the victim enjoyed the experience, Mrs. Chesnut thought it highly amusing.[35]

A packed refugee train with hundreds clinging to the outside was a weird spectacle but not an unusual one. Although railroad officials tried to keep those from going who could not be accommodated within the cars, there was little, if anything, they could do when the pressure was great. Typical of such trains was the one seen passing through east Tennessee when thousands of citizens were in flight South. The "seats, aisles, platforms, baggage cars . . . and tops of cars were covered with passengers . . . and thousands had been left at the depot begging to come." [36] A Georgian riding a similar train estimated that the passengers numbered approximately 1,000, and "people who could not get inside were hanging on wherever they could find a sticking place; the aisles and platform down to the last step were full of people clinging . . . like bees swarming around the . . . hive." [37]

Traveling with the masses in wartime was at best uncomfortable, but there were more private, commodious rail accommodations for the privileged, influential few who could afford them. One or more box-cars could be chartered by a family if the head of the household had proper connections. These were fitted with furnishings from the refugees' home, and the passengers traveled in comparative luxury. They were free from many worries that plagued those in their own conveyances. Thomas Dabney's daughter remarked that the furnishings in the boxcars were "arranged as . . . at home" and that the trip was "the most comfortable long journey" she had ever taken. Dabney had chartered two boxcars, one for his family and the other fitted with kitchen equipment and occupied by his slaves, but these luxurious accommodations cost "several thousand dollars." [38] Very few Southerners could afford to travel in this style. Some who managed to do so lived in the cars after arriving at their destination, but this depended on whether or not railroad officials permitted them to do so. People who could not afford to travel in this manner were nevertheless impressed by those who could, but they also criticized them for having entire cars at their disposal when many refugees could not even get aboard a train. They also complained that chartered boxcars often blocked traffic, and a Georgian noted that cars filled with "the household goods of the refugees" not only slowed travel for others but "literally blockaded" it.[39]

Not to be confused with cars utilized by a single family were those used to transport groups of refugees, especially exiles banished by military authorities. There was nothing private or luxurious about their accommodations, for the passengers, often strangers to each other, were herded together like animals. The boxcar in which Mrs. J. G. M. Ramsey rode out of Knoxville had no seats, "no water . . . no appendages of comfort or convenience more than . . . [were] found on every lumber or coal train." [40] Hundreds of Atlantans banished by Sherman arrived in Macon in boxcars, several families to a car, and because they had nowhere else to go they lived in these overcrowded, makeshift quarters for weeks.

The Confederate Army sometimes made its carriers available to refugees. When it was trying to evacuate an area it often ran a shuttle service, as in the case at Fredericksburg. An officer wrote his wife, "Our ambulances have been running all day, and are now going back and forth, carrying . . . families, who have . . . left their homes . . . rather than risk the chances of the threatened shelling." [41] Government conveyances were also assigned to transport wives and families of high ranking military or political personnel, and this was usually true when they were caught in a battle area. Although army ambulances afforded greater privacy than public facilities, many women privileged to travel in this way bitterly complained about their discomfort. Mrs. Basil Wilson Duke referred to the one in which she traveled as "miserable," and so uncomfortable that she "expected every moment to be jolted to pieces." [42] Prominent personages and their kin were also permitted to ride military trains not open to the public. When Senator Wigfall's daughters were guests of General and Mrs. Joseph E. Johnston in the summer of 1864, it was decided that the young ladies should leave Atlanta and stay with friends in Macon. They had accommodations on a hospital train and, with their chaperone, were the only women on the train. This trip made a lasting impression on Louise Wigfall, and although not a pleasant mode of travel it was a way to get to Macon when others could not get passage on any public carrier. [43]

Those who could use government transportation not available to all were vulnerable to criticism. The social standing of a favored few often enabled them to travel in greater comfort than could the rank and file of refugees. Not only were special conveyances placed at their disposal, but army drivers and escorts were assigned to take them to their destination. This naturally afforded protection and a greater security than most people had, but it also irritated Southerners who had no means of transportation and no one to escort them to safety. Citizens resented the fact that military equipment and personnel needed in battle were assigned to the few women who happened to be related to prominent officers.

Water transportation was used by refugees who found this means convenient, and it often served to transport the people to a point where they could connect with a land carrier. Mrs. Leonidas Polk left New Orleans in a small boat which transported her to the railroad in Mississippi, and many Louisiana refugees left their homes in similar conveyances.[44] One family traveling in a houseboat entered the Mississippi River to find "a seething mass of craft of all kinds and descriptions that could be made into possible conveyances to carry away the terror-stricken people . . . all making a mad rush for the Red River." [45] Canal boats were also pressed into service by the refugees, and this was one mode of transportation used by Cornelia McDonald and her family during their displacement. They traveled by canal boat from Lynchburg to Lexington, Virginia, and because of the lack of space Mrs. McDonald sent most of her baggage by wagon. She carried several pieces of luggage which contained clothing sufficient for the family's immediate needs, and when she arrived at her destination and discovered that the bag containing the children's clothes was missing she was "on the verge of tears." It had taken months to make the clothes and she had only one dollar to her name when she disembarked.[46] Passengers traveling by water were not immune to baggage problems.

Whatever means of transportation the refugees had at their disposal, they had to endure many delays and inconveniences along the way, and in most cases they had not anticipated them. Things might go smoothly until the party reached a river that had to be crossed and the bridge or ferry they had expected to find was no longer there. Rivers and streams normally forded were sometimes swollen or flooded so as to make fording impossible or hazardous, but refugees usually attempted a crossing when they were impatient to be on their way. When wagons were heavily loaded the process of getting across water barriers was complicated, and when ferries or rafts were made by the travelers they were often too light and rickety to carry a heavy cargo. When the Wadleys ferried across the Tensas, the makeshift float was so small that the animals had to be unharnessed from the conveyances to swim or to be run across on the raft, several at a time. Some who were given the privilege of riding jumped off in midstream, and Sarah Wadley surmised that it was because they didn't trust the frail float. Getting the caravan across this relatively simple barrier caused Mr. Wadley to doubt that he would ever make it across the

Mississippi, and he asked all passersby what they thought his chances were but they gave him slight encouragement. One thing he did know: if the Federals refused him permission to cross, he would never succeed at slipping across in the dark of night as so many were doing.

While some refugees crossed the Mississippi with comparative ease, others encountered major difficulties. In this group was a family of refugees who left their flooded Mississippi plantation expecting to cross into Arkansas. They located a man who was capitalizing on the situation and who had supposedly committed to memory the exact times when the Federal gunboats patrolled the river. He agreed to take the family across but he realized it would take two trips. The first was a success but on the second trip he was caught and the refugees were taken to Helena and questioned, after which they were put ashore on the Mississippi side of the river and told to go home. This they did not do, and after finding a "leaky row boat" they crossed successfully, but in the process they had lost all but one slave and many of their possessions.[47]

A party of South Carolinians running from Sherman reached a point on the Broad River where they had customarily crossed on a ferry which was no longer there. A float was borrowed from a farmer, the wheels removed from the carriage, the horses unharnessed, and the wheelless carriage with its passengers was placed on the float and taken to the opposite bank. The servant then took the empty float back across the river, tied the carriage wheels on the horses, and the animals and servant swam back to the waiting party. The wheels were replaced, horses reharnessed, and all were soon on their way.[48] Refugees often handled a water barrier ingeniously but all did not cross with the ease of these South Carolinians. When Josiah Gorgas and his group reached the swollen Catawba River south of Charlotte, they decided to ford it despite the high water. The refugees and the vehicles got across safely but a part of their furniture, together with "tin basins, water pails, [a] bag of useful things, corn," and other items floated off downstream during the crossing.[49]

Some of the worst traffic jams of the war occurred at crossings when hundreds of people arrived at about the same time and facilities were inadequate to meet the demand. This often happened if entire communities fled by a single road as when hundreds of people left their homes in the Cumberland River Valley after they heard that Fort Donelson had fallen. They headed for Nashville, and when they arrived at the river bank opposite the city, they found insufficient ferries to take them across. Bedlam prevailed as they crowded "the landing for ferriage in small, . . . insufficient scows that . . . had to make do for bridges." [50] When hundreds of citizens fled simultaneously from Huntsville, Alabama, a similar situation developed, but here the extortioner went to work. As refugees lined up for miles waiting their turn to be ferried across, the wealthier ones who could pay as much as $500 were taken across first. Those who could not pay this unreasonable toll were, in some cases, "delayed for days." [51] Having to pay tremendous costs for simple services which they desperately needed was a major problem for a great many refugees. There were always Southerners who saw their chance to capitalize on the distress of displaced people.

Other factors, including the weather, seemed to conspire against the refugees. The dirt roads in the South fell into disrepair during the war and they were often so deeply rutted and muddy as to be impassable. When Mrs. Meriwether drove through the Mississippi mud it reminded her of an adhesive substance as it pulled at her buggy, clogged the wheels, and enabled her to cover only ten miles a day, about half the usual mileage.[52] The gallivanting Mrs. Basil Wilson Duke was not happy in Abingdon, Virginia, but she decided to spend an entire winter there rather than ride over the roads which were "in frightful condition." [53] And refugees traveling through swamps had an even more difficult time as their conveyances not only bogged down but the wheels broke on concealed roots and stumps. It was primarily the dread of trying to get through the swamps that kept Kate Stone's family from leaving "Brokenburn" earlier. When they eventually overcame this obstacle, they were confronted with others on the road to Texas. On several occasions wagons had to be unloaded and passengers had to get out and walk so that the vehicles could get through the mud.[54]

Probably no traveler had greater reason to complain about poor road conditions than did Joseph LeConte when he escorted the party of women and children out of Georgia. Burdened with an excessive amount of baggage, they jogged over the muddy roads which the military had left so deeply rutted and in such "dreadful condition" that in one afternoon they were stuck "half-a-dozen times." Once when the mud was exceptionally deep, LeConte and his servant had to remove every article from one of the baggage wagons in order to extricate it and then the muddy items had to be reloaded before the refugees could resume their journey. When they neared Milledgeville, the party was caught in a traffic jam as the road conditions brought hundreds of travelers to an abrupt halt. LeConte commented that never before had he heard such a "babel of noise and confusion" as he did that day.[55]

Refugees who traveled with heavily loaded wagons filled with household goods may have had greater difficulty getting through swamps, over muddy roads and across rivers, but they did not usually have to depend on wayside lodging. Some who carried camping necessities nevertheless expected to find accommodations along the way, but failing this they could manage. However, all displaced people moving through areas in which they had no personal contacts could never be sure of finding a place in a private home or commercial establishment at the end of the day. Kate Stone's family had a great quantity of household equipment with them yet expected to find lodging of some kind en route to Texas; before they left Louisiana they learned that rarely would this be their good fortune. Not only did people refuse them rooms regardless of what they offered to pay, but they often treated the Stones with contempt "as though the very name of traveler was a disgrace." The family had no choice but to camp out, and although they were so tired by night that it didn't matter where they slept, Kate took a dim view of the "myriads of ticks, redbugs [and] fleas" with which they had to contend.[56]

The Stones were less prepared for the hostile attitude of those who lived along the road because, as strangers, they had been cordially received in the home of the Wadleys when they first fled from their plantation. Here Kate formed a lasting friendship with Sarah Wadley, and, remembering the hospitality, Kate was disillusioned to find that such a welcome did not await them in homes across the state or in Texas.[57] Yet there were many Southerners who were as generous to refugees as their circumstances permitted. A Vicksburg citizen who traveled with her family to Alabama later recalled that they had stopped "at friendly houses" all along the road, and their hosts were often already accommodating other displaced people.[58] But no one could be sure of such a reception and for this reason Bishop Lay, who had experienced the problems of wartime travel, made plans to leave Little Rock ahead of the mass exodus. He thought his chances better for finding lodging.[59] So eminent a person as Joseph Davis had to camp out many nights as he moved across Mississippi. Once when he and Mrs. Davis found a room in a boardinghouse, they stayed three weeks, but their party, including their granddaughter, had to live in an abandoned cabin because they could not find rooms.[60]

Refugees recognized that while lodging was desirable, food was vital, and it was very difficult to buy meals or provisions in many areas. One of the greatest shocks experienced by the displaced people was their discovery that "room" and "board" were often separated during the war. To obtain the former did not necessarily mean one could contract for the latter, not even for breakfast. If the refugees did not have food with them they could never be sure of eating and, as one refugee said, "Everyone carries his own provisions; . . . you can get nothing if you do not. . . ." [61] Joseph LeConte's party had this problem also when, after their third day on the road, they gave out of provisions. For the remainder of the trip they existed on a scant supply of bacon and bread which they could buy and on occasional handouts from sympathetic people, most of whom were themselves refugees. It is no wonder that when the LeContes stopped with Professor Holmes, after leaving the others, they were impressed with his bounteous hospitality bestowed on a total of twenty guests, most of whom were refugees and strangers to Joseph LeConte. It took several hours to prepare the breakfast the morning after they arrived, but LeConte said that the meal "was so large" that it was well worth the delay.[62]

Refugees who camped out and prepared their own meals usually ate only twice a day, and both meals were as substantial as supplies permitted but usually so plain and monotonous that it was difficult to tell one meal from the other. Most refugees who took along household equipment had taken time to prepare food for the trip, but this was soon eaten and they then had to resort to a simpler diet. However, even the plainest meal tasted good to weary refugees, as an Arkansan later recalled. Although only a child at the time her family refugeed to Texas, she said that her most vivid memory of their trip was the aroma of bacon frying over an open camp fire and the deliciousness of meal after meal which consisted of nothing more than bacon and biscuits fried in the bacon fat.[63]

There were additional problems which confronted the refugees, and one of these was trying to find the way in strange areas, especially when roads were in disrepair, nonexistent, or inadequately marked. It took one group nearly four months to cover approximately a hundred miles in Arkansas, during which time they lost their way many times and had to retrace their steps.[64] Rain and snow were also delaying factors, and for those camping out this was a serious problem. Not only did heavy rains make roads impassable and swell rivers and streams, but they made it virtually impossible for the travelers to keep themselves and their baggage dry. Campers had difficulty finding dry wood with which to make fires and keep them burning. A newspaperman visited an encampment of Texas-bound Louisiana refugees who had been traveling in rain for more than a week when they reached the Sabine River. The steady downpour continued as they tried to make camp and build fires which would do no more than smoke and smolder. The reporter saw mothers holding their young and hovering around the smoking heaps in an effort to keep warm. Their household goods were thoroughly soaked in the open carts and wagons, and their laundry was "satyrically [*sic*] hanging out to dry." One planter family was seen sitting under a wagon, the father writing, the mother knitting, the daughter reading, and all three "defying the elements." Farther down the road was an open baggage cart stalled in the mud, the owners "nearly desperate" as they tried to free it.[65] This was not an unusual scene in the wartime South, and nothing could make a party of refugees appear and feel more dismal and dejected than a long siege of inclement weather.

The lack of water, as well as too much, was a problem in certain areas and in certain seasons. Not only was it needed for drinking purposes but also for bathing and laundering, and refugees who had never experienced a water shortage were surprised to be confronted with this problem. Those moving through drouth-stricken areas or into Texas, where distances between rivers were greater, were thrown into a state of shock because of the scarcity of water. Dry areas also afforded less grazing land for cattle—another source of great concern. Even when water was more plentiful, the tired, dirty travelers who wanted to bathe usually lacked the necessary facilities and the privacy to which they were accustomed. A bath suddenly became a luxury and because those who camped out usually slept in their clothes, it seemed a necessity. Sarah Wadley had never before endured such primitive living conditions as when she spent three days and nights in the same clothes, including her corset. At the end of the fourth day the family encamped near a house and, taking "all the requisites for washing and dressing," Sarah marched herself to the front door and asked the owner if she could have the use of a room in which to bathe and change clothes. The request was graciously granted, and after Sarah completed her toilet she reported that her spirits were greatly improved.[66]

A potential danger always confronting the refugees was death on the roads, and this was more to be expected than in ordinary times. The enemy was one possible threat, but lawless bands in some areas preyed upon travelers without regard for life or property. The danger to one's person was the problem most often expected and feared by the refugees, whether traveling singly or in groups. There were several instances during the war when trains carrying large numbers of refugees were fired upon by the enemy, and whether deliberate or accidental, the stories were repeated, reprinted, and interpreted as diabolical acts. One of the most widely publicized incidents was the shelling of a refugee train leaving Fredericksburg, and although no one was killed, it nevertheless caused Southerners to be even more afraid of the enemy. Judith McGuire was a kind, gentle person and not inclined to repeat rumors or atrocity stories, but when she heard of this incident she expressed sympathy for the travelers and sadly commented, "The sufferings of wandering women and children are great." [67] This understatement was nevertheless a profound truth. Almost as widely publicized as the Fredericksburg incident was the shelling of a refugee train leaving Fernandina, Florida, where two passengers were killed.[68] However there were fewer refugee casualties from enemy fire than might be expected, especially when so many people waited for an attack to begin before leaving home.

Fright and overexertion were more often cited as causes for death among the refugees. When Cornelia McDonald was caught in the midst of "sick men, hungry men, and women with crowds of children" all in flight before the enemy, she saw the body of a man who stopped to rest but "never rose again." The passersby, fearing for their own lives, merely glanced in his direction; no one "took time to stop." [69] One of the refugees leaving Columbia and traveling in a party which included an "elderly grandmother" and an "invalid father" was convinced that the death of both came because of their extreme fright and exertion.[70] Many refugees died in flight but the exact cause of death was not always determined. The Yorkville (South Carolina) *Enquirer* on March 16, 1865, reported the death of a prominent Charleston lawyer who had been a refugee in Lancaster. His body was found "concealed in a ravine" near the town, and it was assumed that he had been murdered by the passing Federals, but in this case and many similar ones the conclusions were drawn in the heat of war.

So afraid of the enemy were the refugees that if he approached they might hide for days and even weeks in nearby woods to escape his clutches. This was a miserable and often almost unendurable experience. They were afraid to build fires because the smoke might be seen, or to make any noise lest they bring the foe down on them. Trying to keep quiet was especially difficult when babies and animals refused to be disciplined. A party of Arkansas refugees caught in this situation lived in the forest for weeks, for as one group of Federals left the area and the travelers made preparations to resume their journey, another appeared.[71] Displaced people hid not only to protect themselves but also their possessions, and they hid from the Confederates as well as Federals, for the "friendly" forces often impressed their wagons and stock. In the thinking of most refugees it made no difference who took their valuables, for when they were gone they could seldom be replaced.

Guerrilla bands organized under a heartless leader were more to be feared than the Federal army. These ruffians could easily terrorize and overpower the refugees, many of whom were at the time in flight to avoid them. There were several notorious guerrilla leaders who operated in remote areas of the Confederacy, but one of the most ruthless was Cullen Montgomery Baker, a bloodthirsty renegade who preyed on poor people living in western Arkansas and those traveling the road to Texas. He determined that the residents living in his territory must stay at home because he exacted money and produce from them in return for "protection," and when they left, his income diminished. Settlers who had been bled "white" by his extortion and intimidation sometimes banded together and started toward Texas. In 1864 a group of about two hundred set out and got as far as the Saline River when they were slowed down in crossing. About half had crossed when Baker and his gang overtook and ordered them back to their homes. Several men refused to obey and were shot, after which the others turned back. Additional members of the party who irritated Baker on the return trip were killed and all in the group were terror-stricken.[72]

Primarily because of the innumerable problems and dangers, most refugees preferred to travel with others, but the desire for companionship was also strong. Women left without male protection wanted both company and the safety of numbers, and when they could do so attached themselves to a party. Those with children were more willing to start out as a single family, but women traveling alone, especially in private conveyances, were relatively rare. It was because women preferred a male escort that Joseph LeConte found himself with a party of strangers who had attached themselves to him. The Wadleys were requested to let a neighbor go along with them and the generous family at first agreed, but when Wadley discovered that she had a tremendous quantity of baggage and no vehicles of any kind, he refused her request. Sarah Wadley expressed sympathy for the lady but admitted that her own "charity" did not "go far enough" to accept her company under these conditions.[73] Mrs. Meriwether left Memphis with only her two small sons and a servant, but when a second move was later necessary she was relieved to have the company of others although she thought their caravan an amusing sight.[74] There were a few stout-hearted women who would travel alone in their own conveyances, and one of these was a Mississippian who was so afraid of the Federals that she was determined to leave her home with or without company. Neighbors tried to discourage her going and one thought her "very unwise," but she went despite their protests.[75]

Young people were usually not concerned with the problems of overloaded conveyances or feeding and getting along with additional people, some of whom were "free-loaders," but what they so often wanted were others of their own age for company. Kate Stone expressed the wish that she might join a party because it "would be so much more enjoyable." [76] And a young lady in Virginia watched a caravan of refugees pass her home, and they seemed to be having such a good time as they sang "Dixie" and laughed that she wanted to be a refugee and enjoy the gaiety. She soon was, but she found that it was not as much fun as she had thought it would be.[77]

The refugees were introduced to the meaning of their displacement as they traveled away from their homes, and in most cases their trip was a rude awakening to the realities of war. Adults usually started the journey with a heavy heart, for it was not easy to leave one's home and head toward an uncertain future. As they traveled, whether by road or rail, singly or in a caravan, in comfortable conveyances or on foot, every mile was a potentially dangerous one. Days on the road were long and trying, whatever the season, and even the people who were normally optimistic and adjustable grew tired and irritable as they battled the elements, inconveniences, and impediments. None anticipated genuine happiness at the end of the line; safety and comparative peace were all they expected in a temporary abode which they never intended to be "home." Many refugees were bitter that a war for which they felt no responsibility was compelling them to make a move they had never planned, and this bitterness and frustration usually increased rather than diminished as they traveled through the wartime South. Spirits sagged, bodies ached, tensions mounted, and tempers flared in proportion to their problems. Jorantha Semmes aptly described a typical flight of displaced people as one of "clashing carriage wheels and conflicting interests." [78]

. . . *the fascination* *of brick and mortar*

Where would a refugee go? As Judith and John McGuire rode away from Alexandria, neither spoke until they reached the first crossroad, and it was not surprising that the minister broke the silence with the statement: "It makes not the slightest difference which road we take—we might as well drive to the right hand as to the left." [1] Where, indeed, would a refugee go? The McGuires were among the first to raise the question but they would not be the last, for thousands of displaced Southerners were faced with the same problem. And most refugees were confronted with this situation more than once, for rarely was their first move their last.

At the time of their first displacement the people usually fell into one of three categories: those who had planned their flight with a specific destination in mind; those who had no definite plans but expected to be received in the homes of relatives or friends; and those who had no idea where they would go. Many refugees experienced all three as the war repeatedly uprooted them, and even those who had carefully planned their first move eventually discovered that circumstances prevented their later relocating themselves in an orderly, organized manner. Very few refugees were permitted to remain in one spot long enough to feel at home, and as they migrated from place to place within the contracting Confederacy they created problems for themselves and others. This floating population contributed appreciably to the breakdown of homefront morale as it aggravated the economic and social conditions in the wartime South.

Refugees who gave any thought to the future had many decisions to make when they left home. They must decide how far they were willing to travel, whether or not they wanted to live with friends or relatives, what type of accommodations they preferred, and whether or not they would need employment. They also had to choose between towns and rural areas, a decision depending on their wishes and needs, but what they wanted and what they were compelled to accept were two entirely different matters, if not in the beginning, before the end of the war. Because their first decision very often proved to be an unwise one, their ideas changed and for this reason the refugees appear to have been inconsistent. Some who went first to the city later found the country more to their liking, and others moved first to rural areas and then to the towns. But the war altered circumstances, and the uncertainties of the period were not conducive to the development of consistency when the people were pushed along with the crowd.

Displaced people made many decisions which were shortsighted, if not foolish, but most were natural mistakes which would be made by any people caught in an enemy invasion which they had not anticipated. They had been reassured many times by the politicians, press, and pulpit that the South would be defended, and they believed it in the beginning. Even as their homes fell within enemy lines they were certain that a Confederate counterattack would soon free them, and for this reason most people were reluctant to stray too far from home. As they edged away by degrees, keeping a short distance ahead of the Federals, they were soon living like gypsies, always on the move and never rooted anywhere. Most refugees were hesitant to take a giant leap in the beginning and unwilling to leave their native state except as a last resort. Their records indicate that many would have preferred to transplant themselves in a foreign country rather than cross the state line. Matthew Page Andrews, like many others, advised his fiancée to find a refuge in Virginia, for he had a "perfect dread" of her leaving the state.[2] This was the reaction of most Virginians and South Carolinians, but some from other areas often felt the same way. Refugees usually preferred to move a half-dozen times within their own state rather than settle themselves in another, but they sometimes had no choice in the matter.

Newspapers frequently commented on this preference of the displaced people, sometimes condemning and at other times praising their provincialism. When South Carolinians from the coastal areas moved to the interior, they were often caustically critical of the residents whom they accused of being unfriendly. It did not seem to occur to them that they might find a pleasant life in Georgia or North

Carolina; they often reported their situation to the Charleston newsmen who then editorialized on the subject. A typical item was one which reminded the upcountry citizens that the refugees were not foreigners but South Carolinians who had chosen to remain "in their own Carolina." For this reason, if for no other, they merited a hospitable reception. "The heart of an exile," wrote the editor, "revolts at seeking a home, however temporary, outside the parental territory." [3] This attitude proved to be an unfortunate one in many cases. Although no one could foresee the course the war would take, many displaced people could have saved themselves several moves had they been willing to travel a greater distance in the beginning. But most refugees believed that they would soon return to their homes and the nearer they were to them the sooner they could get back. As they fled they were dazed, disillusioned, and afraid, and all seemed to think that although displacement had happened to others, it could not happen to them. They were in search of temporary shelter and they wanted it to be near home and in their own state.

Refugees who had family and friends in safer areas had to decide whether or not to seek refuge in their homes. For some it was a logical solution to their problem and for others it was the only solution, but for many it was the least desired arrangement. This was the reaction of many mothers of young children who had been accustomed to supervising their own homes and raising their young according to their own ideas. When they were required to live in another's home where several families were housed, young matrons felt as though they were relegated in an inferior position. Overcrowded wartime homes called for the occupants to exercise patience and emotional control, but this was even more difficult because of the uncertainty and insecurity of the period. When families were not compatible the situation was trying for all concerned, and when the refugees feared trouble they were reluctant to move in if there was any other solution to their problem. It was often at the husband's insistence that the wife took the children and went to her parents' home, but this arrangement was not always satisfactory. Letters and diaries indicate that the most common complaints were that the grandparents spoiled the children, interfered with maternal discipline, and constantly gave advice which was not sought or appreciated. If conditions became unbearable, families sometimes separated, the disgruntled refugees moving elsewhere.

But the forces of war brought many families together, for it was natural that loved ones would want to be with one another in time of stress. Not only did refugees move into the homes of relatives, but several families refugeed together when this was necessary. A cousin of Mrs. Basil Wilson Duke wrote that his wife was coming out of Kentucky and he wanted her to go directly to Mrs. Duke who was herself displaced. He asked that she "learn" his wife the fine points of refugeeing and instruct her "on all the good places" for refugees to live.[4] Homes, temporary and permanent, stretched to accommodate homeless friends and kin, and despite family disagreements, there were many instances of several families living together in peace. As previously noted, Mrs. Leonidas Polk threw open her doors to her children and their families, and all lived together in harmony. For almost a year, the McGuires shared a small cottage with several families, and despite the overcrowded conditions and innumerable problems, Mrs. McGuire thought that this was the most pleasant period of her displacement. The conditions within a congested refugee establishment depended on many factors, not the least of which were the occupants.

Whether to live in a city or in the country was another decision which many refugees had to make. The merits of each was a major topic for debate in the Confederacy and the people, whether displaced or not, expressed definite views on the subject. Within a ten-day period, two Confederate officers advised their wives to pursue an opposite course in selecting a refuge, and each was positive that he was right. One urged that his go to a city because she would be "much safer there than in the country."[5] The other warned his wife against towns because the cost of living was much higher and she would not be as safe as in a rural area.[6] Newspapers also argued the pros and cons of the matter, and while generally encouraging that townspeople graciously receive refugees early in the war, editors more often discouraged their coming later. They blamed many of the city's problems on the displaced people and tried to pressure them into the country. An Atlanta correspondent for the Augusta *Chronicle and Sentinel* asked, "Why do refugees insist on swarming around crowded cities, when the country offers so much cheaper and better retreat?" He believed they would be more comfortable in a log cabin than in a "congested tenement," and he could not understand "the fascination of brick and mortar." In his opinion nothing could equal the rural areas "especially for refugeeing."[7] By 1864, Georgia was feeling the full effects of the refugee infiltration, and the editors desperately tried to remove the homeless from overcrowded towns by stressing the higher costs, the danger of living in railroad centers, and the risks involved should the communities have to be evacuated. One newsman warned the refugees on all these points and cautioned them that they would probably have to move many times if they insisted on staying in cities.[8] A Milledgeville editor not only pointed out that supplies were cheaper in the country but also that taxes were lower.[9]

Editors in Georgia and elsewhere in the Confederacy might just as well have saved their energies, paper, and ink, for the refugees ignored their pleas and continued to be "fascinated by brick and mortar." It has been previously noted that urban areas were attractive for many reasons. Most important were the greater opportunities for employment, better transportation and communication facilities, companionship, protection, and charitable organizations. Early in the war cities offered more adequate and varied housing facilities, but this situation soon changed as thousands flocked into areas accustomed to accommodating hundreds. Despite the seriousness of the times, many refugees went to the cities for social reasons, and nowhere was this more true than in Richmond. Hundreds of Maryland refugees congregated here and one, Hetty Cary, was the toast of the capital. As stories spread over the Confederacy of the gaiety in Richmond and other cities, many young women living in remote areas away from others of their age wished that they could spend the war years in the social centers. They were embittered that the conflict had denied them male companionship and it was presumed that towns would afford them suitors aplenty. Some young refugees were drawn to urban areas for this very reason. The Wigfalls sent their daughters to Greensboro, North Carolina, when Richmond was endangered during the Peninsular Campaign, and Louise was anticipating the change for two reasons. She was happy to be leaving her mother's watchful eye, and she was delighted at the thought of living in a college. Her parents had made reservations for the girls in the Methodist College which was open to refugees. Upon her arrival in Greensboro she was shocked and disappointed to find that it was "a *Female* not a *Male* College." [10] This was a cruel blow to the teen-ager who had been so eager to be a refugee.

Not only did the larger towns attract displaced people, but villages also became overcrowded. This was especially true of those served by some form of public transportation and maintaining mail service. Resorts and college towns were popular because they afforded living quarters. Resorts usually had a hotel and cottages while college communities offered boardinghouses and college buildings which were open to refugees, especially when the institution closed or when its enrollment declined appreciably. Another attraction of the villages, especially if located in a rich farming area, was the more abundant and less expensive supplies. The high cost of living in larger cities sent many refugees into smaller, more remote towns, but as the community became overcrowded rents rose until they were often as high as those in the city. When General Lafayette McLaws urged his wife to leave Augusta because of the high cost of living, he suggested several towns in Georgia which would make a much better refuge. His choice was Sparta because it was off the railroad and telegraph line and therefore should be safer and less congested. But the *"six* good schools" in the town also appealed to him, for he was always worried about the possible disruption of his children's education.[11] Parents were often drawn to towns affording educational opportunities for their young, for as a North Carolinian expressed it, "education must be considered." [12]

The smaller towns were the ones more likely to need the services of professional people, especially ministers. When James Earl Bradley, a refugee from New Orleans, heard that he could be a supply preacher in Summit, Mississippi, he went there. Later when he heard of the need for a full-time minister in Arcola, Louisiana, he moved to the town and served a congregation composed "primarily of refugees." [13] When a great many South Carolinians flocked to Edgefield, those who were Episcopalians were disappointed to find no rector. The local newspaper called on a displaced minister of the faith to make the village his refuge for the duration of the war, assuring him that a church with organ awaited his coming.[14]

Rural areas were far less popular with the refugees than were cities and villages, but many plantation homes were nevertheless crowded with occupants during the war. Women without male protectors were especially reluctant to rent or buy property in the country because they would be unguarded and would lack companionship. They also would be less likely to get word from their husbands and to obtain services they might reasonably expect in towns. But they would be able to live more cheaply. Supplies were more plentiful and, if necessary, they could raise some food themselves and many problems of city living would be avoided. When trying to sell property, realtors made rural living very appealing by directing their announcements to the refugees, with captions reading "of Interest to Refugees," or simply "Refugees!" The wealthier people, especially those who had a man at home during the war, often bought country homes or moved to their own plantations in an area removed from battle lines. Small farmers who had no other way of making a living, and could afford to do so, usually wanted to buy or rent farms when displaced, for they were not at home in the cities. The Briant family from northern Georgia is typical of this group. They were first run from their little farm in Fannin County, and settled for a time in Bartow County, but during the North Georgia Campaign they were again uprooted. They found another farm for rent in Banks County and the family settled there, but living on three different farms in four years made it difficult for them to prosper.[15] Most refugees who lived in rural areas during the war were those who had moved in with family and friends, and these homes were often as crowded as any to be found in cities.

Because propagandists for the small towns and country so often emphasized the greater abundance of supplies to be found there, it would seem that a larger percentage of economically hard-pressed refugees would have chosen either in preference to the city. Some did remove themselves from urban areas, but the number leaving for this reason never approximated the number arriving. In several cities groups of people, including some refugees, tried to solve their food problems by organizing mutual aid societies which undertook to obtain and sell supplies at below market price. Among the more successful organizations were those in San Antonio, Houston, and Columbia. A group of refugees wrote the editor of a Columbia paper about the local Mutual Supply Association in which they owned stock. So successful did they think it was that they were urging that a similar organization be established "for the purpose of reducing rents" in the city.[16] Refugees usually complained far more about high rents than about the scarcity or high price of food, but seldom did this deter their coming into cities. In the thinking of the refugees, the advantages of the larger towns outweighed the disadvantages, and although some people moved into the country after first settling in a city, most refugees "town-hopped" when the enemy repeatedly threatened their safety.

Individual preferences and inconsistencies confused the movement of refugees to such an extent that it is difficult to determine just what they sought. Perhaps a Texas editor got to the heart of the matter when he stated that those coming to Texas were looking for a place where they would find "corn aplenty and Yankees scarce." [17] Although this might have satisfied most of those going to Texas, it does not explain why thousands were attracted to the cities. In every state there were dozens of communities, large and small, which were refugee centers for varying periods of time, but the course of the war determined how long they were popular. A community which was congested in one year might be almost deserted the next, but some remained havens for displaced people until the end of the conflict. During the last year of the war there were fewer areas into which refugees could go if they were determined to live under the Confederate flag, but Southerners stayed on the move whether or not they had promise of shelter in the congested communities. As they did so, however, they less frequently referred to their "friendly" receptions.

Everywhere in the Confederacy towns which were attractive to a few refugees were likely to be attractive to many, and so it was that the "centers" developed. There were hundreds of these communities in the South, but none was more popular or crowded for the entire four years than Richmond. A city of 40,000 in 1860, its population doubled in the first year of the war and refugees continued to arrive throughout the conflict. In addition to the advantages found in most cities of this size, it was both the Virginia and Confederate capital and naturally attracted political and military officials and their families as well as thousands of persons seeking employment in the government offices. Richmond was also the social center of the Confederacy and therefore appealed to many people who contributed little or nothing to the war effort. Foreign travelers, always on the lookout for the unusual, were astounded by the congestion in the city. One noted in 1863 that Richmond "was never intended to hold so many people," and another referred to its population as "unnaturally swollen," while both contended that the refugees were primarily responsible for this condition. Judith McGuire reported Main Street "as crowded as Broadway," and a newsman said that it took very little imagination to pretend he was walking "among the throngs of Broadway, . . . refugees are here in swarms." [18]

In the summer of 1864, the influx of Petersburg citizens caused a Richmond resident to remark, "Fredericksburg, Norfolk & now Petersb[ur]g taking refuge in Richmond, to say nothing of many exiles from Maryland." In desperation she asked, "How many people are to be fed or lodged?" [19] Local editors had been raising this same question for months and their comments were becoming more caustic as they appealed to the refugees to stay out of the city and requested those already there to leave. When their emotional, patriotic, and logical pleas fell on deaf ears, they resorted to satire, insults, and vituperation in an effort to uproot them. One went as far as to refer to refugees as "rag, tag and bobtail," moaning that Richmond was having "to pay

through her nose for her greatness." [20] As the editors ranted about
the congestion, high prices, and innumerable other problems which
they blamed on the displaced people, they no doubt concluded that in
this instance the pen was not mightier than the sword, for the homeless
remained and others kept coming.

Towns and villages near Richmond were also popular refugee centers, and it was Ashland's proximity to the city that brought hundreds
into this community. Because there was daily railroad service to and
from Richmond, those working in government offices found it easy
to commute the twelve miles to their jobs. Living costs were not as
high as in the city and life was more placid. A visitor to Ashland was
impressed with the number of refugees, most of whom were "of the
better class," and with their pleasant life "in cozy cottages." [21] But
what he did not realize was that there were not nearly enough "cozy
cottages" to accommodate the people, and several families were living
in the ballroom and billiard room of the local hotel, as well as in other
makeshift quarters.[22] Petersburg was also crowded because of its
nearness to Richmond and its direct transportation line to the city.
Army wives and others from coastal Virginia and North Carolina
arrived early and displaced people continued to infiltrate until war
came to its gates. When Mrs. Roger Pryor went to the city midway
in the war she was astonished to find so many refugees there, some of
whom were living in the homes of her friends who had moved to
safer areas.[23] When Mrs. E. P. Alexander had to move out of the war
zone, she planned to go to Petersburg, but hearing that it "was already
filled with refugees" she decided to remain in Richmond until she
could find a less congested town.[24] When the siege of Petersburg
began, hundreds of the residents and refugees fled from the city. Some
went to Richmond and elsewhere, many camped just outside the city
or crowded into nearby country homes, and those remaining in town
endured hardships second only to people caught in the siege of Vicksburg.

Although parts of Virginia were battle areas throughout the war,
the state probably accommodated as many refugees as any other in
the Confederacy. Included in the group were displaced Virginians and
those from all other areas of the South. Communities of all sizes received homeless people, but some were more popular than others.
Fredericksburg was crowded with refugees when the order for evacuation was issued late in 1862. They left with citizens of the town and
so many found refuge in country homes nearby that a Confederate

surgeon reported none could be used as hospitals and the wounded soldiers had to be taken to Richmond.[25]

A great many towns in the interior of Virginia boasting direct railroad lines to Richmond were popular havens for women who desired access to the city but who did not want the inconvenience of having to change cars. One of these was Danville which had the advantage of remoteness from battle lines and therefore greater safety than many other communities, but it was too far removed from Richmond to appeal to some women. It did attract many refugees, however, and in June, 1862, a newspaper correspondent noted that its population had doubled during the war and that it then had six thousand residents, most of the newcomers being refugees.[26] Amelia Court House was another community with a direct railroad into Richmond, and General E. P. Alexander urged his wife to go there for this reason. But he cautioned her not to confuse this village with Amelia Springs, where so many refugees were settling, because the hotel at the Springs had once been commandeered and might be again, in which case she would be displaced. He wanted her to settle permanently somewhere.[27] He also suggested that she might go to Danville, but it was too far from his camp to suit Mrs. Alexander who chose Farmville instead. When she arrived, the town was already so crowded with refugees that the homes were filled and many of the homeless were "boarding in the country." [28]

Among other popular refugee centers in Virginia was Staunton which Fitzgerald Ross visited in 1863 and found overflowing with a great many "prominent citizens" who had been displaced.[29] Lynchburg was also a favorite refuge from the time of the Peninsular Campaign until near the end of the war. As the Richmond citizens arrived in Lynchburg in 1862, the residents were leaving in large numbers, fearful that if the capital fell, their homes would be in danger. A lady who sent all of her children out of town during the scare filled her home with refugees from Gordonsville. When asked why she had not gone with the children, she said she had stayed to guard her home, and if the enemy came she had no intention of interrupting him and doubted that he would interrupt her.[30] Charlottesville was naturally a popular refuge because of the University buildings opened to refugees and the boardinghouses anxious to accommodate displaced people during a period when there were too few students to support them. Among those who lived in Charlottesville at some time during the war were the McGuires, the Wigfalls, and Betty Herndon Maury,

daughter of Matthew Fontaine Maury and wife of Will Maury. It
was here that the Maury's daughter was born.[31]

Throughout the war, communities in southwestern Virginia sheltered refugees from other areas of the state and from Tennessee, Kentucky, and North Carolina. Bristol and Abingdon were especially
popular centers for those driven from their homes by the Federals,
their Unionist neighbors, or lawless groups which roamed the mountain areas. After Sheridan and Hunter endangered the Valley and
Grant settled down outside Petersburg, additional numbers flocked into
southwestern Virginia. During the last year of the war there were
few safe regions in the state, but a great many Virginians were still
trying to find security within its confines.

There was less dislocation of North Carolinians than Virginians
because only the eastern area was endangered and invaded during
most of the war. The port city of Wilmington, guarded by Fort
Fisher until early 1865, was a refugee center. Those in search of commercial opportunities, employment, or passage to a foreign country
flocked to the city, but never were hundreds banished from Federal
lines dumped on the city at one time as in the case of Charleston,
Savannah, and Mobile. Refugees came from all areas of the Confederacy—James Ryder Randall was surprised to find several New Orleans
families living in his boardinghouse. These, he said, "were birds of
passage" who hoped to get to Nassau.[32] Although Wilmington was
crowded throughout the war, hundreds of people in flight before
Sherman arrived in its last months. A local citizen referred to this last
influx as "the most serious difficulty we have had to contend with,"
and she estimated that "thousands . . . [representing] all classes and
grades . . . [came] from *all* directions," and were being "put in
every nook and corner" of the city.[33] Although many Wilmington
citizens moved to the interior of the state, the greatest single evacu-
ator was not the enemy but the yellow fever epidemic.

North Carolinians living in the coastal areas eased away from their
homes, going only as far as seemed necessary at the time, and the
first points of concentration were communities relatively near the
coast. Goldsboro and Windsor were two of the more popular havens,
but refugees in Windsor were "constantly . . . excited by rumors of
the enemy's landing" in the area and soon moved away.[34] One of
these was Mrs. John Benbury from Edenton who left Windsor at
her husband's insistence and went to Warrenton on the Virginia line.
Refugees crowded into the village early in the war, and a lady from
Wilmington gave her reasons for liking the town. There was a "pleas-

ant hotel" in which she had a room large enough for a "promenade–
a waltz–a polka, or a quadrille," and the food was "good." But she
was also pleased to find a physician in the town and other congenial
refugees "all of whom were members of the Episcopal Church," and
all of whom loved to talk.[35]

Hillsboro in Orange County was not only a refuge for displaced
people but also an example of a village crowded with them. It took a
Wilmington refugee seven months, midway in the war, to find even
a room in the town.[36] Other refugees were living in the schoolhouse,
bank, Masonic Hall, outhouses, and other makeshift quarters. This
was the situation when General William D. Pender wrote his wife,
a refugee in Hillsboro, to find accommodations for the family of a
West Point classmate. He said that the lady insisted on a place in a
boardinghouse for herself, nine children and a servant. This was an
impossible order for even a devoted wife to execute.[37] But conditions
were almost as bad in nearby Chapel Hill despite the fact that it was
a University town with housing facilities for the displaced. A resident
who was trying to persuade her sister, a refugee from Nashville, to
come to Chapel Hill said that it was "the safest place in the Confederate States." She emphasized the lower cost of living there by
comparing prices with those her sister was paying in Atlanta, and
she noted that when steak was selling at seventy-five cents a pound
in the Georgia city it could be had for ten cents in Chapel Hill.[38]
But her campaign was unsuccessful because her sister preferred to
be near her husband who was stationed in Atlanta.

Raleigh, like other state capitals, was very early a mecca for refugees
from the coast, but in the spring of 1862, many Richmond people
displaced by the Peninsular Campaign came to the city. In the group
was Mrs. Jefferson Davis who with others from the Confederate
Capital were only temporary residents of Raleigh. Greensboro also
absorbed a number of Richmond refugees at the same time, but when
they came the town already had many of the homeless from the North
Carolina and Virginia coast. When Louise Wigfall arrived she immediately concluded that the North Carolinians were "uncouth," and
she wrote her mother that she had "always thought N. C. was not
good for much," but was "more convinced of it" after coming to
Greensboro. Although she was not one of the many refugees who
sought employment in the ordnance plant or government factories,
the young men working there and the officers stationed in the town
appealed to her, and after meeting several she found the community
to be a "sociable little place." [39] When J. G. M. Ramsey came to

Greensboro late in the war, he was interested in finding only a room for himself and a vault for his valuables. The latter posed no problem but he had about given up the idea of getting a place to stay when he met a friend who offered to share his bed with the banker. After leaving the city Ramsey's troubles increased; when he arrived in Salisbury he found that refugees had filled every room in town, so he spent the night under a table in the lobby of the hotel. "The entire floor . . . was covered with men—some snoring—some drunk—some sober," and after a night on the floor he arose sore, stiff, and convinced that "the planks of Rowan County were sawed out of very hard wood." Food was as difficult to obtain as shelter, but Ramsey managed to get breakfast when he assured the proprietor that he "had silver to pay for it." [40]

Throughout the Piedmont and mountain areas of North Carolina there were refugee colonies from the beginning of the war, but they grew in number and size late in the conflict. As early as September, 1861, Charlotte was making room for Carolinians from the coast, and less than a year later a correspondent for the Richmond *Dispatch* wrote, "Charlotte is filled up with refugees" who wanted to work in the government factories. He assured his readers that "everyone" could obtain employment in the city, a statement which may or may not have inspired others to come to Charlotte. The largest single migration of displaced people to the city came in February, 1865, when refugees from Columbia arrived in droves. Mrs. Joseph E. Johnston was in this group and she wrote friends that over three hundred women on the train with her were unable to find lodging. "The sight of the town is lamentable," she wrote, "women [are] hunting in every direction for shelter—and the people themselves beginning to move off." [41]

Charlotteans were moving toward the mountains because they feared that Sherman would march on the city, but even this area was already crowded. A year before, a man in Lenoir had been unable to find any kind of accommodations for friends anywhere in or between his home and Morganton.[42] Flat Rock, Asheville, Morganton, Lenoir, Shelby, and other communities were bulging with refugees in the winter of 1864–65. But the most popular haven for the Columbia refugees was Lincolnton, a refuge for Mary Boykin Chesnut, Mrs. Joseph E. Johnston, and members of the Middleton, Rutledge, Preston, and Ravenel families. Although referred to as an "out-of-all-routes-place," Lincolnton was, as Mrs. Chesnut said, "in a regular line of strategic retreat from Sherman." [43] It was also in Lincolnton that Bishop Henry Lay selected a home for his wandering family, giving as his reasons that the people were like their friends in Arkansas, the rents were reasonable, and fuel was plentiful.[44] But one refugee from South Carolina who followed the crowd to Lincolnton could not agree with Bishop Lay. He thought its major drawback was the extortioners; also, because of its name, he thought the community an unsuitable refuge for Confederates.[45]

Because only the coastal areas of South Carolina were invaded prior to 1865, most of the state was in a position to accommodate a great many of her own low country citizens as well as those from other areas. Thousands settled in the interior, and the Piedmont became a giant sprawling refugee center, but communities in the eastern part of the state also absorbed the coastal folk wanting to remain near their homes. Even Charleston was at times crowded with displaced people, and midway in the war a Confederate officer noted that it did not "have the appearance of a besieged city. . . . The promenade has almost the same appearance it had years ago." [46] When hundreds of banished Floridians were brought to Charleston, housing accommodations were scarce, but the increasing number of homes listed for rent or sale in the local papers seem to indicate that the city was not as congested as some.[47]

In the area between the coast and Columbia refugee centers developed as the low country people settled as near their homes as possible. Cheraw, Sumter, Orangeburg, and Barnwell attracted this group, but it was Sumter that first became congested. A local editor noted in the spring of 1862 that it was now a city and no longer a village and he appealed to the residents not to commercialize on the homeless.[48] One of the Charlestonians then in Sumter complained bitterly about the high cost of living and disliked the town because of "the prevalence of sand and Jews." Almost as soon as she arrived she started planning to leave and thought of going to Camden, Anderson, Spartanburg, Pineville, or Chester because she had refugee friends in all of these communities. Her next move was to Camden.[49] This was a popular refuge for Charlestonians who may have been attracted by the local hotel's invitation to refugees which was inserted in the Charleston papers during the first years of the war. These announcements stressed the comfortable accommodations, excellent cuisine, and referred to Camden as "an asylum of delightful repose." Throughout the war and especially during the last year, Cheraw received so many displaced Georgians and South Carolinians who were fleeing from the Federals that, in March, 1865, its population was said to have been "composed in a large part of refugees." [50]

Columbia absorbed a larger number of refugees than any other South Carolina community but no more in proportion to size than smaller ones in the upcountry. It had excellent transportation and communication facilities, hotels, boardinghouses, government ordnance plants and laboratories, and other attractions which normally enticed people to a city. The press often editorialized on the great number of refugees coming to Columbia and, in 1863, a visitor commented that there "was not an unoccupied house in the town." [51] The following spring an editor estimated that the population had more than doubled since the beginning of the war. Mrs. Chesnut noted the increase in population, referring to the refugees as "pleasant people" who contributed to the "glorious social life" of the city.[52] Most citizens did not react in this fashion; however, Mrs. Chesnut was not including the rank and file of the people. Columbia was in no position to take care of the thousands that flocked into town early in 1865 to avoid Sherman. They presumed his destination was not the South Carolina capital, but when it developed that this was exactly where he was going, the refugees, citizens and government workers all tried to depart at the same time and created a traffic jam such as was seldom seen even in the Confederacy.

Villages and rural areas in upcountry South Carolina were filled with displaced people from the first year of the war. During this period the local press encouraged their coming, but most of these invitations ceased after the early period. However, the Edgefield paper was always hospitable and kindly disposed to the refugees as it advertised the advantages of the village. These included living quarters, properties for sale, churches maintained in the town and, early in the war, "several excellent schools" which would be kept open "at all costs." [53] Not until February 22, 1865, did the *Advertiser* announce that the "tide of refugees" which had been arriving during the war had "entirely ceased." Also in the Piedmont, Greenville and Spartanburg were exceptionally popular havens for displaced peoples. A great many prominent low country families including the Hugers, Gilmans, Jerveys, and Porchers were in Greenville hoping to find safety and expecting to find adequate housing and food supplies. But one refugee preferred Greenville because of its "abundant supply of gas" which he said was "a consideration worthy of mention" when candles were in short supply.[54] As early as 1862, visitors to Spartanburg noted the

The citizens of Atlanta, ordered from the city by General Sherman, load their household effects on U.S. Army wagons, from *Frank Leslie's Illustrated Newspaper*.

Women refugees encamped near Vicksburg during the siege, from *Frank Leslie's Illustrated Newspaper*.

Georgia refugees in flight before Sherman's army during its March to the Sea.

Flight of the Charleston citizens during the bombardment, 1863.

The flight of civilians from Savannah in December, 1861, when attack appeared imminent.

"Southern Refugees Moving North from Arkansas and Southern Missouri," from *Harper's Weekly*.

Courtesy Henry E. Huntington Library,
San Marino, Calif.

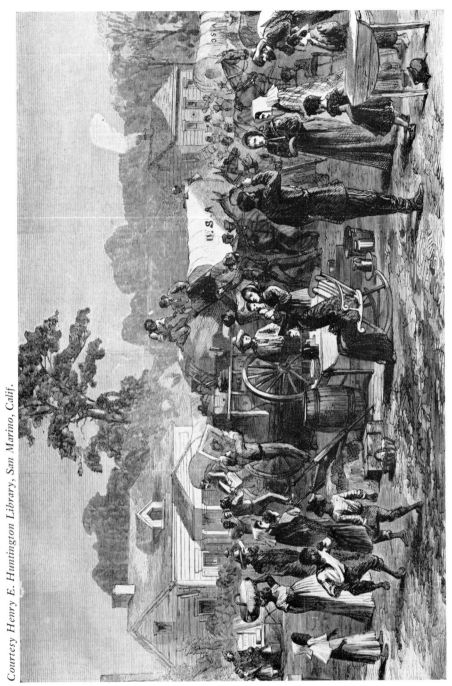

"Refugees Moving South from Atlanta, 1864," from *Harper's Weekly*.

"Registered Enemies in New Orleans Taking the Oath of Allegiance to the United States in Order to Avoid Banishment by Federal Authorities, 1863," from *Harper's Weekly*.

"Refugees in
Kingston, Georgia,
1864," from
Harper's Weekly.

"Unionist Refugees in the Swamps of Louisiana," from *Harper's Weekly.*

"throngs" of refugees who "filled all the houses" in the village.[55] A displaced Charlestonian verified the town's crowded condition many times during the war, and when those from Columbia arrived in early 1865, he told of their having to find shelter in country homes on "the Charlotte Road." [56]

Piedmont South Carolina abounded in small resort communities which were also taken over by the refugees. One of these, Limestone Springs, was typical of most in that it had a large hotel and many cottages. The hotel was purchased by William F. Calcock as a refuge for his own family as well as those of his brothers and nephews. During the war forty or fifty people were always in residence there. Supplies for the hotel came from a nearby farm also purchased by Calcock, and the children continued their education at Limestone Academy which had been an important factor in bringing the refugees to the Springs.[57] Chester and Winnsboro were heavily populated centers throughout the war. Hundreds of Columbia refugees hoped to find accommodations in the villages but only a few could do so while the others had to press on into North Carolina.

Although most refugees in South Carolina during the first eighteen months of the war were natives of the state, by 1863 an ever increasing number were arriving from other invaded areas. As previously noted, the fall of New Orleans brought many of its prominent citizens to South Carolina, including the Palmers and DeBows. The 1864 movements of the Federals in Georgia contributed appreciably to the state's refugee population, many of these coming from the far corners of the Confederacy and on the move for the second, third, or fourth time. During the last year of the conflict the thousands of displaced people in South Carolina created a major problem for the state.

Georgia was always attractive to refugees from the Deep South, Tennessee, and Kentucky, and the most congested city in the state was Atlanta which boasted all the attractions the homeless looked for in an urban area. It was thought to be safe from invasion, and even when the Federals were working their way toward Atlanta most people thought that because it was so valuable to the Confederacy the city would be held at all costs. During the first year of the war Atlanta had gracefully absorbed those who came, but during the second year pressure developed. J. G. M. Ramsey arrived midway in the conflict and had difficulty finding a room because the town was "full of refugees from Louisiana, Florida, Alabama, Arkansas & especially from Tennessee." He eventually found accommodations in a boardinghouse where "crowds" of the "*Elite* of Nashville, Memphis [and] Knoxville" were living.[58] Conditions within the city continued to grow so much worse as the war progressed that a farm woman who arrived from north Georgia in 1864 reported, "There is a haep [*sic*] in Atlanta . . . [living] in tents." [59] She might have added a number of other makeshift accommodations.

In Macon, south of Atlanta, the problem of displaced people was not of major concern until the Atlantans flocked into town during the summer and early fall of 1864. Those who arrived before Sherman's evacuation order managed to find living quarters, but when the exiles were dumped on the community in September, the situation became serious. A local editor noted that before affairs "got so bad in Atlanta," Macon had only "the accustomed few perambulating the sidewalks." The evacuation of Atlanta put the sidewalks "in a bustle, while numberless wagons and drays" were disturbing the peace and "tearing up the dust." He expressed the hope that Atlanta would "soon be retaken from the Yankees," for its people were "used to dust, . . . the citizens of Macon . . . to quiet streets." [60] Milledgeville in the same area was a refugee center through all of the war, and as early as the spring of 1862 the community was reported to be crowded with the homeless from "Maryland, Kentucky, Tennessee and Louisiana." [61] By the time the Atlantans began to arrive they were told that Milledgeville had "no vacant houses." [62] Nor were conditions any better in Athens, for it had also accommodated displaced people from as broad areas as had Milledgeville. Some had found adequate quarters in the Franklin College buildings as well as in private homes, and the reception in the community was exceptionally hospitable. Many of the refugees were attracted by the intellectual atmosphere of Athens. Those with children were pleased with the educational opportunities in the village. Although the college was closed, Lucy Cobb Female Institute and the Collegiate Institute remained in session.[63]

Augusta was another center whose problems with displaced people increased after the North Georgia Campaign got underway. The city appealed to large numbers of the displaced who wanted employment in the factories and ordnance plants. The mayor and journalists were concerned for the refugees and community because those coming from the mountains of Georgia were usually destitute when they arrived in Augusta. Through most of 1864 they came, and in the summer and fall Atlantans arrived, followed by those from Savannah during the winter. Then in January a great many South Carolina farmers and planters were driven from their homes, not only by the Federals but by the flooding of the Savannah River. A resident noted at this time that "scarcely a morning passes but a long train of wagons, horses and mules, accompanied by negroes on foot, and followed by their owners in carriages can be seen passing across the bridge coming from South Carolina." [64]

Along a line running from Rome to Bainbridge, Georgia, refugees crowded into the towns and rural areas for as long as they were safe. When an invasion threatened, the civilians fled to an area as yet untouched by the enemy. A Confederate chaplain who visited Rome in the summer of 1863 was surprised to find so many refugees living there, but when he returned the following February he said the community looked like "a deserted village," the people having fled before the invader.[65] Newnan on the West Point Railroad was a meeting place of travelers as well as the wartime home for many refugees. Those who came to town often commented on the number of displaced people living there. As previously noted, Senator Oldham was surprised to find many old friends in Newnan, and both Fannie Beers and Kate Cumming, who were nurses in the army hospital, told of displaced people living in and passing through Newnan. In nearby LaGrange there were refugees from far-reaching areas of the Confederacy, but the Louisianians composed the largest group. One of this number estimated that there were sixty families from New Orleans in the village.[66] Many prominent personages and their families were at some time temporary residents of LaGrange, including Philip Phillips, Clement Claiborne Clay and Mrs. William Joseph Hardee.[67]

Along the same line and farther south were other communities whose situation was similar, among them Columbus which was especially attractive to Alabamians, Louisianians, and Floridians. There were employment opportunities, and, in the beginning, ample housing in the city, but when several hundred New Orleans exiles arrived in 1863, all commercial establishments were filled. Townspeople were urged to open their homes to the unfortunates as the local editor noted that there were many private homes not yet "too crowded for comfort." [68] When Mobile citizens left home at the request of military authorities, many went to Columbus where they could keep their toes on the Alabama line. Lumpkin, Georgia, was also a popular retreat for this group partly because the cost of living was cheaper than in Mobile or Columbus. One observer stated that it cost only one-fourth as much to live in Lumpkin as in the Alabama city.[69] Although these and other communities located in western Georgia were especially significant as refugee centers, villages and rural areas throughout the southern part of the state also absorbed refugees from elsewhere in the state, from Florida, and eventually from other parts of the Confederacy. After the LeGrand sisters left New Orleans, they paused briefly in Mississippi before being driven to LaGrange and finally to Thomasville, Georgia, where they spent the last year of the war.

Because Florida was so sparsely settled, its position was unique. When war came to the coast, citizens left their homes for the interior of the state or out-of-state areas. Those banished by Federal authorities in northeastern Florida were transported by the hundreds to points in Georgia and South Carolina and were usually put ashore in the Savannah-Charleston area. A sufficient number settled down in these port cities to further complicate the problems there. However, many refugees moved to the interior. A lady living on the St. Johns River reported that most of her neighbors had already moved inland by the spring of 1862. Her son was trying to get the family to leave Florida and settle in Georgia or the Carolinas, but his parents moved to Lakeland instead and rented a farm on which was a small, primitive house. They had many refugee friends in the area but their wartime problems were numerous.[70] Most displaced Floridians moved out of the state and few from other areas came into it. Before she was banished by the Federals for refusing to take the oath, Mrs. Frances Kirby Smith, mother of the general, had tried living first in Madison and then in St. Augustine. Some refugees from eastern Florida went to Tallahassee, but when the city was endangered many moved on to safer localities. An eighty-year-old resident of Tallahassee wrote a friend in South Carolina that she had packed her belongings and was ready to flee if it became necessary, and she had also burned all personal papers she could not take so that they would not fall into the hands of the enemy. She mentioned many of her friends who had already left the city, noting that the refugees who had come from Jacksonville were in no hurry to depart.[71]

While it is never easy or safe to generalize on the refugees or their movements, it is even less so when discussing the situation in Alabama, especially the northern area. It was this region that first felt the pressures of homeless people as they drifted in from Tennessee and settled in the mountain communities, resorts, and in the major city, Huntsville. Although the fall of Fort Henry prompted hundreds to flee from their Tennessee Valley homes, it also opened the river to the Federals who were not long in coming to the Huntsville area, causing the flight of the people from the town. When the Confederates returned to control the area many of these refugees also returned. The military and civilian history of the region is one of repeated advances and retreats, the result being that the population was as well churned as that in any part of the Confederacy. Huntsville was the first place of refuge chosen for Bishop Lay's family, but they had been there only a few months when they were compelled to move a second time.

Central Alabama was out of the battle zone for most of the war, and its communities were populated by its own displaced citizens, as well as those from other states. Montgomery had a large refugee colony when Kate Cumming visited the city in early 1863. She found the hotel in which she was staying "filled with . . . fashionably dressed" refugees, most of whom were from Florida. One of these, the Reverend J. J. Scott, was a friend of hers and at the time an assistant pastor of St. John's Church. When Kate was again in Montgomery two years later, she found that the minister had his own church which was "wholly supported by refugees." On another of her visits to Montgomery, Kate had to sleep in one of the boxcars placed on a siding to accommodate the overflow of refugees, and she so enjoyed the experience that she said she would never again be sympathetic to those "living in cars." But a group of Mobile refugees with whom she talked in Montgomery were so unhappy about living conditions and refugeeing in general that they were planning to return to their homes.[72] Montgomery was a haven for many Mobile citizens, and because of the number in the capital an organization was founded for the specific purpose of rendering aid to the "Non-Combatants of Mobile" arriving in the city. The committee surveyed homes in the area to determine what facilities were available and studied the problem of provisioning the destitute.[73]

Despite its being vulnerable to enemy attack, Mobile was the major refugee center in the coastal area of Alabama. Refugees came to the city throughout the war since it did not fall until April, 1865, and were usually unmoved by the officials' pleas that they go elsewhere. The largest mass invasion of displaced people came when thousands banished from New Orleans arrived in the city during 1862–63. The local press referred to this as "the largest wholesale exile of people to be witnessed in modern times." [74] A British traveler in Mobile at the time recognized the problem confronting officials who had to find living accommodations and provisions for the poor and homeless people. He noted that this ingress contributed to the frustration and exasperation already felt in Mobile, a situation which led city officials to think the time had come to hoist the "black flag" and admit no more exiles.[75] When General Dabney Herndon Maury was desperately trying to persuade the city's residents to leave, he reported that it was more difficult than it might have been because Mobile had become a "refuge to homeless people from other parts of the Confederacy." [76] Many who did leave returned when its defense seemed assured, and once back home they were not so easily moved a second time. An editor facetiously wrote, "The Yankees are coming to Mobile, and now they ain't. But it is all the same to the people of Mobile. They have heard the cry of wolf so often . . . that the recent outgivings . . . have produced no visible effect." [77]

Numerous other towns in Alabama were also crowded with refugees. Selma had hundreds, many of whom were Mississippians wanting to get only as far away from their homes as necessary, but displaced people also came to Selma hoping to find jobs in the government plants. Cahaba was another popular center which one displaced person said had "almost as many refugees as Selma." [78] Tuscaloosa absorbed several hundred of the homeless, but unlike most university towns, housing was a major problem throughout the war because the institution remained open and enrolled an increasing number of students. Quarters that might have been assigned refugees were in use and the newcomers had to find accommodations wherever they could. Mrs. Meriwether was fortunate in having located even a ramshackle cottage in a poor area of town, but other refugees housed in similarly uncomfortable structures were her neighbors and all were grateful to have a roof over their heads.

Mississippi was so ravaged by war that most of the refugee centers which developed in the first two years were depopulated in the last two. As previously noted, Jorantha Semmes went from Memphis to Canton, Mississippi, and when it was necessary to move elsewhere she briefly debated returning to Memphis and enduring Federal rule, but she eventually went with others in the family to Gainesville, Alabama.[79] Before the fall of Vicksburg, Mississippians sometimes crossed into the Trans-Mississippi area, but after mid–1863, most of them had to move eastward. Until Jackson fell, it was the major refuge in the state and this complicated its evacuation as similar situations did in other Confederate cities. Trains took the refugees from Jackson to Mobile, Meridian, or Vicksburg, and all cars were reportedly filled to capacity. The passengers to Vicksburg were families of Confederate soldiers stationed there or those who thought they might be able to cross the Mississippi. Most refugees who rode west out of Jackson were soon caught in besieged Vicksburg and the only homes they knew were the caves or the battle-scarred houses and public buildings of the city. Civilians who had remained in town when asked to leave were caught in the line of fire and in constant danger of being killed by falling shells or starvation.

As Grant approached Jackson many of the displaced Mississippians who had edged away from their homes and into the capital were compelled to move still farther if they were to escape the Federals. Most of these fled to Columbus and other communities in the state or just across the line into Alabama. Mrs. Meriwether arrived in Columbus before the Jackson refugees but still had great difficulty finding a place to stay. However she did eventually find a room in a private home, and it was here that her third son was born on Christmas Night, 1862. There were many displaced people from Tennessee, Missouri, and Arkansas who settled in areas around Columbus and to the north and east of the town, but most of these eventually moved on to safer regions. In the spring of 1862, the little village of Okalona was reported "filled with refugees," most of whom lived in "private dwellings." [80] Rural homes throughout the area were also accommodating displaced relatives and friends of the owners, and many planter refugees from Arkansas and southeastern Missouri moved their slaves and transportable properties to Mississippi where they bought or rented farms and hopefully settled themselves for what they expected to be the duration of the war. When the family of a twelve-year-old girl in Springfield, Missouri, decided to send her into a safer area, she was permitted to join a party of planters going to Mississippi. Her destination was an uncle's plantation on the Yazoo, but within a year she and her uncle's family were forced out by floods.[81]

Most of Tennessee was either lost to the Confederacy early in the war or subjected to so many battles and raids that few Confederate sympathizers sought refuge in the state after the first year of the conflict. Kentuckians and Missourians fled to Memphis, Nashville, Knoxville, and smaller communities in 1861, but by mid–1862 they were being pushed farther south. There is no indication that the Tennessee towns were congested in the early days, and not until Fort Donelson fell did Nashville become suddenly overrun with the homeless. They went elsewhere when the city fell. Many civilians who did not leave before the enemy's arrival were later banished for refusing to take the oath, and Nashville remained a Federal center throughout the war. Those who left in the winter of 1862 moved to communities in southern and western Tennessee, Alabama, Georgia, or Mississippi. Many went to Memphis, but in June of that year this city also was captured. Chattanooga had long been congested with displaced people when the battles began around the town, and most of these refugees moved into Georgia. A witness to the coming of the homeless to Chattanooga after the fall of Nashville told of their arriving in an almost constant stream, most of them destitute and carrying only a few belongings. When they could not find accommodations, many of the refugees slept in the depot, other public buildings, and wherever they could find a place.[82] Knoxville changed hands so often and the surrounding area was so insecure that few Confederates went into east Tennessee and many whose homes were there left. During periods when the Confederate forces held the city some did go to Knoxville, among them the Huntsville editor, James W. Clay, and the Confederate spy, Belle Boyd. But for most of the war it was a Unionist refugee center.

No sooner had the war started than many residents of southern Missouri and northern Arkansas fled into the area around Little Rock or through the state to Louisiana or Texas. Planters along the Mississippi who wanted to cross the river into Tennessee and Mississippi found this increasingly difficult after the fall of Memphis in 1862; therefore many went to Little Rock where they found a great many refugees from other areas. In November, 1861, a local paper mentioned a number who had come from Maryland, Kentucky, and Virginia as well as from Missouri and northern Arkansas.[83] After the fall of the city, two villages in the southwestern part of the state attracted many more displaced people than either could accommodate. One was Camden where ordnance plants were located, and the other, Washington, became the wartime capital of Arkansas. Hundreds also moved into northern Louisiana and Texas, and Bishop Lay wrote his wife about the citizens' leaving Little Rock for these states two months before the city fell. It was in this period that he thought of going to Hempstead County in which Washington is located, but he decided instead to cross the Mississippi to be nearer his family.[84]

All refugees were, to a degree, confused and uncertain as to what they should do, but none were more so than the Louisianians whose great port city was lost early, whose southern area was rapidly overrun by the enemy, whose escape eastward was cut off or endangered by the Federal gunboats, and whose northern neighbor could furnish little in the way of security. Those who did not want to live under Federal rule had only two choices: to move from place to place in Louisiana, which most preferred to do, or go to Texas, which was thought to be "the end of the earth" by most displaced Louisianians. They believed that Texas had nothing to offer but heat, dust, wind, reptiles, insects, and uneducated, boorish neighbors—nothing else, that is, but safety from the enemy. And it was this last inducement that drew thousands of Louisiana-loving citizens to Texas.

When New Orleans fell in the spring of 1862, it had a great many refugees who had been easily absorbed in this largest of Southern cities, but very few of these people or residents were able to get away before the appearance of the Federals. Therefore Baton Rouge and other communities in the area did not have time to be overrun with the homeless from New Orleans. As soon as word reached the capital that the port city had fallen, Baton Rouge was hastily evacuated by government officials who fled to Opelousas where the provisional capital was established. Many residents of Baton Rouge were unable to get out of town before the enemy arrived, but some left as soon as they could and others followed months later when the battles centered around the city. For a time Opelousas was crowded but when it was endangered the people and government again fled, the latter moving to Shreveport. A resident of Opelousas wrote his sister of his plans for leaving that area should the Federals arrive, and his thinking on the matter of where to go is typical of many other displaced Louisianians. He planned to "go to North Louisiana where corn is abundant, living cheap" and where he could rent a small farm. Realizing that it would only be a matter of time until "that portion of the state becomes unsafe," he planned to go to Texas eventually and it would be easier to get there from northern Louisiana than to "start out from [Opelousas] across prairies and pine woods with nothing to eat except what you take with you." [85] Many of his neighbors had already left for northern Louisiana in the hope that they would not have to go to Texas, but if they did the trip would be easier from that area.

Both Sarah Wadley and Kate Stone told of the hundreds of refugees from southern Louisiana who filled the homes in the area around Monroe and who lived on the roads leading to Texas. After Shreveport became the capital and the headquarters of Kirby Smith, it was a congested refugee center. Many Arkansans lived there during the war as did Louisianians, and a correspondent reported twenty families from New Orleans in Shreveport in 1864.[86] New Orleans citizens managed to stray all over the Confederacy—many of those who first left the city went only as far as Tangipahoa Parish, located between Lake Pontchartrain and the Mississippi. The village of Arcola was said to have been composed almost entirely of New Orleans and Mobile refugees, and nearby Amite was also overcrowded with them. A Tennessee refugee living here was amused to see so many New Orleans people going up the river to Memphis in the belief that the bluff

city would be impregnable, for she had just come from there, convinced that it would soon fall.[87]

The most pitiful of the displaced Louisianians were those who
floundered about the state, trying to stay within its bounds and out
of the reach of the enemy. Mrs. Louis A. Bringier received no assistance from her husband who told her only what she must not do and
where she must not go, so she sought the advice of General Joseph
Lancaster Brent. The general recognized the grave economic plight
of Mrs. Bringier and her family, but when she suggested that they go
to Texas with a party of refugees, he discouraged this move and urged
her to go into Federal lines rather than "stray too far away." But this
her husband would not permit her to do.[88] Thousands of Louisianians
who wandered over the state, enduring frequent moves and innumerable hardships, eventually saw no alternative to taking the road to
Texas.

Texas had at least one asset that other Confederate states could not
equal in degree—space. Louisiana refugees from all walks of life
migrated there during the war, but a great many were planters who
transported their slaves to the state, placed them on land they rented
or bought, or leased them to others. Planters and small farmers usually
rented or bought farms, with or without slaves to work them, and
set about trying to provision their families. It was primarily in the
eastern third of Texas that the refugees settled, along the Brazos,
Trinity, and Sabine rivers, or along the coast. Those from southern
Louisiana seemed to have preferred the coast, but some who settled
too near the Gulf were ordered to move farther inland by the military
authorities. One of these was John Leigh who first settled in Wharton
County near Matagorda Bay, where there was a colony of Louisianians
"too numerous to mention." When he was ordered to move, Leigh
took his family to Robinson County on the Brazos, and the letters
he wrote to friends back in Louisiana indicate that he was pleasantly
situated. He told them of the "most succulent" foods he was producing
and especially of the melons being harvested in "overflowing abundance." Although first disliking Texas, he became a propagandist for
the state, and one of his most pleasing discoveries was that the climate
did not produce chills and fever so common in Louisiana. "This is to
be esteemed above all other blessings," wrote the refugee.[89]

Those who preferred town life settled in eastern and central Texas—
in Tyler, Rusk, Marshall, Waco, Corsicana, and other villages. In
October, 1863, a Marshall paper reported that refugees from Arkansas

and Louisiana were "pouring in," the roads into town being "lined with them," and the houses filled to their capacities.[90] But even before Arkansans and Louisianians began to arrive in appreciable numbers, Missourians had settled in the communities. One young Missouri girl who came midway in the war had already lived in refugee homes in Mississippi and Arkansas and had been unhappy in both, but after arriving in Waco she enjoyed her displacement primarily because there were other refugees her age in the town.[91] The homeless, who insisted on living in communities which were only villages, created housing problems. Kate Stone mentioned the scarcity of living quarters in Tyler, but she preferred any inconvenience to having to live in Paris where the family first settled. It was too near the Indian Territory to suit Kate, who commented that she had no desire to lose her "scalp in addition to everything else." [92]

Houston was the major refugee center along the coast, but the largest single contingent of displaced people to arrive in the city came from nearby Galveston. Houston had been alerted to this movement and city officials thought they were prepared for the onslaught; however, there were hundreds more than anyone had anticipated, making both the housing and supply problem serious. In the spring of 1863, a British traveler was astonished to see so many refugees in Houston; more than a year before he or the Galvestonians arrived, a Houston paper had commented that all hotels were filled "from garret to basement" and, in the opinion of the editor, there were enough refugees in the city "to whip any Yankee force that may be sent" to Houston.[93] San Antonio was as crowded as any town in that area. Refugees began arriving early in the war and continued to come throughout the conflict. In the last winter of the war a displaced Virginian living in the town wrote the editor of his hometown paper, "All hotels and boardinghouses are filled" and there "isn't a vacant house to be found," but refugees were still arriving in San Antonio.[94]

Although newspapers and other records afford greater information about the refugees in towns, the letters and diaries of those living in rural areas refer to crowded conditions in many country homes. Yet it seems certain that an overwhelming majority of the refugees lived in urban communities at some time during the war. With only a few exceptions, most of these were small towns and villages, and those designated as cities in the Confederacy would rarely merit this status today. But with the addition of thousands of refugees, towns often doubled or tripled in population during the four years and were confronted with typically urban problems. There can be no doubt that the displaced people were attracted to "the brick and mortar" for a great many reasons, not the least of which was their desire for companionship. They proved the old adage true: misery does love company.

. . . cabined, cribbed, confined

Refugees described their living conditions in various ways, and most of them were especially critical of their temporary homes which were usually inadequate, overcrowded, and uncomfortable. A displaced Charlestonian, apparently fond of alliterations, referred to herself as "cabined, cribbed, confined." [1] Other displaced people were in similar circumstances and most lived in quarters which were inferior to those they had occupied before the war. If they were accustomed to spacious, comfortable homes, they found it very difficult to adjust to makeshift accommodations. Typical was Mrs. John B. Grimball who had always lived in luxurious plantation homes and town houses. When she and her husband arrived in Spartanburg, they moved into a rambling, unfinished college building which in no way resembled their previous dwellings. Mrs. Grimball tried to conceal her dissatisfaction from those around her, but she poured forth her discontent on the pages of her diary. Realizing, however, that nothing could be done about the situation, she wrote, "I may consider myself at home any where my family and trunks are." [2] All refugees might have benefited from adopting this philosophy, for finding adequate shelter was the major problem, and very few could hope to live either in elegance or comfort.

John and Judith McGuire's struggles to find accommodations were similar to those of other refugees. For eight months after leaving Alexandria the couple had to make their home with friends and relatives, and during this period the Reverend McGuire searched for employment. For thirty-seven years he had been a minister and educator, but his health did not permit his accepting a chaplaincy in the

Confederate Army and he could not find a teaching position. He accepted an appointment in the Post Office Department although the salary was small, and the McGuires moved to Richmond in February, 1862. This was the beginning of their housing problems. They had not made previous arrangements for a place to live, and it was Mrs. McGuire's responsibility to locate accommodations. Because his salary was their only income, she knew that they must be satisfied with a room and board, but she did not realize that already even this combination was difficult to find. For two weeks she walked from door to door, following every lead given her by friends, before she found a room. On the first day of her search she was surprised to find a displaced Alexandria neighbor living in "an uncarpeted room . . . poorly furnished," but she was stunned when the lady referred to herself as "*nicely fixed*," for before the war she had always lived in a "handsomely furnished home." During the rainy, cold two weeks, Judith McGuire grew "weary in mind and body" as she met with rude receptions from those to whom she was referred, and she concluded many times that there was not "a vacant room in Richmond." Finally she found a room on Grace Street in a building which, until recently, had housed schoolboys and was now open to refugees.

The McGuires lived there until summer when Mr. McGuire became ill and the couple went to Lynchburg and Charlottesville. In the fall he was sufficiently recovered to resume his work in Richmond, but this time they moved into a cottage in Ashland and he commuted to his job. There were five families of refugees sharing the house, but in spite of the crowded conditions they were happy. In 1863 the cottage was sold and the McGuires could find no other accommodations in the village, so they returned to Richmond only to find that housing conditions had worsened since the preceding year. Again Mrs. McGuire went from door to door, and eventually found two rooms which had "remarkable circumstances" in that the house had been her girlhood home and one of the vacant rooms had been hers at the time of her marriage twenty-nine years earlier. They were not given board but did have kitchen privileges; however they were not allowed to remain there long. Mrs. McGuire soon was looking for other quarters. Although she had managed to find places in Richmond only by walking from door to door, Judith McGuire had many things in her favor that the average refugee did not have. Richmond was her hometown, she had friends there and contacts throughout Virginia, and the McGuires were a quiet, genteel, middle-aged couple with no small children. By any standard they would make ideal tenants.[3]

Had the Reverend McGuire been alone he could have more easily found accommodations, for landladies preferred to house and feed men. A Richmond editor noted that "animosity . . . is exhibited against females," for the owners of boardinghouses would "rather die than feed a lady." He explained that women were usually more critical of the food, insisted on using the parlor which then had to be heated in the winter months, and were nuisances because they stayed at home all day, offered advice, incessantly asked questions, made demands for special services, and otherwise irritated the proprietor.[4] Yet couples generally found it easier to rent rooms than did single women, for even a man encumbered with a wife was a welcome tenant when there were no other men in the house. The refugees who had the greatest difficulty finding living quarters were women with small children, for many property owners refused to rent rooms or houses to them, and the larger the family the more reluctant were the owners to take them as tenants.

When Mrs. Cornelia McDonald left Winchester with her six children in the summer of 1863, she traveled toward Amherst Court House which had been suggested to her because of "its abundance of provisions and because it was out of the way of the armies." Whenever she passed an attractive cottage along the way she wondered if she could find her family as pleasant a place to live, but even then she had her doubts because her funds were limited, as they would be throughout the war. She did not predict, however, that her children would also complicate the situation. When Mrs. McDonald arrived in Amherst Court House the friend who was to have assisted her in finding a home was too ill to help, but an acquaintance suggested that she take rooms in an old, dilapidated hotel which had not been used as such for years, but which was now available to refugees. Despite its sagging ceilings, sinking floors, decaying fireplaces, and gaping rat holes, Mrs. McDonald was prepared to move in when she was called to the bedside of her husband in Richmond. While in the city the couple talked about the family's plight, and it was suggested that she go to Lexington where they had friends who could assist her. This she did, and when the family arrived in the town Mrs. McDonald took rooms in a local hotel, but these were to be only temporary quarters because she could not afford to live there permanently.

Accompanied by a loyal friend who had contacts in Lexington, Cornelia McDonald began to make the rounds, and after a few days she found four rooms over a shop, but the owner refused to rent it to anyone with children. As she continued her search Mrs. McDonald worried about the cost of living in the hotel and of storing a wagon load of furniture that had arrived in the meantime. Finally, after much pleading, she and her friend persuaded a minister and his wife to take the family as boarders, but she was told that they would accommodate her for no more than ten days. However, they remained for a month until Mrs. McDonald rented a ramshackle house that was within her limited means. They lived in this crude abode until October when the fall rains "poured through" the roof and autumn chill proved that the house could not be adequately heated. Again Mrs. McDonald canvassed the town and this time moved her family into a more comfortable house where they lived until 1867.[5] Her struggles, like those of Judith McGuire, indicate that even refugees with personal contacts had a difficult time finding housing in the war-torn Confederacy. But the displaced people who strayed far from home and who had no one to assist them had an even harder time.

After one family was driven from its Louisiana plantation, it lived in many makeshift homes, among them a houseboat, several uncomfortable hotels, a ranch house, and an adobe hut. Unlike the McGuires and McDonalds, "there was no question of money" for they could afford the finest accommodations but could not find them. After they drifted into Texas and settled on a ranch, they hoped to repair the "shanty" but could not locate the necessary materials at any price. It was in Laredo that they had to settle for an adobe hut, but not until they had sought lodging in "every decent-looking house" in town, promising to pay "large sums of money" to anyone who would accommodate them. The lady in the family was disgusted with the hut which had a dirt floor and sleeping quarters "like those of immigrants on board transport ships." There were six berths along the walls, no furniture, not even a looking glass, and for "all toilet purposes" they had to go "to the public fountain in the patio," where they bathed "under some difficulties." [6]

Refugees who arranged for living accommodations before they arrived in a strange community were assured shelter but it was often so unsatisfactory that they immediately tried to find other quarters. Jorantha Semmes reported that their first home in Alabama was so "unfit" that they were seeking another place, but their major complaint related to the size of the house which was inadequate for their needs. They moved to a larger house on a plantation, but it was not as large as Mrs. Semmes desired and she was especially inconvenienced because there was no fireplace in her room. When a neighboring farm was made available to them, one family moved there and the others remained where they were. This relieved the congestion and Mrs. Semmes was happy to be living apart from the cousins with whom she most often disagreed, but even this arrangement did not afford her all the space she desired.[7]

Mrs. Leonidas Polk was also able to improve her living conditions but in a different manner. As the family circle expanded she realized she should have a larger home, but houses were scarce, rents were high, and large homes were difficult to find in Asheville. However, the Polks had a stroke of luck when a new friend offered to share her nineteen-room house with the family. The owner refused rent because she wanted their company and would feel safer with a man in the house, but Hamilton Polk insisted that he pay the taxes on the place and attend to various chores in return for the accommodations. This was agreed to and the Polks moved into this spacious home, shared the produce from the forty-acre plot, and lived in far more comfortable circumstances than most Southern people, although they were not without other problems.[8]

Many of the Louisiana planters who rented places in Texas "sight unseen" were dissatisfied with them. One who contracted for a farm in Polk County arrived to find the house uncomfortable, the land poor, and the rent so high that he soon moved to another farm more to his liking. He complained that the rent was still too high, but the land was fertile and the house new. His wife was especially impressed with the latter because it was painted, "all of the rooms . . . [were] finished off," and she proudly wrote relatives in Louisiana that they had the "nicest home" she had seen in Texas.[9] From the moment the couple moved into these more comfortable quarters their spirits soared despite the many inconveniences they had to endure. They were no different from other Louisiana refugees who found most of the houses in Texas primitive and lacking in both comfort and beauty.

Uncomfortable, exorbitantly priced living quarters, grasping, meddlesome landlords, and disagreeable neighbors were among the most common complaints of the displaced people, and any one or a combination of these could send them in search of something better. Some were able to improve their living conditions, but many who moved to get away from an unpleasant situation very often discovered that they were in worse circumstances. Emma Holmes and her family moved from their first haven in Sumter because they were not satisfied with the town or its people, and when they arrived in Camden they rented a ten-room house thinking they had greatly improved their situation. This house met Emma's standards in every detail, but the family had not lived here long when the landlord doubled the rent, knowing that he could get twice as much because so many refugees were coming to town. The indignant Emma called him an "extortionist" and rebuked him for expecting "refugees and burnt out people" to pay the rent he was asking, but it was several months before the family could find another house so they remained there and feuded with the landlord. Financial considerations eventually compelled them to take the cottage in which Emma was "cabined, cribbed, [and] confined." After a few months they rented another more comfortable place only to have it sold, and they again became displaced.[10] This was the pattern of a great many refugees who never accepted the fact that they could not live in their prewar elegance, nor could they live anywhere for long, unless they handled their landlords with respect and courtesy, for an owner could always rent his property to others.

All refugees were not searching for the same type of living quarters and most had difficulty finding the kind they preferred, but the common complaint of the displaced people was lack of space. The McGuires' eight-room cottage in Ashland accommodated five families and they were not as crowded as some households. General Lafayette McLaws wrote his wife of the congestion in the homes around Fredericksburg. In one house he found five families in five rooms and in another dwelling a mother and seven children shared a single room.[11] Similar conditions were reported elsewhere in the Confederacy, and it isn't surprising that so many people compared their homes to "India rubber," for they seemed to stretch beyond anything the builder had planned.

Whether townspeople or rural folk were the more willing to lodge refugees is a moot question, for in the cities and in the country were those who opened their doors to as many as they could care for, but there were others who refused to accommodate anyone. Rural homes were often filled to the rafters with relatives, friends, and sometimes strangers, but the refugees who stood the best chance of getting rooms were those who were personal friends of the owners or who came with references from mutual friends. Although the ability to pay rent cannot be entirely discounted, neither could it always guarantee shelter. Money was generally more powerful in the city than in rural areas where planters and farmers received friends and even strangers with references and no cash, but often turned away others who offered to pay. Perhaps it was because Mrs. McGuire had been welcomed by her rural friends but rebuffed by so many Richmond people that she concluded country homes had a "greater elasticity" than those in the city. She had seen country houses accommodate "any number who may apply" whether friends or strangers, and sofas and couches were "sheeted for visitors" whom the host had never before seen. Although Mrs. McGuire's statement was not entirely accurate and her experience was limited, she was nevertheless correct in saying, "If the city would do more in that way, there would be less suffering." [12] City people were more likely to charge the refugees for all commodities and services, including shelter, and the homeless who wandered into an urban area without friends, references, or money were in a sad situation.

Many refugees who brought along their furniture expected to rent houses in a small town or in the country, but they tended to steer clear of the larger communities. Although some displaced people went to cities hoping to rent a furnished house, most who stayed preferred or settled for a room with or without board. Hotels and established boardinghouses were soon filled, but home owners sometimes opened their doors to the homeless for a price. Most of those accommodating roomers for the first time did so only because they were in need of an income, but they were extremely reluctant to admit this as their reason, preferring to explain it as a contribution to the war effort. Proud Southerners were ashamed to publicize their economic plight and tried as best they could to save face. Many homes opened to lodgers did not supply board, and others that had customarily done so abandoned the service because food shortages and rising prices made it difficult to get food and impossible to set its cost for more than a few days at a time. There were also the problems of standing in line at the markets, getting fuel for cooking purposes, and hiring servants. Most refugees who rented a room then had to find some way of eating, for most could not afford to take their meals in restaurants or hotel dining rooms. Refugees who early in the war had thought themselves underprivileged when not finding entire houses were later grateful when they could get room and board under the same roof.

Because it was difficult to find a place to board, refugees in cities rented a room and used it for all purposes as they would a house. When the landlord permitted, they cooked their meals in the same room where they slept and entertained. "Cooking in bed-chambers," wrote a Richmond editor, "is all the vogue. Small marketing is the rage. Solitary feeding is the order of the day." [13] When one refugee was asked if she were keeping house, she replied, "No, I room-keep," and many others might have answered in a like manner. [14] It well suited the needs of a great many displaced people who lived one day at a time in a temporary refuge and on a limited budget.

As universal as "room-keeping" became, it was too crude and inelegant for many of the more refined, sensitive ladies. When they rented a room which did not include board they usually requested kitchen privileges but seldom got them. Judith McGuire, in search of living quarters in Richmond for the third time, found two dingy rooms which her husband could afford but the landlady refused to board them. She asked if she might use the kitchen but was told that the stove was not large enough for the tenants to use. She could, however, cook in her rooms if she so desired, but Mrs. McGuire informed the owner that such a thing was unthinkable, and that she must have "*a part of the kitchen.*" She confessed to her diary that this arrangement was not satisfactory and was "the most annoying thing to which refugees . . . [were] subjected." [15] But refugees neither shared another's kitchen nor cooked in their rooms through choice.

Enterprising persons sometimes rented or bought homes or hotels and catered specifically to refugees. In most cases they were investing in a business from which they expected to derive a profit, but those who were displaced themselves were at the same time providing housing for their families. This was a practical arrangement for refugees with sufficient capital, and if the location turned out to be removed from the battle lines it could be a profitable undertaking. One displaced woman bought a farm in North Carolina and converted the house into "a boarding establishment for Refugees." No sooner had she announced her intentions of going into business than "numerous" applications came from those who asked to be accepted as paying guests. A few weeks after its opening this "Paradise resort" was filled to capacity; some of the owner's friends could not understand why the venture was so successful when the patrons "were paying *only* $75 a month for room and board." [16]

The more affluent refugees often chose to live in hotels, but the number who could do so decreased during the war. Even those who might have afforded these accommodations were unable to find them and had to settle for something less comfortable and convenient. As a rule hotels were overcrowded and owners found it more profitable to rent to transients. New arrivals in a community often went to hotels until they could find cheaper or more spacious quarters as did Cornelia McDonald. Many of the low country homeless in Spartanburg went first to the hotel but had no intention of remaining there, for as one said, it was "not nice" and the rates were unreasonable. [17] Other refugees lived in hotels throughout the war and a Charlestonian with rooms at a Camden inn referred to the establishment as "a most charming place of refuge." [18] But there were many who complained about the poor service and high prices in the Southern hostelries.

The wealthier refugees sometimes bought hotels for the sole purpose of providing their families with housing and with no intention of commercializing on the property. As noted, William Calcock purchased the hotel at Limestone Springs, South Carolina, and issued invitations to his kin to join his family in their refuge. Southerners frequently mention in their records other refugees who bought hotels for this same purpose. Like most Louisianians, Frances Fearn's family expected to remain in the state and, for this reason, purchased a hotel near Alexandria. It was bought without the family's having inspected the property, and although spacious enough to accommodate two or three hundred people, it was in a terrible state of disrepair. There was almost no furniture in the building, and the refugees were not sure whether the previous owners or pillagers had removed it. Even the stove had been taken, and the refugees had to cook their meals in the open.[19] Had the course of the war not compelled the family to move, they would probably have done so anyway. Many of the hotels bought by other refugees were scarcely fit for human habitation and most were inadequately furnished.

Displaced people appropriated any space which could be utilized as living quarters. Parlors, libraries, and dining rooms were converted into bedrooms, and if these did not afford sufficient accommodations, basements and attics absorbed the overflow. An observer in Richmond noted that many Southerners who had "a superabundance before" the war were now grateful for places "in garrets," and Mrs. McGuire's friends who were "accustomed to every luxury" had to live in a "damp cellar" because they could afford nothing better.[20] Mrs. Roger Pryor was dissatisfied with the overseer's cottage in which she lived during the siege of Petersburg, but many of her friends were reduced to "coal cellars" and other makeshift quarters.[21] In refugee centers throughout the Confederacy, factories, banks, stores, offices, and similar buildings were converted into temporary homes for displaced people.

In both rural and urban areas churches afforded refuge for thousands. When a community was under attack, as in the case of Vicksburg, residents fled to the churches because they were usually sturdily constructed and the people believed they were less likely to be shelled deliberately by the enemy.[22] Pews were converted into beds, pallets were strewn about the floor, and if the attack was prolonged the people stayed on, attending to their domestic duties as they would at home. When refugees fled from towns they often headed for a nearby church, expecting to find a refuge there until they could return. A Fredericksburg citizen who was among the last to leave the town went directly to a country church a few miles away. On arriving she found the building already filled with displaced people and hundreds more encamped on the grounds. There was no room for her and she had to press on in search of shelter.[23]

When college and university buildings were opened to refugees, the early arrivals usually appropriated several rooms as did the Grimballs who occupied an entire wing of the college building in Spartanburg. They soon discovered that these quarters were not conveniently arranged for keeping house, a major complaint of the displaced people who lived in similar structures. Eleemosynary institutions also afforded temporary havens for those whose homes were endangered. Hundreds of Columbia citizens fled to the mental institution on the outskirts of the city as Sherman's forces approached and fires were started. All space within the building was soon filled and several hundred clustered about the grounds and watched the burning town. So hysterical and distraught were the refugees that it was impossible to distinguish them from the inmates of the institution.[24] When Sarah Morgan's family fled from their home in Baton Rouge, they found shelter in the "Deaf and Dumb Institution" on two successive nights. The first Sarah thought exciting but by the second night she found the beds more uncomfortable, the insects larger and more numerous, and the experience very distasteful.[25] She learned, as did most refugees, that it didn't take long for the novelty of refugeeing to wear off as it became more tiring than thrilling.

In their search for living quarters the refugees did not overlook carriage houses, stables, slave cabins, and similar structures. The occupants were often many miles from their homes but sometimes they were the owners whose residences had been destroyed. Although the tenants were frequently charged rent for the use of the property, some owners permitted refugees to live on the premises free of charge. If the property was abandoned, the passersby usually appropriated the buildings often intending to spend only a night, but if no one evicted them and they liked the quarters they might settle down indefinitely. A great many honorable, honest refugees became squatters before the war had run its course. Structures of this kind were always preferable to tents which were used not only temporarily by travelers but also permanently by refugees who had no other shelter. Tent "cities" sprang up near embattled towns as the citizens tried to stay as near their homes as possible. The encampment outside Petersburg included hundreds of people, some of them prominent Virginians, who had waited too long to leave the city and could get no other accommodations.[26] In the environs of the town owners of rural homes opened their doors to many of the refugees and permitted others to camp on the premises. A young woman recalled that her father had let the tenters use his land and she was especially impressed by the number who had two or more tents furnished with whatever possessions they had been able to bring with them.[27]

Most refugees improvised tents from blankets, rugs, quilts, or any heavy material, but in some cases the armies furnished groups of displaced people with military tents. This was more often true of the Federals who provided in this way for those coming into their lines, and General Alexander Asboth reported from Barrancas, Florida, that he had sheltered "609 destitute" refugees in condemned army tents.[28] When the Atlantans swarmed into Augusta in 1864, homes were already accommodating hundreds of displaced people. The city officials opened the race track and parade grounds to those who brought or could devise tents, and here also a tent "city" sprang into being.[29] When other Atlantans arrived in Macon, the Confederate Commissary furnished them with as many tents as could be spared, but so pathetic were those living in tents and boxcars that a local editor suggested that all be transported to southern Georgia where they could live more comfortably in "pole tents." He was anticipating their even greater discomfort when winter came and thought it wise to settle them in a warmer climate.[30]

Boxcars have been mentioned as a mode of transportation and also as living quarters at the terminus. Atlanta had refugees living in cars long before the evacuation of the city, and many of these people had come from Chattanooga. Residents and other homeless people mention their living on sidings in the railroad yards, but when little "Loulie" Gilmer, daughter of Jeremy Gilmer, visited them in September, 1863, she was so fascinated with the sight that she wrote her father about them. She said that there were "at least 30 familys [*sic*] just liveing [*sic*] in old box cars. They are refugees from Chattanooga & about." [31]

The happiest solution to the housing problem, but one that few people could afford, was to build or have built a wartime home. An Alabamian built a cottage on his plantation for his daughter and her children so that they might have his protection as well as their independence in their own house.[32] This was an ideal solution to the problem but a very rare exception to general practice. Even had the refugees been financially able to do so early in the war, many hesitated to invest money in property which they thought would be only a temporary home. Those who did build a retreat usually settled for a cabin which they could later abandon without great financial loss. Several states rendered limited assistance to refugees. One of the more interesting projects developed in Georgia, where state funds were used to build log cabins for the Atlanta refugees who congregated in Macon. These homeless people created problems for all because, as one editor stated, there were "nearly a thousand children" who with their parents were destitute and without shelter. He called on the authorities "in the name of justice" to do something for them, and at his urging a meeting was held at which "between thirty and forty thousand dollars" was collected. But this did not solve the housing problem, and Governor Joseph Emerson Brown appointed Colonel Ira R. Foster, Quartermaster General of Georgia, to find a suitable location for a log cabin village which the state expected to construct for these displaced people. The place selected was in Terrell County and the settlement was known as Fosterville in honor of the Quartermaster General.[33]

There was careful screening of settlers assigned to Fosterville, and only refugees from Atlanta were permitted to live there. All residents were told that "the strictest order and morality would be enforced at all times." To assist the residents in earning a living, "implements of industry . . . and cotton cards" were distributed. "Between 75 and 100 families" had moved into the housing project within a month after it was opened. Its location was said to be "beautiful," and it afforded "the best water in Southwestern Georgia." The log cabins, measuring sixteen by eighteen feet, were situated on plots sufficiently large to permit every family to have a garden and the colony had a resident physician, churches, and "Sabbath schools." [34] When the legislature met in November, Governor Brown reported on the project, stating that he had taken money from the military fund to purchase the tents and build the cabins.[35]

Caves were among the more primitive shelters used by refugees. A Confederate nurse in Atlanta told of women and children who "cowered . . . trembled . . . hungered . . . and thirsted" in them, and cave dwellers were reported in all hill and mountain areas of the South.[36] They attracted the attention of journalists, especially those from the North, but no displaced people living in this fashion were more widely publicized than those in the caves near Vicksburg. On July 5, 1863, the New York *Times* published an account of the town's last days under siege, and the writer commented that the "most noticeable feature" of the area was the "group of caves on every hillside." These did not seem to be "very desirable bed chambers," but he noted that they had "answered a very good purpose." A Knoxville paper noted that it was not only the poor of Vicksburg who sought refuge here but many prominent citizens also "burrowed in the ground like animals." [37] Few of the caves were natural ones, for most had been dug by professional diggers and some were multiroomed affairs, sufficiently high to permit the occupants' moving around within them in a standing position. They were inconvenient but the women went about the chores in as near their usual manner as possible, one lady recalling that most "carried on as cooly and calmly as though the abode was one of choice." [38]

Mary Webster Loughborough, caught in Vicksburg because she was determined to remain near her husband, was one of the town's cave dwellers. Her first underground home was a large "T-shaped" dugout with living and dressing rooms "high enough" for even the "tallest person to stand perfectly erect." The cooking had to be done out of doors, and although the arrangement was not ideal, Mrs. Loughborough found it "more comfortable" than she had imagined it would be to live "under the earth in that fashion." Because her husband feared that she would be caught in the crossfire, he found her another cave nearer the lines but more secluded by trees and vines. This was larger and lighter than the first, and after she added a rug and other furnishings she felt very much at home. But in time, the life became monotonous and she concluded that she was not "made to exist underground," for she was growing "wan, spindling and white" as she "vegetated" day after day in her cave.[39] Others who experienced this same primitive mode of living complained about the dampness, seepage, darkness, cold, and "grave-like silence" which made a Vicksburg cave "a living tomb." [40] A Northern traveler in Vicksburg after the war talked with several people who had lived in caves, and one lady told him that refugees at first felt ill at ease and were reluctant to undress at night, but after a few days they "grew accustomed to undressing and retiring regularly." [41]

The housing problem confronted all refugees, but it was easier for some to find housing than for others. Those who fared best were not necessarily the wealthy people nor the ones who at first moved into

spacious, comfortable homes. The most fortunate were those endowed
with abnormal foresight or an uncanny amount of good luck who
settled in areas remote to the battle lines and stayed there through most
or all of the war. In most cases, every move made by displaced people
served only to complicate their lives and worsen their living conditions.
Because their financial problems increased with each year of the war,
there was an ever-widening gap between what they had to buy and
what they had to spend, and the higher rents posed a real problem for
those who were still transplanting themselves in new communities
during 1864–65. Although the spiraling prices affected all Southerners
and not just the refugees, the latter were especially vulnerable to the
consequences when searching for accommodations in strange communities where they had no friends. Their chances of finding shelter
were never encouraging, and late in the war nearly all refugees were
compelled to consider the price of lodging.

Thousands worried about the soaring rents and many once affluent
people were forced to sell their personal property and family treasures
in order to pay rent and other living expenses. Cornelia McDonald
gradually parted with all of her prewar finery, jewelry, and china
because she needed cash or commodities. Newspapers carried notices
of refugee possessions for sale, usually omitting the name of the person and identifying him only as "a refugee" from a specific town or
state. Typical of these announcements was that of "A REFUGEE
FROM NEW ORLEANS" in Mobile who let it be known that she
was compelled to sell her fur neckpiece in order to pay her living
expenses. The editor reminded his readers that it was only two weeks
until Christmas and suggested that the furs would make "the best
and most serviceable present . . . to be found in the city." He hoped
that a buyer would step forward, help the deserving refugee, and in
so doing make another woman happy.[42]

Although shelter was a basic need of the refugees, there were other
factors which determined living conditions. A great many necessities
were difficult to obtain, and keeping house in wartime was complicated
by innumerable shortages and mounting costs of the most common-
place items. Refugees who were living among strangers had the most
difficult time supplying their needs, for scarce articles were usually
reserved for long-standing customers and gifts of food were usually
bestowed on friends instead of strangers. Although there were exceptions, in most cases the displaced people struggled much harder
to supply their families than did the permanent residents of a community. If they had little or no money with which to purchase the

necessities the refugees were pitiful in the extreme, but even when they had sufficient funds they very often could not buy commodities which were in short supply.

The food problem was a serious one, not only because there were acute shortages in many areas but also because staple foods were those most likely to be hoarded. People on the run could not transport huge quantities of food, yet the staples had to be regularly replenished. Fortunate indeed were refugees who had friends nearby willing and able to share produce with them. The McGuires were often given farm products by their friends living near Richmond; without these generous gifts they would have gone hungry late in the war. Cornelia McDonald worried constantly about providing her children with a sustaining diet, often going hungry herself in order that the young might share what little the family had. Therefore she was especially grateful whenever friends brought her even small quantities of plain food. A Columbia refugee in upcountry South Carolina, who was also concerned about feeding her family late in the war, noted, "We have to restrain the children's appetites and limit our own." [43] Katherine Polk Gale remembered the generosity of the Asheville people in supplying them with food, but even so the family "many, many times" had nothing to eat but corn bread and milk, and the latter they had only because a friend had loaned them a cow.[44] One of the few refugees who mentioned having a cow was John B. Grimball. He bought one for $24 when he realized that food was going to be a problem in Spartanburg. Until the creature "went dry" the family had an abundant supply of milk and butter.[45] Friends and foresight kept many refugees from starving.

Displaced planters who took their slaves with them were not in an enviable situation. The workers had to be fed but even when their masters located them on a farm or plantation it was not always possible to produce sufficient provisions. Those taken into towns were a burden unless they were leased out to others in return for their keep. Mrs. Grimball worried incessantly about feeding the Negroes they took to Spartanburg. She reported that they consumed "10 quarts of Meal and Clabber for breakfast," and for the other meals they had soup "made from half a Cow's head" which she bought for ten cents at the local market.[46] She was concerned that the time would come when even this plain fare would be unobtainable. Jorantha Semmes, cognizant of this problem, wrote her husband, "What an immense expense these refugees must meet who . . . carry their servants without anything to feed them." [47] It was primarily the cost of feeding slaves that compelled many owners to lease them to others who needed a laboring force and were willing to board them. Many Louisiana planters who took their slaves to Texas solved the supply problem in this way. Mrs. Leonidas Polk leased twenty of her Negroes to men in Asheville, specifying that food and not money be paid her, and that the workers be given their board and keep.[48]

It is strange that so many refugees gave no thought at all to the food supply in the communities where they settled. Although some mention adequate supplies as a reason for going to a specific area, most selected their wartime home for other reasons and rarely because of available provisions. Women seldom gave a thought to this feature; menfolk were usually more practically inclined. This was not always because the refugees completely ignored the problem but because so many were pulled along with the crowd and had no time to check on conditions until they arrived at their destination. However, even those who carefully selected a refuge with thoughts of the food supply soon discovered that abundance in one year could change to scarcity the next. As additional people moved into a customarily well-supplied area, the constant drain could soon deplete stocks of foodstuffs; even the most productive region was often not geared to furnish food to so many hungry folk. The refugees who were more realistic about the food problem frequently tried to rent homes which had a garden plot, and realtors with such properties for rent or sale were careful to mention this asset in their advertisements. Few wartime acquisitions gave the refugees a greater sense of accomplishment than having a patch of land which could be converted into a garden, for whether or not they used it for this purpose, it made them feel more secure.

Displaced people might haul tons of housekeeping equipment, clothing, and other personal possessions in the hope that they would be comfortable and well-supplied in their new homes, but all had to be fed by the area into which they went. They could stretch many prewar items to last four years, but inadequate transportation, lack of refrigeration and storage space made it impossible to store large quantities of perishable supplies. In an effort to spur the farmers to greater productivity and also to discourage people from coming into a community lacking adequate provisions, newspapers often noted this situation. In one of its many editorials on the subject a Mobile paper, in the fall of 1863, declared that "doubtless 400,000 persons . . . [had] been thrust into the Confederacy without any provisions. They . . . may have brought money with them, but they most certainly did not bring provisions." The editor called on farmers to produce more and bring their products into the city, and asked food speculators to cease their selfish activities.[49]

Refugees who boarded were able to avoid many problems relating to the purchase and preparation of food, but they were aware of the shortages and rising prices as the cost of board mounted and meals became plainer and more monotonous. Before Augusta was overrun with Atlantans, refugees were worried about the increasing cost of board, one noting that within a few months it had risen from "$90 to $200." She was especially concerned about its effect on the New Orleans citizens living in Augusta who were "at their wits end" because of the rapid rise in prices.[50] It was the combination of high prices and plain, unappetizing food served in boarding establishments that often compelled the refugees to "room-keep" or forsake the city's advantage for the more plentifully supplied rural areas. Very few displaced people liked boarding for long, and most voiced some of their bitterest complaints against these establishments. A Nashville refugee in Atlanta told of the number of boardinghouses in the city, and although there were many which were "exteriorly . . . very handsome," they served "very poor fare." She maintained, "Even the best are miserable," and because many of her friends could not "stand boarding," they were looking for other accommodations.[51] Yet those who were most caustic in their criticism had seldom encountered the problems of marketing and preparing food during wartime; most who had were satisfied to board.

Complications other than finding shelter and obtaining food also plagued the refugees. Unless they had brought sufficient furniture and other housekeeping essentials with them, the displaced people were apt to be inconvenienced at some time. As Southern homes stretched to accommodate the homeless, the hostess invariably had to improvise beds by using pallets, sofas, chairs, and even tables, and the refugees lived out of trunks and valises. Privacy and real comfort were luxuries few people could afford during the war, and although children looked upon refugeeing as an adventure, their elders were less enthusiastic about what it was doing to their way of life.

From the description of a planter's caravan and list of items hauled by some refugees, it would seem that if they arrived at their destination with their possessions intact, they could want for nothing. But even the best organized people who had planned their flight slowly and methodically invariably forgot something which they considered vital. Some learned to do without the articles, but others sent for them. Letters requesting that the items be sent were posted or conveyed by trusted servants, or some member of the family retraced his steps to bring them out of the endangered area. Friends and neighbors who had stayed behind were sometimes driven to the point of distraction when they were asked to locate and send the forgotten possessions. The time it took to follow orders depended on circumstances, but these "stay-at-homes" who were requested to locate the items sometimes wished that they, too, had left. A family of Charlestonians who refugeed in Clarendon County arrived with several wagons of household paraphernalia, but they did not have everything they wanted. A son in Charleston was contacted and asked to pack and send additional furniture, including "2 bedsteads with 13 slats, tester posts, 5 bundles of mahogany chairs, 2 setees, 1 desk board, 1 easy chair, 1 bundle of pillows, 1 tub, pots, foot-tubs, [and] 2 sofas." As his mother wrote, these were absolutely necessary if the family were to feel "at home." [52]

Mentioned more often than any other household necessities was the lack of sufficient bedding, especially in the more crowded homes. When Mrs. Polk first learned that Mrs. Gale and her family were coming to Asheville, she told her that the house was so well furnished that there would be no need to ship any furniture to North Carolina. She did, however, suggest that Mrs. Gale bring an ample supply of sheets, blankets, quilts, and towels, for there were not enough in the house to take care of all. [53] The lack of floor covering was also a source of complaint, but many rugs and carpets had been donated to the army and converted into other items. Many ladies felt that it was almost indecent to live where the floors were bare, and Mrs. McGuire was one who always stressed the point when displaced friends lived in uncarpeted rooms. She once had to rent a carpetless room, but a friend gave her a rug and few gifts received during the war pleased her as much as this one. Because of a rug's many wartime uses, refugees who took along household equipment usually had one or more in their cargo.

Another problem mentioned frequently was the inadequate supply and high price of wood used in heating and cooking. A refugee in Greenville, South Carolina, complained bitterly about both, and in the fall of 1862 she said that she was spending a dollar a day for wood and at this price she should be able "to keep warm." [54] A Culpeper, Virginia, refugee was delighted that he had chosen Charlottesville as his refuge because there were so many interesting refugees there, but he doubted that even this offset the problem of getting sufficient wood to heat his quarters. He attributed the scarcity to the hard rains which had made the roads impassable and to the impressment of wagons and horses by the Confederates. For these reasons country people were not bringing wood into town, and there was widespread suffering in the community.[55] Mrs. Roger Pryor reported that during the last winter of the war her refugee neighbors were using fence rails for firewood, and those in other parts of the Confederacy resorted to the same practice.[56] Wood was one of the items often distributed to the poor by charitable organizations, although there was never enough to go around.

Keeping warm during winter months was a problem in many refugee households. Lack of warm clothing as well as the lack of wood was responsible for the people's being cold. A great many displaced people were unable to bring sufficient clothing with them and some had only what they were wearing when they left home. Like others in the Confederacy, refugees patched, darned, and improvised clothing, and if they could make garments hold together most were, at best, threadbare before the end of the war. Shoes were scarce and children were especially prone to wear out or outgrow theirs. In carpetless households with inadequate wood for fuel the problem was a serious one. When refugees moved into colder climates than those to which they were accustomed, the lack of adequate clothing and shoes worked a real hardship on the family. This was the situation of Mrs. Gale and her children who were unprepared for the cold Asheville winters, and once for four weeks in midwinter the youngsters had to go barefoot because they could not get shoes. Mrs. Gale reported that their feet were "partially frozen" and she was almost desperate until a friend made several pairs for the children. It was during this same period that she patched the baby's wrapper *"one hundred times,"* hoping that it would hold together.[57]

The people displaced with only the clothes on their backs were always in a sad predicament, but those who had left home in warm weather were especially pitiful. This was the situation of a Norfolk refugee who wrote a friend for money with which he could buy winter clothes. He explained that his were locked in his home "and the damed [*sic*] Yankees have the keys." [58] A Fredericksburg woman, who fled from her home in such haste that she had no time to get a coat, wrapped herself in an ironing board cover as she went out the door. For weeks this was the only wrap she had, and when her clothes had to be laundered, she stayed in bed while friends performed the chore.[59]

One fact is certain: the refugees were faced with a host of problems as they tried to provide themselves with the essentials of life. In most cases their problems increased in number and intensity as the war progressed and as they moved again and again. Although all Southerners were called on to endure many daily privations and inconveniences, those who were displaced usually suffered greater hardships, all things considered. Yet several factors should be noted, one being that there was no "average" refugee. A person's financial situation, personal contacts, place of refuge, ingenuity, adjustability to changing conditions, and his good fortune or lack of it combined to make each refugee's circumstances distinctive. Finding shelter was a basic problem for all and their surroundings had a bearing on daily life and attitude, but most refugees thought of their wartime home as only temporary, and even those who might have improved their situation were not usually interested in doing so. They were merely "camping" until they could go home. Most refugees at first did not try to adjust to the community or make friends with the permanent residents, yet they did eventually recognize the value of friendship during their displacement, after they discovered it could get them many things which money could not buy. Because most refugees had grave financial problems before the end of the war, they came to fear inflation as much as the enemy, and their bitterness, frustration, insecurity, impermanence, and homesickness contributed to their increasingly pessimistic view of life. Those who were "cabined, cribbed, confined" were not overjoyed with their situation, yet some concluded that they must learn to be "at home" wherever their family and trunks were.

. . . *how many sad hours we have*

The refugees had won but one battle in their war for survival when they provided themselves with the material necessities of life. They fought others of a personal nature which in many instances were even more frustrating and tiring. They were challenged daily by innumerable unpredictable and complex problems which tested their endurance, faith, and courage. All had moments of depression, but with some it was a chronic state and as pressures increased and tensions mounted the refugees suffered from their own peculiar type of battle fatigue. The number of "sad hours" experienced by the individual depended on his inherent qualities and particular circumstances; the war years were unbearable for some, only tolerable for others, and happy for none.

The displaced people's major problem was adjusting to new living conditions, especially those found in the congested homes of the Confederacy. When several families were living in space meant to accommodate only one, all had to exercise patience, understanding, and consideration if frayed nerves and intemperate outbursts were to be avoided. It took superhuman tact and selflessness for even the most devoted, congenial group to live together in complete harmony. The war years were not conducive to the creation of a calm, placid atmosphere within or without the home. When there was natural friction between members of a household, life could be miserable for all. Women accustomed to being mistresses of their own homes were the ones most likely to be dissatisfied in that of another. This would have been true in some instances at any time, but the worries and tensions of wartime served only to make matters worse.

The letters written by Mrs. Benedict Joseph Semmes to her husband reflect her own reactions to an unhappy domestic situation, and they are not unlike those of other women caught in similar circumstances. Mrs. Semmes wanted more than anything else to move nearer to her husband, and this probably explains why she insisted on his knowing of her daily problems which must have seemed trivial when compared to his own. Another factor contributing to her discontent was the overcrowded home which at one time was shared by three families totaling seventeen people, including Mrs. Semmes and her five children. She was living with her husband's cousins whom she did not like and who she believed felt the same toward her. From the moment she arrived at their home in Canton, Mississippi, Jorantha Semmes concluded that she and the children were unwelcome, and after all moved together to Alabama she had no reason to alter her opinion. Semmes believed that his wife only imagined this and perhaps she did, but she may have been less than cordially received because she was a Northerner by birth, the cousin of Federal General John A. Dix, and inclined to be both positive and aggressive. Whether or not justified in her views, Mrs. Semmes frequently alluded to herself as "a nuisance," and regularly made such statements as, "I can only try to live in harmony with all and try to swallow all feelings of annoyance at the discomfort I cause." She assured her husband that she was trying to adjust, was bearing her share of the expenses although she had been assigned the "poorest room in the house," and was placing herself "in as little a troublesome position as possible." [1]

In answer to this letter, her husband reiterated that she only imagined herself unwelcome, but unless she could rid herself of this complex she should use the direct approach and ask his cousins if they preferred her to move elsewhere. However, he said nothing about her coming to his headquarters in Chattanooga. Rather he admonished her, "You ought to be grateful to God for having the opportunities for safety and protection as you now have." Later, in answer to a similar complaint, he wrote that he felt sure his cousins were "like others in the same position . . . willing to share . . . as thousands of others are doing throughout the south." Trying to impress upon her the stern realities of the period he stated, "You must expect great discomfort in such times as these and I do not see how you can better yourself no matter where you go." Therefore he urged her to practice self-control and accept graciously that which could not be changed.[2]

This letter aroused rather than calmed his unhappy wife, who again outlined in detail her major causes for complaint, including the congestion and lack of privacy. She wrote, "On all occasions I think I do control myself and behave as amiably as possible," but she also emphasized her dislike of his relatives, the Alphonso Semmeses, whom she called "Bena" and "Phonso." Jorantha Semmes was especially irritated that the couple insisted on disciplining her children as well as their own, but she also resented the pregnant Bena's temper which made Jorantha "afraid to mention the news of the day lest her evil auguries and hyper-criticisms" make her even more despondent. She resented "Phonso's drinking and smoking too much," becoming "very irritable when the children are fretful," and whipping her children as "he and Bena do theirs." Mrs. Semmes thought that this stern discipline did not make their children "really better . . . though they . . . were more obedient" than hers. The letter also predicted trouble when winter came and all the household had to huddle around a single fireplace, each person following his "avocation" and all "debarred from leaving the house" because of the flood which usually "anticipates Christmas." She forecast illness for everyone "at the same time," there already being six patients in the house who needed care.

In this same letter Mrs. Semmes injected a note never before used when she told her husband that she should move because as long as she and her family were there, the cousins' youngsters were denied "the little attentions and indulgences they might otherwise enjoy." Summoning still another argument she wrote, "I am present at all family discussions and quarrels and sometimes when I am trying to make peace I do harm. My words, too, spoken in jest are sometimes misunderstood, or falsely . . . carried from one to the other, making trouble." [3] If this letter revealed Mrs. Semmes's dissatisfaction, her next did nothing to counteract it. She reported the "children crying with cold," Bena suffering with diarrhea, two others in the family with pneumonia, "Phonso" with a toothache and neuralgia, and all the adults fearing that Bena's baby was going to arrive early.[4]

Letters of this kind did not ease the tensions or raise the spirits of Benedict Joseph Semmes, but they graphically described conditions in an overcrowded, unhappy refugee home and are typical of thousands written during the war. Two months after these letters were written, Alphonso Semmes moved his family to a neighboring plantation and Jorantha's letters became more cheerful. By the time that her husband established his commissary headquarters in Atlanta in 1864, he was telling his wife how much her "loving letters" meant to him and what "pleasure and comfort" they brought.[5] And her letters did reflect less tenseness and harassment, but they always evidenced her concern about her husband's safety, the family's economic problems, and other wartime worries common to most refugees. Mrs. Semmes was no different from thousands of other women who sometimes lost their perspective and reacted irrationally to abnormal pressures which were a part of their life.

The overcrowding of Southern households fomented more domestic trouble than any other, and this situation was especially apt to develop when hostile in-laws lived under the same roof. Within many homes there were mother and daughter-in-law feuds as in the case of a Nashville refugee who lived in the home of her husband's parents in Atlanta. Letters to members of her own family reveal that the one thing she wanted most was a place of her own. Conditions were especially unsatisfactory when her mother, a refugee from Nashville with nowhere else to go, arrived on the scene. Because she felt that she was unwelcome, the mother remained for only a brief period and then settled in Marietta. Although her daughter resented the cool reception given her mother she could do nothing about it under the circumstances. A major reason for the trouble in this home was the hostess' refusal of money which her son and daughter-in-law wanted to pay for their board and lodging. The couple was treated as guests and therefore felt that they were in no position to make suggestions on domestic matters or to entertain their friends. The young woman felt that she was an imposition and was expressing the views of many others in the same position when she wrote, "I can't be satisfied to board with anyone unless it is a stranger, to whom I can offer to pay . . . and in whose house I can feel at liberty to do as I please. I would rather have a home of my own if it had but three rooms than to be situated as I now am, and this is one of the loveliest places. If it was only mine." [6] Although in this case there is no indication that the daughter-in-law had predicted trouble, many in-laws were so sure that there would be disagreement that they entered the arena dressed for battle and a conflict was then inevitable.

There were refugees who, for personal reasons, preferred to be with their husband's parents rather than their own. One of these was Mrs. George L'Engle who had returned to her parents' home in Raleigh when her husband was killed in action. Although her father was in comfortable financial circumstances, his "low spirits and grumbling . . . on the subject of waste and economy" depressed and irritated her. Her mother took such great pride in her home that she constantly nagged the grandchildren who insisted on playing with the bric-a-brac, and Mrs. L'Engle lived in fear that they might break something. The situation eventually became "unbearable," and she took the children to Florida where she lived with the parents of her husband who were refugees from Jacksonville.[7] When she arrived she found the elderly couple having a difficult financial struggle, but rather than return to Raleigh, she took a job in the laundry to help defray her family's expenses.[8]

Many refugees indicated that one of their most difficult and embarrassing situations was living in another's home and not being permitted to share the expenses, for they were sometimes in a better financial position than their hosts. If their assistance was refused or if it offended the owner of the home, the refugee was in a dilemma when circumstances prevented his going elsewhere. William Pitt Ballenger, a Texas businessman, feared that Houston would be attacked and decided to remove his family from the city. He took them to the home of an aunt in Waco, and then discovered that despite her modest circumstances, she would accept no payment from him. After many consultations he and his wife decided that after his return to Houston Mrs. Ballenger was to write and suggest items he might ship to the aunt as gifts. This was done and he sent huge quantities of food and clothing, always writing that the articles were in abundant supply in Houston but he had heard they were scarce in Waco. Because they were gifts they were graciously received and the refugees did not feel that they were imposing.[9] However, few displaced people could solve the problem in this way.

The question of whether or not to share in the expenses was an especially delicate one in the case of parents and married children, for the former usually wanted to provide for the latter as had been their custom; yet many were in such dire straits that this was either impossible or could be done only with the greatest sacrifice. Many grown children gave little or no thought to the altered economic circumstances of their parents, and going home meant that they would be provided for as they had always been. Young women were often more unrealistic and thoughtless in this than their husbands. A refugee from Charleston who was living with her mother-in-law in Newberry was not especially unhappy in the situation but she wanted to visit her mother and father who were refugees in Spartanburg. When she told her husband, he reprimanded her for not realizing the changed economic status of her parents who had lost most of their property. He understood that she wanted to see them, but he did not want her to spend months there. "You will reduce your father to poverty by

. . . a continued stay," he wrote. *"Let me tell you something, my dear Beckie, the way to make a pleasant visit is to stay only so long as to make your . . . [family] wish you would stay longer."* He told her that she might go for one week but she ignored this restriction and was still in Spartanburg several months later. Her husband ordered her either to return to Newbury or pay board, and he specified that her mother must set the price. If she refused, this would be a sign that she did not want her to stay and "the sooner she left . . . the better." [10] His wife could not see the logic of paying board to her own mother but not to his.[11] The matter was never settled to the satisfaction of both husband and wife, the result being that she spent most of the war shuttling back and forth between the two communities.

Those who made guests of displaced friends and relatives did not necessarily welcome them with open arms. As a hostess watched the approach of unexpected visitors many thoughts crossed her mind. One of the first was likely to be the amount of food on hand; another related to the length of time they planned to stay. The warm handshake and smile which often greeted the wayfarer disguised many inner worries and fears. Sidney Harding, a Louisiana refugee in her early twenties, left her plantation home in St. Mary Parish and lived with her displaced family in a log house in DeSoto Parish. In this modest dwelling were seven people who were too crowded for comfort, but this did not halt the arrival of dozens of friends, relatives, and strangers, some of whom spent weeks with the Hardings even after seeing their pitiful situation. Sidney became increasingly critical of those who further congested their house, ate their scarce food, and placed her mother under great pressure. Mrs. Harding worried constantly about her inability to entertain as she could before the war, and when the family was deluged with guests during 1863–64, Sidney confided to her diary that the lack of food was making a nervous wreck out of her mother. Day after day she wrote, "Ma is very much ashamed of her dinner," or "Poor Ma . . . sat down and cried" when she had nothing to feed the new arrivals. When a cousin and her children settled down for what seemed an interminable period to Sidney, she wrote, "I wish they would go—it looks inhospitable, but the house is so small. Ma is so worried, her room is always full of children . . . I do wonder if they intend staying here all summer. I hope not." [12]

Refugees often had problems with landlords, and for those who had never before rented property this was an unexpected development. They frequently referred to the owners as "selfish," "grasping," and "tyrannical," comparing them to Simon Legree or Scrooge. The most sinister characters sketched in their records were those "money-crazed," unscrupulous creatures to whom they paid rent, and it was the question of money that inspired the bitterest invectives. Rents were too high or were increased without justification and the landlord's pet economies were irritating, but refugees also resented their meddling, breaking agreements, and having annoying personality traits and quirks. They were sometimes accused of being alcoholics, thieves, or narrow-minded, prudish individuals. The displaced Southern homeowners were exposed to a valuable lesson in human relationships when they became tenants during the war.

Mrs. P. C. Calder of Wilmington stayed on the move early in the war primarily because she had trouble adjusting to the landladies with whom she came in contact. After her first encounter with one in Warrenton, her son wrote, "We see that . . . boarding won't do," but he was nevertheless irritated with her for returning to Wilmington and encouraged her to go to the interior, preferably to Hillsboro. He cautioned her, however, that if she were to be happy she must not "be too exacting . . or expect too much" of those with whom she lived, and she "must give as little trouble as possible, and bear little grievances. . . ." Should she live in a private home or boardinghouse in Hillsboro, she must also *"be very careful not to give offense or wound"* the landlady's feelings, for they had to be "handled delicately" now that they were in a position "to command." [13] His words of wisdom fell on deaf ears, and Mrs. Calder had not been in Hillsboro long when she wrote her son that the landlady's "characteristic *selfishness*" and love of gossip was more than she could bear, so she was moving elsewhere.[14] Mrs. Calder found it impossible to live for very long in harmony with others, and it was primarily for this reason that she was miserable in her displacement.

Refugees reacted in many ways to those from whom they rented property. A couple near Lake City, Florida, disliked their landlord so intensely that they made plans to move away from the "quarrelsome, drunken fellow," but they could not leave until the crop was harvested. Meantime the tenants forced him to sign an agreement not to trespass on the property for as long as they lived on it.[15] General E. P. Alexander thought the owners of the boardinghouse where his wife lived both amusing and despicable. The landlady was "a desperately mean old specimen . . . who employed a very thieving set of servants," and her husband was the type "you've seen described in tales of boardinghouses, where the female wears the pants & the male is only tolerated by convenience, to sit at the foot of the table &

carve." Their establishment he referred to as "Mrs. M's hospitable-for-cash mansion." [16]

Those who rented property to refugees also had their side of the story, for many of the displaced people were anything but ideal tenants. Yet once they moved in, it was difficult or impossible to evict them. Mrs. Thomas Hampton, a poorly educated farm wife in Grayson County, Virginia, rented a small outbuilding to a homeless woman for whom she felt sorry, but she lived to regret her action. Letters written to her husband in the army were filled with her problem of trying to force the woman off the premises. The tenant was of questionable character and Mrs. Hampton feared she was a bad influence on the children. "If she is such a woman as a great many thinks she is I don't want such about me," she once wrote. And a few weeks later she reported that the tenant was "going to have a increase in family," the neighbors believing that the father was a mulatto. "Such talk about her and him you never heard. All I ask of her is to get away and not carry my oven off with her." But Mrs. Hampton couldn't budge the woman who said she couldn't move until she could find someone to haul away her belongings, and when she was offered a "waggon [*sic*] & team" and the man in question was told to take her away, "he said that he would not drive a team over the rough roads for Jeff Davis nor no other man." The baby was born on the Hampton farm and Mrs. Hampton wrote that the rumors were apparently correct, for the child was so very dark.[17]

Most complaints against displaced tenants were not as bizarre as Mrs. Hampton's, and the most common was that the refugees were destructive. This was sometimes the result of carelessness or even maliciousness, but more often it was a natural result of too many people sharing too little space in which they slept, cooked, and ate. Buildings and rooms never meant to be used as kitchens, coal cellars, wood sheds, and storage areas were damaged when converted to these uses. It was this reputation for destroying and defacing property that made so many people not want to rent to refugees. Some home owners first removed all valuable furnishings from the rooms and this partially explains why so many displaced people mentioned the bare quarters assigned them. Property damage, whether deliberate or unintentional, was a frequent cause for disagreement between owner and tenant, and the life of a landlord was far from enviable. Refugees who lived in institutions such as schools and colleges were more removed from a landlord's watchful eye and they were especially destructive.

The differences which so often developed between displaced people and local citizens were as disconcerting as any problem of human relations on the homefront. Many of the early refugees were wealthy, prominent personages who moved into a community with their carriages, fine clothes, jewelry, furniture, and retinue of slaves, thus leaving the impression of being far more affluent than the town's residents. They often evidenced a superior attitude, set themselves apart from others, and practiced tactlessness until it became a fine art. They did not try to conceal their disdain for the background, dress, and manners of the natives, and this first group of planters who moved inland from the coastal areas created the refugee image in the minds of the people living in the interior. Many were snobbish and most were convinced that they would not like the people among whom they were going to live. Settling down with this preconceived prejudice, it did not take long for the lines to be drawn as each group glowered at the other on the streets, in the churches, and wherever they met. This situation not only made friendly relations impossible for the early arrivals, but it placed those coming later in a very difficult situation. A Charlestonian in Spartanburg voiced the sentiments of other low country refugees when she said that the citizens were "of low character in Morals." She thought it disgusting that there was "no distinction" between the classes in the village as "all meet on equality." [18] An attitude such as this did nothing to endear the newcomers to the community.

No group of refugees experienced greater shock in their new homes than the Louisianians who went to Texas. Their letters indicate that they were stunned by their first impression of the country and the people, and the one point most often stressed was the tendency of the Texans to brag about their state. One refugee wrote, "The Texans believe they have done all the fighting of the war—gained every victory, and . . . that Texas is the Confederacy." [19] Others were irritated with the Texans' uncouth ways, and this was especially true of the women refugees. One thought Texas women "clever in their way," but she doubted that she would ever find the female companionship she craved. Those she had met were trying to persuade her to "smoke, chew or dip," but she assured her husband that she would adopt none of these habits until she heard which he preferred. She told him of having invited two women to dine with her and midway in the meal one of her guests asked, "You don't dip, nor chew, nor nothing, do you?" So unhappy was she in Texas that she threatened to take up one or all of their habits in an effort "to drown . . . [her] sorrows," and she positively stated, "I wouldn't live in the State for the whole of it." [20]

A ten-year-old girl who had gone to Texas with her family early in the war wrote her sister that she did not like Texans because "the ladies smoke cigars, chew tobacco, take snuff and tilt back on two legs of their chairs!" Her father was no more pleased with conditions. Although Texas was "a good poor man's country," he was distressed that the intellectual and social environment was so unfit for his children. There was "no society above the grade of Comanches, and no schools worth sending children to . . . ," he wrote, and he was anxiously awaiting the day when he could take them away from the "inferior" people.[21]

Whether or not the refugees expressed these opinions in public cannot in all cases be determined, but their records and open letters to editors seem to indicate that they did so in many instances. That as many displaced people and long-time residents eventually came to live in harmony can be explained by the deliberate efforts of both groups to do so and also by the leveling influence of the war. The icy barrier never entirely disappeared, however, and in the beginning it was more often the refugee who was responsible for erecting it. It was also the refugee who suffered most from this line of demarcation, for he was in greater need of assistance as conditions went from bad to worse. He needed innumerable favors and considerations before the war had run its course, and the local citizens were in a position to help him in many ways, but first impressions were difficult to erase and those who had first offended the community were very often unable to win over the inhabitants. These displaced people were the ones who were likely to sulk in loneliness and self-pity as community conflicts became the order of the day.

All local arguments did not develop between refugees and residents; sometimes the contenders on both sides were displaced people. When strangers shared a building they often had their differences which might or might not become serious conflicts. The Grimballs were as reluctant to make friends with other refugees living in the building as with the people of Spartanburg. The family identified only as the Grimball's "nearest neighbors" consisted of the mother, father, and five children. Mrs. Grimball described the man as one "who drinks deplorably, & is the boldest deserter to be found. . . . Sometimes he is brought home in a cart, perfectly drunk, sometimes he crawls in on his all fours." She respected and pitied his wife who kept her family "neat and clean" and was always "cheerful looking" herself, but Mrs. Grimball did not care to cultivate their friendship because of the "drunken husband."²² Ironically yet understandably, refugees unknown to each other and coming from varied social and economic groups, when brought into close contact with each other, would find that their common displacement was not enough to bring them together as friends. Some could go their own way but those who could not often became participants in bitter feuds.

Graciously accepting the residents of a community as they were would go a long way toward helping people adjust to their displacement. When Katherine Polk Gale came to the mountains of North Carolina she had to live in a community and among people who were in some ways different from any she had ever known, yet she often mentioned how courteous, hospitable, and generous they were. She told of their many favors to her family, and she was especially impressed with the gifts and services rendered by the Unionists in the area. Although all were not friendly, Mrs. Gale was surprised that any would be because her father, husband, and brother served in the Confederate Army. Yet many were her "tried and faithful friends to the end."²³ Cornelia McDonald also discovered that political differences could be minimized or forgotten if the parties involved determined it. Once when she was penniless and her children without shoes, a Unionist cobbler in Lexington made a pair for each child and credited her until after the war. This generous gesture she long remembered.²⁴ Although there were exceptions, most refugees found that their own attitude largely determined their acceptance or rejection by the community, but local conditions might be such that they had to go more than halfway in making friends. This many could not do, but all might have benefited by adopting the philosophy of a Louisiana refugee who disliked Texas but nevertheless adopted the motto, "try to extract the sweets from the bitter."²⁵

The disease common to all refugees at one time or another was homesickness, and nothing could have as depressing an effect as a long siege of the malady. It was confined to no one group, and very often the young people, usually more adaptable than their elders, suffered for extended periods from nothing more than the desire to go home. Sidney Harding gave every indication of being a happy, extroverted young woman who managed to enjoy the first year of her displacement as well as anyone could, but by 1864 she was pessimistic and moody for months at a time. She attributed her condition to homesickness and a "distaste for refugee life." In the fall of that year she wrote that her spirits would rise if she could once again see "the green grass and the noble old oaks" of her home. She explained as a reason for her change of attitude, "When I thought it would last for only a few months, I could stand it, but oh, not for years." On the last day of the year she wrote, "I am more, yes much more homesick and gloomy than last year . . . my heart feels often as if it would break with longing for home." [26] Similar thoughts poured from the pens of other displaced people and homesickness reached epidemic proportions in the Confederacy long before the end of the war.

One of the most homesick young ladies in the Confederacy was Elodie Todd, who had more than the usual problems to endure because she was the sister of Mary Todd Lincoln and, as previously noted, was not very warmly received in Alabama. Many times she wrote her fiancé that she was "desperately homesick" for her mother and other loved ones in Kentucky, and because of this she was "perfectly miserable." Early in the war she wrote, "My heart yearns for the love they flourished upon me and which I did not properly appreciate," and on another occasion she cried, "I pine to be in Kentucky. . . ." [27]

Elderly people were especially susceptible to homesickness as they found it difficult to adjust to a new home and a new way of life. Even those who were with relatives in an area relatively untouched by the war yearned to return home. They did not compare themselves with others of the period or take into account the conditions of the day, rather they looked back to happier times in their natural environs, and this only served to make them more miserable. The older people often gave as their reason for not writing to loved ones and for neglecting their diaries and journals that they were depressed by their displacement. The distance between them and their homes had little or no bearing on their attacks of homesickness, for if not under their own roof they were in a foreign land. Louis M. DeSaussure was less than two hundred miles from his home on the coast of South Carolina when he was a refugee in Camden, yet he referred to the area as "a strange land." Although he mentioned many times the cordial reception extended him by his brother and the comforts of his brother's home, he was nevertheless unhappy there. Until 1863, he made regular entries in his journal, but in that year he wrote only once and this was to record his misery and explain his long silence which was attributed to his "having been removed by the force of necessity" from his home. Because he was "an exile in this land of Strangers," he saw no reason to write for posterity. His life was "like that of the Israelites of old . . . in Babylon," and like them, he asked only that he be permitted to return to his "fond home." [28]

Monotony and boredom were the major causes of homesickness and chronic spells of depression. When time hung heavy and the same dull routine was followed day after day, it was natural for the refugees to brood about the present as they recalled the past. Those who were not gainfully employed and who were doing nothing but awaiting the end of the war in an isolated area were the ones most likely to find life monotonous and boring. Those who kept busy had less time to indulge in self-pity, but if the task of providing for themselves and their families was too arduous and the daily battles for survival too frustrating, even the most diligent became morose. It seemed to many of these people that they, like the soldiers, were fighting hard yet losing the war. Busy mothers had little time during the day in which they could think about their situation, but when night came they nostalgically looked to the past and wondered when the monotonous, insecure life as a refugee would end. It was then that they poured forth their inner thoughts and pessimism onto the pages of their diaries. A young woman expressed the thought of many others when she wrote, "There is nothing to mark one day from another now. [It is] always the same. Sew, knit, read. Varied by discussions, sharp words too frequently. Talk about scarcity of provisions and money. Spinning, weaving. Oh, I get so sick and tired of it." [29]

One of the most powerful of the war's depressants was the lack of regular and efficient mail service, and many refugees were completely out of touch with their loved ones. It was the desire to communicate with others that explains why many homeless people settled along mail routes although this did not necessarily insure their receiving the letters they so desired. Because they had changed their place of residence, their whereabouts were not always known to those who might otherwise have written, and when their friends and relatives also became refugees contact was lost. Mail service at best was irregular during the war and complaints were registered by others than the displaced people, but those away from home were especially in need of letters from people who were left behind as well as from loved ones in the service. The one condition that could most easily depress the usually optimistic Katherine Polk Gale was not hearing from her relatives and friends. Although she "tried to possess, [her] soul in patience," this was more easily said than done, for she worried especially about her father and husband on the battlefield. After her father was killed, any interval between letters from her husband seemed interminable, and once in late 1864 she went for two months without news of him. Long after the war she recalled that this was one of the most trying periods of her displacement.[30]

Other refugees endured poorer mail service than did Mrs. Gale who said that there were three deliveries a week into Asheville, and this was one reason her mother had selected the community as her refuge. But when the refugees did not receive letters they expected, they worried and brooded even more. A Louisianian in Texas who had heard nothing from her husband for over two months wrote, "I told you . . . I could not live without letters and I never uttered a greater truth. God spare me from spending two such months again. I could never tell you of my lonely days and miserable nights." After another month passed and she still had not heard from him she wrote, "I am hoping tomorrow will be a brighter day . . . but I have almost despaired of a letter by Texas mail." [31] It was depressing enough to wait for the war to end, but to try to do so without word from one's friends and relatives was a challenge to the most optimistic person. His imagination worked overtime conjuring up disaster and tragedy which did nothing to improve his morale, and the longer the silence continued the lower the spirits sank.

When reassuring letters arrived, morale was sure to rise. A Nashville refugee in Atlanta, who had never been separated from her parents until displacement, spent months without word of them. It was extremely difficult to get letters through enemy lines and when they did arrive they came in batches. With the arrival of every bundle her spirits soared and she immediately answered as if hoping that this would insure her hearing again soon. After receiving several of her mother's letters she wrote, "I wish I could tell you the good your letters do me, for then I know you would never have the opportunity of writing that you would not send me a letter . . . , how *eagerly* I look for it—how disappointed and perfectly *heart sick* I feel when I see no letter from you. . . . Please write me every opportunity." [32] When she once heard that a friend was bringing "a large packet of letters from home," she wrote her sister, "I declare it is tantalizing to have to wait, when a lady is all impatience to receive a letter." [33]

As refugees moved from one place to another and left no forwarding address, it was easy for them to get lost in the shuffle. It was a common occurrence in the war for one to lose touch with members of his family and his closest friends. When a man went to Jackson, Mississippi, to see his father he found the old man gone and was told that he was a refugee, but where he had gone no one knew.[34] A Mississippi refugee in Georgia had not only lost all contact with a sister, but she and her best friends who had left home together had been separated in flight and they were weeks overdue. She was naturally concerned about them and felt she could be "well satisfied" in her refuge if she only knew that they were safe.[35] Among the most pitiful refugees were those who searched for members of their family from whom they had been separated. Sarah Wadley told of dozens of people who stopped at her home asking if the family had seen or heard about their loved ones whom they thought might be in the area. She mentioned a man who had taken his wife and children to a refuge and thought them settled there, but when he returned several months later he found they had gone without leaving any trace of their whereabouts. Sarah's expression, "searching for . . . family," was applied frequently to visitors who came to her door; there were many Southerners who were doing just that.[36] Especially pathetic were soldiers on furlough who made a long trip home only to find their family gone. One South Carolinian, who had served for two years in Virginia, reached his home in Barhamville and was told that his mother had fled, but no one seemed sure where she went. It was a week before he located her in Mc-Phersonville.[37] All searches did not end this happily.

A frequent reason for a refugee mother's being depressed was the abnormally heavy burden thrust upon her by the war. She had to provide for and protect her children, and she worried constantly about the effects of deprivation and displacement on the young. Many women actually grieved over their inability to give the boy and girls a normal childhood and they were at a loss as to how they could explain why the family must live on the run. Mothers were especially dejected when they could not provide gifts and "extras" which children so confidently expect at special times. Christmas, birthdays, and other special occasions were more often dreaded than anticipated by adults for these were times of real heartbreak for most refugee mothers.

Cornelia McDonald lay awake many nights devising ways of feeding and clothing her family, and more than once she was moved to tears when it seemed that the children would have to be distributed among relatives. After her husband's death it looked as though she could not possibly provide for all of them, but she prayed as "never before" that she would find a way to hold them together. An exceptionally ingenious woman, Mrs. McDonald managed to clothe her brood by converting various articles into wearing apparel, but her efforts did not always bring her joy and satisfaction. The most heartbreaking episode occurred when her sons appeared in clothes that were so ridiculous the Lexington boys laughed them off the streets and the children came home in tears. This was an agonizing experience for the mother, but she had many others as she tried to provide for her family's needs and worried constantly about the children's being deprived of a normal childhood.[38]

Similar problems confronted Elizabeth Meriwether who had to care for three sons, Avery who was five when they left Memphis, Rivers who was three, and the third, Lee, who was born while she was a refugee. As the family inched across Mississippi just ahead of the Federals, settling nowhere for long, Rivers asked his mother, "When will we get a house we can h-a-v-e?" His question disturbed Mrs. Meriwether because it clearly indicated that the children were confused about their changed way of life, and it was difficult for her to explain the situation to them. The problem of feeding the children was also with her throughout their displacement, and in the beginning her primary concern was that of a balanced diet, but before long she feared starvation. After arriving in Tuscaloosa she drew corn rations to which she was entitled as the wife of a Confederate officer, but this was inadequate to her family's needs. The newborn baby had to have milk which could not be bought at any price, but she found a "Black Mammy" who had a child of the same age and who nursed little Lee as well as her own. Mrs. Meriwether later wrote that she would never forget watching "the dusky mother nursing her own baby at one breast while . . . [hers] tugged at the other!" Once when she was desperate about the lack of food, Mrs. Meriwether climbed a fence and raided a cornfield belonging to a man who refused to sell her the grain. She was not one to take "no" for an answer, especially when her sons' welfare was at stake, and because of her determination and resourcefulness she emerged victorious from her never ending battle for provisions. Yet her saddest hours were those spent worrying about her children.[39]

Women charged with the physical protection of their children had added cause for concern. When towns were under attack, parents often sent their young to safety, and if they could not accompany them, the boys and girls were entrusted to others. A Vicksburg citizen who could not leave town placed his two sons in the custody of a friend who had a cave near the city.[40] And a group of children were sent out of Huntsville when Federals threatened the community. As the cannons boomed and shells fell, the youngsters were hustled into a wagon and rushed out of town, but when the danger had passed, "the little refugee children . . . returned, all mud and dirt."[41] Children were often sent into the woods or some other secluded area when danger was imminent, and the hours of separation were agonizing ones for the mothers who feared that they might stray too far away or be harmed. When the family was brought together after the ordeal, the relief and joy of the parents evidenced their love and grave concern for the children. When families were in flight, one of the mother's problems was to keep her brood together—often a difficult assignment. As fires started in Columbia, South Carolina, families fled toward the outskirts of the city and congested all roads leading away from the burning town. A mother of four young children had difficulty keeping them together as she tried to hold on to them and, at the same time, carry a few of the family's belongings. The younger children were unable to travel as fast as the older ones and often lagged far behind, but the mother knew that if they were separated in the throng she might never find them. The system she devised was to run rapidly herself, stop and "then wait a few moments" until the smallest one "caught up." The strain and tension of the hegira were implied when she wrote, "And thus we wended our weary way." [42]

As previously noted, another very real cause for parents' concern was the disruption of their children's education. Mothers who could do so often assumed the responsibility for tutoring the young, but their many other responsibilities frequently interfered and made it impossible for them to follow as rigid a routine as was possible in an institution. Thousands of refugee households lacked a person qualified to teach, and although many illiterate or poorly educated women wanted their children to have an education, all of the better educated emphasized the need. Jorantha Semmes was distressed because there were no schools near their refuge in Alabama, and her husband was also concerned about this situation. He once wrote his wife that he considered the disruption of their education to be "one of the evils of the war," and he urged that Mrs. Semmes employ a tutor.[43] He made it clear that he did not think her qualified to instruct the older children and Mrs. Semmes took exception to this, although she had previously written that she felt herself unqualified to handle the problem. But when he agreed, she answered, "Give yourself no uneasiness about their education, I am quite competent to teach them to the full capacity of their years," and as if to prove her point, she itemized the assignments she had given them during the previous week.[44]

Refugee children living in communities maintaining schools usually enrolled in the institutions, but this did not always guarantee their uninterrupted education. The local youth often taunted, teased, or bullied them, and despite children's natural ability to make friends, the refugees were usually set apart from others by their clothes, manners, speech, or superior attitudes. Each group gave evidence of assuming their parents' reaction to the others, and new boys in a community were expected to prove themselves before being accepted by the schoolmates. This sometimes resulted in disputes and violence which created discipline problems for teachers and worried and irritated parents. Sons of a Louisiana refugee enrolled in the public school in Tyler, Texas, and trouble was not long in coming when the Tyler boys referred to them as "refugee upstarts" with ostentatious clothes and haughty manners. The newcomers were tormented in innumerable ways and it was reported that the Texans brandished pistols and threatened the Louisianians, whereupon the mother withdrew the little refugees from the school and did not even permit them to go to church. The boys resented their mother's interference, preferring to handle the problem in their own way, but after this episode, other refugees also withdrew their children from school. The issue soon divided the town into two camps and the "war" was on, with the parents planning the strategy.[45]

When young people went away to boarding school or college they often lost all contact with their parents, especially if battle lines separated them or if the family was displaced. If either the students or the parents heard that the other was in the war zone there were long periods of worry until each party was assured the other was all right. Benedict Joseph Semmes placed his daughter, Julia, in a convent in Columbia, South Carolina, believing that she could complete her education in safety, but after the Federals took the city he and Mrs. Semmes spent several months without any word from or about her. Their letters to each other during this period indicate their grave concern for the young lady. And, a teen-aged Mississippian who attended Judson College in Alabama had only erratic contact with her parents after 1862. Her mother managed to write several letters to her and she expressed concern over the child's safety, schooling, and general welfare. Friends in Alabama were commissioned to pay her expenses and the teachers were expected to care for her, but the mother was never sure that all was well. She urged her daughter to remain in school and reminded her that "education is better than wealth," noting that an "education is all we can give you now." She expressed the hope that school officials were looking after her and cautioned her daughter to be "kind and respectful of them" at all times.[46] Many girls were separated from their mothers throughout the war, but the teachers and administrators attended to their needs as best they could.

Although the refugees experienced a great many more sad, monotonous, homesick days than they did happy ones, those who could approach their problems with a sense of humor made the difficult times easier for themselves and others. Their records include occasional references to amusing episodes and humorous interpretations of people, places, and situations, but these insertions are less frequent than those relating to privations, sorrow, and inconveniences. No one surpassed Charles H. Smith as a refugeeing humorist who could see the ludicrous aspects of his displacement. Writing under the name of "Bill Arp," his accounts were published in several Confederate newspapers and he was able to share his experiences with thousands of others who understood his trials and enjoyed his interpretations, but who must have wondered how he could have found them so amusing. Using a backwoods dialect, he became the homespun philosopher of the Confederacy.

His account of his family's flight from Rome, Georgia, which he referred to as the "eternal sitty," is a classic of wartime humor. At that moment he became a "Roman Runagee," heading first for Atlanta and later wandering over Georgia. He experienced fear and privation as did others but was amused by every predicament and always able to laugh at himself. According to Bill Arp, the "evacuation" of the "eternal sitty" came without warning from the "valyunt Konfederates," and the citizens were therefore "konstrained to change" their residence in the "ded of night." Leaving behind the "usuary things that hold body and soul together," he and his large family began their "dignified retreat." It was at this time that he recalled Shakespeare's lines which he paraphrased, " 'sweet are the juices of adversity,' " noting that so numerous were his adversities that he had "some sweetnin to spare." He doubted the accuracy of the statement, however, concluding that "sich scenes never happened in Bill Shakespeare's day, or he wouldn't have writ that line."

His flight to Atlanta was similar to that of thousands of other refugees, but his account was singular. His first problem was to find transportation for his family, but he discovered that "time-honored friendships, past favors shown, everlastin gratitood, numerous small and luvely children, konfederate kurrency, new shoes, bank bills, and black bottles" counted for nothing at that moment. He could find "nary a korner" on an outgoing train, and with "no rolling stock, no steer, no mule," the family set out on foot "overland . . . which Rail

Roads do not control" nor "Konfederates . . . impress." The road they traveled was "crowded with wagins and teams, kattle and hogs, niggers and dogs, women and children" on their way "to places and parts unknown." The "mules were brayin, kattle lowin, hogs were squealin, sheep were blatin, children cryin, wagginers cussin, whips were poppin, . . . but the grand karavan moved on," as the "everlastin kavalry . . . dashed to and fro . . . spreadin false alarms of the enemy bein in pursuit." The "ten thousand rumors afloat" made everyone even more fearful that the Federals would overtake them, and Bill Arp admitted this made him uncomfortable because he was "afeered of the blue-tailed fly."

When this account was submitted to the "editur" of the Atlanta *Confederacy*, Bill Arp said that he had tried to console and entertain his family during the flight. They "plucked wild flowers, . . . sang songs of merriment, exchanged . . . wit," and these diversions, "together with the comic events that okkured by the way, were safety valves that saved the poor heart from bursting." He wished that someone had composed the refugees' "retreat musik" which would have been a "plaintive tune, interspersed with okkasional comic notes." [47] Others like Bill Arp who could see the "comic events" and hear the "comic notes" could more easily endure the hardships and sadness of their flight.

During the weeks he was in Atlanta, the humorist wrote that he was "remote, unfriended, melankolly," a feeling familiar to many others, and he was searching for a refuge "in some Okeefeenokee swamp, where the fowl invaders cannot travel, nor the pontoon bridges phloat." He seemed to be in no hurry to leave Atlanta, remaining through a part of the battle so that he could witness the departure of the citizenry. The humorous aspects of this event appealed to him as he observed the people's reaction to the "skatterin . . . unfeelin" shells which fell in their midst. "Then came the big panik," he wrote, "people seemed movin in all directions in all sorts of ways with akselerated motion," but he could not be too disturbed because for him it was "the sekund ringing of the . . . bell," and he preferred to remain and "take observations." He spent days at the depot where people were "converging from every pint on the compass," besieging the railroad agents to take them and their baggage on the outgoing trains. Bill Arp was most amused at the mountains of luggage brought to the station and he noted that one lady had a trunk "as big as a niter buro," and another with five small children in tow, three of whom were "cuttin teeth," had a mound of boxes which she asked to be checked to her destination. He heard one Negro, when asked by another what day it was, answer, "I reckon today is Runday from the way the white folks is movin about."

Bill Arp called on several friends in search of human interest stories, and when he reached a doctor's office he found the physician "packin up his vials, pisens . . . and sich like." Seeing "an old skeleton with but one leg . . . swinging from the ceiling," he asked if the doctor planned to leave behind "this mournful emblem of the troubled sitty" and he was told that it would have to remain because of the shortage of transportation. To this Bill Arp replied, "Take the screw out of his skull and give him a crutch. Maybe he'll travel—all flesh is movin and the . . . bones will catch the contagion soon." When the shells started falling "as thick as Governor Brown's proklamashuns," the people began to react with such hysterical, jerky movements that the humorist was reminded of "shakin Quakers going through their pious motions and pekuliar attitudes." He remained in Atlanta until the city "was somewhat purified of its population," and then took his family aboard a train, not knowing where they would go. When the conductor appeared to collect the fares and looked at the size of the family, he suggested that the children be scattered around the countryside since "provisions were scarce." Bill Arp then bought tickets to Covington "to git rid of his impertinence." [48]

After settling his family in Covington, Bill Arp went to Lawrenceville in search of a refuge, but before he was reunited with his wife and children they fled with the approach of Federal raiders and went to the home of friends in Madison. For a time the humorist was out of touch with them, and although worried, he saw the comedy in the episode. He had not been with his family in Madison for long when "the selfish, ubiquitous, infernal Yankees" appeared, but they did not molest the refugees who were on the outskirts of the town. After a week the "Roman Runagee" and his brood traveled out of town on a "dirt road" which he preferred to railroads because the latter were "so liable to be raided, invaded, blockaded and ambuscaded," but their greatest drawback was that "they don't fork often enough." Noting that he had been "partial to forked dirt roads" since being displaced, he said he liked them because they gave "the poor runagee a choice of direction every few miles" and made it easy for him to "change latitude and longitude." Because the family was by this time "konverted to the doctrine of squatter sovreenty," they pitched tents in "the rear of Mr. Sherman's army," far removed from any "unfriendly soljer" who might be "perusin around and axin for papers." Here among the "million majestik pines that stand like tenpins . . . awaitin some cannon ball to . . . knock em down," the family spent several months, and Bill Arp found time to comment satirically on the political feuds going on in Georgia.[49] He returned to his home in Rome after six months of displacement during which time he never lost his sense of humor despite his innumerable problems.

Other refugees eased their tensions by laughing at their predicament. As previously noted, when the Federals arrived in Columbia, many citizens fled to the mental institution on the outskirts of the city, but most accounts of the fire and the flight are filled with the horror and pathos of the event. Two young women who joined the crowd heading out of town managed to laugh at the comic aspects of the movement. Like many others they left home carrying their belongings in their arms, and along the way they dropped several items. Not pausing to retrieve them they shouted, "There goes my last pair of stockings," or "There goes my nightgown." After several such incidents, they stopped, looked at each other and "burst into a hysterical laugh." Arriving at their destination they were amused by the conversations they overheard as other refugees took inventory of the articles they still had with them. One Columbian entertained the group when she laughingly announced that she was wearing her complete wardrobe—three dresses.[50] After the withdrawal of the Federals, the city officials collected the personal effects which were littering the streets and took them to the fire station where the people could claim anything belonging to them. Articles were raised so that all could see them, and if the owner was present she was expected to claim the items, but the women were at first reluctant to acknowledge ownership of a shabby "chemise or pair of drawers." Realizing, however, that they could not be replaced, "necessity soon outweighed modesty," and the women were shouting "mine" when a familiar item was displayed. Those who witnessed this show found it highly entertaining.[51]

Subtle humor characterized the names which many refugees bestowed on their temporary homes. It was rather common for displaced people to designate their quarters as "The Refuge," or "Refugee Hall," and when writing letters, some gave only this as their address. Their descriptions of these abodes indicate that few were spacious enough to be called "halls," but the refugees delighted in resorting to satire and irony. When Katherine Polk Gale and her family were driven from their Yazoo plantation, they found temporary quarters in a small, crude house which she named "Poverty Hall," and from her description of the place and the family's financial status, it was an appropriate appellation. Kate Stone felt compelled to assign each of her Texas homes a name, and her sense of humor is indicated in this instance as in others. The house designated as "Elysian Fields" was a rough, crude structure surrounded by anything but the happy, blissful atmosphere which the name implies, and "The Ranch," the first home of the Stones in Tyler, was so named only because it was spacious. "Bonnie Castle" was more attractive than the family's other refuges, and "The Rest" implies that the Stones were tired of moving from house to house and denotes Kate's wishful thinking that they would not have to move again. Their uncomfortable and primitive abode in Lamar County was named "Vexation," which Kate said was "most appropriate." Once during their travels the family had to spend several days in a rough "two-room affair" on the prairie, and this was designated as "Rescue Hut." None of these wartime homes could compare with "Brokenburn," but Kate enjoyed giving them names, no matter how ridiculous they might be.[52]

At no time in their displacement did the people need a sense of humor as they did when trying to solve their food problems. Substitutes devised for scarce commodities often moved them to laughter, and even those who lacked sufficient food sometimes made light of this situation. A Charleston refugee in Edgefield was noted for telling amusing stories about how the family managed on an inadequate, strange assortment of provisions, and the local editor was so impressed by her sportsmanship and sense of humor that he noted this in his paper.[53] When Mary Boykin Chesnut fled to Lincolnton late in the war, she was confronted with the scarcity of food for the first time. Irritated that she had to struggle to get supplies and especially that the local merchants and farmers refused to take Confederate money, she resorted to bartering her things for food and facetiously commented that she and her displaced friends were "devouring" their clothes. Mrs. Chesnut thought it "quite convenient" that she was in Lincolnton during Lent because she had "nothing to eat," and was therefore free to "fast and pray." Considering Mrs. Chesnut's social and financial position and her comparatively comfortable life, it is a tribute to her sportsmanship that she could manifest a humorous approach to her displacement.[54]

Refugees often made themselves miserable when they permitted their dislike for strangers to become a phobia, but some were more amused than upset by them. Mrs. Chesnut had little in common with the Lincolnton citizens, and although she was critical of some, she was always appreciative of her friends' humorous comments about them. She and Isabella Martin were once stopped by a stranger and told a story about a soldier who had been killed before learning the "sect" of his newborn child. Amused at the woman's misuse of the word, Miss Martin answered by saying that she hoped it would "be Methodist," that being her own faith.[55] Mrs. Meriwether met many ludicrous characters during her displacement, but none more amusing than the Peppercorn family with whom she spent a night on her way across Mississippi. She was disgusted that the mother and her four daughters chewed tobacco, but she was also fascinated by their ability to expectorate the juice ten feet across the room and hit the fireplace every time.[56] Louisianians in Texas were usually amazed by the customs, speech, and dress of the natives. Kate Stone could not get accustomed to those who said "mile" for "miles" or failed to make "year" plural, and when she met a man who made neither of these mistakes she was very impressed with him. She was also amused by the clothing of some whom she met, and once when attending a funeral she stared in amazement at the "oddest-looking crowd" she had ever seen. The women were dressed in a variety of ridiculous costumes, one in "pink tarleton," another in "red woolen," and all bedecked with ribbons and beads. The men were barefooted, wore queer "homemade knit galluses," and slouched wool hats decorated with ribbons and artificial flowers.[57] Some refugees critically and sarcastically described the people they met, but others were kinder and more amused than malicious. It isn't difficult to tell which ones loved and appreciated people.

The refugees approached life in various ways, and all were at some time despondent and homesick as they struggled to hold their families together, to sustain themselves and their dependents, to adjust to new situations and to live with their fears and misgivings. These struggles when combined with their displacement were enough to break the spirit of any person. The war years did not tend to develop humor, yet never was it needed more, and anyone who could laugh at his misfortunes made life more pleasant for those around him. As a Georgian said of Bill Arp, "He actually helped us bear our troubles by his different view of things." [58] Humorists could minimize the depressing effects of the refugees' "many sad hours."

. . . *extremes of generosity and meanness*

Displaced people, not knowing what to expect when they traveled the roads of the Confederacy and settled in strange communities, often met with "extremes of generosity and meanness." They could anticipate rudeness, indifference, insult, and injury from some whom they met, and kindness, sympathy, generosity, and assistance from others, but they did not know when they would encounter a friend and when a foe. Most refugees were greeted with all of these reactions at some time during their wanderings, but the frequency and degree of the various responses depended on the individuals involved.

Southerners who remained at home did not realize that most refugees were embarrassed to the point of mortification when they had to ask favors of others, for they were often too proud to exhibit their true feelings to strangers. A South Carolinian wrote his sister-in-law, a refugee in Greenville, that he had waited too long to make arrangements for his family, and finding no other home for them, he threw himself on her mercy. "As you may suppose," he wrote, "I am deeply mortified at the position I find myself in, unable to provide for . . . my family without the active sympathy and assistance of my friends." [1] All who reacted in a similar manner to their displacement could not bring themselves to speak as candidly to their benefactors, but they often recorded their embarrassment in their personal records. Their humiliation tended to make them more sensitive, and they sometimes imagined hostility where none existed. If this were the situation, they reciprocated in various ways; some brooded alone while others retaliated in accordance with their personality and character.

Although citizens in a refugee center could not be depended upon to react consistently or uniformly to the newcomers, resentment generally increased as the war progressed and it became more difficult to obtain supplies. The more people there were living in a community, the greater was the demand for scarce items and the higher the price. The intensity of this battle for survival in a large measure determined the people's attitude toward the late arrivals. There were also civilians who, on general principles, disliked and distrusted all refugees, but there were others who were sympathetic to them throughout the conflict.

Displaced people had ample opportunity to learn many lessons in human behavior, the first being never to judge others or predict their reactions on first meeting, for most people were inclined to be suspicious of strangers in wartime. Initial dislike for another could be converted into friendship if both parties willed it and left open the door in the beginning, but some of the most critical appraisals were drawn after a single encounter. Refugees also found that at first strangers were likely to judge them collectively rather than individually, and in some instances they could expect never to win acceptance. Many Southerners had old, deep-seated prejudices against specific economic, social, political, religious, and geographic groups, and while some were unable to overcome these biases, others made every effort to do so. During her displacement, Kate Stone's contact with all kinds of people taught her much about human nature, and one of her most interesting discoveries was that "it is not the rich who are most generous." [2] Truer words were never written, as many other refugees learned. Yet the wisest one eventually realized that the degree of "generosity and meanness" they encountered was partially up to them.

When new arrivals in a community intentionally or unintentionally displayed signs of their former affluence, they left the impression of being financially able to pay any price for any item. They were often greeted as though they were vacationers coming to a resort area in season, to be used but not loved, and they were frequently charged higher prices than the citizens had to pay. Therefore the refugees concluded that the primary purpose of the community was to commercialize upon their unfortunate situation. But the poorer people were also caught in this trap when local residents reasoned that if the refugees had to be endured, the merchants, landlords, and farmers might as well benefit economically from their presence. As conditions grew more serious and prices rose, the newcomers became increasingly bitter toward the natives whom they blamed for their predicament. However, a reverse situation arose when strangers came into an area ostensibly in search of safety and later turned to making money in business and speculative endeavors. Marylanders in Richmond and other cities were as often accused of speculating as were the Jewish people, and those participating in blockade running were subjected to caustic criticism, especially when claiming to be refugees. Any person making money during the war was vulnerable to attack, but newcomers who did so were even more likely to be abused.

Everyone seemed to be looking with suspicion on everyone else in the Confederacy. One of the surest ways to make enemies was to leave the impression of having more than others in the community. Because those who amassed stores of scarce items were resented by their neighbors, most hoarders tried to conceal their activities. Although it was easier for people living at home to build up their stock of supplies, some of the refugees were also in a position to do so. A family of Louisianians bought out the entire stock of a store before starting their journey, and one of its members frankly admitted that they wanted to supply themselves abundantly with many items which were already scarce.[3] A refugee whose son traded in blockaded goods received huge quantities of supplies which he had transported by the wagon loads to her temporary quarters in Greenville, South Carolina. He notified his mother as to when each shipment would arrive, which was always after dark, and cautioned her to tell no one about the goods she received. The amount of commodities arriving in Greenville far exceeded the needs of the household, and in a five-month period he sent two barrels of salt, several hogsheads of sugar, and tremendous quantities of black pepper, tea, coffee, rice, cloth, and stockings. He repeatedly encouraged his mother to purchase as great a supply of other items as she could, once suggesting that she buy at least fifty loads of wood. He always instructed her to conceal these supplies from others and "not to speak to anybody" about them.[4] Although this is an extreme example of a refugee's hoarding, other displaced people were guilty of the practice when circumstances permitted, but when their activities were known in the community they could expect to be targets for criticism.

Whatever the reasons for rising prices, refugees blamed the local citizens, who blamed the refugees, with the result that strained relations developed between the two groups. The press, along with individuals, became involved in the controversy and as the displaced people complained to their editors back home about the injustices they encountered in their adopted communities, the hometown editors usually publicized the situation and rushed to their friends' defense. They berated the selfish acts of citizens in the refugee center and wrote emotionally about the "homeless exiles" whose plight was apparently not understood by those permitted to remain at home. Whether or not they succeeded in shaming the hosts for the gross mistreatment of the guests, the newspapers let it be known that conflicts did exist.

The Charleston papers spent most of the war reprimanding the citizens of communities in the interior for their sins against the refugees from the coast. They pleaded with them to recognize the circumstances which sent low country people into their midst, and they often referred to the permanent residents as greedy, selfish, grasping persons who were being disloyal to both South Carolina and the Confederacy. The *Courier* and the *Mercury* published hundreds of complaints from refugees who cited the high rents and commodity prices they were having to pay, and the editors charged the townspeople and farmers with extortion and speculation. In other cities, too, the press was actively at work denouncing those who capitalized on displaced people. Six months before the fall of Atlanta, when Augusta was not yet crowded to suffocation with the homeless, an editor told of north Georgia refugees who had been charged three times the market price for food. He quoted some as saying that they believed it would have been to their advantage to have remained under "Lincoln despotism," for they found the Confederacy "greed-ridden." The editor sharply rebuked those responsible for this outrage and questioned the wisdom and patriotism of Southerners who insisted on hoarding and refused to share, for they were "endangering . . . [the] whole State." He warned that selfish practices of this kind could lose the war for the Confederacy, and as other journalists so often did, he predicted that those who were now treating the refugees with contempt might someday be driven from their homes and would then encounter the same problems.[5] As one editor expressed it, those who "plundered refugees" might soon have "*their* day of tribulation."[6]

When the refugees could not buy what they needed, they often accused the farmers and merchants of holding back these items for their long-standing customers who were paying less than the displaced people had offered for the goods. This situation angered the displaced people as did few other conditions. A Charleston refugee was irate with "the ignorant farmers . . . who regarded the refugees as a bitter foe . . . [and] refused to sell [them] provisions." She was also angry because they refused to accept Confederate money, demanding instead specie or some valuable possession they had brought with them.[7] The latter was a common practice when the finery, luxuries, and jewelry displayed by some refugees were more attractive than the depreciating Confederate money. The person who had commodities to sell was in a bargaining position and could hold out for the payment he sought, a situation which inevitably irritated the buyer.

Many of the displaced people eventually had to part with their prized possessions, not always because this was demanded of them but because they had nothing else with which to make purchases. Cornelia McDonald gradually swapped most of her prewar finery and heirlooms for necessities; Elizabeth Meriwether traded nearly all of her cherished personal possessions for food. Some who resorted to barter believed that they got a fair exchange, but most were disappointed when they received so little in return for articles they prized. When they felt themselves cheated they were even more critical of the local people with whom they bargained, but few were more irate than Mrs. Meriwether when she negotiated for a little sugar with which to make Christmas candy for her sons. The Tuscaloosa speculators were selling the commodity for $30 per pound, a price she could not afford. When she heard that a lady had been hoarding sugar and might be willing to sell some of it, she approached this "lady of the sugar barrel" with a deal. The woman's daughter wanted a pair of satin slippers Mrs. Meriwether owned, and the refugee offered to swap the slippers for forty-five pounds of sugar. There were weeks of bickering, innumerable complications, and for a time it seemed that there might be litigation before Mrs. Meriwether finally settled for fifteen pounds of sugar. Years later, the scars of the transaction had not healed, and "the lady of the sugar barrel" was still referring to the refugee as "that terrible Mrs. Meriwether." [8]

Both Mrs. McDonald and Mrs. Meriwether were determined women who used all of the resources at their command to get necessities for their children, but they did not flaunt whatever luxuries they possessed. There were others who did, however, and most lived to regret it, for it created the impression of being both wealthy and snobbish. Women who wore silk and satin instead of homespun to make a prewar wardrobe stretch over the war years, usually did not explain this, either because they saw no reason to do so, or because they preferred to convey the idea that they were in better financial circumstances than they actually were. Expensive clothing often made them targets for extortioners, and they had greater difficulty winning acceptance in the community, when if their true situation had been clarified they might have been better understood. A young woman who was a refugee in Chester, South Carolina, aptly described this situation when she told of the coolness and indifference her family encountered in the village, explaining that this was due to their having left the impression of being "rich people who could not possibly be in need of assistance." [9]

As the refugees built their case against the local citizens and won the support of the press, their opponents were also telling their side of the story and bringing editors into their camp. Journalists publishing in the overcrowded refugee centers usually supported their neighbors and criticized the refugees; none was more outspoken than E. A. Pollard of the Richmond *Examiner*. He was a man with very positive views on this and other subjects, who could not claim moderation of speech as one of his virtues, and to whom the word "refugee" was a red flag that could provoke him to charge forth in unrestrained fury. He blamed many of Richmond's problems on the displaced people living there, accusing them of being primarily responsible for the shortage of food, the high prices, the terrible congestion, and even the scarcity of fodder. Once when bemoaning the poor transportation facilities in the city he declared that the refugees were responsible because "at least one-half of the long forage" brought to town was used to feed the horses which refugees rented for "purely social purposes." His implication was obvious when he stated that this was a luxury which "cannot be afforded by honest people, . . . only by negroes, thieves and refugees." In another editorial he referred to the displaced people as "vultures who are now preying upon the community." [10]

Few editors used the caustic language of Pollard, but those in other towns came close when pointing out that local problems, and especially the congestion, were due to the presence of large numbers of refugees. These same journalists also came to the defense of the displaced people when circumstances merited, few holding as consistently as Pollard to the antirefugee bias, but most were known to move from one extreme to the other. Southern editors were generally sympathetic to the plight of the homeless but frequently opposed their settling in the community. When the absorption point was reached, they were quick to suggest that the people move on to some less-congested region, but if they heard that the areas they had suggested were unfriendly to the newcomers, they did not hesitate to criticize those responsible. Late in the war when Columbia was the most over-crowded city in South Carolina, a local editor urged that the overflow move elsewhere. But when word reached him that those who took his advice had met with a cool reception in the Piedmont, he wrote one of his most caustic tirades of the war. Captioned "Refugee Haters" and reprinted in many other newspapers, it referred to the up-country people as so "cold . . . unsympathetic . . . and positively unfriendly" that they were no better than the "Yankees." The editor said that if he used the strongest language applicable to the enemy, it would not be strong enough to describe the South Carolinians who mistreated refugees. He noted that "the Yankees, as bad as they are, have some sense of what they owe their kind." Although they were known to "steal, cheat or lie in behalf of their fellows-in-arms," he felt that this was "far better than the selfishness of those cold Southern hearts which" he was then placing "under the editorial dissecting knife." The editor reminded his readers that his contact with refugees had assured him that they sought "no charity," but were willing to pay a fair price for commodities, and he reprimanded those refusing to sell at the market price to displaced people.[11]

Other newsmen who thought this editorial to be of universal inter-est reprinted it in their papers, a Fayetteville, North Carolina, editor adding the comment that he was distressed that Southerners were guilty of "such acts of unkindness to refugees." He cautioned the people that "no one can be exempt from the liability to this misfor-tune as long as the war lasts." [12] Most journalists who cited their Columbia colleague were in agreement with his views, but his readers were not always in accord with his opinions. One correspondent ad-mitted that there were people guilty as charged, but he resented the editor's generalizing and including citizens of only one area. "Many a poor refugee who had never set foot in the upper part of South Carolina has suffered bitterly from the inhumanity of those around him," he wrote, "and that many of the low country refugees have been coldly received . . . must be attributed to the haughtiness and arrogance which some have exhibited toward the people who would have otherwise treated them with all possible kindness." [13] The original editorial set off a chain reaction as both sides presented their views. Just what effect this and other battles of words had on the situation is not known, but chances are it was not improved. If the issue was serious enough to trigger a debate, however, there can be no doubt that trouble existed in the communities.

Although the Southern press was always ready to publish complaints from displaced people, it also attempted to explain the reasons for the seeming discrimination. When a New Orleans refugee in Columbia protested vigorously against the mistreatment of the homeless in "the fiery little State," he emphasized particularly the refusal of Columbians to open their "spacious homes" to those from other states. He saw no reason for this when the refugees were willing to pay a fair rent, and he assured the editor that most were "able to pay at reasonable rates and would not accept charity." He was irritated when South Carolinians offered their sympathy but refused to render positive assistance. This letter was published with the editor's comment that he hoped the townspeople would take the criticism to heart, but he also reminded the writer that Columbia was "overcrowded with refugees" from the coastal areas and was "hardpressed for room." [14]

Refugees could not be expected to be entirely objective when discussing the local people's reactions to their coming into the community, but when so many voiced the same complaints there is sufficient evidence to substantiate the fact that they often met with a cold and even a hostile reception. Kate Stone told of the Tyler citizens' hostility toward the refugees and of the conflicts between the two groups. Mrs. Basil Wilson Duke wrote that Virginians were so rude to those from other states that many of her friends were posing as Virginians in the hope that they would meet with a more friendly reception.[15] A Confederate officer cautioned his wife against going to Alexandria, Louisiana, because the inhabitants were "selfish [and] mean" to refugees, and other men in the service warned their families against settling in specific communities for the same reason.[16] A doctor in Albemarle County, Virginia, was accused of posting signs that "no refugee should put foot within his enclosures," because he hoped to make "thirty thousand dollars" from his farm that year and "could not afford to be feeding strangers." But he was charged with turning away friends as well as those he did not know, and when his college roommate sought refuge in his home he, too, was refused admission. The story was circulated in the press and a Georgia editor commented, "Such a fellow ought to be tied to the tail of a cart and whipped out of the country." Pondering this situation the editor concluded, "The extremes of generosity and meanness developed by this war have certainly been remarkable." [17]

Families who were requested to share their homes with refugees were often divided on the question of whether or not to receive them. Men were more inclined to take them in than were their wives, and the marital battles resulting from this difference of opinion often became heated affairs. When Mrs. Roger Pryor and her children were drifting around Virginia, she found an unusually sympathetic farmer who invited the family to board in his home. He assured Mrs. Pryor that it would be agreeable with his wife, but when the refugees arrived at the house it was immediately apparent that she had not been consulted. The reception was far from cordial and the situation grew worse during the weeks the Pryors were there. The hostess did not mince words when reiterating that she did not want displaced people in her home, and as soon as other arrangements could be made Mrs. Pryor left. She long remembered that while the family lived in the home "everything combined" to increase her "discomfort and wretchedness." [18] Mrs. Meriwether had a similar experience in Mississippi when a kind, hospitable farmer invited her and the children to come to his home where they would be safe since it was located "off the main road." He assured her that the family would be welcome, but as they neared the house he grew quiet and when they rode into the yard he got out of the buggy, sat down near the well and left Mrs. Meriwether to make the introductions. Her meeting with his wife, "a woman of forbidding presence," was unpleasant and embarrassing. She stood in the entrance "glowering" and eventually asked them in but assured the refugees that she was opposed to having strangers in the house. Although the farmer had agreed to take them for "a month or two," the hostess limited the hospitality to one night, retired to her room and was not seen again until the Meriwethers were ready to depart the next morning.[19]

Displaced civilians were never as well treated as the Confederate soldiers, and very little was done for them as they traveled through the South. Organizations administering to their needs were fewer in number than those established to aid the servicemen. Although fund-raising drives were conducted to assist the mass displacements, most courtesies extended individuals were on the person-to-person basis and the majority of refugees were entirely on their own. When the public's attention was called to the plight of large groups of homeless people the most earnest appeals for donations often came from areas not faced with the need for accommodating them. The mass displacement of citizens from Fredericksburg, New Orleans, and other cities inspired newspapers hundreds of miles away to seek contributions for their relief. Thousands of dollars were raised, but when the refugees began to drift into some of these same communities in search of food, housing, and jobs, they were rebuffed. They might be given charity and refused those things they really wanted, but perhaps they were asking too much when they sought understanding, friendship, acceptance, and a chance to make their own way. Many refugees who were a part of the mass evacuations were for the first time indigent but still proud, and they resented being treated as charity cases as they so often were in areas where they had no personal contacts to help them. The townspeople's lack of understanding of the predicament of these people was natural, although it did contribute to the lack of empathy between the two groups.

Southerners who observed displaced people moving into the area, either singly or en masse, often recorded or openly reflected the prejudices which refugees accused them of having. A Charlestonian wrote his wife, "The refugees eat up pretty much everything that is raised in the neighborhood." He blamed them for most of the evils in the city.[20] A young woman delivered lengthy tirades against all refugees but especially those whom her mother had taken into the home. She resented their intrusion and her own lack of privacy after she was compelled to share her room with one of them. She evidenced her jealousy of the guests when she wrote, "Nothing arouses my temper more than seeing a stranger have greater privileges or . . . consideration paid her than is paid to some others in the household." Her resentment of the refugees mounted to the point where she felt genuine animosity toward members of her own family who befriended them.[21]

Southerners who derived an income from catering to refugees were sometimes critical of them in private, if not in public. The owner of a boardinghouse in Charlotte frequently discussed his tenants in letters to his family, and although they were his major source of livelihood, he took every opportunity to make unflattering personal comments about them. He described one group as "the ugliest set of girls" he had ever seen. There were forty-three of these refugees living in his home at the time, with nine more expected momentarily.[22] When hundreds of South Carolinians descended on Charlotte in early 1865, another resident wrote her son that so many came to her door in search of accommodations that she had reached the point where she hated "to hear the bell ring." She explained, "I feel sorry for them but still can't love my neighbors better than myself." The truth was that she had never been fond of South Carolinians and was now especially critical because they did not stay at home and defend their state. "The South Carolinians," she wrote, "who made all the fuss are now the *swiftest* of foot," but she was not the only one in her household who did not like the southern neighbors. Another son, critically ill at the time, was too "weak and . . . sick to speak on other subjects," but at the mention of " 'refugee' or South Carolina," he would rise from his bed and "hold forth." [23]

As previously noted, male refugees who appeared to be sound in mind and body were usually looked upon with suspicion when they arrived in a strange community. When they came ostensibly to locate their families in temporary quarters, the residents had little to say about it, but if they remained and failed to offer their services to the Confederacy, the townspeople were likely to criticize and even mistreat them. Their presence may have been consoling to loved ones, but they were seldom accepted by the community. An Arkansas editor called attention to men who had escorted their families out of endangered areas and settled them in Little Rock, but who had remained and were doing nothing for the Southern cause. He distinguished between those who needed to remain so as to provide for their dependents and those who were affluent or had relatives financially able to care for them. The latter group were enjoying a life of "inglorious ease" as their homes were being overrun by "the hirelings of Lincoln," and the writer could only conclude that they were "cowards and deserters." He resented their "putting on immense airs and seeking offices in the State," and he said that any citizen who would vote for these undeserving refugees merited execution. As the situation in northern Arkansas became critical, the editor even more caustically criticized the displaced men who were "lounging on the streets and about the hotels with no visible occupation except to abuse General McCulloch and reproach Arkansas for not going to the help of Price." He suggested that they leave the state because they were engendering "ill feeling where there should be harmony." [24]

Newsmen elsewhere launched similar attacks, one in North Carolina referring to the men as "able-bodied refugees from God knows where." [25] A Wilmington editor condemned the city's native sons who left for safer areas and suggested that they never again "be permitted to live in our community and exercise the right of citizenship." [26] One in Sumter, South Carolina, stated that "men . . . who fly from their threatened homes, and leave strangers to defend their property . . . and meet the shock of battle," deserve nothing but harsh criticism. But what he resented most about the male refugees were their "words of ill-boding . . . and prophesies of disaster." For this group he had "unutterable contempt" because they were "a traveling agent of the enemy; a circulating engine of mischief." [27] Any man who did not bear obvious signs of an infirmity was vulnerable to this sort of accusation.

All editorial diatribes and insinuation did not go unanswered. When an editor in Yorkville, South Carolina, criticized the refugees, and especially the able-bodied men, one in the group referred to the verbal assault as "unjust." He reminded the journalist that although other piedmont communities had been rude to the refugees, Yorkville had never before indicated displeasure with them. The local citizens had received them "with nothing but uniform kindness," but if the editor had spoken for the community the displaced people had no alternative but "to seek new homes." [28]

Another source of unhappiness for many refugees was their cool reception in the churches of strange communities, reflected many times when they were denied a choice of pews. Several young women who went to Lynchburg were shocked to find that the "people were not kindly disposed to refugees," and this was especially apparent when "the wanderers ventured to occupy their pews in church." The first Sunday they were in town, the newcomers seated themselves downstairs and were promptly asked to move to the balcony. When the minister arose to address the congregation he stated that hereafter "refugees would find seats in the gallery." Hurt and bewildered, the ladies found places in the area assigned them but soon made light of the situation when they joined in singing a hymn, the last lines of which were

> Haste my soul; Oh haste away
> To seats prepared above.

This brought giggles from the gallery as the faces of those on the lower floor "reddened perceptibly." The next Sunday when the refugees arrived at the church, they were invited to occupy pews on the first floor but they declined, saying that they preferred "the seats prepared above." [29] All refugees confronted with a similar situation did not think it amusing, and most were shocked when they were not graciously received in the churches. Many displaced people did not understand that in some Southern churches families had occupied the same pews for several generations, and these were almost as sacred to them as their faith. Therefore when the recent arrivals into the community were asked to sit elsewhere, they often construed it to mean that they were not welcome.

Refugees who had experienced or heard of churches rebuffing newcomers sometimes wondered how the congregation would react to their presence. If the reception was cordial they were both relieved and happy. They appreciated this courtesy as much as any extended them, gravitating toward any one church which had a reputation for welcoming displaced people. A Tennessee refugee noted that many of his neighbors and friends attended the First Presbyterian Church in Atlanta because they were made to feel welcome. He was pleasantly surprised to find that "a number of pews" in the central part of the sanctuary "were set apart" for their use.[30]

The question of seating was usually no problem for those who had friends or family willing to share their pews with the refugees. A young lady who went to Camden, South Carolina, wondered whether or not she would be permitted to rent a pew in the church of her choice, but an uncle arranged for her family to occupy one "rent-free," and this she said was a "very kind and liberal" gesture which she deeply appreciated.[31] Displaced people who were unable to break the ice in the churches often congregated together in one of their own, bringing "refugee" churches into being, usually under the direction of a displaced minister. However, this made them vulnerable to the charge of being clannish. They were also accused of this for other reasons, sometimes with justification and at other times without cause. But when they separated themselves from the local citizens, understanding between the two was less likely to develop.

A great many of the displaced people had reason enough for complaining about the lack of hospitality and understanding in strange communities, but very often they failed to take into consideration that their own actions and attitudes were contributing factors. If they came to a new area and openly criticized the mores of the people and the other ways in which the surroundings differed from those to which they were accustomed, the refugees were creating ill will whether or not this was their intent. Their statements were construed to be ridicule, for the inhabitants of poorer, more backward regions were sensitive and sometimes ill at ease when thrown in contact with those from richer, more progressive areas. When the sensitive refugees confronted the sensitive residents, both had to exercise the greatest tact if trouble were to be averted. Many of the disputes between the two groups stemmed from simple misunderstanding of each other, and usually neither thought himself in error. But all meetings were not unhappy ones, and most refugees had many heartwarming experiences that helped to keep alive faith in their fellow man.

Just as some people refused to take strangers into their homes, others opened wide their doors to those in need. A man in Charleston wrote his fiancée that four hundred displaced people, all unknown to him, were expected to arrive from Savannah the next day, and he was thinking of taking some of them into his home "if there are no better places" available. "If they will come . . . [I] will offer," he wrote, and the following day he was at the dock when they disembarked. He reported that Charlestonians were there "to help the ladies off the boat," and a local physician was supervising the handling of the baggage which "was no small job." The young man assisted in unloading the luggage while others greeted the arrivals, assigned them to quarters, and aided them in other ways.[32] The real test of a person's attitude toward refugees came in situations like this when he was confronted with requests from strangers. Most Southerners felt an obligation to relatives and friends whether or not they really wanted them in their homes, but they were not as likely to feel themselves compelled to assist strangers. Refugees were more intuitive than some of their friends and family realized, and they could sense whether or not they were welcome, but when a stranger opened his home to them they were sure it was because he wanted to do so.

Before Thomas Dabney and his family were driven from their Mississippi plantation, he inserted a notice in the Vicksburg papers inviting "any and all citizens desirous of leaving the city to take refuge" on his estate. Prior to this blanket invitation, he had already permitted a family of Louisianians to settle on the premises, and after his public announcement, others accepted his generous hospitality.[33] In and around Raymond, to the east of Vicksburg, citizens organized a committee to scout the area for possible places where the refugees might live. Residents were urged "to open their doors to the fugitive women and children" and render whatever aid was in their power to bestow, free of charge, if possible. One man near Raymond was reported to have filled his home "to the utmost capacity" and had refused to accept payment from his homeless tenants.[34] As previously noted, the Wadleys also opened their doors to all who came, and once when the home was already so crowded that there seemed to be no room for additional refugees, Mrs. Wadley took as guests two women and their babies because "the circumstances of their case were so sad." Their home had been burned and they had come to Monroe in search of relatives who were "scattered about" in the area.[35] Few Southerners could afford to house and feed a great number of people, and those who dispensed such bountiful hospitality were necessarily wealthy, but others graciously shared what they had with displaced people.

Refugees going into a strange community did not always react to the people in the same way. Some criticized their coolness while others reported a warm reception. A Charlestonian who settled in the upcountry said that "refugees from the seacoast have a kind welcome," and the residents were always ready to perform "acts of courtesy which are always so gratifying to the heart of a stranger in distress." [36] Although many Louisianians in Texas thought the people strange and inhospitable, one young lady wrote that she was "agreeably disappointed in the Texas." Her choice of words leaves something to be desired but her meaning was quite clear when she explained, "We have been very kindly treated everywhere we have been & have not heard a single complaint of refugees. . . . The people here are the most sociable folks I have ever met. . . . They visit and treat us just as if we were old settlers." [37]

Those who sought a wartime refuge in the mountains frequently criticized the natives for being openly hostile to strangers, mentioning the suspicious nature and indifference of the mountaineers. However, one of the refugees in Asheville told of their "inexhaustible" hospitality. He was impressed that "the accursed greed of gain . . . sweeping over the land" was not to be found in the mountain areas and that the people "still had an open house and a welcome hand for the exiled refugee." [38] Katherine Polk Gale noted that she and her family had a pleasant sojourn in Asheville and that many "charming friendships" were made there during the war.[39]

Mrs. Meriwether met all types of people during her displacement, including many who were of great assistance to her. She remembered with deepest gratitude the lady who gave her lodging in Columbus, Mississippi, and nursed her through the birth of her third son. She recalled also the many kind and generous folk in Tuscaloosa who helped her find housing and gave her furnishings which they could scarcely afford to part with at a time when the items could not be replaced.[40]

Although some refugees received only half-hearted invitations to live with relatives and friends, and others received none at all, there were many who were tendered such warm, genuine invitations that there could be no doubt as to their sincerity. The prospective host was often so persuasive and convincing that he uprooted the recipient who had not as yet decided to leave home. It was such an invitation from Alabama friends that decided Bishop Lay to send his family to their home, and it was a similar appeal that caused the Wigfall girls to go first to Mrs. Joseph E. Johnston's Atlanta home and later to that of other friends in Macon. Sarah Morgan and her family were cordially received by several families in Louisiana before they decided to go to her brother's home in New Orleans. But one of the most sincere and touching invitations of the war was extended to Mrs. Elizabeth Eggleston by an Alabamian whom she had nursed in a Vicksburg hospital. After his discharge he went to his parents' home in Cahaba and wrote Mrs. Eggleston inviting her and her family to be his guests for the duration of the struggle. There could be no doubt as to his sincerity when he wrote, "You shall have a home at my house and such comforts as I have myself as long as I have hands to work." He offered to divide "to the last" all that he had, and closed his letter by saying, "I insist upon your coming to Alabama to live." [41]

Wartime invitations often included qualifying statements that made the recipient wonder if he were really wanted, for the person ex- tending the invitation was sometimes embarrassed that he could not promise greater comfort and happier conditions than were possible under the circumstances. They forewarned their invited guest that he would be crowded or would lack the fare of better days or would in some other way have to adjust to unusual conditions. Yet this was inserted to prepare him for the changed status of his host and the in- conveniences he would encounter. Although some displaced people interpreted this as a cool attitude, most of those already displaced understood it as a realistic approach to the situation. Refugees who invited others to join them were usually in worse circumstances than those as yet in their own homes. One of these temporarily located in South Carolina invited a cousin to live with her but asked that she bring whatever supplies she could for her own use. She reiterated throughout the letter, "I will share with you what I have," but she emphasized the shortage of commodities in the area. She also asked that her cousin bring her "most useful servants" to make her more comfortable, for the hostess had none in her refuge.[42] In this case the invited guest had not left her own home in Atlanta, and those who were not yet familiar with the life of a refugee were less likely to understand the problems incurred by displaced people.

Just as refugees were sometimes justified in criticizing those who made it difficult for them to obtain provisions, so they had reason to be grateful to others who came to their assistance. They were often the recipients of food, clothing, and other essentials bestowed on them by old friends and even by strangers in the area. A family in Greenville, South Carolina, periodically received turkeys, ducks, chickens, sausage, bread, and confections from their more fortunate neighbors. But one of the most cherished gifts was "a large cake of myrtle wax" which was used to make candles.[43] Friends of the McGuires who lived in the country very often delighted the refugees with gifts of food which could not be procured in the city markets. After Mrs. Meriwether's unhappy encounter with the farmer who refused to sell her corn, she had her faith in mankind restored when a local citizen heard of her trouble and came to her assistance. Although he was at first a stranger to her, he brought her many baskets of food in the months that followed and refused to take any payment for the produce. Mrs. Meriwether remembered him as a "dear, good old man . . . so kind, so generous." She felt that "no man ever deserved God's favor more" than this kind farmer whom she "knew in Tuscaloosa. . . ."[44]

Many refugees were justified in their complaints against particular churches and congregations which reacted in an unfriendly manner, but there were also religious forces at work in their behalf. Ministers often sermonized on their plight and pleaded with their parishioners to aid them. The displaced people were also included in their prayers just as were the soldiers and leaders of the Confederacy. A Charleston clergyman, reviewing the first year of the war and stressing its effects on the Southern people, emphasized the trials of those who had "retreated from . . . towns and river banks," and warned his congregation that they might someday have to flee and "entrench" themselves "among the hills." He stated that this displacement of noncombatants was one of the worst disasters of the war, and that the refugees were suffering as much as the soldiers in the field. He urged his flock to do all it could for them and to give them the understanding they merited.[45] Not long after the Reverend W. B. W. Howe delivered this appeal, members of his congregation began to leave Charleston, but he lacked the money to send his family to safety and relocate them in the interior. However, the vestry came to his assistance and raised $800 to be used for this purpose. He must have felt that those who heard his plea in behalf of displaced people had taken his words to heart.[46]

Church conferences were held erratically during the war, but when they convened the refugees were topics for discussion and prayer. The Presbyterian Synod of Virginia, meeting in the fall of 1864, devoted much of its program to the problem. One of the pastoral addresses had as its theme the problems of those who were driven from their homes. "Let the exiles be cared for," commanded the speaker as he explained the circumstances which had made thousands homeless, emphasizing that many had chosen to leave home rather than take the oath of allegiance to "the enemy government." He stressed that these people needed the "kind consideration" of all true Southerners, for many had left behind the material comforts of life to come "in poverty" to strange communities. He cautioned, however, that they did not ask charity but only "a livelihood by proper exertions in some proper employment." After this persuasive address, the Synod charged the churches "to give them the assistance they may need in finding employment," and to show "a becoming spirit" toward them. All people who rendered aid to the refugees were promised that they would be "ever . . . remembered" for their kind deeds.[47]

The religious press also articulated on this subject and requested Southerners to understand the peculiar situation of the displaced people. When editors heard that the homeless were meeting with something less than cordiality, they rebuked those responsible and urged that the strangers be hospitably received. Like the secular press, religious journals published letters from refugees who were either complaining or praising the communities into which they went. In an editorial appearing in the *Confederate Baptist* midway in the war an editor wrote that he "deeply sympathized with the hard lot of the sufferers who are now exiles from their pleasant homes." He sought "to bespeak for them the kindly offering of those among whom their lot may be cast." [48]

Just as the secular press frequently criticized and exhibited an inhospitable attitude toward the displaced people who came into the community, so it interceded in their behalf. The time, local conditions, and editor determined the tone and slant of the comments, but as previously noted, most newspapers in crowded refugee centers reflected a less friendly approach to the problem. The Charleston *Mercury* referred to the first refugees arriving in the city as "victims and martyrs of this war, . . . sacrifices upon the altar of patriotism," and the editor asked that "every door and heart be opened to them, . . . for to desert them is to desert the cause." [49] This same paper, however, later became more critical of those arriving in the city, as was generally the case in most communities late in the war. An editor in Atlanta wrote at length on the subject of hospitably receiving the Kentuckians in the early months of the conflict, and he caustically criticized the residents of the city who were "encased . . . snail-like . . . in their luxurious abodes . . . averse to the trouble of having boarders." Because "the black winds of winter" were pressing down on the city, he asked that the citizens practice the Golden Rule and open their homes to the refugees.[50] Other newspapers lectured their readers on the meaning of Southern hospitality and Christian principles as they pleaded in behalf of the displaced people. A Raleigh paper noted that anyone who fled from enemy territory carried "a sure passport to our kindest and best attentions," and another in Lynchburg, Virginia, asked the local people to see that "their condition . . . was made more comfortable." [51]

All suggestions made by the press were not as general as these— some were very specific. Editors frequently supported the establishment of relief programs which ranged from serving meals to the refugees as they passed through the town to setting up agencies to deal with the provisioning problems of those settling in the area. A Columbia editor suggested that local delegations meet incoming trains and escort the refugees "to places . . . where a smile of welcome should greet them." [52] When loud and bitter complaints were voiced by those who could not get the necessities, local papers pleaded with farmers to bring produce into town and sell it to the refugees at reasonable prices. The Vicksburg *Whig* urged the rural people to take supplies to those living in caves who were suffering from hunger because no provisions were available to them.[53] In many communities the press suggested that committees be formed to go into the country, buy food, and sell it at cost to the refugees. A Winnsboro, South Carolina, editor insisted that this be done, explaining that the permanent residents did not understand the pitiful conditions of the newcomers whose "nature, education and class" make them reluctant to publicize "their real and positive sufferings." [54] When the Galvestonians descended on Houston, the press begged Texas farmers to send additional supplies to the city, and it requested the citizens to meet their displaced neighbors, take them into their homes, and render all possible aid.[55]

Although the refugees at times felt that newspapers were their sternest critics, they also might have thought of them as their best friends. The press played a major role in familiarizing the civilians with the peculiar problems and needs of the homeless people in their community as well as those living in other areas. Journalists often sought to break down the selfish provincialism when they asked that donations be sent to refugees in other states. When an Atlanta editor called on his readers to send aid to the South Carolinians, he impressed on them that the Carolinians "had always given a helping hand to the distressed in other lands," and it was now up to the Georgians to render assistance to them.[56] His words clearly indicate that many Southerners thought of neighboring states as a "foreign land." And another editor informed his public that they were just as responsible for helping refugees from other states as they were for assisting those from Georgia.[57]

The words of crusading editors sometimes fell on deaf ears, for the writers were often guilty of wishful thinking. A Spartansburg editor who witnessed the arrival of the first refugees from coastal South Carolina envisioned all sorts of wonderful developments which would take place when the two groups were brought together by the forces of war, hoping that they "would see the better qualities of each other, and thus remove much of the prejudice which existed between the inhabitants of the same State." [58] But in this case, as in others, the animosities were too deep-seated to be easily overcome, and the wartime situation in Spartanburg gives no indication that the editor's hope was fulfilled. Perhaps he knew that his words would have little or no effect on the populace, but he preferred to look at the situation optimistically. Certainly it did not make matters any worse and in a few instances he might have improved conditions. The increasing problems of the period complicated life to such an extent that it was even more difficult than it might otherwise have been to overcome existing prejudices. In refugee centers, as elsewhere, the winning of friends and the making of enemies was largely an individual matter.

As the refugees grew more bitter and critical with the continuation of the war, they were more inclined than ever to blame local citizens for their troubles. It seemed the natural thing to do. Very few wrote such glowing accounts about their refuge and neighbors as did Constance Cary. Midway in the war she enthusiastically commented, "I love Richmond." She found the town "full of hospitable souls," noting that if there had been "a little jealous feeling between the 'residents' and the 'refugees'," she had not experienced it. "I don't wonder that those everlasting 'refugee' wails and pleas grow fatiguing," she wrote. "I must confess our class is at a discount, and . . . the exile privileges have been abused." She assured her readers that she was having "a capital time" in Richmond "chequered though it . . . [is], by the saddest scenes of my life." [59] Few were this enthusiastic about their adopted home, but Miss Cary had many reasons for being happier than most refugees. She was one of the wealthy, socially prominent young women who moved in official circles, and it was while she lived in Richmond that she met her future husband, Burton Harrison, secretary to President Davis. She was very much a part of the city's social life, and she should have been as satisfied with her surroundings as any displaced person could be. Had she found a refuge in some remote area where she had no contacts it is doubtful that she would have reacted so enthusiastically.

Refugees learned that human relations could be complicated by innumerable factors, and for those unaccustomed to contacts outside their limited circle of friends the lesson was often a heartbreaking one. When coming into strange areas, a cool reception hurt them, mistreatment angered them, and lack of appreciation for their social position and misfortunes shocked them. If they met with exceptionally kind treatment and understanding, most were gratified and some were surprised, but many took it as a matter of course and failed to show their appreciation. The refugees' personality defects and idiosyncrasies stood out clearly to those they met for the first time and were often topics for conversation among the citizens of the community. But the newcomers also criticized those among whom they lived, and they too often went into a community without any intention of modifying their views to conform with those of the residents. Some displaced people conditioned themselves to their surroundings, but others were never able to do so; most of them at some time during their displacement experienced the "extremes of generosity and meanness."

. . . the times . . .
have duties for all

The Civil War presented a challenge to Southern civilians as well as soldiers, and to displaced people as well as those who stayed at home. A Charleston editor noted that there were "duties for all," and although the refugees were in some ways distinctive, they were not immune to wartime responsibilities. They were expected to sustain themselves to the best of their ability, to support the war effort, and to maintain a positive outlook that would contribute to a high morale—the duties of the homefront in any war. Displaced people who stayed busy making positive contributions to their country, community, and loved ones were usually the ones who had less time to brood, complain, and criticize. They were also the ones most likely to adjust to new situations, to benefit personally from their endeavors, and to win the respect and affection of those with whom they came in contact.

Unfortunately there were refugees who idled away the war years either because they preferred to do so or had little choice in the matter. Those trained for a specific profession or line of work were sometimes unable to continue with it during the war and refused to try another. Women who were accustomed to a life of ease, and thought it disgraceful to take a paying job, did not seem to realize that they were living in an age which expected them to assume greater responsibilities. Although most women worked harder than ever before in the home, on the farm, or in the business and professional world, others were too proud, lazy, or spoiled to face the challenge realistically. Many in this group felt as though they had made their contribution when they gave up their homes, and they lived only for the day they would return. There were also both men

and women who lacked the imagination and ingenuity to create jobs
or diversions for themselves, and in their long, empty hours they
became bored, critical, and homesick. They were the "croakers" so
often mentioned by their contemporaries, and this was the group of
refugees to whom the Charleston editor addressed his reminder that
the war had "duties for all." [1]

People who might otherwise have kept busy were often confronted
with many wartime impediments, not the least of which was the
scarcity of money, supplies, equipment, and countless other commodities and facilities. Those who were constantly on the move
could not establish themselves in a permanent job, and those who
settled in communities affording employment often had to compete
with hundreds of others who were seeking the same position. The
older refugees were usually handicapped because they lacked the physical endurance to perform regimented assignments, although the elderly women could busy themselves within the home and be more
contented than could the men. Refugees who settled in rural areas
had fewer opportunities for gainful employment, since the only occupations open to them were farming and domestic pursuits. All displaced people who "sat out" the war did not do so through choice,
but most people who were imaginative and energetic could manage
to keep occupied.

A great many refugees worked diligently and contributed appreciably to the communities in which they settled. Some continued
their customary line of work, and this was especially true of displaced
ministers. They were sometimes assigned permanent positions, but
more often temporary ones, and in either case they were called upon
to render professional services. Contemporary accounts often mention their unselfish devotion to duty, and their willingness to serve
without remuneration. It has been previously noted that there were
many clergymen in the refugee ranks, and most stayed busy administering to the needs of others. Although the Reverend John B. McGuire
depended on a government job for his livelihood, he organized an
Episcopal church during his year in Ashland, and his wife credited
him with administering the first Episcopal sacrament in the village.
She proudly noted that his flock consisted of fifty families, most of
whom were refugees, and she said that he neither expected nor received any salary for his services.[2] Other displaced preachers established
churches which very often were attended primarily by refugees. As
previously noted, the one organized by the Reverend J. J. Scott in
Montgomery was supported by homeless Floridians.[3]

When a minister came into a community which had need of his services, he might settle there for as long as the forces of war permitted him to remain, but he sometimes found that his income was insufficient to his needs. It was not unusual for him to hold a second position, usually teaching. His classes were sometimes held in the local schoolhouse, in his home, or in the church, and they were well attended. One refugee commented that a displaced preacher had assumed this double responsibility in Cuthbert, Georgia, because he needed two salaries to provide for his children who numbered "a full baker's dozen." [4]

Primary and secondary teachers and tutors were also in great demand during the war. Many men who had taught prior to the war went into the armed forces, or, if Northern sympathizers, left the South; therefore the field was open to Southerners and primarily to women, who during this period entered the profession in greater numbers than ever before. Among them were many refugees. Teachers were not required to have college training, and judging from some who taught, little more than literacy was expected, but young women who had very little formal schooling were often exceptionally well read and thoroughly qualified to teach the younger children. Professors had greater difficulty finding positions because a great many colleges closed during the conflict, but they sometimes conducted classes for the younger students, and a few managed to find positions in other institutions. But it was the mothers or other members of the family who usually assumed responsibility for the children's education. One who held classes for her own sons and daughters sometimes permitted other children to attend, but usually these sessions were held in the home where the mother could attend to her domestic duties as she taught. Women who had never instructed before frequently confessed to their lack of confidence in themselves, but they were willing to assume this responsibility in addition to others if this were the only way for their children to get an education. As previously noted, Jorantha Semmes taught her young, and Kate Stone tutored her younger brothers. The teaching profession had an advantage for women in that it was a ladylike occupation; many positions opened to women during the war were not thought suitable for the Southern female.

After her husband's death, Cornelia McDonald realized that she must find employment from which she could derive an income. She had a natural artistic talent and had practiced drawing during her displacement, so when friends suggested that she teach classes in her home, her favorite diversion became her profession. It was difficult for her to begin her teaching so soon after Angus McDonald's death, for she hated the thought of the "daily interruptions" of students coming into the home, and "of being obliged to meet strangers," yet she also knew that the classes would help to take her mind off her grief as well as bring in the much needed income. She had only a few students at first but soon others were added to her rolls, and within weeks she was teaching poetry and history in addition to art. She conducted her classes during the morning and afternoon and somehow managed to attend to her other chores. "Only in this way," wrote Mrs. McDonald, "was I able to provide my family with bread, beans . . . [and] a little fat bacon." [5] She was so happy in her work that she continued teaching after the war.

Many refugees who became teachers had no previous plans for entering the profession, nor did they have a burning desire to make it a career. It was thrust upon them when they had to make a living, and it could not be said that they were "called" to the service. Sarah Morgan was typical of those who assumed her first teaching position with an uninspired, desperate, gloomy outlook, for she had long feared that this would be her fate when her late father's estate was lost. Although she had received only ten months of formal schooling, she was an exceptionally intelligent, well-read young lady who wrote and played beautifully. Yet the fact remained that she did not want to teach, and the thought of devoting her life to the profession caused her to exclaim, "I would rather die than teach." She thought it was a "hopeless, thankless, task," and her heart had always "ached" for any governess, but when she went to her brother's home in New Orleans she took a teaching position rather than be entirely dependent on him. After she started her work she confessed that her classes kept her so busy that she had no time for "melancholy reflections," and for this she should have been grateful. [6]

Other young women who were raised to be ladies of leisure, expecting their father to support them until their husbands took over, were rudely awakened during the war to the need for earning a living. Most of them met this challenge with greater courage and cheer than did their parents who were shocked and embarrassed when their daughters took jobs. Among the refugees confronted with this situation was John B. Grimball, whose business affairs had suffered to such an extent that he was having a difficult time provid-

ing his family with the necessities. His daughter decided that she
could relieve him of a part of his burden if she accepted a teaching
position in a "female academy" in the nearby village of Union. She
seemed to be very cheerful about the prospects, but her parents were
saddened by the turn of events. After he had seen his daughter on
her way to the school, John Grimball wrote of his unhappiness but
admitted that he was in no position "to oppose . . . [her] effort to
support herself." [7]

Refugee lawyers usually had greater difficulty pursuing their profession than did ministers and teachers, but they often utilized their
legal training in government work or followed other interests. Because most attorneys had to leave their law books at home, they found
it impossible to practice unless they were accorded the use of a colleague's library. Philip Phillips was among the lawyers who let nothing
deter them from following their profession, and for him the war
years were busy ones. He left Washington and went to New Orleans
shortly after the outbreak of hostilities and was living there when
General Butler took command of the city. Mrs. Phillips irritated the
General who accused her of laughing at the corpse of a Federal
soldier and had her imprisoned on Ship Island. Upon her release, she
and her husband joined the refugee colony in LaGrange, Georgia,
where they rented a comfortable cottage situated on a plot of land
large enough for a garden. Phillips was so successful as a gardener that
his neighbors dubbed him "Cincinnatus of the Plow," but his agri-
cultural pursuits did not occupy all of his time. He made frequent trips
to Mobile where he had several clients, and he pleaded a number of
cases during his displacement. One of these brought him a fee of
$15,000 which he invested in cotton and mining stock. He sold
the cotton at a profit after the war and still owned the mining
stock ten years later. Writing after the war, Phillips commented,
"My fees during my . . . years in LaGrange enabled me to support my family abundantly and furnished the means to begin a new
life." [8]

Physicians seem to have been as scarce among the refugees as they
were on the homefront at large, but they are sometimes mentioned
as among those who fled from the enemy. Kate Stone and Sarah
Wadley mentioned doctors who moved from southern Louisiana to
other points in the state. One of the Louisianans who went to Texas
and settled in Tyler was a close friend of the Stones, and it was while
he was a refugee that he died. Many of the younger physicians went
into the service, and throughout the war in all areas of the South

there was a shortage of medical men. Even a superannuated doctor coming into the community usually had no trouble finding patients if he chose to practice. When a displaced Atlanta physician opened his office in Milledgeville, the local editor was so elated to have him in town that he editorialized on his coming and expressed the gratitude of the local people for his having chosen Milledgeville as his wartime home.[9]

Women had to assume responsibility for tending the sick, doing their best to replace the doctors and pharmacists as they concocted medicines from indigenous plants. When a refugee came into a strange community and made known her nursing talents or her simple "cures," she was likely to be appreciated by those who needed her assistance. These were often the poorer farm women from remote areas who might otherwise have been ignored or snubbed by the citizens, but when they rendered a valuable service to those in need, they were almost sure to win friends. Women refugees were also among those who dared to run the land blockade and bring scarce medicines into the Confederacy, concealing these under their hoop skirts. Hetty and Constance Cary crossed into Maryland several times and brought back to Richmond many contraband articles, including medicine. Doctoring and nursing one's family and friends was but another task for the Southern woman to perform, whether or not she was displaced.

In other fields there were refugees who practiced their customary occupations during displacement. Some of the artists continued to paint, and one who left Jackson, Mississippi, before the Federals arrived took with him his paints, easels, and canvas. He settled in Athens, Georgia, where he set up his studio in a college building and earned a livelihood by painting. The local press was very enthusiastic about his work, and one editor referred to his Madonnas as "exceptionally beautiful," and his portraits of Confederate Generals as "life-size . . . living copies of the great originals." The Athens citizens were urged to patronize the homeless, "courteous, affable" artist.[10]

As colorful, exciting, and dedicated as any group of refugees were the journalists who voiced their opinions and aired their views wherever they paused long enough to set up their presses. Out of dingy, shell-gutted buildings and out of boxcars came issues of Southern newspapers on the run. No newspaper published for a longer period against greater odds than did the Memphis *Appeal* which came to be known as the "Moving Appeal." Leaving Memphis, it paused for a time in Granada, Mississippi, before going on to Jackson where it remained long enough to print an edition the very morning the Federals entered the city. As soon as the journal was on the streets, the editor and his staff packed "everything essential to the publication of the paper" and fled from the town. The exodus was described as a "masterful one, . . . accomplished without loss, notwithstanding a number of shots . . . fired across the Pearl River . . . by the disappointed Yankees." [11]

The editor's determination to keep his paper alive won for him the admiration and profuse praise of his colleagues throughout the South. The Richmond *Whig* referred to the *Appeal* as "a sterling paper," [12] and the Natchez *Courier* called it "one of very best papers in the Southern Confederacy," and certainly "the ablest conducted paper." When the editor of the *Courier* wrote so glowingly he had already moved into the Federal camp, and he suggested to the staff of the *Appeal*, then in Atlanta, that it not try another move when the enemy came to that city. Noting that "the Confederate road has been a rough one" for the paper, he questioned if it would not be well for it "to remain stationary . . . , and let the United States come to it," for a third move was sure to bring "a break up and grand smash." [13]

Throughout the spring and summer of 1864, the determined editor of the *Appeal* reiterated that come what may he wasn't moving again, and when other Atlanta newspapers fled or ceased publication he stood his ground as the "Yankee missiles" fell around him.[14] However, in August the paper moved out of the city in a boxcar and during the last nine months of the war published in Montgomery, Macon, and Selma. A Columbus editor, commenting on a Montgomery edition, said that wherever the paper had been published in its stormy career, it had "always sustained its high character and interest." [15] When the Federals approached Selma, the editor of the *Appeal* fled to the hills and, according to one student, when he was captured by the Federal Cavalry he had "saddle bags filled with type, all that remained of the once prosperous *Appeal*." [16]

Although no newsman evidenced greater determination than the editor of the peripatetic *Appeal*, others moved frequently and published in several communities. They were among the busiest refugees, and as a North Carolina journalist wrote, "The dispersion of the column of the press" have made them true "moveable columns as they work their way from one side of the Confederacy to another." [17] When this was written in the summer of 1864, the Knoxville *Register*, had its offices in Charlotte after leaving Atlanta, and the Chattanooga

Rebel which had published in Chattanooga, Marietta, and Atlanta, was then in Griffin, Georgia, and was yet to publish in Columbus and Selma. The Atlanta *Intelligencer* was publishing in a boxcar in Macon, the *Southern Confederacy* (Atlanta) in Columbus, and the Jackson *Mississippian* in Selma. Withers Clay, publisher of the Huntsville *Democrat*, was also displaced but as a refugee he had edited the *Daily Huntsville Confederate* in Chattanooga, then Marietta, and finally in Dalton where publication was suspended in February, 1864.[18] Clay, like other newsmen, supplemented his income by doing job printing. Although countless editors ceased publication or went into the enemy camp, an impressive number adamantly continued in the profession for as long as they could possibly do so. They did not, as one journalist phrased it, "console themselves behind pipe and speculations." [19]

The displaced press always manifested sympathy and understanding for the refugees and in many cases became their spokesman. After the Galveston *News* fled to Houston it carried appeals for aid to the homeless people who flocked to the city. While the Knoxville *Register* had offices in Atlanta, a displaced Tennessean said that its headquarters was a meeting place "for East Tennessee refugees." [20] However, the fugitive press was not always praised for its flight; this was most apt to be the case when editors remaining within Federal lines caustically criticized their wandering colleagues. The Natchez *Courier* many times printed sniping remarks aimed at the Jackson *Mississippian*, and other editors, often embittered by their own problems, referred to those who refugeed as cowards. But if the displaced press had its critics, it also had friends among other refugees who looked upon the editors as men of courage.

It was not unusual to see editors at work during their displacement, but it was less common to find displaced educators relocating their schools so as to keep them in operation. This possibility was considered more often than it was accomplished, for the problems involved appeared to be insurmountable in most cases. The Board of Trustees of Randolph-Macon held several meetings to discuss moving the institution to an area where supplies would be more plentiful, but it was finally decided to close the school for the duration of the war, after which it was moved to Ashland.[21] It was also the shortage and high price of food that resulted in the removal of the Bingham School from Orange County, North Carolina. In December, 1863, its founder, William Bingham, wrote an enrollee's father that he was planning to transfer the school to "a cheaper boarding place," not because he intended to profit personally from the move but because this seemed the only way to keep it in session.[22] It was the winter of 1864–65 before Bingham, the faculty, students, and college equipment were settled in Mebane, North Carolina.[23]

State political officials who had to flee to provisional capitals were kept busy moving themselves, their families, and state properties to the new locations, and performing their accustomed duties, often under the worst of circumstances. When a state government located itself in a new community, it was almost certain to complicate life for everyone concerned as congestion, inadequate facilities, and scarcities were sure to develop. Local residents were not inclined to greet the displaced officials with open arms because they realized what the outcome of their arrival would be, and they were also fearful that when the town became the capital it would be more vulnerable to enemy attack. State officers were usually criticized when they abandoned the established capital and especially if they crossed the state line. Those finding refuge in neighboring states were looked upon as cowards rather than determined, dedicated men performing their duties in exile.

When the fall of Jackson was imminent, Governor John J. Pettus arranged for the archives to be sent first to Meridian and later to Columbus and Macon, but when he stepped into Alabama, a Mississippi editor asked, ". . . who's the Governor of the State of Mississippi in Alabama?"[24] Arkansans started criticizing Governor Harris Flanagin even before he had left Little Rock, but an editor rushed to his defense and assured the citizens that the "Governor of Arkansas has not fled," but because the city could not be held, he had already sent "the archives of the State to a place of safety."[25] The flight of public officials was seldom construed as a patriotic act, nor were the problems incurred in the execution of their duties fully appreciated by their constituents.

As previously noted, bankers often performed their usual tasks and acted as custodians for the institution's assets during displacement, but none had greater wartime responsibilities than J. G. M. Ramsey. He had obligations to the Bank of Tennessee's stockholders and depositors and also to the Confederate government which had designated the bank a depository. Ramsey was in Atlanta during most of the war, and although he worried about his family who had to leave their east Tennessee home, he considered his first duty was to the bank. Before Sherman's arrival in Atlanta, he left the city and went to Augusta, then to Charlotte where he named his fugitive institution the "*Bank on Wheels.*" When the local bankers started packing for flight, he moved on to Greensboro only to be caught in "a stampede" from that city. He then retraced his steps back to Augusta where he was when the war ended. Ramsey made many personal sacrifices in order to shoulder his business responsibilities, and he was too busy to devote much time to brooding or dwelling on his personal problems.[26]

A great many refugees who moved their businesses to new locations were not identified by name in the records of their contemporaries, but their wartime services were mentioned. There were frequent references to machinists who somehow managed to move their equipment out of threatened areas and open their shops elsewhere. Both political and military officials recognized their value to the South, and for this reason encouraged their moving ahead of an invasion, often at government expense. The Texas state government ordered machinists out of Galveston and told them to settle in the interior of the state, but in this instance the military command did not concur because it needed their services.[27] Owners of machine shops were made aware of their importance during the war, and the equipment they hauled in flight was far more valuable than the plunder transported by most refugees. A New Orleans machinist was extended a warm welcome when he arrived in Atlanta with his machinery. After opening his shop in the city, he went to work making gun carriages, cannon balls, and shells for the army, a patriotic contribution which one editor said merited "the praise of all Southerners." In this case, the machinist had "removed the valuable tools from an occupied area and put them to work for the Confederacy." One of his Louisiana colleagues had made a similar move to Montgomery.[28]

Merchants seldom undertook to transfer their stocks to another community, primarily because of the bulk and lack of adequate transportation. Nor could they be sure they would be able to reopen an establishment elsewhere. If they did move, it was sometimes to a point nearby, possibly in the same town as in the case of Vicksburg where stores were moved "farther back from the river."[29] When confronted with displacement, most merchants sold their merchandise, usually at auction, packed and stored the goods where they hoped they would be safe, or took the most valuable merchandise with them. Those who did not flee but kept their businesses open hoped for the best and very often prospered under Federal control. When merchants closed shop and ran, new ones arrived to take their place. Most mercantile houses founded during the war were not owned by Southern sympathizers but by persons who came in the wake of the Federals. As noted previously, however, many men who went into business by speculating or trading in blockade goods referred to themselves as refugees.

Displaced agriculturists frequently followed their customary occupation, sometimes for a profit, but more often simply to provision their families and slaves. If those with several plantations had one situated out of the reach of the enemy, they usually transferred themselves to the holding and centered their activities there for as long as they could do so. Others rented or bought farms, but the refugees who found land to till were often handicapped by a lack of farm equipment, which was heavy and bulky to transport and impossible to buy. A Louisianian who rented a farm in Texas encountered this problem, but his landlord generously loaned him the essential tools for working the plot.[30] Despite the shortage of equipment and numerous other obstacles, most small farmers were inclined to continue farming if they possibly could do so, but they were often compelled to find other employment.

Hundreds of refugees tilled the soil for the first time, but they were usually gardeners rather than farmers and were primarily interested in producing food for their families. A few women tried gardening because it was considered both patriotic and fashionable to garden during the war. But the greater portion of those who cultivated the soil did so from necessity. If temporary quarters did not include land enough for a garden, the refugee sometimes rented a small plot to be used for this purpose. Cornelia McDonald leased an acre on the outskirts of Lexington and raised potatoes which became the family's staple food during the winter.[31] Mrs. McDonald, like others who gardened for the first time, took great pride in her accomplishment and derived personal satisfaction as well as produce from her efforts.

Refugees in need of remunerative employment often had to go where the jobs were, for not all communities afforded the displaced people opportunity for work. Those trained in special occupations might find it impossible to continue in the same work and necessary to transfer to some other, but getting a job in the Confederacy depended on being in the right place at the right time. Among those who might easily starve were the professional auctioneers, unless they went into a port city or large community where blockade goods were sold at auction, or unless they happened upon an opportunity to use their talents. Because people sometimes sold their personal property and possessions at auction when it was impossible to carry them to

another community, there was need for an auctioneer to preside at
the sale. Although an amateur was given the job if no professional
was available, the latter was preferred, and there are hundreds of
references to "refugee auctioneers." A Virginian told of his mother's
selling her possessions before leaving home, and he mentioned that
"a refugee from Culpeper cried the estate." [32]

In those areas where workers were needed and refugees were known
to be living, employers publicized available jobs in the local newspapers under announcements captioned "Notice to Refugees." In
most cases such appeals were made for day laborers, but women,
children, and elderly or infirm men could not perform this heavy
work. If there were younger, more able-bodied men who might
qualify for the strenuous tasks, they were often too proud to take the
job. Sometimes refugees put their slaves to work as manual laborers
but the employers did not always want Negroes, especially if they were
slaves. A typical advertisement for workers, and in this case road grad-
ers, was that of the Macon and Brunswick Railroad which appealed
specifically to "men driven from their homes" and needing employment. It implied that the railroad was seeking white laborers and
assured interested parties that the tracks were "secure from . . . the
enemy and healthy for residences." [33]

Among the new positions created with the establishment of the
Confederacy and the outbreak of war were those in the government
offices in Richmond. These opportunities attracted thousands of displaced people to the city, but many more sought work than could
find places. During the first year of the conflict it was fairly easy to
get appointments, but it later became more difficult. In the fall of
1863, Christopher Memminger told Judith McGuire that one vacancy
brought "a hundred applications." She was at this time desperately
trying to get office work, for her husband's income was insufficient
to their needs, but Mrs. McGuire waited for almost a year before she
received an appointment. She was irritated when she had to take a
qualifying arithmetic examination and justify her need for the job.
As to the latter she remarked, ". . . no lady would bind herself to
keep accounts for six hours per day without dire necessity." She
attributed her eventual success to a cousin's intercession and to a
draft call which took several men out of the offices.[34]

Hundreds of other women refugees worked in the Richmond
offices, there being thirty-five in Mrs. McGuire's. This entrance of
genteel women into the business world was one of the most noticeable,
and to some, shocking developments of the war, but many indigent

ladies could not afford to think in terms of prewar propriety. Even more disconcerting to some people were the office workers who commuted daily to and from their jobs in Richmond. Emma Mordecai told of sitting next to an elderly Fredericksburg refugee in a train bound for the Capital. The lady had boarded in Ashland where she was living because it was cheaper than in the city. Miss Mordecai was shocked that an old woman would have to ride the train every day and work in a public office.[35]

Many refugees had to work at any job they could find, and it was not unusual for entire families to seek employment. A lady in Augusta, who had lived in comfort before the war, wrote a friend about the economic misfortune her family had experienced in their displacement. Each individual was trying to find work or had already taken a position—her husband in the local arsenal, her two sisters in schools in South Carolina and Georgia, and her father was hoping to find employment but as yet had been unsuccessful.[36]

There were never enough jobs for all who sought them, but some women who might have found employment could not be away from home all day. Those with small children or invalids to care for, or those too old, infirm, or proud to work in public often utilized their talents within the home by making articles which might have market value. When humiliated by their poverty most of them were at first reluctant to sell their products, but if friends urged them to do so, they often relented. If their creations won favor, the women soon forgot their embarrassment as they found pride in their accomplishment. There were many ways in which ingenious, determined ladies could commercialize on their talents, and among the more popular were sewing and millinery. Mrs. McGuire, who sensibly realized that false pride had no place in the war years, was delighted when her friends evidenced a practical bent. She mentioned many times her once affluent refugee acquaintances in Richmond who made hats for a living, and one young lady earned enough in this way to provide for herself and her mother. Others "with fair young fingers which had not been accustomed to work . . ." were selling hats for twenty dollars each, but their "pride in their handiwork" pleased Mrs. McGuire more than their economic success.[37]

During the last winter of the war, Jorantha Semmes plaited hats which she sold for fifty dollars each, and when she told of this pursuit she radiated the happiness she felt in being able to supplement the family income. Early in the war she did not have serious financial problems, but by 1865 the wartime inflation had brought the annual cost of feeding the family to $4,800, and she expected to make $2,000 that year selling hats. But this domestic enterprise did more than bring in a much needed income; it brought her a sense of satisfaction which she had not experienced previously. She noted also that the children were less troublesome now that they were helping in the project.[38]

Women with special culinary abilities had their opportunities limited because of the food shortages; those who did commercialize on these talents discovered that it was usually a seasonal occupation. It seems that most women specialized in jellies or relishes, thus making use of fruit and vegetables in season. A lady in Richmond sold her pickles and catsup to local merchants and restaurants, and another was famous for her gooseberry wine which was said to have sparkled "like champagne." [39] Some women who could not derive an income from the finished product, sold their wartime recipes which called for substitute items guaranteed to produce dishes just as delicious as "the real thing." When newspapers inserted hundreds of these offers in their "for sale" columns, it was revealed that all of these enterprising citizens were not women, nor were they all refugees. Most wives and mothers did not market either their food or their recipes but stayed busy devising ways to feed their families. This time-consuming task was the major domestic activity of the women.

Another of the more popular home industries was soapmaking, the process of which was usually unfamiliar to the upper classes. But during the war many women learned to make this scarce commodity and some profited from the sale of their products. During her displacement Judith McGuire sold soap for a dollar a pound and taught others in Ashland the art of making it. One of her refugee "students" spent her evenings and weekends manufacturing soap, and twice a week she carried baskets of the finished product into Richmond where she delivered it to customers before proceeding to her regular work in an office. These two jobs, clerical and domestic, enabled her to provide for herself and five children.[40]

Although women often depended on their hands to earn them a living, there were a few who capitalized on their literary abilities. It was while Constance Cary was a refugee in Richmond that she began the literary career she was to follow after the war. As a regular contributor to the short-lived *Southern Illustrated News*, she wrote a column which was primarily directed to women readers. It included items relating to fashions, social events, cooking, expedients, and makeshifts. Whenever she or her cousin Hetty Cary returned from a blockade-running expedition in "Yankee-land," she transmitted to the Southern ladies news of the latest styles beyond the lines. Constance Cary often suggested ways for altering and renovating garments so as to keep them in style—vital information for the fashion-conscious, poverty-stricken Southern female. She wrote so cleverly that her columns make interesting reading today, and her optimism and sense of humor offset much of the gloom and pessimism found in the newspapers of the period.[41]

Elizabeth Meriwether also utilized her literary talents to good advantage. While living in Tuscaloosa she read that the displaced *Mississippian*, then publishing in Selma, Alabama, was sponsoring a short-story contest, and the first prize was to be $500, a small fortune to Mrs. Meriwether and one well worth competing for. Despite all of her other responsibilities, she wrote an account in story form of her experiences since leaving Memphis and entitled it "The Refugee." Her entry won first prize and was so well received that the editor asked her to write a second story for which she would be paid $800. Within a few weeks she had completed "The Spy" and sent it to the *Mississippian* where it and the paper's offices were destroyed by fire. Unfortunately this venture was a total loss because the author had no copy of the story. However her first story had done more than win a prize; it brought her a friend in the person of Joseph Davis who read "The Refugee" and was so impressed with it that he introduced himself to Elizabeth Meriwether and continued to call on her for as long as they both were in Tuscaloosa. He assured her that her story would live because it was an accurate account of the "troubled times" in which they lived. His weekly visits brought great enjoyment to Mrs. Meriwether as they talked about "almost everything under the sun, from the myths of the ancient Greeks to the latest ailment of . . . Baby Lee." [42]

When refugees went into the hotel business they very often catered to other displaced people. A Kentuckian who bought the Perry House in Columbus, Georgia, announced through the columns of the local press that he had been driven from his home by the enemy and had invested everything he had in his business. He hoped that the enterprise would bring financial rewards, but he wanted other refugees to know that he would especially welcome and be sympathetic to them because he understood their problems.[43] A Louisianian who opened a hotel in San Antonio reported his business venture to another refugee in Crockett, Texas, and requested that his friend tell other displaced Louisianians about the hostelry. He hoped that they would come to San Antonio and patronize his establishment, for as he reminded his friend, Louisiana refugees "must stick together." [44]

Many displaced people who, for one reason or another, were not gainfully employed realized nevertheless that there were many other jobs that needed doing. They evidenced common sense when they reasoned that if they were to be accepted by a strange community, they must give something in return, and these same refugees also knew that they would be happier if engaged in worthwhile pursuits. They did not always find what they sought from the local citizens because they were sometimes overshadowed by other newcomers who were less civic minded. Yet in the long run, the cooperative ones benefited in some way from their efforts.

Male refugees often took an active part in the home guard units and other local defense groups. When an enemy raid threatened Lynchburg, Virginia, both refugees and residents responded to the call for assistance.[45] And more than a hundred Marylanders, under the leadership of Walter Lenox, offered their services in the defense of Richmond during the Peninsular Campaign. Lenox was himself a refugee and the former mayor of Washington.[46] After the Galvestonians escaped to Houston the men organized two home guard units, and when an editor facetiously inquired of them "what home" they were guarding, the response was "our adopted home." [47] Displaced people often exhibited this same attitude but received little or no credit for their deeds. Although it is doubtful that home guards contributed very much to the defense of towns, men who participated in these activities felt as though they were making a contribution to the war effort. The periodic drills not only afforded the volunteers a pleasant diversion, but also gave the townspeople comic relief, for these drills were among the most humorous sights of the war. Had the units done nothing else but make people laugh, they would have been worth the time and effort expended.

Displaced men sometimes went into military service after they left home, thus offsetting to some extent the men who fled to avoid the draft, but rarely were they accorded the attention given the dodgers. A Mississippi editor noted that so many of the exiled New Orleans men went into service that Southerners should express appreciation to General Banks who had banished them. The journalist was probably exaggerating when he said that "several thousand" of these refugees had joined the Confederate Army before the summer of 1863, but he was so pleased with the number of enlistments that he exclaimed,

"Banks . . . as a recruiting agent . . . is bon. He has no superior. Three cheers for Nat!!!" [48]

Many displaced men who did not affiliate with the army organized in groups to harass the enemy, but these guerrillas often did more harm to Southerners than they did good. Some partisans, however, worked effectively against enemy fortifications, transportation lines, and military installations, and a number of the refugees from Memphis were efficient saboteurs in northern Mississippi and western Tennessee. According to one newsman, they knew "every foot of the country around Memphis" and were therefore able "to annoy . . . the enemy considerably." [49] Yet they were also largely responsible for the Federal retaliatory policy of sending noncombatants into Confederate lines after their attacks.

Refugee women rendered comparable wartime services more in keeping with their sex when they volunteered as nurses or otherwise assisted the Confederates. They often received and cared for soldiers in their homes, but an impressive number became professional nurses in the army hospitals. One of these, Fannie Beers, was visiting her mother in the North when her husband enlisted in the Confederate Army. Not only was she unhappy to have the battle lines separating them, but she was miserable to be in Union territory where old friends criticized her because of her Southern sympathies. Therefore she went into the Confederacy, offered her services as a nurse, and throughout the war moved with her hospitals, enduring the problems of a refugee. Other nurses in field hospitals were kept on the move, including Kate Cumming, who left her home in Mobile not as a refugee but with the intention of being an army nurse. She often referred, however, to displaced women who either became professional nurses or helped care for the men when a hospital was established in the community. Before leaving Canton, Mississippi, Jorantha Semmes served as secretary to the Soldiers' Relief Association and regularly visited the local hospital where she assisted in the care of the wounded and sick soldiers. She was happy to be doing this volunteer work from which she derived great satisfaction, and she could not understand why her husband's cousins disapproved of her war work. After a heated argument on the subject, Mrs. Semmes wrote her husband that she wished "Cousin Bena" would take an interest in such worthwhile activities rather than spend her time criticizing her patriotic work.[50]

Most displaced women seemed to enjoy participating in fund-raising drives for worthwhile causes. Amateur theatrical productions and bazaars for soldiers, refugees, or indigent persons, or for the purchase of military equipment engaged the time and interest of thousands of refugees. The younger women were especially anxious to participate in these affairs because it made them feel as if they had a part in the war and also afforded them a social diversion, but the refugees had difficulty getting parts in the tableaux, recitals, or plays. If they were not already in the social swim, they were usually ignored or assigned the lesser roles or that of stage hand, and this they resented. The line of demarcation between the displaced people and the local citizens was clearly drawn despite the production's being for a worthwhile cause. A great many young women recorded this unhappy state of affairs, but some eventually managed to cut through the ice. Kate Stone dated her family's acceptance into Tyler society from the time that her mother was invited to direct a program to raise money for a soldiers' home. Kate had long been chagrined that her mother's talents had been overlooked, for she believed that Mrs. Stone knew "more of such things than all the rest of . . . [the townspeople] put together." After her first production was a success she was invited to assist with a second, and from this moment until they left the city, the Stones came in contact "with all the *creme de la creme*" of Tyler. It isn't known whether or not this change in social status made her mother happier, but for Kate it was the turning point of her displacement.[51]

Confederate women by the thousands, including refugees, spent their spare time knitting and sewing for soldiers. Mrs. Chesnut once commented that she did not know that she had "seen a woman without knitting in her hand. 'Socks for the soldier,' " she wrote, "is the cry. . . . It gives a quaint look, the twinkling of needles [with] the everlasting sock dangling." [52] Mrs. McGuire also noted the amount of knitting that was done by the refugees who shared her cottage in Ashland. When a friend remarked that Southern ladies were getting more like the Germans because they always had with them their "everlasting knitting," Mrs. McGuire mused that she wished it were "everlasting," for the "poor soldiers in their long marches strew the way with their wornout socks." [53]

Included also among the contributions of the women refugees was their willingness to shelter and feed the passing soldier, often at a great sacrifice. Although they were sometimes suspicious of those who traveled singly or in a small group, far from their companies, the women nevertheless pitied almost any Confederate soldier. In the last "gloomy and melancholy" March of the war, Cornelia McDonald watched "the men coming home . . . in squads, in couples, or singly, all leaving the army." That many of these men were deserters Mrs. McDonald knew, but when they asked for food she always gave them "a share of such as . . . [she] had," although she could not help feeling a certain amount of scorn for them.[54] Many refugees were as generous as Mrs. McDonald and they very often shared with soldiers when they refused all others. They also joined with local citizens in meeting troop trains, serving the soldiers food and drink, and helping with the wayside homes which were maintained in many cities. They often gave shelter to the passing service men when they could possibly accommodate them and rendered assistance far in excess of their means. Refugees were just as generous to the fighting men as were those who stayed at home and, ironically, they were often more hospitable to them than to other displaced people.

Very few refugees were as financially able to attend to the soldiers' needs as John Edwards Caldwell and his wife. Driven from New Orleans early in the war, they made their home at "The Refuge" near Lynchburg, Virginia, and their sole interest seems to have been to make this the headquarters for enlisted men from Louisiana. The couple attended to the needs of the sick and wounded, counseled the confused, cheered the homesick, welcomed the weary, and encouraged all arrivals to remain as long as they wished. They charged nothing for this abundant hospitality which they considered their personal contribution to the war effort. Throughout the war and long after, their guests paid tribute to these refugees who ignored their own misfortunes to help the common soldier.[55] As noble as this undertaking was, other refugees gave proportionately as much when they shared their meagre supply of food and makeshift quarters with those coming to their door.

The precarious economic circumstances of most refugees did not always deter them from contributing money to various fund-raising drives, and many who kept records left an account of their contributions while others remained anonymous. In the list of contributors published in the newspapers were hundreds of donors known simply as "a refugee." Among the many wartime charities to which displaced people subscribed were the Free Markets established to aid the indigent families of soldiers. During the first two years after the opening of the Charleston Free Market, 145 contributors listed in the local press were designated only as "refugees," but it would stand to reason that many whose names are given were also displaced people. Mrs. John Grimball sadly noted that her husband very much wanted to contribute to this charity but because of their economic embarrassment and his many other donations, he was unable to send money to the Free Market. Mr. Grimball had been philanthropic beyond his means, and after moving to Spartanburg he had given fifty dollars to a hospital in Richmond, a hundred dollars to those who had lost their homes in the Charleston fire, and substantial sums to solicitors who came to his door. Mrs. Grimball worried about his generous inclinations for she feared that they might soon be objects of charity themselves. "We have no income," she wrote, "and are in a fair way of getting to an end of what we have. . . . I tell him he has first to consider his own family." [56]

Donors who preferred to remain anonymous naturally incite the curiosity of anyone perusing the rolls in the newspapers of the day. When a contributor was designated simply as a "burnt-out refugee," "a victim of Butler," or "a refugee widow," one feels as though there must have been a pathetic story which merits telling. Among the more appealing donations to the Charleston *Courier*'s fund-raising campaigns was that of a little girl identified only as "a ten year old refugee." She sent "twenty-five dollars and fifty cents" with a note written in childish scrawl. She had raised the money by selling her doll house, and stipulated that five dollars was to go to the Free Market, the remainder "to the soldiers." [57] Southerners generally contributed more generously to all projects early in the war than they did after conditions worsened in the Confederacy. In a five-week period in early 1862, dozens of refugees were listed as donors to the South Carolina Ladies Gunboat Fund. One of these was an elderly woman from Fernandina, Florida, who was known only to the editor but who had been driven from her home of fifty years and was then living in middle Florida. But there were also unidentified refugee contributors from Edisto Island, Port Royal, Beaufort, and Bluffton, and one family from "the banks of the Broad River" had made and sold palmetto cockades and given the money to the gunboat fund. Another sent the editor of the *Courier* a quilt she had made, asking that he dispose of it "as he thought best" and deposit the profits in the same fund.[58] Examples of generosity such as these were not exceptions, for in other areas anonymous displaced people made similar contributions, and in proportion to their numbers they seem to have supported worthwhile causes as enthusiastically as the civilians who stayed at home.

Although all refugees could not be depended upon to assist others in their group, displaced people were often the recipients of many kindnesses from homeless strangers. One in Richmond noted that "each refugee family shared what it had with another." [59] Joseph LeConte discovered that those who had experienced displacement were most willing to help others in similar circumstances. Sidney Harding, who knew so many "sad hours" in her log refuge, told of dozens of refugees unknown to the family who were given lodging and food as if they were old friends. As the Hardings' financial problems increased so did the refugees who came to their door, and all were fed even when the hosts were "almost reduced to starvation." [60] Cornelia McDonald was in dire circumstances when called upon to feed other refugees, friends, and strangers, but she always shared what she had, which was never much and always was plain food. However, she "tried to make things appear as well as possible," and made it a policy to "keep unpleasant things from the eyes and ears of the weary." [61] It might be expected that all displaced people were not this generous, but there was usually a common sympathy and understanding among the refugees, the existence of which is stressed in contemporary accounts. Although Kate Stone found the "stay-at-home" people often unfriendly, she thought other refugees were exceptionally kind, although she did know some who were not. One, a former Louisiana neighbor who also lived in Tyler, became increasingly selfish late in the war when the Stones asked to buy some of the huge stock of supplies she had brought with her.[62] Kate could not understand this change of attitude, but it was rather common during the war for people to become more possessive with what they had. They realized the difficulties involved in getting replacements.

The patriotism and views of refugees were sometimes questioned by other civilians who did not understand them or their predicament, and displaced people were often accused of shirking their duties, but none of these charges were justified in the majority of cases. Stephen Mallory once wrote his wife about those in Richmond from "comfortable, . . . splendid homes" who now had nothing; "yet their patriotism burns brightly." [63] Newspapers also cited individuals who proved their devotion to the Southern cause, and even the carping Richmond *Examiner* occasionally recognized a refugee who had done something "above and beyond the call of duty." In the fall of 1863, it mentioned one from Winchester who had sold cotton goods "at cost" when he could have made a profit "of $10,000" on the deal.[64]

The more articulate refugees, usually ministers and editors with firm convictions, sometimes felt that they must speak out in a strange community whether or not their beliefs were those of the local citizens. In most cases, there would be people in the audience who would agree with the person's views but this did not necessarily imply that the majority concurred. An individual in this category aired his opinions and led crusades because he felt it his duty to do so despite public opinion. Whether he was made to appear disloyal, cowardly, courageous, or only strange depended upon the beliefs and attitudes of those who read or heard his words. A displaced Baptist minister rode the circuit in Georgia pleading with his congregations to "petition Congress in reference to Sabbath Keeping," but in some instances he met with an indifferent or cold response. One lady who heard him disgustedly remarked that she was "neither interested or edified" by what he had to say, but to him this was a vital issue which could, at least indirectly, have a bearing on the outcome of the war.[65] Others who aired their views on politics, religion, morals, and economy may or may not have had an appreciable influence on the people they addressed, but they were doing what they felt compelled to do although it left them vulnerable to criticism.

Despite the charges made against those refugees who contributed little to the war effort or their adopted community, there were many who did what they could to cooperate and who worked diligently to sustain themselves under the most discouraging circumstances. Only a minority could say, as did Mrs. Hugh Lawson Clay in referring to herself and her sister-in-law, Mrs. Clement Claiborne Clay, "We deserve *no* credit for *any thing*. We have done *as little* for our country as any two worthless women I know." Although they were refugees, "their manner of life was as little changed as possible by war conditions"; they were safe, had no serious food problems, and were "well supplied with clothing and many luxuries that came through the blockade." They visited hospitals only twice during the four long years and did "no war work." [66] There were others who might claim a similar record, but most women could testify to a far different life during their displacement. They worked as hard, if not harder, and were as patriotic and philanthropic as those who stayed at home. The majority of both the male and female refugees indicated by their activities that the age did, indeed, provide "duties for all."

. . . *the most enjoyable life*

In their daily battle for survival, refugees were not likely to find much time for making merry, yet all of them participated in some kind of social activity, and the more affluent ones often appeared to be unaware that a war was being fought. In some cases this impression was given by those who were "drowning their sorrows," and in others it was a manifestation of the individual's natural epicureanism which he refused to abandon even in time of war. Few people reacted consistently as they endured their ups and downs, but most found that recreation and other social diversions helped them to forget the stresses and strains of the moment.

There were a number of factors which determined the social activities of the displaced people. One was the individual's character and temperament, and this did not tend to change fundamentally during his displacement. Another was the person's age, the older ones usually finding their pleasure in quiet diversions such as sewing, knitting, visiting, and talking with friends. Some adults who worked outside the home managed to make their jobs a kind of social activity as they enjoyed the contact with others. But time often hung heavy for the young, single women if there were no others of their age nearby, yet this was the group which evidenced greatest originality in creating pastimes. The place also conditioned social life, for in the larger communities there were group activities which were usually lacking in small villages and rural areas. Time was another factor, and most people were gayer and more socially inclined early in the war than they were after hardships, weariness, and despondency took hold of the South. All people's social activity and enthusiasm did not lag chronologically, however, but depended on circumstances such as the length and frequency of displacement, their social and economic situation, and their personal tragedies and shocks.

The social life of Richmond officials and other prominent personages was not typical of that of most refugees. As Mary Boykin Chesnut and her displaced friends were being wined and dined in the capital, and the Cary cousins were attending elaborate, extravagant parties and balls, the vast majority of the displaced people were deriving social satisfaction from simpler, less costly activities. All Southerners were inconvenienced in some way by the war and for the elite this was often its only noticeable effect, but the group not touched deeply and directly composed only a fraction of the population. All of the prominent, wealthy citizens did not "dance" their way through the war, however, and many of the upper class refugees learned the hardest lesson of their lives—that a war on the homefront has a devastating effect on class lines.

Just as conflicts developed within overcrowded households, so did companionship as families were drawn together in work and play. When they had no other companions, displaced relatives who lived together for extended periods often found that they had a great many common interests. Mothers discovered in their children a new source of satisfaction and comfort as they traveled with them, taught them, and watched the young assume abnormal responsibilities far in advance of their years. They marveled at their adaptability, cheerfulness, and appreciation for little favors, and many displaced parents mentioned that it was only their boys and girls who enabled them to survive the ordeal. Entirely dependent on each other, many refugees discovered how many happy hours could be spent with others whom they had never before taken the time to know. But whether the group was composed of family, friends, or both, most wartime social activity centered in the home.

It is a tribute to the refugees that so many of them could enjoy any part of their displacement, but when one reads of the social activities in some communities and homes it would seem that they were but little altered by the war. However, this was not the general situation, for the people were often doing no more than making the best of a bad situation and living only one day at a time. The little village of Ashland, Virginia, was described by a Richmond editor as a gay social center for displaced people who participated in an exceptionally varied program. Held regularly were "tilting matches" over which refugee belles reigned, and both formal and informal dances. Despite Federal raids, fire, and robberies during the spring and summer of 1864, it was reported that there was "still a cheerfulness . . . in the appearance of every person" and the social life was enhanced by frequent entertainments at the Masonic Hall, performances by the "thespian corps," delicious dinners served at the local hotel, "gay pomenading parties," and "regular concerts of cotillon [*sic*] music" rendered by a "fine band." [1]

The parties given in Richmond and attended by prominent refugees and others were famous throughout the Confederacy. The displaced Mrs. Basil Wilson Duke noted, "The cities are gayer than before the war—parties every night in Richmond, suppers costing ten & twenty thousand dollars. . . ." [2] It was this lighthearted extravagance that worried Judith McGuire who "wish[ed] these things were not so." En route home one evening, after having spent several hours at the bedside of a dying soldier, Mrs. McGuire passed a house which was gay with laughter, music, and dancing. "The revulsion," she wrote, "was sickening. I thought of the gayety of Paris during the French Revolution, . . . [and] the hall at Brussels the night before the battle of Waterloo, and felt shocked that our own Virginians, at such a time, should remind me of scenes which we were wont to think belong only to foreign society." [3] During the same winter in which Mrs. McGuire commented on the merriment in Richmond, Mrs. Roger Pryor reported that Petersburg had "none of the gayety of Richmond." Yet she later recalled that "ball followed ball in quick succession. 'The soldier danced with the lady of his love at night, and on the morrow danced the dance of death in the deadly trench on the line.' " [4]

In many other communities where refugees congregated, ostentatious parties were sometimes given but they were the exception rather than the rule. A number of displaced people lived in Tuskeegee, Alabama, which was safe from enemy depredations for most of the war, and here the inhabitants seemed to fare much better than those in most other areas. A Kentuckian who chose to live there so she could be near her husband enjoyed the social life in the village. She told of having attended many extravagant, glittering parties, but one given by "a refugee from Mississippi" especially impressed her. Although the host claimed to be "camping out," the lady was overawed by the "wealth, style, beauty and taste" of the home and by the "evening clothes and jewels" worn by the hostess and her guests. A beautifully appointed supper table was centered with "a pyramid of flowers in a silver stand," and the meal consisted of three kinds of cake, a variety of breads, "calf's foot jelly, turkey, chicken salad and ham." The guest list was composed almost entirely of refugees "from a distant state," and all gave the impression of having a carefree, wonderful time. Overwhelmed by this display, the Kentuckian exclaimed, "And this is the starvation in the South!" [5] Whether or not she was aware of the fact, most refugees did not live and entertain in this manner.

Nothing could so stimulate displaced people as being with old friends and neighbors. The family of the attorney, Philip Phillips, and the other Louisianians in LeGrange, Georgia, formed a "pleasant social circle." The men had their "Boston Club" while the ladies had their parties, music club, and war work. According to the Phillips' daughter, "In spite of the War, we had . . . merry times." [6] A Nashville refugee discovered that she had "an advantage living in Atlanta" because she could visit with so many friends who passed through or settled in the city. She sought to entice other friends and relatives to join her for this reason and also because of the gaiety to be found in the town. [7] Other Tennesseans in Atlanta mentioned the good times they had getting together with each other, and the only entertainment they asked was quiet conversation.

Extended periods of homesickness could often be avoided if refugees could be with congenial friends who shared the past, as well as the present, with them. Meta Grimball could temporarily forget her unhappy situation in Spartanburg when she was with her Charleston friends, the only people with whom she maintained close association during her displacement. Mrs. Grimball could not entertain lavishly, nor could her friends, but they could spend happy hours chatting about their mutual acquaintances and their days before the war. Mr. Grimball once decided against buying a small country cottage because he knew that his wife would be even more miserable away from her friends in town than she was in her makeshift quarters. [8] Whether the meetings between friends were chance occurrences or regular events, the displaced people pooled whatever information they had about others, and this was the source of many rumors and news items cited in their diaries and letters. Few women could resist writing to relatives and friends when they heard about or saw mutual acquaintances, and it did not matter whether it was tragedy or comedy, they hastened to tell the story.

Kate Stone made it a wartime hobby to find other displaced people, a diversion which she called "refugee-hunts." It did not always involve great effort on her part because, as she said, "No matter where we may go, we are almost sure to meet old friends and acquaintances." But this young lady did not wait for strangers to make the first move, nor did she confine herself only to refugees from Louisiana. Before the end of her sojourn in Texas she had made friends with displaced people from widespread areas of the South, and these new acquaintances offset to some extent the rebuffs she received from many Texans. Like most young ladies in their twenties, she liked gay parties but when she was unable to participate in these she found pleasure and stimulation in being with people of all ages. Once when a group of Tyler refugees dropped by, conversation lagged until someone thought of fining the individuals "for each lapse of grammar." This did enliven the evening for a time and made everyone listen to what was being said, but it was finally abandoned because the participants feared that they would soon be "bankrupt in both purse and temper." [9] This was only one of many simple diversions which the Stones originated in an effort to avoid boredom.

When a group of women gathered for an afternoon or evening of conversation, they often brought with them their sewing, knitting, or other handwork, sometimes applying themselves to their individual projects, but at other times working as a team on articles for one of the group or for a worthy cause. It always eased the burden and helped the hours to pass more quickly when chores were performed in groups. Sidney Harding often organized groups to make recreation out of sewing, plaiting hats, knitting, and searching the woods for sumac berries which were used in dye. Although she got "so tired" of these activities and "never worked so hard" before, she thought it more enjoyable when everyone joined in the task.[10] Women who engaged in hospital work usually thought of this as a kind of social diversion because it enabled them to get out of the house and be with others. Elodie Todd was amused by the young, unmarried women's sudden interest in nursing after a hospital was established in Selma. On one of her visits there she found eighteen men recovering from measles, none in a serious condition but all being "killed from excessive kindness" bestowed by the Selma belles. The girls had brought so many flowers that "the mantelpiece was perfectly crowded," and many were visiting the hospital more than twice a day although none of them seemed sure as to what they were expected to do. Miss Todd concluded that they must be starved for male companionship to be willing to devote so much time to "the roughest men" she "ever saw," for they were the type that most of the girls would have avoided before the war.[11]

Much of the women's war work appealed to both their patriotic and social natures. Sometimes greater emphasis was placed on the latter, notably in the staging of dramatic and musical productions, and few homefront activities generated as much enthusiasm or aroused greater jealousy than these. As previously noted, these were often arranged and performed by the local girls while the refugees pouted, ranted, and feuded with those in control. A Charlottean noted that a tableau was being planned "for the benefit of the poor of the town" and specified that both "refugees" and "ladies" were taking part, but she failed to mention which ones were assigned the leading roles.[12] Judging from the number of programs presented during the war, it would seem there would have been choice parts for all who were interested, but the same young women were usually the stars in all of the community productions. However, this situation might be said to have stimulated activity of a sort since groups were formed to compete with each other. Selma, Alabama, was divided into classes, each being numbered, and Elodie Todd resented being omitted from "the number one class." This was the group that snubbed the refugees and refused to let them participate in their tableau, and after one feud, Elodie wrote her fiancé that "many persons" did not speak to her, and that she and her sister were no longer being invited to "the surprise parties." Therefore she was speaking "*only when . . . spoken to.*" The eventual outcome was that a "reconciliation" tableau had to be presented and this brought peace for a time, but it didn't take much to rekindle the furor in Selma.[13]

Elodie Todd's fiancé repeatedly assured her that he did not care whether or not she was in the "number one class," and at times he urged her not to associate with the group. He discouraged her taking part in the theatricals even when invited, and he asked her not to accept the post of secretary in the newly organized Aid Society. "I am opposed to all female societies," he wrote, "as I have never seen one, not even a Bible or church society, where unpleasant controversies did not arise." He believed that she could best serve the Confederacy and the community if she rendered aid "independently" and refrained from exposing "herself to the calumnies of the evil-minded." In trying to impress upon Elodie how strongly he felt about the matter he quoted from a letter which he had recently received from a ten-year-old girl who said, "I go to the Aid Society every week and the people do nothing but talk." It was what they said at these affairs that worried him, but Elodie's desire to socialize was both natural and unaffected by his opinions.[14]

When Kate Stone's mother directed her first amateur production in Tyler her daughter was not invited to take part but was "permitted to attend all rehearsals," and the affable young woman was grateful for this concession. It gave her an opportunity to meet and converse with others, and during the rehearsals Kate managed to satisfy her curiosity about a number of townspeople. By the time the show was ready for presentation she knew "most of the love affairs in Tyler," an attainment which gave her great satisfaction, and she had also made many new friends. Among these were poetess Molly Moore, a refugee in Tyler, and Lieutenant Bry Holmes who had the leading role in the tableau. She and Molly became inseparable friends and she and Holmes were later to marry. Kate was immediately attracted to the young officer but was discouraged from seeing him because he had a reputation for being "so fast." She was not to be discouraged and during the remainder of his stay in Tyler, Holmes was a frequent visitor in the Stones' home and, according to Kate, was "behaving all right" and remaining "perfectly sober." Lieutenant Holmes also starred in Mrs. Stone's second production, this time as "Prince Charming," and Kate was even more regular in her attendance at rehearsals. Although she was soon the target for the Tyler gossips, it did not seem to worry her, for she was sure the stories would "die out after a time." Despite Mrs. Stone's fear that Holmes was "too dissipated," Kate saw him regularly in Tyler and as she was en route home after the war. When they met in Louisiana she refused to marry him because she thought it a "dreadful risk for any woman to take," but during the next four years the risk apparently decreased and she married him in 1869. The Stone's participation in the Tyler tableau did more than bring Kate into contact with the *"creme de la creme of the city."* [15]

No other situation on the homefront had a more depressing effect on young women than the scarcity of eligible young men. Most girls considered it one of the major tragedies of the war, and because there was keen competition for all available men, girls living in a community resented refugees who tried to captivate the local boys. One reason that Elodie Todd had trouble in Selma society was that she won the affections of Nathaniel Dawson when several young ladies claimed him. The jealousy they felt for Miss Todd might have developed in any age, but because her conquest came during a time of scarcity it seemed to justify harsh retaliatory measures. Although Kate Stone evidenced no jealousy when she mentioned two refugees near Monroe who were "the belles of the country," it cannot be assumed that other young women did not resent them. The sisters were not only "enjoying themselves exceedingly," but their refuge was "a favorite resort for the officers" with whom the girls walked and rode "every day." [16] This sort of situation usually had local repercussions.

All refugees were not successful in finding escorts or potential husbands and they poured their innermost frustrations into their diaries and journals. When a young Charlestonian moved into a house so small that one of the drawing rooms had to be converted into a bedroom, she noted that this really would work no hardship on her or her sisters. "There will be no need for a second drawing room to entertain lovers or even gentlemen visitors," she wrote, "the latter being very scarce here." [17] The teen-aged Louise Wigfall judged every town by the number of unattached males who knocked on her door, and for this reason she was never happier in her displacement than when visiting Mrs. Joseph E. Johnston in Atlanta. Here she had contacts that only a general's home could afford, but when she was sent to Macon she found no one in whom she was interested, and she disgustedly wrote her mother that there was "no entertainment except going to church." [18] One of the few officers she met in Macon was a young man with a "serious turn of mind, who [cared] little for the society of the more frivolous sex," and Louise was not inclined to be interested in this type. She and the other girls did, however, enjoy playing "mischievous pranks on him." [19] Although this furnished the gay Miss Wigfall with a diversion of sorts, it was not what she would have preferred.

When Sarah Morgan was moving around Louisiana as a refugee, she had a happy social life until a back injury curtailed her activities, but even after the accident she had several young gentlemen friends who called on her. After going to her Unionist brother's home in New Orleans, she missed male companionship but refused to socialize with those who were not of Confederate sympathies and there were "no Southern men left in town." In deference to his sister's views, her brother did not invite Unionists to his home, but he did worry about the gap in her social life. He tried to remedy this situation by getting her interested in an older man, a veteran of Shiloh, whom Sarah referred to as "Brother's 'safe Old Secesh.'" This man of fifty-three was considered "a compromise between the stay-at-home youths and the Yankees," but as monotonous as her life was, Sarah could not be driven to the extreme of seriously concerning herself with "Old Secesh." [20]

Comments made by both Federal and Confederate soldiers indicate that Southern girls were not without beaus because they were unattractive. A soldier in Montgomery told an editor about the many displaced young women in that city who were the most attractive he had ever seen. "I did not know there were such specimens of beauty and perfection . . . as I have seen here," he wrote. "They hail from Alabama and Mississippi. The young lady refugees . . . are pictures of beauty, and possessed of rare accomplishments. . . ." [21] When his comments were published, the girls who read them were no doubt encouraged by his views, but it must be assumed that this was but another example of vicarious pleasure.

Literary pursuits occupied the leisure hours of a great many refugees, but these were somewhat restricted by the scarcity of paper and ink. Although more of a chore than a pastime to the poorly educated people, most displaced Southerners wrote letters during the war. For those of all ages it was a way to keep in touch with friends and relatives, and for the younger women it provided a contact with young men in the service. When a young Mississippi student at Judson College was asked by a soldier to exchange letters, she wanted to do so but the rules of the institution forbade the girls writing or receiving communications from boys whom their parents had not approved. The young lady could not reach her parents to ask their permission so she sought that of her brother, who was stationed nearby. She referred to the soldier's comment that because they were both cut off from their homes the exchange of letters "*might* be interesting and *perhaps* beneficial," [22] but this did not bring her brother's approval because he did not "think it best for school girls . . . to correspond with young men." He felt sure that if she would explain to the soldier that she could be expelled for writing to him that he would understand. [23]

Although this schoolgirl was prevented from writing in this instance, thousands of Southerners wrote letters and kept diaries during the war. It was a favorite diversion for the better educated people, and while many stated that their reason for keeping records was to preserve their experiences for future generations, many noted that it was also a way of easing their tensions and spending their leisure hours. Diaries and journals, especially, were safety valves, for it was often easier to write one's thoughts than it was to express them orally. Some of the most revealing accounts were kept by the busiest people, among them Judith McGuire, who wrote regularly in her diary despite her office job and volunteer war work. Most women with small children found it more difficult to keep complete daily records, but even they somehow managed to write letters to loved ones and many kept creditable journals. But some of the most complete and illuminating accounts were those of young women and girls who had fewer responsibilities and more time. Whatever the age and circumstances of the writer, however, there was one factor that could deter their writing more than any other—monotony. When they had nothing worth reporting or when they became lethargic because of boredom, they were likely to lay aside their pens until the situation remedied itself. When Sidney Harding once let her writing lapse for five days she explained it in this way: "There is nothing to write about. One day has been pretty much like another. Work, eat, and sleep." [24]

Reading was another very popular activity with the educated refugees, and they enjoyed reading alone or aloud in groups. A number of displaced people mentioned organizing book clubs, and one of these was Emma Holmes who did not anticipate the "long dull" winters in Camden and thought they could be more pleasant if such an activity could be started. An avid reader herself, she spent many hours of her displacement reading anything she could find but was especially fond of history, poetry, travel accounts, biography, and "anything by Sir Walter Scott." [25] Elodie Todd found a refuge in reading, safeguarded in this pursuit from the slings of local society, but she assured her fiancé that she did "not read *for show* but from *a love of reading*." [26] But the lack of books was one of the greatest handicaps of the refugees who loved to read. They could seldom take their personal libraries with them, and unless they made friends with those in their adopted community who had books, they had to forsake this diversion. Sidney Harding had great difficulty borrowing books, and although she many times reported having "spent the day reading," she also noted that she was "famished for something to read but there are no books in this miserable piney woods country." [27]

Kate Stone could manage the inconveniences and miseries of her displacement as long as she could find something to read. In pursuing her favorite pastime, she engaged in "hunts" for reading material just as she did in locating other refugees. Early in their displacement Mrs. Stone rented books from a woman who otherwise refused to lend them to strangers, but Kate was not very impressed with the collection of this "regular skinflint." However, she once tried to buy a copy of Shakespeare from the lady because, as Kate said, the family would then have "a good library, Shakespeare and the Bible." The owner asked fourteen dollars for the volume and Kate thought this unreasonable, but while she was still yearning for the copy she heard that the woman had leprosy and the Stones suddenly became uninterested in her collection. A brighter day dawned for the family when Kate made friends with a doctor and his wife in Tyler. Not only did the couple have an excellent library but they were exceedingly generous with it so that within two months Kate had read every volume at least once, and because so many were histories she said that she felt "as dry as those old times." But she had also "nearly memorized Tennyson and read and reread . . . Shakespeare" of whom she never tired. Despite Kate's deep-seated Confederate sympathies she missed the Northern periodicals and was irritated that "good" Southerners were discouraged from reading them, but whenever she could get a copy of *Harper's Weekly* or *Frank Leslie's Lady's Magazine* she read their every word. She once noted that Northern literature was to the Stones what "the 'flesh pots of Egypt' were to the wandering Israelites—we long for it." [28]

Even before the war, Southerners had long looked upon church services as both a spiritual and social outlet, and they continued to do so during the conflict. For many refugees it was their primary social activity when they saw others whom they could not be with during the busy week and heard news they might otherwise have been months in hearing. Despite the refugees' complaints that they were sometimes made to feel unwelcome in strange churches, many of them either found great cordiality or satisfied themselves with the spiritual benefits derived from attending services. The displaced people were restricted when there was no church in remote areas, when the services were irregular, or when they refused to attend one of another denomination, but most were as regular in attendance as circumstances permitted. The only gatherings which Sidney Harding attended with regularity were church and Sunday School, but after returning from these her Sundays nevertheless seemed "so long." [29] Refugees who lived in towns had less difficulty finding a church than those in rural areas and most attended services as a matter of routine. Those who moved from urban communities into the country or a village were sometimes dismayed at the irregular services when a single preacher divided his time between two or more churches. The Grimballs were annoyed that the clergymen who served Spartanburg also served Union, and services could be held only every two weeks. Mrs. Grimball saw no reason for this inconvenience when there was another ordained minister of the same faith in Spartanburg, but the residents suspected him of Northern sentiments and would not invite him to preach.[30]

When refugees moved into a more primitive area than that to which they were accustomed they were shocked, amazed, or amused by the religious services. As might be expected, the observant Kate Stone experienced all three sensations. Shortly after their arrival in Texas the Stones attended a protracted meeting held in a school-house named "Paradise," which Kate said must have been given it "in mockery." Although the women's styles were passé and they looked ridiculous walking around barefoot in hoop skirts, she thought that they presented a better general appearance than others she had seen. The services overwhelmed her, however, for she had never before witnessed such an open display of emotionalism. "The scene [was] . . . most striking," she wrote, ". . . the anxious, excited faces . . . the groans and shrieks and wild prayers of the mourners, mingling with the shouts and hallelujahs of the newly professed." While admitting to being thrilled and interested in the event, Kate nevertheless noted that she preferred to take her religion "more quietly." [31] Throughout their displacement, the Stones attended church regularly, and when the first rumor of the war's end arrived in Tyler, Kate paused to write in her journal before going to church. Her comment made on that quiet Sabbath was also the sentiment of other displaced people during the war and after: "It behooves us to ask aid from Our Maker when all else is failing us." [32]

In their social activities as in other ways, the refugees struggled to maintain their old way of life in so far as circumstances permitted. Yet many affairs bore little resemblance to those of prewar days except that they furnished the participants with hours of enjoyment. The shortage of men on the homefront did not deter women from having dances although they had to dance with each other or await their turn to dance with the few available men. Grand balls could be held only where there were escorts, as in Richmond, and orchestras or bands to provide the music, but most refugees contented themselves with less lavish affairs, dancing happily to the music of a single fiddler. Mrs. Roger Pryor liked dances, and when she was living at the hotel in Amelia Springs the proprietor arranged one for his guests. It was typical of wartime with the fiddler and no men for partners, yet Mrs. Pryor and the others enjoyed it.[33] When Senator Williamson Oldham was en route to his home in Texas he joined in the social activities of displaced friends living along the way. While a guest in a farmhouse near Newnan, Georgia, he attended a dance that brought back memories of his youth. The participants included "a half-dozen hearty rosy cheeked country girls . . . three or four young men," and a lone Negro fiddler. "I had not witnessed such a country frolic since my boyhood days in Tennessee," wrote Oldham. "The tunes were the same, and the dances the same as those I had heard and seen of yore." [34]

The refugees more often danced in the home than they did in public, but this depended in part upon where they were. Families and neighbors joined in the activity which was usually spontaneous, and these affairs often served to break the monotony. A Louisianian told of her family's dancing after supper and neighbors frequently dropping in to share in the fun. The nine-year-old daughter in the home was noted for the way she rendered the "Wild Irishman" and never had to be coaxed to perform. [35] When dances were held outside the home mothers were sometimes reluctant to let their daughters attend, not necessarily because they opposed public dances but because they thought them out of place in time of war. However, young people seldom considered the sad times as sufficient reason for curtailing their enjoyment and they pleaded and cajoled to be allowed to go. A refugee in South Carolina wrote an older daughter that she was going "to martyrize" as a chaperone at a public dance which her younger daughter was to attend. She wanted the child to enjoy herself despite the sorrowful times and although she was young to be going to a dance the mother said, "She has such a dull time . . . that I do not like to curtail her opportunities for amusement." [36]

Party refreshments underwent a marked change during the war as "starvation parties" replaced lavish banquets as a form of entertainment. Friends gathered together knowing that only the simplest refreshments, or none at all, would be served because of the scarcity and high price of even the plainest foods. [37] Although "starvation parties" were not confined to refugees, they were popular with this group. Nor was an elaborate array of delicacies the only thing missing even at the so-called dinner parties, for displaced people often lacked the essentials usually thought necessary for such an event. Sidney Harding told of being invited to "an informal dinner" given by other displaced people. When seated at the table the guests had "no knives or forks or plates" but they ate with their hands and had "a glorious time." [38] Picnics were not easy to plan if one thought of this entertainment as primarily the enjoyment of good food, and many refugees who mention attending picnics note that there was no food or that it was far different from that one might normally expect. These affairs might be more accurately referred to as outings rather than picnics, but they were popular with the displaced people. A lady from Roanoke Island who spent a part of the war in Hillsboro said that picnics were a favorite diversion among the homeless people in the community.[39] Others were unable to attend these affairs because they refused to go when they could supply none of the food, and Sidney Harding was one who had to decline an invitation for this reason. She was told that she must bring her own and her only comment was, "Asking poor refugees to bring eatables!" [40]

In the lives of all displaced people there were special occasions which would have called for elaborate celebration but which now had to be greatly simplified. In this category were wartime weddings which were usually very simple affairs but often planned by the entire community so that they would be as memorable and beautiful as the circumstances permitted. Few social affairs could so stimulate the women to activity as these, for as Judith McGuire said, "Neither war, pestilence nor famine could put an end to marrying. . . ." [41] The interest in a wedding extended beyond the family circle, and the kindness of those in the community often helped the displaced people to renew their faith in mankind. It seemed that everyone wanted to have a part, and this was an event which women enjoyed describing at great length in their diaries and letters.

Although Judith McGuire felt that there was "a perfect mania on the subject of matrimony," most women did not take as pessimistic a view as she did. Mrs. McGuire noted that in Richmond the churches were kept open day and night "for bridals," and she attended one held before "the dawn of day." Because the groom had to return to his command, the bride wore her traveling "costume," and after the wedding a breakfast was served before the couple rushed to the train that was to take them South.[42] It concerned Mrs. McGuire that weddings took place under these circumstances. One of the most brilliant nuptials held in Richmond was within two weeks one of the greatest tragedies, and this is what Mrs. McGuire so often feared might happen. Hetty Cary was married to General John Pegram late in the conflict, and Confederate officialdom was there to pay homage to "the most beautiful woman" in the city and her handsome officer.[43] Pegram returned to the battlefield immediately following the ceremony and two weeks later was killed in action. Few shocks hit Richmond society harder than this, and Judith McGuire recalled the couple's recent "bright and beautiful" wedding which had been solemnized before "a crowd of relatives and friends," who were now called on to return to the same church for the groom's funeral.[44]

Katherine Polk Gale's sister married William Huger while the family lived in Asheville, and it seems that most of the town contributed something to the occasion. It took great ingenuity to get together a trousseau for the bride, but old clothes were hauled from trunks and renovated. It required, as Mrs. Gale said, the "thinking caps" of everyone to make this a memorable event. Friends who had vehicles let the bridal party use them to ride to the church; the Negro cook somehow managed to make a "delicious wedding cake" which a neighbor iced, and the supper consisted of "excellent" chicken salad without a "trace of olive oil, celery or lettuce." [45] Jorantha Semmes wrote her husband about a refugee's wedding she attended and noted the interest friends had shown in the affair. She told him that he would have been "astounded" at the supper of "magnificent turkey ($10), stuffed choate, lamb, broiled birds, tongue, bird pie, giblets a la Marie, lettuce and other vegetables, jelly cake, custard, conserves, puddings, strawberry pie, etc. etc." But Mrs. Semmes was even more interested in the decorations which consisted of wild flowers and Confederate flags.[46] When LaSalle Corbell married General George Pickett friends gave the wedding supper, and among those contributing was Mrs. Robert E. Lee who made "a beautiful fruit cake." Another friend gave one she was saving for her fiftieth anniversary but preferred to contribute to the affair. One of the most interesting facets of this story was the way in which the sora were killed. Paddles were used, as the bride said, because "the expenditure of ammunition could not be afforded to shoot the birds when there were so many more important targets to be found." [47] No other social event was as important to women as a wedding and none so stimulated them to devise, contrive, and sacrifice as did these occasions.

Christmas also called forth special efforts which taxed the mind and the ingenuity of the women, for despite the shortages, inconveniences, poverty, and tragedy in the lives of most of them, parents left no stone unturned as they tried to find some special remembrance for their children. A great many mothers went to bed on Christmas Eve saddened because they had nothing for the youngsters, and they were heartsick at their children's disappointment in being "forgotten." Others worried for fear that their little token gifts would disappoint their sons and daughters, but when morning came and the boys and girls were overjoyed with makeshift toys, the mothers knew that their efforts had been well rewarded. Katherine Polk Gale knew this feeling after she and others in the family spent weeks getting ready for Christmas and were greeted on Christmas morning by the children's "shouts and screams of delight." The adults had decorated the tree with candles made of myrtle wax and held in place by potatoes secured to the tree by thorns and with cornucopias made from a roll of old wall paper and filled with popcorn balls, walnuts, sorghum candy, and apples. The older members of the family did not think it "a very beautiful" tree, but it and the homemade toys and knit clothing brought "happiness, unalloyed happiness . . . to eight precious children." The weeks of preparations had also done something for the adults, according to Mrs. Gale who wrote, "They helped us to pass the anxious, weary days." This and the feeling that they were "more than repaid" for the time and "trouble" gave the parents satisfaction.[48]

Benedict Joseph Semmes's family had Christmases very similar to the Polks and Gales, and just as important to them was the tree which, in 1863, Mrs. Semmes decorated with spools of bright colored thread which her husband had sent to her for other purposes. But having nothing else with which to hide the bare places in the tree she had used them, knowing that he "would have been very much amused" could he have seen her decorations.[49] Mrs. Semmes always wrote at great length of the family's Christmas as she told her husband about the simple gifts everyone received, about the antics and reactions of the children, and about the joy she derived from having been able to make them happy.

Elizabeth Meriwether's first Christmas spent as a refugee was the most memorable of her life. When she left Memphis a few weeks before, she thought to bring marbles, books, tin horns, and "a tiny sword" for her two boys. These and a little candy, which she made from a pint of sorghum given to her by her landlady, constituted her gifts. The children played with their toys all day, and after they went to bed Mrs. Meriwether wrote her husband of the day's events and then settled down to "reading Macauley's comments on Moore's *Life of Byron*." Reflecting on Byron's exile "from the land on which his genius had shed immortal glory," she realized that her "third child gave notice that it meant to make its appearance on the stage of this turbulent world." Before midnight her son was born and named Lee for the Confederate military leader.[50] Mrs. Meriwether was to know two more Christmases as a refugee, and although neither would be as significant as the first one spent in Columbus, Mississippi, she would always manage to have some little treat for her sons. It was in her struggle to get sugar for Christmas candy that she had her troubles with Tuscaloosa's "sugar lady."

Some displaced people were confronted with such a cheerless Christmas that they wished it could be forgotten, and such was Kate Stone's attitude during the two normally festive seasons passed in Texas. On one of these she was relieved that her younger brothers had an invitation to spend the day with friends, for she wanted "the little fellows to have a pleasant Christmas," but her first one away from home was sad. Like so many other refugees, she was much more inclined to be depressed at this season than at any other, for homesickness overtook displaced people as they reminisced about the way they had once spent the holiday season. On this first Christmas Kate paraphrased Tennyson in her journal:

> Tears, idle tears, Tears from the depth of some distant time,
> Rise in the heart and gather in the eyes,
> In gazing o'er the dreary winter fields
> And thinking of the days that are no more.

This Christmas for the Stones "passed most quietly, not a cake, not a visitor," and no one but the servants enjoyed the "mean whiskey" which she said, "smacked of Texas." [51] On her second Christmas she made no entry in her diary for six weeks during December and January, and when Kate was silent for an extended period it usually meant that she was depressed. The same was true of others, and while Sarah Morgan wrote at some length and with enthusiasm about her first Christmas as a refugee, she did not mention it at all in either 1863 or 1864.[52]

The Christmas season was the inspiration for many editorials which stressed the religious significance of the occasion, encouraged the citizens to remember the poor and displaced people, and reflected the gaiety among certain groups. Although often criticizing the extravagance displayed in most cities, the papers also told of elaborate parties, some of which were given in honor of refugees. The Richmond *Dispatch* described "a blow-out for Refugees" which was hosted by prominent citizens for "the refugee members of the Legislature and Congress." Those who attended were sumptuously wined and dined on an "abundance of eggnog and other beverages, and a bountiful supply of edibles." After dinner the gathering was "edified by speeches from various gentlemen," and Mayor Joseph Mayo was complimented for having made "the strangers feel at home in Richmond." The editor noted, "Such remembrances of the homeless will not be lost on the refugee patriots who have already sacrificed so much for the cause of the South." [53] Appeals to Southerners to remember displaced people were especially numerous at this season, and the Charleston *Courier* asked its readers to do something for those who had been "driven from their homes by the ruthless enemy." It was this group, he said, that would be most unhappy as they compared their Christmas in displacement with those they had known before the war. These memories would be certain to "aggravate their present ills and add grief to their sorrows." [54]

When Southerners seemingly forgot the religious meaning of Christmas and the seriousness of the troubled times, critics stepped forward to rebuke them. Judith McGuire was both devout and sensitive to the tragedy of the period and could not bring herself to celebrate Christmas with the abandon of many others. For her it was a time of religious dedication, and although she tried to provide a few delicacies for the family's dinner, she was not as effervescent and buoyant as were some of her friends. On the last Christmas of the war she told of the cheerfulness of others around her, but said that she found it extremely difficult to "exert" herself to be merry. [55] She regretted the excessive extravagance and frivolity which so many people insisted on at this season, but Mrs. McGuire never caustically criticized them, for such was not her nature. She was only saddened by their conduct which she felt hurt rather than helped the Confederacy. Editors were often of the same opinion, and weeks before Christmas they began stressing the seriousness of the times and urging the citizens to observe the season quietly.

The refugees' records reflect many reactions to wartime Christmases, and some told of celebrations that were so shocking to them that they questioned whether loyal, refined Southerners could be guilty of such conduct. It was especially at this season that some wondered if Southern society were not being degraded by the conflict. Meta Grimball heard of a Christmas party held in Charleston which prompted her to condemn the participants as "fast." This affair was "attended by a gay collection of young people," most of whom were not Charlestonians, but it was held in the home of a prominent citizen. The group arranged a mock wedding, which was a popular form of entertainment at the time, but in this case "a Magistrate" read the "Episcopal Marriage service." Mrs. Grimball noted that "in the consideration of many people" this had been a "real wedding," and she blamed the host who had permitted the event to take place in his home. [56] It took several months for the story to reach Spartanburg and during the transit it probably disgusted others as it had Mrs. Grimball.

No other annual occasion excited as much interest as Christmas. Birthdays are seldom mentioned as cause for celebration among the refugees, because gifts were rarely exchanged and even the displaced people who kept regular records usually omitted all mention of their own and others' birthdays. There were exceptions, of course, especially when a gift received by one refugee was so unusual and expensive that it merited mention in several Southern newspapers. This lady's husband gave her a breast pin about an inch and a half square which was "made of gold" and faced with enamel. It was the likeness of the Confederate flag with small diamonds for the thirteen stars. She and her gift were seen going through Selma, Alabama, and it was reported that the jewelry had been ordered from Paris and had come through the blockade in time for her birthday.[57]

Special events were held in all communities throughout the war, but most refugees were primarily dependent on themselves and those around them for daily diversions. Some people never participated in organized activities outside the home, and the responsibility for finding leisure time pursuits rested largely with the individual. Those with varied interests could usually manage to occupy their time in some kind of simple, inexpensive activity. Among the popular games of the period were euchre, checkers, backgammon, and chess, and these engaged a great many refugees who were so fortunate as to have the essentials for playing. Another diversion which took nothing more than originality, interest, and energy was charades which many of the young and old enjoyed for hours at a time. Teen-aged girls were especially interested in fortune telling and never seemed to grow tired of hearing their future predicted, probably because a young man always showed himself in the period that lay ahead. It did not seem to matter that the same man rarely appeared twice, for to see any male in one's life was a consoling thought to girls on the Confederate homefront. Sarah Morgan, Sidney Harding, and many others became very excited about fortunes told them and could "float" for days after an especially encouraging one.

Children played their usual games and most of them enjoyed having stories told them. Nor did they mind hearing the same ones again and again, although they had often committed them to memory. As a rule, displaced youngsters did not have many books or toys because of the difficulties involved in transporting, repairing, and replacing them. Grace King, later a prominent literary figure in the South, was ten years old when she and her family left New Orleans. Because of the baggage problem, each child was permitted to take only one toy of his choosing, and although she made no mention of her selection, she told of a woman's handing her "an ugly, heavy, cumbersome, . . . hideously dressed" rag doll when the family drove away from their home. As she played with it, the doll soon began to come apart at the seams, and upon investigation Grace found a note and money stuffed inside. The recipient was instructed to send the money to a soldier whose address was given, and this Grace's parents did, but the doll was never the same after the removal of the bills. The young refugee continued to play with it, however, and as it developd, this was the last doll she ever had.[58] If children received any new toys during the war, they were usually homemade from whatever materials were available, but even those that were simple and crude pleased their young owners.

A very popular diversion for refugees who lived along the railroads was meeting the trains stopping in the town. Some people gathered regularly at the depot, often hours before the train was due to arrive, and they conversed with each other in the interval. After it pulled into the station, they chatted with the conductor and passengers and in this way heard the news and rumors from farther up the line which they hastened to spread with tongue and pen. Their eagerness to see new faces and hear the latest happenings was both amusing and pathetic, but displaced people often indicated that the hour or so spent at the station was the highlight of the day. Philip Phillips made it a habit to meet the trains coming into LaGrange, and he was following his customary pattern on May 10, 1865, when he first heard that his friend Clement Claiborne Clay, then in town, was being sought as a conspirator in President Lincoln's assassination. When Clay decided to go to Macon to face and deny the charges, Phillips went with him as his attorney.[59] Travelers frequently commented on this practice of meeting the trains. A soldier who was en route from Montgomery to Mobile was surprised to find so many "women and girls . . . coming from God only knows where—looking with strange unsophisticated looks at passengers." He thought that they betrayed "in gait and habit, the poor, simple, uncultivated" people, but this was by no means the only group which congregated at the depots.[60]

Many of the refugees were fond of music and some were talented performers. Those who settled in the larger towns had ample opportunity to attend musical programs, provided they were financially able to do so, but those in the rural areas were dependent upon themselves for musical diversion. In some of the refugee centers the displaced people banded together to form music clubs, as did the Louisianians in LaGrange. But others were sometimes handicapped by the lack of an instrument and sheet music, and while many instrumentalists could play from memory certain selections, young women were especially anxious to learn the popular war songs. Elodie Todd had her fiancé looking for copies of "Maryland, My Maryland" and "The Bonnie Blue Flag." On one of his return trips to Richmond he stopped in Augusta, Columbia, Charlotte, and Raleigh trying to find copies, but it wasn't until he reached Richmond that he found the words and music of "Maryland, My Maryland." He bought two copies and mailed them separately, hoping to insure the arrival of one.[61]

Refugees who were either amateur or professional pianists were made miserable in their displacement when they had no piano. Those living in the home of friends and relatives who had one, could use it, but many had to forego their playing during the war. Sidney Harding was one who missed her piano to such an extent that her family tried unsuccessfully to rent one for her. As previously noted, Julia LeGrand was unable to practice during her displacement because none of her temporary homes had a piano, and this was one reason she doubted her ability to teach, as she had done before leaving New Orleans. Smaller musical instruments could be more conveniently taken by the refugees but were easily damaged and irreplaceable. The instrumentalists may have been inhibited during their displacement, but the vocalists —trained and untrained—could indulge in their pastime. Group sings in the home and in public were popular, and impromptu sessions could be held whenever the spirit was willing. Almost always this outlet improved the participants' dispositions, and Kate Stone's family often relied on this activity to fill their hours. One of the first friends Kate made in Texas was a young woman who knew many old ballads, "Barbara Allen," "Willie Over the Lea," and others, and she sang for the Stones "nearly every night," much to the delight of her audience.[62]

In their social activities, as in other spheres of their lives, the refugees had to make many adjustments. Thrust as they were into strange communities and often removed from close contact with others, they were likely to be as dependent on themselves socially as they were economically. There were several personality traits, the possession of which would help a displaced person to develop a more satisfactory social life for himself. If his interests were varied, many avenues would be open to him and he would be in a position to take advantage of social opportunities planned by others. Another asset was the ability to adjust to the preferences of others and to his own peculiar situation, but it also helped him if he had imagination, originality, ingenuity, and qualities of sportsmanship. Refugees who had these traits usually managed to derive a great satisfaction from their leisure hours. Although very few displaced people had an exciting social life and most had times of depression there were always those who got enjoyment from simple activities.

Kate Stone represented the small group of displaced people whose interests, accomplishments, and temperament were such as to make life more pleasant for herself and those around her. She loved people, made friends easily, and possessed not only curiosity about others but also cultivated an interest in them. Although her family suffered losses during the war, was touched by death, and endured inconvenience and privation, she was always ready to participate in social activities. When they were not suggested to her, she originated them, but she did not have to be with others in order to be contented for there was nothing she would rather do than read. Her journal consumed hours of time as she attended to it with amazing regularity except during periods of depression, but even in those "darkest hours" of her life when most refugees had ceased to write, she not only continued to record the happenings but also noted, "we are having the most enjoyable life." [63] Yet, not once during her years in Texas did Kate Stone attend an extravagant ball or party; she depended on simple amusements and diversions to fill her leisure hours. She was like many other refugees who were unable to indulge in their usual prewar gaiety but who always tried to make the best of the circumstances.

. . . *the rights a general may exercise*

Federal and Confederate military policies relating to the unfriendly citizenry were often similar and sometimes identical. Because the Federals succeeded in overrunning the South, a far greater number of Southern sympathizers bore the brunt of enemy orders than did Unionists, but when Confederate officers went into areas where there were many Northern sympathizers they did not hesitate to play the role of the conqueror. Yet neither army ever adopted consistent policies in dealing with the people, and for this reason the civilians never knew what to expect. The war proved beyond any doubt that both Confederate and Federal generals could exercise certain rights when dealing with the foe even when he was not in uniform. In this category were tens of thousands of displaced Confederate sympathizers who were directly affected by Federal military measures at some time during the four years.

The refugees were shocked to find that even when they had left home in the advance of an enemy invasion they were apt to be overtaken before the conflict ended. And, as previously noted, noncombatants who remained at home might at any time be exiled by military orders. Southerners were both confused and embittered by the Federals' actions, and despite their displacement most people never completely comprehended the full meaning of this war. They did not understand that the Confederate and Union forces had but one goal: to win. Because this was the all-important object civilians were relegated to a secondary position and their welfare could not be considered if it interfered with the military program. The people were expendable and could not expect to live according to what they believed to be just and logical. Nor could military policies follow a consistent, prearranged pattern, but had to be altered to fit the time, place, and people; no part of the Federal military policy was more contradictory and inconsistent than that pertaining to the refugees. Therefore it is only natural that they were bewildered by the enemy's actions.

Displaced people also confused, surprised, frustrated, and exasperated the enemy. Military reports indicate that Federal officers were at times overwhelmed by them and uncertain as to how to handle the problem. Officers were caught off guard by the immensity and complexity of the situation and they hastily issued thousands of orders in desperation. Their policies were developed piecemeal, which was not conducive to consistency, and their orders were issued, modified, withdrawn, countermanded, enforced, and evaded. When commanders changed, the citizens wondered and worried about what the new appointee would do. If stern measures were immediately modified this did not mean that people could completely relax, for they found that the new official often reverted to the policies of his predecessor. Yet, it might have been of some comfort to the refugees had they realized how very irritating and confusing they were to the enemy.

As previously noted, the right to banish citizens was a powerful weapon in the hands of the Federals. It was applied to one person or to thousands and might be wielded at any time in an occupied area. Early in the war its primary purpose was to create a docile citizenry within Federal lines, and this could best be done by ridding the area of hostile Southerners. If all were not forced to leave a community, a sufficiently large number could be exiled to subdue those remaining, or so the enemy thought. Midway in the war, however, wholesale banishment of people into Confederate lines was recognized as an even more powerful weapon, for the pushing of greater numbers into the contracting, congested, hard-pressed Confederacy would break the people's spirit, create grave economic and military problems, and hasten the end of the conflict. When this policy was followed many docile citizens who would have given the enemy no trouble were ensnared in the military strategy and became the pawns of war.

Federal commanders gave many reasons for banishing both individuals and groups, but few managed to describe the adversaries as well as General John Schofield whose problem was the Southern sympathizers in Missouri. He referred to them as influential, wealthy, "bitter enemies of the Government" who made no attempt to "disguise their sympathy for the rebels, and yet [are] too shrewd to commit any act for which they can be punished." Because they were potential con-

spirators, Schofield favored sending them "down the river beyond
. . . [Federal] lines." General Henry Halleck approved the plan but
cautioned Schofield to use his power "sparingly" lest he "increase the
ranks of the enemy." [1] And noted later will be this question of the
advisability of sending able bodied men into the Confederacy, for it
was a point of disagreement throughout the war.

Adopted early was the policy requiring that individuals leaving
Federally controlled areas obtain a pass from the local provost marshal.
This would be automatic with those banished but others who wanted
to go into Confederate lines were expected to adhere to the rule;
however many people managed to slip away without getting a pass.
Thousands preferred to take the risk rather than face the provost
marshal and his staff, for this was a terrible ordeal for most civilians.
Julia LeGrand seriously thought of leaving New Orleans while General Butler was in command, but she was afraid to approach his provost
marshal. When General Banks replaced Butler she was pleased to hear
that his appointee was much kinder and more understanding, and it
was during the period of Banks's command that she left the city. But
she had waited so long to go that she could not get to her brother's
home in Texas as she had hoped to do.[2]

The banishment of civilians was very often used as a retaliatory
measure by the Federals and was imposed on the families of Confederate soldiers, notably those of officers. This practice was often
followed after partisan and guerrilla attacks on Federal properties,
railroads, boats, and Northern sympathizers. The situation in and
around Memphis caused the military commanders to resort to this
measure, but even before it was applied in retaliation General Grant
thought it advisable to banish all citizens who had a father, husband,
or brother in the Confederate Army, or who were widows or orphans
of Southern soldiers. When Grant's order to this effect reached General M. Jeff Thompson in Mississippi, he vehemently protested "in
the cause of humanity," saying that its enforcement would include
"nine-tenths of the people of Memphis." [3] Before Thompson's protest
reached Memphis, the order had been modified but was not yet a dead
letter.

When General William T. Sherman took command of Memphis he
announced that he intended to make the city "a safe place of operation
for the army" and had no intention of relinquishing his right to banish
citizens just to suit "the personal convenience of even a large class of
ladies." By this second summer of the war Sherman already realized
that a hostile populace could threaten his military plans and divert

troops from the battle lines to police duty. Therefore, he determined to use whatever force necessary to create a tractable citizenry, and when guerrillas in northern Mississippi fired on "unarmed boats carrying passengers and goods," he decided to banish noncombatants in retaliation. Sherman ordered that "for every boat fired on, ten families must be expelled" from Memphis, and the provost marshal was instructed to maintain at all times a list of thirty unfriendly families from which the exiles would be selected. He recognized that the punishment "would sometimes fall on the wrong head," but the order would nevertheless be enforced. When the Confederate officials protested, Sherman asked, "How would you like it if we were to fire through the houses of . . . [your] wives and families as . . . [you] do through the boats carrying our wives and families?" [4]

This was the policy that made refugees of Elizabeth Meriwether and her sons. Mrs. Meriwether had managed to get along with Grant and had respect for him, but she and Sherman disagreed with each other from the beginning and she thought he was a "monster." The major point of dispute related to an order which prevented Mrs. Meriwether from collecting rents on property she owned unless she took the oath of allegiance, which she refused to do. She and the general had several heated sessions after which she thought of leaving Memphis, but a friend dissuaded her from acting too hastily. When Sherman ordered the first ten families banished after an attack on the Federal boats, Mrs. Meriwether was notified that she was in the group. Given only twenty-four hours to get out of town, she asked permission to remain until her Negro driver was well enough to take the family to Mississippi, but this request was denied and she was threatened with imprisonment if she did not leave within the allotted time. She left Memphis "at once" driving the buggy herself.[5]

Other commanders retaliated by banishing civilians from their lines and although these orders are similar, nearly all of them have a distinctive provision. Major John McDonald exiled both the Southern sympathizers who had committed "outrages" against Unionists and those who did not take measures to prevent these attacks.[6] General Don Carlos Buell, in 1862, ordered "all persons who had aided or abetted the invasion of Kentucky by rebel troops" sent to Vicksburg.[7] When General Stephen A. Hurlbut assumed command in Memphis he continued Sherman's banishment policy, and after guerrillas attacked a train carrying "women, children and citizens," he ordered from the city "rebel sympathizers . . . of greatest wealth and highest social position. . . ." Hurlbut believed that "no Southern sympathizer should be allowed" in Federal lines and he did what he could to rid the area of them.[8] General Gordon Granger was so successful in promiscuously banishing families of suspected saboteurs and guerrillas that to do so came to be known as "Grangerizing" an area.[9]

Women who were banished were not always innocent bystanders, however, for many were themselves guilty of sabotage, espionage, or subversion, and some willingly admitted their guilt. A Mrs. Hunter and her daughter, Tennesseans, not only confessed to having helped burn a bridge but told the Federals that they expected to do it again. They were immediately ordered to leave Federal territory.[10] Other officers eventually realized, as did Sherman, that hotheaded Southern females could be a formidable foe, and although at first reluctant to punish women by banishing or imprisoning them, the authorities were soon treating them less gently. They were more often banished than imprisoned, but as previously noted, Mrs. Philip Phillips was among those sent to prison, and in her case to Ship Island. Marylanders who were accused of aiding the Confederate raiders in 1864 had their homes seized, their furniture sold, and the men were sent to prison in Wheeling and the women into Confederate lines.[11]

Southerners were often spared banishment if they took the oath of allegiance to the United States government and if they settled down in peace under Federal rule. But in this instance, also, there was a lack of consistency, for taking the oath did not always insure a person's being permitted to remain at home although his chances for doing so were improved. Nor did the failure to take the oath necessarily subject him to exile. In many instances Southerners were not asked to take the oath and in others it was sometimes months after the occupation before they were required to do so. It was more often used in towns than in rural areas, and in many communities excessive pressure was applied for a brief period and then relaxed after examples had been made of a number of recalcitrant individuals. The people did not know where or when they would be confronted with the choice of taking the oath and remaining at home or refusing to subscribe to it and being banished.

New Orleans, of all the Federally controlled Southern cities, contributed the greatest number of refugees to the Confederacy when thousands of its citizens refused to take the oath. It was not only the largest Southern city but it fell too suddenly to permit an appreciable number of its residents to flee in advance of the Federals, and too early in the war for civilians to realize what an enemy occupation could mean. When General Butler took command, New Orleans was a tinderbox filled with thousands of belligerent pro-Confederates, many of whom were women. It would take only a spark to inflame the citizens and Butler provided that when he tactlessly and sternly tried to handle an indignant people. He announced that no one could leave the city without a permit and called for loyal residents to step forward and take the oath. Only 27,929 had sworn allegiance to the Federal government during the first five months of the occupation, but others voluntarily left with or without passports, and hundreds were banished or imprisoned in this period.[12]

In September, 1862, General Butler put into effect the Confiscation Acts which required the registration of persons who had not taken the oath, these people now being classified as enemies of the United States. Their property was listed at the time of their registration and they were given an opportunity to take the oath if they so desired. During the next four weeks 39,991 additional residents took the loyalty oath and "somewhat less than 4,000" registered as enemies.[13] During his rule of New Orleans Butler suppressed, imprisoned, banished, threatened, terrorized, and intimidated Southern sympathizers while he fed, sheltered, and employed thousands of indigent citizens and refugees. He insulted the women because "the fiery little Creoles," as Mrs. Chesnut called them, were insolent and disrespectful to his soldiers, and when this failed to subdue them Butler herded both men and women into prison or Confederate lines. Julia LeGrand felt that he deliberately determined to humiliate women and she said that "they never knew what would happen to them." Although neither Julia nor her sister took the oath, she noted the temptation to do so and told of many who did. Some of these wept and others "went away crazy" after having sworn allegiance to the enemy government.[14] But hundreds preferred to leave New Orleans, among them Mrs. Leonidas Polk and Reverend Benjamin Palmer. Shortly before he was relieved of command, Butler ordered all registered enemies to leave the city, but his successor, General Banks, cancelled the order.

When Banks took command, a great many citizens had complied with the Butler order and were making preparations to leave. Some had disposed of personal possessions and were packed for flight when Banks changed "the entire program" thus creating even greater confusion.[15] Within two weeks, however, he gave the registered enemies, excepting men of draft age, permission to leave, and even some of these men slipped out of New Orleans. Once Banks realized the problems involved in dealing with a large group of subversive people, he put into effect a program that won him the distinction of banishing from a single city more non-combatants than did any other Federal officer. His order banishing all registered enemies unless they took the oath by May 10, 1863, came after most Southern sympathizers had settled down in the belief that Banks's cancellation of Butler's order meant that he would not forcibly uproot them. It was during the first ten days in May that women appealed to the provost marshal to be exempt from taking the oath and still be permitted to remain in the city. A reporter for *Harper's Weekly* watched them "constantly flocking in to see if there was no way of avoiding the dreadful alternative of starvation in Dixie or bowing to the horrible Yankee flag." He was amused at the ladies' tactics and manners as some had "despondent faces," others were "very haughty," and a few appealed to the provost marshal as daughters would to a father. The reporter noted that a great many "wasted their bewitching smiles" on one of the handsome young members of the staff, but no matter what means they employed, the women were either "sworn or banished." [16] The majority of these refugees set adrift by Banks descended on Mobile, creating innumerable problems for that community.

Although New Orleans affords an extreme example of a people's being banished by the thousands for refusing to take the oath, it is typical of other communities in which Federal policies varied according to the wishes of the commander. Citizens who would not take the oath were never sure when new orders would change their lives. In Nashville the Federals did not require the oath as a condition for remaining until more than a year after the city fell. When it was thought necessary to order that it be taken, many residents were sent out for refusing to do so. A refugee who had voluntarily fled from Nashville early in the war was worried about her elderly parents who had stayed at home. The father was too ill to travel and was not forced to leave, but his wife was banished when she refused to take the oath, and the couple never saw each other again, for the husband died before the end of the war.[17]

Commanding officers were most apt to issue and enforce their orders when they suspected or had proof of widespread subversion in the community. These would continue to be enforced as long as necessary to check the activities and then perhaps become a dead letter. An interesting example of intimidating the enemy with a threat of banishment was the order in March, 1863, which exiled "citizens . . . of Williamsburg and vicinity" for refusal to take the oath. This came as a result of their having participated in recent Confederate raids, and in itself was not unusual; but when the raids continued, General John

A. Dix wrote Governor Henry A. Wise that if they did not cease he was going to send to Richmond a group of noncombatants who had not been included in his earlier order—the "inmates and employees of the Eastern Lunatic Asylum" whom the Federals had been supporting.[18]

As the war continued the oath was more frequently required of refugees entering Federal lines. In many cases men who refused to subscribe were imprisoned, and women were turned back in the direction from which they came. In 1864, General Francis J. Herron warned women who tried to come into Brownsville, Texas, without taking the oath that they must return to their homes, and if they tried again to cross into Federal territory they would be "treated as spies." [19] All refugees wanting to go into Federal-held areas were not Unionists, and this was especially true after the first two years of the war when an ever-increasing number of Confederate sympathizers were going home or to a region where they would be safer and more abundantly supplied with necessities. Some who were in dire circumstances took the oath but were not sincere. They had supported the Confederacy and still did so, but they could no longer support themselves in its confines. Officers frequently reported their trying to cross the lines late in the war. General George W. Morgan told of the son of "a member of the rebel legislature" of Virginia seeking entrance into his area of command and requesting to take the oath. In this case the man was trying to find safety away from the battle lines.[20]

When General Sherman decided to expel the Atlantans they were not given the choice of staying in the city, whether or not they took the oath, and this is one of the distinctive features of this development. Although more than half of the citizenry had left Atlanta before the city fell, to banish virtually all who remained created one of the most startling episodes of the war. The people in the contracting Confederacy were thrown into a state of shock and those living along the Federals' later line of march through Georgia and the Carolinas expected to have their communities ridded of the populace in the same way. Hundreds of Southerners fled ahead of the enemy and many more would probably have gone but had nowhere to go. The Confederacy was running out of safe areas and accommodations for refugees. But when Sherman did not repeat his Atlanta policy in either Savannah or Columbia, the people were again confused. He knew that Savannah was filled with dedicated Southern sympathizers, but he also realized that "the war was rapidly drawing to a close, and it was becoming a political question as to what was to be done with the people of the South." Therefore, he did not force them out as he had done the Atlantans but gave them the "option to remain or join their friends in Charleston or Augusta." Sherman reported that only about 200 of the 20,000 Savannah residents requested permission to leave the city.[21]

The most thoroughly studied chapter in the story of the refugees is that relating to the Atlanta exiles, but because it is also a unique episode it merits cursory mention. Throughout the North Georgia Campaign General Sherman had forcibly evicted noncombatants from their homes, usually permitting them to go North or South as they preferred. One of his more spectacular group banishments was that of 400 women workers in the Roswell mills, whom he ordered arrested "no matter what the clamor" and then escorted "under guard to Marietta" from which point they would be sent by train "to the North." Sherman knew that they would "make a howl," but he gave them permission to "take along their children and clothing provided they had a means of hauling." If any of the refugees seemed "dangerous" they were to be "imprisoned for a time," but none could be saved by taking the oath.[22] Sherman had already adopted the policy of mass banishment even before he reached Atlanta, for he was now convinced that an unfriendly populace in the rear of his army could be dangerous.

These tactics, coupled with a natural fear of the enemy, alarmed the Atlantans to such an extent that thousands left before the city fell. Those who remained when Sherman took command were primarily the people who were too poor to flee, who had nowhere to go, or who for some reason did not want to leave and were willing to adjust to the occupation. Some of these were refugees who had settled in Atlanta and who had decided that they had nothing to gain by running again. Presuming that if they gave no trouble they would be permitted to remain, the citizenry was thrown into a state of shock when the general announced his plans to clear the city of its occupants. Not only did he plan to rid his lines of a large and possibly hostile group of people but he realized that an indigent population thrust into Confederate lines could help to hasten the end of the war.[23] When his policy was made public it brought protests from General John B. Hood, the Atlanta officials, citizens, and the press, but Sherman stood pat. He and Hood carried on a heated correspondence on the matter and finally agreed that a ten-day truce would be declared so that the noncombatants could be removed to a railroad junction south of the city where they would be turned over to the Confederates. Permission was given for the refugees to take "clothing, trunks, reasonable furniture, bedding, etc.," as well as any Negroes who went voluntarily. The Federals provided transportation for "705 adults, 867 children and 78 servants, with 1,651 parcels of furniture and household goods." [24]

There were many and varied reactions to this expulsion of the Atlantans, but most Southern sympathizers condemned Sherman's actions. There were exceptions, however. Major William Clare of General Hood's staff thanked Sherman for "the uniform courtesy" extended to him and his "people" and expressed the hope that he could "reciprocate" the general's "courtesy . . . and positive kindness." [25] As might be expected the Southern press was generally brutal in denouncing Sherman. Typical of many editorials published in the Confederacy was that which referred to the orders as "the most unfeeling, inhuman, domineering document . . . since the commencement of the war." Of Sherman the newsman said that he was "a Yankee Hanan, a hell-deserving General" with a "black" character and "atrocious" policies.[26] However, a Macon editor quoted exiles arriving in that city as saying that they experienced "generally kind personal treatment from General Sherman and his officers." He also told of one exile who requested permission to remain in her home because she was ill, and although Sherman denied her request, he called on her and had his soldiers pack her possessions. She reported that the baggage was "bound up nicely and transported" to Confederate lines and that she had been permitted to bring along everything she wanted, "even her washtubs." She had nothing but praise for the man who exiled her.[27]

Bishop Henry Lay, himself a refugee, received permission from Sherman to re-enter Federal lines a week after the end of the truce period and also to go to visit "old and destitute friends" in Huntsville, Alabama. While in Atlanta Lay dined with Sherman and quoted the general as saying that "exiling the citizens . . . was the most merciful thing he could do" because his supply lines were so extended that he would have been unable to feed the people and there was nothing for them to eat in the area. He thought it was to their best interest to be sent out "in good weather, with their stores and baggage and with the appliances of both armies to aid them." [28] Most Southerners did not agree, even though they did not know Sherman was then planning his march across the state and that he did not want a hostile population left in the rear of his army. The march from Atlanta to Savannah is both famous and infamous for what in Sherman's opinion amounted to $100,000,000 damage done by his troops, bummers, and stragglers who foraged and plundered along the way. When the movements of the Federals were known or even suspected, hundreds of people living in their path fled in terror and others wished they had done so. Many refugees who had settled in this part of Georgia were caught in the maneuver, and some uprooted themselves again hoping to avoid the enemy.

General Sherman not only serves as an example of an officer who made use of the unfriendly people in order to reach his goal, but his policies reflected certain inconsistencies which confused the citizens. As noted, he did not repeat his Atlanta program in either Savannah or Columbia, although many expected him to do so. His troops lay waste to wide areas of Georgia and the Carolinas, yet he was known to befriend individuals. A Columbia family, who fled to the outskirts of town upon hearing of his coming, was sent for and received by the general at his headquarters. He gave them his own suite of rooms, invited them to dine with him and his staff, and was especially kind to the children whom he seated next to himself at the table. Before leaving Columbia he gave this family "six hams, two bags of rice, and one of wheat flour" which the Southern sympathizers "were glad to accept." [29] He also left with the mayor of the city 500 head of beef to be distributed among the poor of the city.[30] Another inconsistency which showed itself in other instances was Sherman's appeal to Southerners to remain at home. A year after he had banished Memphis citizens he advised the people in northern Mississippi "to stay home, gradually put their houses and contiguous grounds in order, and cast about for some employment or make preparations on a moderate scale to resume their former business or employment." [31]

Other Federal officers who had banished people at one time did not hesitate to ask that they stay at home when this was to the army's best interest, and this was often the case when they were needed to supply the troops. Not only did the Federals implore Southerners to raise food and keep businesses open, but they were known to recall those who had fled in advance of their coming. The army was at a disadvantage when supplies were lacking, transportation disrupted, and business halted, but there was also the problem of feeding the unemployed workers who had not left. The day after Memphis fell, military officials "exhorted . . . residents who may have fled their homes to return," and others who had "abandoned the businesses" to reopen their "stores and shops." The only exception were "those dealing in intoxicating liquors." [32] General Samuel Curtis was so concerned about the lack of provisions and business in northern Arkansas that he urged the "thousands" of Arkansans to return home and follow their normal pursuits.[33] In these instances and hundreds of similar cases, nothing was said about requiring the citizens to take the oath, but only that they be "peaceable." However, when subversion or violence later developed the same citizens who had remained or returned home would be liable to banishment if they did not swear allegiance to the United States government.

As previously noted, the Confederates approached the problem of evacuating Southern communities in an entirely different manner, and because most of the residents were friendly there was no idea of punishment in their orders. They were primarily interested in the safety of the people and in defense of the community. And in most instances, the orders were not rigidly enforced. General Lee was more successful than most officers when he had the citizens removed from Fredericksburg, but the presence of the Federals and falling shells were also influential in ridding the town of its more adamant residents. Yet in 1864, when Lee wanted Richmond evacuated of "all the population whose presence would impede or endanger" the military program and those who "increased the consumption of public stores without aiding or strengthening the army," he was unable to win the support of Secretary of War Seddon. Although agreeing with Lee in principle, Seddon said that when he had previously recommended such a step to President Davis nothing had been done. But the Secretary noted that by 1864 the "grave character" of the problem made it inadvisable because there was no way to guarantee the indigent displaced people food and shelter within Confederate lines. He reminded Lee that refugees had come "to be regarded with less sympathy than apprehension, for they are looked upon as diminishing the means and increasing the privations of the communities to which they flee."[34] This was, indeed, an accurate evaluation of the circumstances and partially explains the Confederate officials' reluctance to forcibly exile the citizenry at any time, but especially late in the conflict.

When Confederate commanders pressured noncombatants to leave an area, most Southerners understood that it was done as a military necessity; when there was criticism it was not usually as caustic or widespread as that launched against similar Federal measures. Yet there was some criticism. When General P. O. Hébert ordered the removal of Galvestonians in May, 1862, a native of the city, whose family was already displaced, referred to the order as "wrong and inhuman." He thought any disloyal persons should be dealt with "boldly and directly; but to remove the great mass of noncombatants & poor people . . . and force them into the country and destroy their cisterns, cattle, poultry & *property itself* . . . advances no public good." To make "refugees and exiles" of civilians not only hurt these people but also those "among whom they went." The critic cited cruel treatment of the refugees by the authorities and admitted that he was "bitterly indignant toward the policy pursued at Galveston." Yet Hébert's orders did not get all of the residents out of the city, for when the Federals seized control the same critic reported hundreds of noncombatants arriving in Houston.[35]

Confederate officers also urged that citizens stay at home and carry on their customary work, and they did it primarily for the same reason as the Federals. None exerted greater pressure on the civilians than General Edmund Kirby Smith who pleaded with Louisianians to remain on their farms and help provision his troops. From the time of General Banks's Red River Campaign in 1863 until the end of the war, Kirby Smith reiterated this plea. He was badly in need of supplies, for a large part of Arkansas and Louisiana had been ravaged by war, deserted by the Southern sympathizers, and occupied by the enemy, and it was becoming increasingly difficult to transport commodities from Texas. Kirby Smith finally issued an order forbidding planters in southern Arkansas and northern Louisiana to go to Texas, and the displaced editor of the Galveston *News* supported the general by telling the farmers that the task allotted them was "that of raising food." But he also reminded Smith that the Confederates owed these "agriculturists . . . all the protection the military authorities" could give them.[36]

When either army ordered an area evacuated there was the problem of transportation for the people who could not supply their own. The Federals usually furnished some means for conveying those they banished and sometimes for those who left voluntarily. However, the refugees were unceremoniously deposited at some point offering access to Confederate lines, and unless the Confederates arranged transportation beyond that point the people had to continue their journey as best they could. The carefully arranged plan of Sherman and Hood in the Atlanta evacuation was the exception rather than the rule. A more common practice was that used with the New Orleans exiles who were landed at Pascagoula and told to get to Mobile by any means available. In the evacuation of Fredericksburg Lee ordered that army "wagons and ambulances" be used, and although these were kept busy day and night they were insufficient to the needs and many people left home on foot.[37] When Beauregard was trying to remove the Charlestonians, "refugee tickets" were made available to the indigent and others who had no way of leaving the city.[38] Boats were occasionally assigned to take the refugees away from stricken areas, and sometimes those commissioned for other purposes were appropriated by the people. In the fall of 1861, a Confederate vessel was sent to Beaufort, South Carolina, to be used in removing records, papers, and military stores, but it returned to Charleston not with this cargo but with hysterical citizens and "their voluminous properties." [39] It has been previously mentioned that army conveyances were sometimes used by the families of high ranking military and political officials, but in most cases the Confederates lacked sufficient facilities to transport large numbers of displaced people.

People banished and traveling in Federal conveyances often complained about the type of transportation, the congestion, mistreatment, search of their persons, and baggage restrictions. But there were others who commented on the consideration and kindness displayed by the officers. A Confederate sympathizer in Missouri who refused to take the oath was served her "papers of exile." She was, however, given the use of two army wagons which shuttled back and forth hauling her personal possessions some miles from town where they were left in the care of a friend, and she was given transportation to her destination. This was to be as comfortable travel as she was to know during her displacement.[40]

A major problem for both armies was that of refugees coming into their lines. There was always an element of risk involved since the officers could never be sure whether they were bona fide refugees seeking safety with friends or enemies bent on espionage. General Braxton Bragg was convinced that the lines around Shelbyville, Tennessee, were "filled with spies, admitted by . . . pickets as refugees from Nashville," and he ordered that no more be admitted without his permission.[41] Officials in Mobile had reason to believe that persons posing as refugees were spying for the Federals and the order was issued that all "suspected" persons trying to enter Confederate lines be returned "immediately to the lines of the enemy." [42] Union commanders were also concerned about the espionage problem and for this reason came increasingly to demand that the oath be administered to those coming into their territory. Both armies also resorted to careful interrogation of refugees seeking to cross the lines, and one reason for this measure's being used frequently was to determine the person's loyalty.

There was another reason for interrogating displaced people: to get information about the opposing forces. Vital facts were sometimes given willingly by these people and sometimes inadvertently. Reports might be accurate but were frequently misleading, erroneous, or exaggerated. Yet many officials thought them of possible value and issued orders that all refugees be interrogated. Typical was General Banks's order which called for a careful examination of all incoming people by a "discreet officer" who would have the information "compared, collated, and reported." [43] General McClellan was one officer who placed too great a reliance on the reports of refugees, whether gathered by himself or by his scout, Allan Pinkerton. McClellan's communiques frequently cite information obtained from "contrabands, deserters, refugees and prisoners." It was the testimony of a Leesburg refugee that McClellan submitted as evidence against General Charles P. Stone after the Ball's Bluff "disaster," and it was information provided by others that caused him to overestimate Confederate strength during the Peninsular Campaign.[44] Confederate officers also utilized reports of displaced people, and General Beauregard was one who ordered that they be questioned and the name taken of any who brought "important intelligence of the movement of the enemy." [45]

The phrase, "confirmed by refugees," appears in thousands of military reports emanating from both armies, and the information given relates to such matters as the opponents' movements, strength, policies, plans, and the area's internal conditions. Because so many refugees could carry bits of vital information into the enemy area, some Southerners questioned the advisability of promiscuously granting passes to leave the Confederacy. Midway in the war a Richmond editor criticized the War Department's "issuing an unprecedented large number" of passports for parties to go North because he believed that they could "bear away . . . information." [46] The editor noted that while no one person might add appreciably to the enemy's knowledge, shreds of information might be collected, and when combined, it could injure the Confederacy. Whatever the reasons were for examining the refugees, those questioned were bewildered when no explanation was given as to why they were interrogated, and civilians were usually frightened during these encounters with military officials.

Displaced people who flocked into the lines of either army presented an economic problem for the command if they had no means of support. They often had to be fed from military supplies and because this proved to be a drain on the commissary the Federal officials sometimes ordered that only those refugees willing to take the oath would be provisioned. General John Schofield encountered a confusing situation in Missouri where it was especially difficult to determine positively the people's true loyalties. In 1863 he ordered that all persons seeking sustenance must "give proof" that they had been "loyal since the breaking out of the present rebellion," and that no refugee could expect to be provisioned for more than a limited period but must eventually sustain himself.[47] Despite commands of this kind from headquarters, most soldiers found it difficult to let people go hungry. They tended to agree with a Federal lieutenant who said, "Refugees, like other people, must eat or starve." [48] And it was not unusual for troops to share their rations with displaced civilians without asking where their loyalties lay.

The Federal forces were called upon to feed a greater number of homeless people than were the Confederates, but they also had more ample supplies from which to draw. As the Southern armies retreated into heavily populated areas they were often competing with refugees and others for food, and the displaced people congesting the region were often responsible for the soldiers' being inadequately provisioned. Reports of Confederate officers indicate this situation, and typical of hundreds of other comments was that of General Humphrey Marshall who said that refugees "eat up the food of the country, and are a positive nuisance." [49] It would probably have been to the advantage of the Confederacy had civilians stayed at home, and late in the war the supply problems could have been minimized had it been possible to force displaced people to return to their homes. This could not be done for many reasons, but their presence within Confederate lines aggravated the already serious provisioning problem.

One supply policy followed by many Federal commanders had a direct bearing on the displacement of Southern sympathizers. As thousands of indigent people flocked into Federal-controlled areas and the provisioning of these refugees became a major problem, the military officials tried to shift the responsibility to the unfriendly civilians. This sent thousands of Southerners into Confederate lines. Early in the war General Halleck was called on to feed thousands of Unionists who fled to St. Louis to get away from their pro-Southern neighbors and guerrillas. He ordered that these "stripped, . . . plundered, . . . barefooted, half-clad, . . . destitute and starving" refugees be provisioned "at the expense of the avowed secessionists and of those who are found guilty of giving aid, assistance and encouragement to the enemy." To implement his plan he ordered that Southern sympathizers who did not volunteer aid would be assessed their proportionate share and also be fined if it became necessary for military authorities to auction their property to raise the amount due. Any person resisting Halleck's orders would be tried by a military commission.[50]

Coming as they did before most civilians realized the meaning of this war, Halleck's orders shocked the Southern people who vehemently protested his action. However, Confederate commanders understood that such measures were sometimes necessary and although they did not openly support the enemy's orders, some made the effort to view the matter objectively. One of these was General Jeremy Gilmer who wrote his wife that although Halleck's orders seemed to be "pretty harsh," they were nevertheless "one of the rights a General may exercise in time of war." [51] When General Ben Loan adopted similar measures in southern Missouri the following year, the cash payments required of Southern sympathizers were so high that Loan reported hundreds of these people to be fleeing South.[52] Similar policies were followed by other Federal officers including Generals Prentiss in east Arkansas, Hurlbut in Memphis, Grant in the Chattanooga area, and McPherson in Natchez.[53]

The problem of what to do with male refugees was always a confusing one. Some of these men sought to enlist while others were fleeing from conscription, but there was always the question of whether there were spies among them. When General Humphrey Marshall asked Secretary of War Randolph whether or not he should "seize" male refugees and hold them as "conscripts," Randolph replied, "Do what you think best with them." [54] And this is what was done in most cases—whatever the commander thought best. When General Kirby Smith realized that men were fleeing to Texas to avoid conscription, he ordered a regiment to the frontier to apprehend them and enforce the draft law.[55] Although many of the refugees were trying to evade military service, some were entering Federal lines to enlist in that army. One officer was so astonished by the number of Alabamians asking to enter Federal service that he was at first "incredulous as to their good faith," but when they continued arriving in large numbers he "at last became convinced that the matter was worthy of notice." [56] Yet most Federals were skeptical of Southern volunteers, and General Grant is an example of an officer who followed no consistent policy in regard to their enlistment. Immediately after the passage of the first Confederate Conscription Act, he believed that refugees of draft age who came into Federal lines should be inducted, and a year later he ordered that all "draft-dodgers" fleeing into Hurlbut's district be "immediately pressed into service." By 1864,

however, he would only "reluctantly admit the propriety of enlist-
ing deserters and refugees." [57]

While at times hesitant about inducting refugees, both the Confederates and Federals were more willing to use them as guides and
scouts. As such the displaced men could render a real service and at
the same time earn their keep. Orders were often issued which assigned refugees to scouting details. General E. B. Brown used many
displaced Arkansans for this purpose when the Federals were ma-
neuvering in the northern part of the state.[58] One displaced Arkansan
who served for a time as a scout in Tennessee requested transfer to his
home area when the Federals invaded the region. Noting that he was
familiar with the country, he believed that he could be of greater
service to the troops, and his request was granted.[59]

The military policies relating to property, as distinguished from
those relating primarily to personal contacts between the armed forces
and civilians, will be discussed later; but because they did bring the
Federal officials face to face with the people and did cause the displacement of many, brief note is made here. The Federals frequently
commandeered homes which were at the time occupied by Southern
sympathizers, and although both armies followed the practice of taking
over buildings for military purposes, the evicting of women and
children from their homes was always shocking to civilians. General
Robert Huston Milroy made his reputation for ruthlessness early in
the war when he evicted Mrs. Lloyd Logan and her five daughters
from their home in Winchester, Virginia, so that he might use the house
as his headquarters. He gave the family only a few hours to leave the
premises, and they were taken to the edge of town and "set down by
the roadside, destitute of everything." Cornelia McDonald noted
that his action "shocked and outraged the town." Accounts of the
Logans' displacement were carried in the Confederate press and used
as an example of the enemy's vindictiveness.[60]

Mrs. McDonald later had direct contact with General Milroy when
he wanted her home for a hospital, but she called on him and boldly
but tactfully protested his order. He informed her that she should
leave before the "exodus begins" for he momentarily expected orders
to banish all "rebel sympathizers," and said, "By G—— I will do it."
Mrs. McDonald remained silent as he ranted about Confederate sympathizers in general, and soon Milroy was speaking more quietly
and rationally. It was then that she reminded him that he was the
commandant in Winchester, that no one would "interfere" with his
commands, and that he was the only person who could decide what

should be done with her family and her home. When Milroy offered her transportation out of town Mrs. McDonald replied that she had nowhere to go, but she thanked him for his kindness. Because of the way in which she handled the situation, she was permitted to remain in her home. Leaving the interview, Mrs. McDonald noted that she "could almost have kissed his hand," and admitted that he had been very considerate of her, but she also realized that "others had felt the weight of his hand." [61] She, too, might have felt this weight had she approached him with the haughtiness, disdain, and hatred which so many Southern women evidenced under similar circumstances. Yet Cornelia McDonald never once denied that she supported the Confederacy nor that her husband was an officer in its army, but she calmly explained the family's economic plight, listened quietly to Milroy's initial outburst, flattered his ego, and won her case.

Buildings commandeered by the Federals were very often used to house refugees coming into their lines, for the problem of sheltering the displaced people also confronted the military officials. General Butler had no hesitancy about using private homes and other structures for those coming into New Orleans, and the policy was continued after he was removed. Two years after he left the city the Commercial Hotel, which came to be known as "Refugee's Home," was still housing 150 refugees, and in 1864, the provost marshal was told that too many displaced people were being permitted to stay there for indefinite periods and that the practice must cease. It was ordered that these people were to remain only overnight except in rare instances and that "as soon as the oath was administered" they should be sent on their way. Those refusing to subscribe to the oath should be given rations "until they can be returned from whence they came," but during the interim they were not "allowed the freedom of the city." [62]

Typical of the more cautious Confederate orders with regard to commandeering occupied buildings in friendly areas was that issued in the spring of 1862 by General John B. Magruder. Needing buildings for hospitals, he first ordered vacated homes to be taken, and then houses occupied by "males alone." If these did not suffice he ordered "all public offices [seized,] the occupants [to] go into tents," after which hotels would be commandeered before "private families are forced to give up residences." [63] The implication is clear, however, that should the necessity arise even the friendly civilians would have to be evicted. When Confederate officers needed the homes of Southern sympathizers they seldom found the people willing to displace themselves as a patriotic gesture. Many civilians refused to rent their property "at any price," and some who consented asked "exorbitant rents." [64] But a great many Southerners, including refugees, permitted the soldiers to share a part of their home even when they would not displace themselves for the military convenience or need.

Refugees became a greater problem for the armies as the war progressed. Their ranks were composed of all kinds of people and not necessarily just those who were victims of the war. Many who posed as refugees were actually spies, gamblers, smugglers, or prostitutes, and all were nuisances. Federal officers issued an ever-increasing number of orders to send all unnecessary individuals out of camp. In 1862, General Buell commanded from Nashville that "all persons . . . whose presence interferes with the discipline, efficiency and safety" of the army be turned "out of camp." [65] The people who "had no fixed homes" were often classified as "undesirables" and ordered to be on their way. General Sherman had such a problem with this group in northern Mississippi that he commanded "all hangers-on" to leave and not to come again into "any camp under any pretext whatsoever" or they would be sent to Memphis or "put in the work gang." [66] The good and the evil, the exploiter and the indigent, the spy and the loyal supporter were all looked upon in much the same way when they wandered into a military encampment. When the well-meaning people were treated with contempt and suspicion they were embittered and indignant, but the officials were often too desperate to try to distinguish a bona fide refugee from an "undesirable."

Throughout the war refugees in flight became enmeshed with the troop movements and chaos invariably resulted as the displaced civilians were shoved about and the soldiers delayed. Bill Arp facetiously described the "Roman Runagees' " entanglements with the "Konfederate Kavalry," and Cornelia McDonald told of the Winchester refugees being pushed off the roads by the retreating army, and there were many others who reported similar situations. Newspapers frequently commented on the congestion and confusion resulting from soldiers and civilians trying to evacuate a community at the same time, and military reports indicate that this was a serious problem. General Franz Sigel, who was noted for both his military defeats and his recruitment of Germans into the Federal Army, explained that his "masterly retreat" after the Battle of Wilson's Creek was "broken by crowds of refugees, wagons, horses, mules, cows etc. which got mixed up with troops in such a manner that it would have been very difficult to have made any disposition for battle." [67] Knowing that such conditions as these were likely to develop, the military officials wanted the civilians out of the way before a major engagement and it is not surprising that they urged the evacuation of communities. Refugees were inclined to be critical of either army who rode roughshod over them as they traveled the roads of the South, but the troops had a job to do and that came first.

Tens of thousands of displaced Southern sympathizers had personal contact with the armies and it was seldom pleasant. By their very nature civilians wanted to avoid the enemy but most were unable to do so, and his actions in dealing with them were generally interpreted as both unnecessary and diabolical. Many Southerners found that war was not as glamorous as it first seemed to be, especially for the people who were losing, and they sickened of the conflict as well as the enemy long before it ended. But the noncombatants also baffled the Federals who came to realize that they must contend with dedicated Confederates other than those encountered in battle, and in trying to handle this problem, the generals exercised the "rights" accorded them "in time of war."

. . . my property and yours

To Southerners, property was one of the causes of war. Even the refugees, who tore themselves away from certain of their possessions, carried a sense of property with them. In fact, the determination to protect that which was theirs was a major reason for many people refusing to leave home until they were compelled to do so. While thousands were fleeing at the mere mention of "Yankees," the calmer folk paused to consider what might happen to abandoned property—homes, lands, slaves, supplies, and other personal possessions. Southerners not faced with the decision until late in the conflict were more reluctant to leave that which they owned, for by then it was common knowledge that deserted homes and unprotected valuables were more vulnerable to pillage, theft, and damage. Yet those who stayed at home and were then banished left behind far more than most earlier voluntary exiles had been required to forsake. Regardless of when or why they deserted their homes, displaced Southern sympathizers lost millions of dollars worth of abandoned property.

The destruction and damage was not the work of a single group. Although much of it may be attributed to the soldiers, it was not always the Federals who misused, plundered, and stole, nor was it altogether their policies of confiscation and commandeering that resulted in military use of private property. The Confederates were much more willing to make use of their wartime prerogatives in the case of property than they were when dealing with the person of friendly people. The Federals did adopt the theory that the victor owns the spoils, but the Confederates were also known to accept the idea that abandoned possessions belonged to anyone who claimed them. And, in addition to the troops, there were many instances of damage and destruction by other Southerners, slaves, and even the refugees themselves.

Military officials in both camps gave as a reason for the peoples' staying at home that they stood a better chance of protecting their property. They noted that it was difficult or impossible to discipline their men to respect unguarded homes, for their natural curiosity led them to investigate vacant premises and appropriate that which had been left behind. The poor, tired, hungry soldier was always sorely tempted to disregard orders which restricted him in this respect, but he was less likely to ignore them if the owner was at home. There were exceptions, but because the commanders understood the situation they called on the people not to leave their property and often urged those who had done so to return.

General Samuel Curtis discovered that thousands of Arkansans had abandoned their homes "for the victors," and he was "much embarrassed" by his inability "to preserve discipline . . . as these circumstances offered extraordinary temptations." He announced that if "peaceably disposed citizens will stay at home or return . . . much of the havoc of war will be avoided." [1] General Alexander Asboth bluntly informed the Floridians that "deserted Firesides can not be guarded. . . . None therefore should depart. The absent should return." He promised that "every house containing a living soul will have protection." [2] Other officers made similar promises to the people —General McClellan stated that "all" Virginians' homes and "property rights" would be "religiously respected." [3] Regardless of how sincere the officer might be, pledges of this kind could not be guaranteed when the war was being fought on the doorsteps, and any civilian who believed that the guarantees applied to all future time was extremely naïve. Yet many Southerners became bitter and

Cotton was a valuable possession of many Southern civilians, and the question of what to do with this commodity when the owner faced displacement was a major one. If left intact it would be of value to the enemy, but it was too heavy and bulky for most refugees to transport any distance, therfore it became a common practice for the cotton to be burned before it could fall into enemy hands. But fires intended to burn only the cotton often spread to buildings and fences before they could be brought under control. General Thomas West Sherman, incensed by this practice of South Carolinians living critical when the promises were broken.

in coastal areas, ordered that all cotton "in any part" of the state "deserted by the inhabitants" be seized as "property of the Federal Government." [4] This made the people even more determined to destroy their cotton and the practice became widespread over the South. Bales accumulated in the cities were sometimes deliberately fired just before the arrival of the enemy and at other times were accidently ignited during a bombardment, but these conflagrations often spread through blocks of the town and destroyed millions of dollars in property and displaced hundreds of residents. Although the enemy was usually blamed, the origin of cotton fires was not always determined, and in many instances Southerners were responsible.

One of the most foolhardy acts committed by displaced people early in the war was the destruction of their own homes in order to keep them out of enemy hands. They were encouraged in this by many editors who informed the people that it was their patriotic duty to destroy anything that might be of value to the foe. An editorial in the Richmond *Examiner*, in June, 1861, sermonized on this subject and suggested that the people read history, especially the effects of the Russians having burned Moscow before the arrival of Napoleon's forces.[5] The writer urged loyal Southerners to emulate this policy, and a great many other newsmen made an identical comparison and offered the same advice.

Hampton, Virginia, was one of the first victims of the torch, and Confederate General John B. Magruder justified his order that it be burned because it was "a harbor of runaway slaves and traitors" and could not be defended by the Confederates because it was "under the guns of Fortress Monroe." He stated that "the gentlemen of Hampton seemed to concur." Therefore he ordered civilians to leave and "the town was fired in many places and burned to the ground." [6] General Butler, in command of the Federal forces, denounced "the secession inhabitants of Virginia" who had "chosen to . . . destroy [Hampton] . . . under circumstances of cruel indifference to the inhabitants." He reported that during the two months the Federals had occupied the town they had not done more than "$100 worth of damage to the buildings," although his men had "appropriated some furniture from *unoccupied* houses." [7]

The Richmond press made heroes out of the parties responsible for burning Hampton. The *Dispatch* editorialized at great length on the subject, boasting that the village had been "burned by our own people" and warning the enemy that this was "evidence of the readiness of Southern men to sacrifice property . . . rather than surrender it for . . . [his] benefit and advantage." It was predicted that if the "people of the South . . . cannot keep back the enemy, they will give him a desolate country to traverse." In this case, the Hampton citizens were said to have "acquiesced cheerfully" to Magruder's orders and had "set fire to their buildings." Two days later, the same paper encouraged others to do as the Hamptonians had done, for patriots must be willing to destroy their property for the cause just as mothers were willing to sacrifice their sons to the fighting forces. The writer hoped that "no southern father" was so greedy and materialistic that he would "not give up his property even more cheerfully than he would give up his son," and the editor called on the people to light the path of the enemy with "our burning cities." [8] The *Enquirer* voiced the same sentiments, and a reader was so impressed by the editor's impassioned plea that he referred to it as "no less just than eloquent." He noted, however, that many of the Hampton families "are now suffering for their self-sacrifice," and needed assistance which he hoped would be forthcoming from others in the state.[9]

In the first year of the war there were many editorials pleading with people to burn their homes as they fled and praising those who did so. After Elizabeth City, North Carolina, was burned, a Wilmington paper told of the residents having set the fire "rather than permit the Yankees to have" the city, and the editor shouted, "That is the spirit North Carolinians!" He suggested that the homeless "be sustained and reimbursed out of the property of those who . . . ran away" from Wilmington during "the hour of danger." His editorial brought criticism from the more rational, practical folk and in a few weeks he reconsidered his earlier words. As he cited Moscow, he also noted that Paris had never been burned by its inhabitants and was "more proudly the French capital than ever." He offered several modified suggestions to those who were in the path of the enemy: remove all cotton from near the coast "*at once*," put the bales on rafts and "have rosin and turpentine placed on the rafts ready to cast adrift if necessity arises," remove all food and other stores from threatened areas and destroy anything that might be of use to the enemy. Qualifying his earlier statements he reasoned that the possession of buildings "would not advance the cause of the enemy, nor could their destruction retard . . . [his] progress." He also cautioned the people not to act in haste and panic when emergency arose.[10] Pressure from his readers had caused him to advocate a more moderate approach to the problem.

An increasing number of newsmen, officials, and citizens condemned the burning of one's home to keep it from the enemy, but through the summer of 1862 the debate raged. When the Federals were dangerously close to Richmond in the Peninsular Campaign, the *Examiner* continued to insist that "it were better that Richmond's fate be that of Moscow's than that Richmond . . . be inhabited by the invader"; it was confident that the citizens' "patriotism . . . is equal to the sacrifice." [11] When Nashville fell, the *Mississippian* criticized the city's residents for permitting the town to fall to the enemy and said that he "should have been greeted with fire and sword, and if Nashville could not be held, a heap of smoldering ruins should have been the only spoils left to the victors." Recognizing that this would be a difficult choice for a man who had "an idolatrous devotion to his property," the editor declared that for a true patriot "it would be a work of love." The only "sure road to independence" lay in sacrifice of one's possessions and he urged Southerners to "emulate the example of Russia during the French invasion." [12]

All of the supporters of arson were not to be found in newspaper offices. Political leaders urged owners to destroy their property if the enemy approached. In January, 1862, four eminent Georgia leaders addressed their neighbors on the subject of the obligations of the individual to the Confederacy. Howell Cobb, Robert Toombs, Martin J. Crawford, and Thomas R. R. Cobb included as a patriotic duty the destruction of property before permitting it to be taken by the enemy. "Let every woman have a torch, every child a firebrand," ran the instructions; "let the loved homes of your youth be made ashes, and the fields . . . be made desolate. Let blackness and ruin mark your departing steps, . . . and let a desert more terrible than the Sahara welcome the Vandals. Let every city be levelled by flame and every village be lost in ashes." [13] There is no indication that the Georgians took this sermon to heart, but had they done so their grievances against Sherman would have been minimized. He did what the Georgian leaders had suggested and was condemned. Ironically, Sherman made his headquarters for a brief period in the unburned home of Howell Cobb and his men foraged on the "corn, beans, peanuts and sorghum molasses" they found there. They made fires from the fence rails and carried off "an immense quantity" of Cobb's personal possessions. What was left of the property was then confiscated.[14] Clement Claiborne Clay expressed virtually the same sentiments as did the Georgians when he paid tribute to the Carolinians and Virginians who had burned their homes and urged that the Alabamians do likewise.

He told them, "If our arms fail us, *fire will not. The torch can consume what the bayonet may not defend!* Emulate the noble Carolinians." [15]

With so many articulate Southerners goading the people to burn their property it might be supposed that those opposed to such a policy had difficulty counteracting these suggestions. But their language was just as strong and their ideas made sense to the property-conscious people. Six weeks before New Orleans fell, the *Bee* noted that "not the slightest parallel could possibly exist between" the burning of Moscow and the burning of Southern towns, for to "doom to flames a Southern city would afford the most exquisite pleasure to the Yankees." The editor raised the question as to what would be gained by burning New Orleans. "Where would its vast population . . . be sheltered? What city is there within reasonable distance that could receive them?" He urged that anyone setting fire to the city be "shot down or strung-up to the nearest lamp-post." [16] The *Delta* agreed with the opinion of its colleague and pointed out that whereas the French soldiers needed Moscow's buildings to shelter them from the Russian winter, the Northern soldiers "were doing very well in tents" and were not affected by Southern winters. He argued that it would be easier to starve the enemy if he were bottled up in cities rather than encamped in rural areas, and he reminded his readers that "if a city can be taken, it can be retaken." When this was done, the returning refugees would need their homes.[17]

Among the opponents of burning one's property was the editor of the Raleigh *Standard* who questioned both the "policy and propriety" of the Elizabeth City residents because he believed the owners hurt themselves more than they hurt the enemy. "Returning fugitives" who had destroyed their homes as they departed would be "a burden to their friends" who must accommodate them. He referred to those who advocated arson as "hair-brained people" who owned no property themselves. There were only two groups who would encourage such foolish action, "those enemies who wanted to go North to be with friends or those pessimists who expected to be driven into the Gulf of Mexico." However, the people who were "determined to stand and fight the invader would want their homes after the war." [18] Sarah Morgan would have agreed with the Raleigh newsman in this matter of the "hair-brained" folk who had no property but were anxious for others to burn theirs. She said that the people who were most anxious to burn Baton Rouge were "those who had no interest there," and she noted that the farther she moved from the city, "the more ardent the people were to have it burned." Pensively she wrote in her diary, "There is the greatest difference between *my* property and *yours*." [19] The war was to prove the truth of her words, for this simple statement could be applied to the treatment of property in general and not merely to its burning.

The Southern people did great damage to their own property. Jorantha Semmes wrote her husband just before the fall of Memphis, "We are in danger of being burned out by the violent Secessionists who say they will only let the Yankees possess the Ashes of Memphis." As she wrote she could see the "cotton and sugar burning on the bluffs." [20] Perhaps one reason the city was not burned was Mayor John Park's earlier ultimatum that under no circumstances was Memphis to be burned by her citizens. He proclaimed that any person who "attempts to fire his neighbors house or even his own . . . will, regardless of judge, jury or the benefit of clergy [be hanged] to the first lamp post, tree, or awning." He reminded the public that he had the power "to carry out the above individual proclamation." [21] Although the Mayor of Memphis may have thwarted plans for burning that city, H. H. Hoeg of Jacksonville, Florida, did not prevent some of the residents from setting fire to their homes before they left that community. He not only appealed to them not to start fires but urged them to remain at home and go about their usual pursuits, for he felt sure that if they did not resist the enemy, "private property would be respected." [22]

Although fires were responsible for damage and destruction in all parts of the Confederacy, other wartime forces were also at work on the refugees' property. Among these was the Confederate impressment policy to which the displaced people attributed great losses. They realized that they could expect to have the enemy confiscate whatever he might want or need, but when their own army resorted to this practice the civilians were confused and embittered. They looked upon impressment as running counter to the welfare of the very people who supported the Confederate forces, and they believed the troops were responsible for protecting the property as well as the persons of loyal Southerners. Long before the war ended, however, many of these people concluded that it did not really matter which army controlled an area, for both were responsible for the loss of property.

Confederate impressment agents drove civilians into self-imposed exile, preyed on refugees in flight and, like most other problems encountered by displaced people, followed them to their temporary

quarters. Although General Kirby Smith discouraged citizens in northern Louisiana from going to Texas, he assisted others from the southern
and central parts of the state when it seemed that their transportable
property could be saved in this way from Federal confiscation. If
they could evade the enemy and settle on farms in Texas they could
produce food for the Confederacy and he was ready to see them go.
Yet many of these Louisiana planters complained that as soon as they
crossed the Sabine River impressment agents swooped down on them
and took their slaves, vehicles, and animals. Some of the refugees
reported losing from one-third to one-half of their slaves who were
impressed to work on fortifications and perform other services for
the Confederate Army. It was reported from Alexandria in 1863 that
because so many displaced Louisianians were having their wagons,
teams, and Negroes impressed en route to Texas many planters were
refusing to move out of the path of the enemy. Others who had started
for Texas had returned "preferring to live with the enemy" rather
than risk property losses along the way.[23]

General Magruder had ordered the impressment of Negroes belonging to Texans and therefore felt justified in taking those of displaced
people crossing into the state. When Kirby Smith instructed him to
wait until the Louisianians were settled in Texas before impressing
their slaves or other property, Magruder answered that he was in
urgent need of all the Negroes he could get and did not think it right
for the Texas citizens to be forced to give theirs when the refugees
were exempt. He made it very clear that he had no intention of permitting the displaced Louisianians to interfere with his military program.[24] Kirby Smith thought it very unwise to impress private property of those en route to new homes, and in November, 1863, he
ordered that the practice cease. His orders read:

The great abuse of authority by officers in impressing wagons, teams etc.,
belonging to persons changing their homes, and the annoyance arising
therefrom, demands the most stringent orders and rigid enforcement. Hereafter refugees with their property must not be interfered with or molested
in any manner whatever until they have acquired a home.

The punishment for any officer disobeying this order would be immediate court martial.[25]

Elsewhere in the Confederacy refugees had similar troubles with
impressment agents and even those who went to Mexico were often
confronted with the same problem. Although many people who
crossed the Rio Grande were Unionists, others were Southern sympathizers or persons with no deep-seated convictions. They were

leaving Confederate territory for economic or personal reasons and as they traveled toward the border they often reported that Confederate impressment authorities followed them. When they crossed into Mexico these agents sometimes reported to Mexican officials that the refugees had stolen horses and they had been commissioned by Confederate authorities to return them to their rightful owners. This may have been a just accusation in some instances but in others it was not, and the agents were accused of using this means to impress the animals for army use. General Napoleon J. T. Dana, when confronted with this situation, demanded an investigation and learned that not only had the refugees been deprived of their horses but had also been imprisoned in Monterey.[26] Refugees testified, as did others, that it mattered not where they went, they could not escape the impressment agents.

Most Southerners resented the policy of impressment as a violation of their property rights, and despite the hard-fought war going on around them, they thought of these rights as being the same as they had enjoyed in time of peace. They were often angry when compelled to part with anything they owned and they could not understand why the friendly army would force them to give that which they had not offered voluntarily. However, there were individuals who took a more positive view of the situation, as did a refugee from Memphis who settled in a colony of displaced neighbors near Demopolis, Alabama. By 1864, most of these friends had returned to their homes within Federal lines and were encouraging that she and her husband also come back because provisions were more plentiful and conditions more settled there. The couple determined to remain within Confederate lines so as to maintain contact with their sons in the army, but the mother worried constantly about her boys not having enough to eat. When she heard others complain about the impressment agents taking provisions from farmers in the area, she wrote her son that she wished "the government . . . [would] impress every lb. of bacon in . . . [Alabama] and Georgia" for the use of the Confederate Army.[27] Her statement must be interpreted as a mother's natural concern for her sons, and under other conditions she might have less ardently supported impressment, for most refugees vehemently protested the policy.

Displaced people had difficulty protecting the possessions they had with them, but their abandoned property was even more likely to be impressed or confiscated by the armies. The Confederates may have been more reluctant than the Federals to take over occupied buildings but they did not hesitate to use those which were vacant. Both armies used houses and other structures as barracks, hospitals, stables, and storage depots with the result that the property was damaged, whether through carelessness, maliciousness, or hard use. Soldiers had no personal interest in the property and concluded that the owner must consider it of little value since he had left it to its fate. Therefore no attempt was made to care for it and the buildings were often defaced, the furnishings damaged or stolen, and edibles consumed by ravenous soldiers. There was little if any difference between the destructive inclinations of the Federals and the Confederates when they appropriated abandoned property, often under orders from their commanders. Typical of such orders was that of a Confederate in Arkansas who instructed his officers to billet their men in any deserted farmhouses found in the area.[28] No question was raised in this instance nor in thousands of others as to whether or not military use of private property was just or legal, for during war the issue is not important to anyone except the owner.

Southern sympathizers criticized the enemy for appropriating property for any use whatever, but the Confederates adopted the same policy. A chaplain entering Bowling Green, Kentucky, with Terry's Rangers, noted that many of the "wealthiest inhabitants . . . [had] joined the exodus to the North," leaving their beautiful homes unguarded. "As each palatial mansion is vacated," wrote the chaplain, "it . . . becomes a home for some refugee, the headquarters of some officer, or a quiet resting place for the sick soldier." But he also emphasized that many of the most luxurious houses were assigned to the "refugees from the Lincolnized portion of Kentucky who . . . sought safety" within Confederate lines. Later, when the Confederates and their friends were forced to retreat, he was shocked to see these refugees set fire to the homes they had been occupying, and he reported that he had never witnessed "such consternation, confusion and alarm" as he did that day.[29]

When displaced people received word that their abandoned property was being used by either army they very often registered protests where they felt it would do the most good. A refugee from coastal South Carolina heard that the military authorities were not only using his home and grounds but had also permitted a soldier to be buried in his family's private cemetery. This was more than he could stand and he protested to the military authorities in Charleston: "When the citizen is called upon to part with his property for the benefit of the country at large, it is his duty to submit patiently," but at the same time the "military authorities should defend the same while they occupy it." He let it be known that he expected the commander in charge to see that the body of the soldier was "disinterred and . . . placed in its proper burial grounds." There was no room for even a Confederate soldier in the family plot.[30]

Because civilians recognized that abandoned property was more likely to be damaged, stolen, or destroyed, they tried to make arrangements for its protection if time permitted. Transportable possessions were often left with trusted neighbors and servants who remained behind, and sometimes they were taken great distances and deposited where it was presumed they would be safe. As previously noted, Sarah Wadley's father sent many of the family's cherished possessions to Marshall, Texas, and once considered shipping them to Germany. Others transported various items to the home of friends or relatives, but usually they were deposited somewhere in the general area. People indicated by these actions that they expected destruction in their absence and yet they were indignant when it occurred. Others who had been more trusting and less realistic were shocked to see the damage wrought by the armies, especially the friendly forces. A refugee who left Washington to live within Confederate lines took his family to his wife's estate in Virginia, and he was dismayed and embittered by the way the Southern soldiers had demolished the property. The house had been pillaged, personal papers and other possessions stolen, and outbuildings and fences destroyed. His wife "grieved over the vandalism" because many of the missing items were family heirlooms. The incensed refugee commented, "The country around here is more like an enemy's country than the homes of loyal citizens. The whole place will have to be deserted." Yet he did not know where he and his family of seven children would go.[31]

Nothing was more disillusioning than having a friend act the role of the foe. Editors in many communities criticized the misuse of the refugees' property by the military and condemned malicious destruction by others. Those in Charleston frequently cited cases of unnecessary demolition by the Confederates after the property "had been visited and respected by the Yankees." They told of "spoilation from the hands of those who should have been protectors," and reminded the Confederates that they owed the refugee positive protection of the homes they had left behind. Readers were told that "a very fine piano" left in one of the plantation homes had been "cut to pieces by [Confederate] soldiers for the sake of procuring the wire cords as pipe cleaners." [32] Stories of this kind circulated in the Southern press were intended to reprimand the guilty parties, but they served also to disillusion and embitter the displaced people who were always concerned about their property.

Although the Federals cannot be blamed with all destruction done to the refugee's property, they were responsible for much of it. Their officers often ordered that it be demolished and at other times they condoned or ignored destruction and looting by their troops, but it was frequently a case of being unable to keep their men in line. Individual soldiers were known to act on impulse, as did those who fired the home of John Letcher in Lexington; and Sherman's order that his men were to "forage liberally" on their march across Georgia was interpreted in its broadest terms. In an unchallenged military movement of this kind, the victorious troops celebrated as they advanced and committed a great many diabolical acts which were not specifically called for nor condoned by the leaders. Although the commanders were not always blameless, many charges were made against them which should have been leveled at men who were often acting counter to orders. Colonel John B. Turchin, who ordered the complete destruction of Athens, Alabama, stands out as an example of an officer who was directly responsible for wholesale, unjustified spoliation of property. And others left the way open for greater damage when, like Sherman, they implied it in their orders. The same was true of Grant's statement that if Hunter had to retreat down the Valley of Virginia he was to remove "every particle of provisions and stock, . . . [and] eat Virginia clear and clean . . . so that crows flying over it for the balance of the season . . . [would] have to carry their provider with them." [33] Orders of this kind encouraged Federal soldiers to commit depredations when they might otherwise have hesitated to do so.

Newspapermen accompanying the Federals into the South frequently commented on the damage done by the troops. These accounts, when reprinted in Southern papers, served a double purpose: to inform noncombatants as to what they could expect should the enemy reach their doors and to arouse their fighting spirit. The reports originating in the Federal camp were graphic portrayals of the damage done. A correspondent for the Chicago *Tribune*, who accompanied the Federals to Fort Henry, referred to the march as "a disgraceful one." He noted that the people had fled ahead of the invasion and that their homes had "been stripped of everything portable, useful or otherwise, and that which was not portable, . . . destroyed." The soldiers took "every domestic fowl, calf, pig or anything living" which could be used as food.[34] It was a St. Louis reporter who told of the firing of Alexandria, Louisiana, and of General Banks's refusal to take the homeless citizens away from the burning town.[35] These horrifying descriptions and the valuable military information divulged by newspapermen explain why the officers so often questioned the advisability of promiscuously circulating these reports. The archenemy of the correspondents, William T. Sherman, once told a Cincinnati correspondent, "We don't want the truth told about things here—that's what we *don't* want." [36] Peace-loving, humane Northerners could become critical of needless, wholesale destruction and pillage.

Negroes were also responsible for damage done the property of refugees. When a few trusted slaves were left by the owners to guard the possessions they could not always carry out the assignment if others in the area were bent on destruction, and it was often the Negroes from neighboring plantations who sacked and looted the homes of displaced people. Much of the damage to plantations in coastal areas of the Carolinas and Georgia was that of the slaves whom Thomas West Sherman referred to as "hordes of apparently discontented blacks." [37] General Ambrose Burnside reported that nine-tenths of the damage done in New Bern, North Carolina, must be attributed to the Negroes who pillaged and looted the refugees' property before the Federals arrived.[38] Negroes ransacked Kate Stone's home and the presence of these unruly slaves, as much as that of the Federals, provoked the family to flee from "Brokenburn" in the middle of the night. The Stones, having stayed at home long after many of their neighbors left, witnessed the Negroes' destruction and pillage of abandoned property. When the family finally decided to flee Kate noted that only two "half-grown" slaves were willing to accompany them and that the remainder stayed behind to do as they pleased.[39] The opportunity to ransack the homes of their recent masters and mistresses was a great temptation for most Negroes, and if they did not divide the spoils among themselves those from neighboring plantations would probably do so. Despite the problems involved in transporting one's slaves with the family it was sometimes a precautionary measure.

Negroes who remained on the property frequently gave vital information to the invader. They told where prized possessions were hidden, where food was stored, and often identified the owner of the property. When the absentee landlord was a prominent military or political official or an ardent secessionist his property was almost sure to receive rough treatment from the enemy, and the home was frequently burned. The families of these leaders were the ones most apt to flee, and yet their abandoned property was especially vulnerable to Federal depredations. When they left trusted servants in charge of their homes they hoped that their ownership would not be divulged, but if some Negroes were loyal, others were not, and all were so afraid of the Yankees that most could be easily pressured into telling anything. Often without meaning to do so they could embellish the facts to the detriment of the owner.

As dangerous as the slaves might be, they were no more so than vindictive neighbors who stayed at home and awaited the enemy, for these people were also guilty of looting the abandoned property and aiding the Federals. General Grenville Dodge reported that his men were joined by "a large group" of Unionists and Negroes who combined talents for the destruction of "the garden spot of Alabama" which they "rendered useless." [40] Sarah Wadley was both shocked and disgusted with her turncoat neighbors who managed to benefit themselves by getting into the good graces of the Federals. They took over valuable property left by the refugees and one man, whom Sarah identified as "Old Montague," especially angered her with his activities. She said that he was "a perfect traitor to the country," and that he had enriched himself by "working several plantations owned by refugees" which he obtained only after ingratiating himself to the enemy.[41]

Similar indictments were made in all areas of the Confederacy. A Federal officer marching into Manassas Junction in 1862 reported the village deserted "except for a few citizens with two or three wagons [who were] loading the spoils left by the rebels." [42] During J. G. M. Ramsey's displacement, his home was burned and many of his papers, manuscripts, and books were destroyed in the fire, but others were stolen earlier. After the war he happened to see a part of his library for sale "in a Book Store on Gay Street in Knoxville," and he was not sure who was responsible for the theft, but he made no attempt to reclaim the volumes nor run down the culprit. He preferred to leave the books "to bear evidence of some one's atrocious dishonesty." [43]

Some refugees managed to dash back to their homes during the war and dash away again. Their curiosity and concern over their property was so great that they were willing to take whatever personal risk might be involved. When Mrs. Elizabeth Meriwether slipped back into Memphis in 1864, she found that her home had been confiscated and rented to persons who paid rent to the Federal officials. She did not go into the house but was pleased to note that it appeared to be undamaged. A building in the business district had also been confiscated but the grocer to whom she had rented it was still there, and she was overwhelmed to learn that he had paid only a part of the rent to the Federals and the rest he was saving for her. This he gave in gold to Mrs. Meriwether when she visited Memphis, and the refugee was grateful for the unexpected windfall and for the loyalty of her friend.[44]

Mrs. Meriwether's brief return to her home was far happier than was that of most others who made a quick tour of inspection. Sarah Morgan's visit to hers in Baton Rouge was heartbreaking. The Morgans had stayed at home for three months after the Federals occupied the city, and during the period their property and persons were guarded by sentries. Mrs. Morgan and her daughters talked of leaving the city during these months but they knew that their chances were better for protecting their home if they remained. However, when the Confederates attempted to retake the city, the family left and when Sarah and her sister made a quick trip back they found that it had not been burned or possessed by Negroes as had others, but it had been ransacked. A neighbor told her that he had tried to prevent the looting and because of this his own home had been sacked. Sarah reported that her home had been so "shockingly treated" that "strangers and friends flocked in to see the ravages . . . ," and one man asked for a piece of mirror as a memento so that he might take it with him to show people in Mississippi "a specimen of Yankee Vandalism." Clothes, books, furniture, keepsakes, papers, and other possessions were gone or strewn about the floors, broken, torn, or ruined. Family portraits were slashed and "every book of any value or interest, except Hume and Gibbon, were 'borrowed' permanently." [45] Although her sister had visited the house earlier and warned Sarah of what she would find, she was nevertheless shocked and saddened as she stared about her in disbelief.

Others reported on the condition of their property during the war. A refugee from Galveston made a business trip back to the city while it was in Confederate hands and was surprised to find no great damage done to his home, but he feared it would be if Confederate troops were billeted there as planned, for as a vacant house it was liable for impressment. He was dejected by the neglect of the grounds which were "overgrown with weeds," but he did not report theft or damage to the furnishings.[46] Despite his reassurances his wife worried constantly about their possessions, and this was both natural and justified, for even when the houses were left intact and showed no great damage, the furnishings were very often taken. Federal troops were reported to have "carried off a considerable quantity of furniture from the deserted homes" along the Georgia coast, and many abandoned "houses of rebels" in the Pensacola area were filled with furniture which was ordered brought into the town and "distributed among officers at their quarters" or taken "to the hospital." [47] From Fernandina came the report that the refugees' abandoned property had suffered great damage, the fences and weatherboarding used as fuel and the vacant buildings taken over "by the military authorities and homeless people." The correspondent stated that "most of the property abandoned by the 'secesh,' both real and personal, has been disposed of at auction," and two of the finest homes in town had been sold for "$5 each and . . . occupied by Yankee teachers." None were sold for more than $100, according to the reporter.[48]

Governor Henry W. Allen of Louisiana appointed a commission to investigate and report on damages done by Federal troops in western Louisiana during 1863 and 1864, and the commission's findings clearly indicate that the greatest damage done in this one area occurred after the owners had left their homes. The report states that "instances [of destruction] were rare where . . . dwellings were occupied. . . . The country was full of deserted houses from which families had fled," and these were carelessly treated. But when the houses were occupied the residents were usually not molested, and even in instances where the enemy needed the building for military use, the occupants were simply confined to several rooms and were rarely evicted. In certain cases during the winter of 1863–64, "all unoccupied buildings . . . [were] torn down and consumed for fuel." [49]

It mattered little who did the damage to the abandoned property, the fact remains that it was done. When soldiers used the houses, they were indifferent as to the grandeur of the dwelling and the richness of its furnishings. They did not care where their tobacco juice landed nor what effect their rough, muddy boots had on the upholstery. They often wrote on the walls and used fences, shutters, furniture, or anything else they could find to build their fires. A Texas editor, and others, protested the way in which Confederate soldiers tore down "fences and out-houses" to use for fuel and commented that such depredations were less likely to occur if the owners were present. He maintained that although the commanders might try to protect the property "fires must be made . . . [and] fences and houses disappear every week" for this reason.[50]

Sarah Morgan was correct in saying that there is "the greatest difference between *my* property and *yours*," for the only person likely to protect it was the owner, and most people cared little what happened to that of others. Abandoned possessions belonged to no one and to everyone, and those using the property could not be expected to treat it as they would their own. Those who under more normal circumstances never would have thought of taking that which did not belong to them reasoned that what was left would be claimed by someone else if not by them. Therefore, the first on the scene had first choice. War is never conducive to the preservation of property situated in the battle area where civilians as well as soldiers are expected to guard the homes, and so it was during the Civil War. When the people fled by the thousands they deserted their property, as one correspondent noted, "to the great destroyer—war." [51]

. . . the greatest sufferers

The Confederacy was slow to recognize a need for a refugee relief program. In fact, such a need did not appear to have occurred to the Southern mind in the war's first months. No preparation was made for the care of displaced people until the necessity for an aid program was so great that it could no longer be ignored. Even then nothing was done about establishing a centralized agency whose responsibility it would be to assist the homeless people. As the problem became more serious the states formulated various programs designed to aid refugees within their borders, but it was only in the last two years of the war that most states specifically provided for the displaced people. When large groups were set adrift, as in the case of the Fredericksburg, New Orleans, and Atlanta citizens, appeals were made for relief contributions, but after a few months and long before the need had disappeared each of these programs died and nothing more was done in the way of organized assistance until another mass displacement attracted public attention. Although individuals rendered an undetermined amount of aid to the refugees, organized charities were few in number and relief legislation was inadequate.

Newspapers proved to be friends to needy refugees, and even those editors who rued the day they settled in the community were often the first to call attention to their needs. They supported fund-raising drives, collected and dispersed thousands of dollars in aid, publicized meetings and entertainments to raise money for refugee relief, and called on legislatures to assist the indigent displaced people. Newspapers devoted space to editorials on the subject, to listing donors to the various funds, and to commenting on those whose story or predicament would be sure to arouse human interest. Had it not been for the newspaper crusades the refugees would have experienced even greater suffering, yet it was not until midway in the war that the press made a concerted effort to educate the public on the hardships of this group. This peculiar wartime problem dawned slowly on the editors as it did on others, but as the number of displaced people increased and as the Federals more boldly banished thousands into Confederate lines, it could no longer be ignored. The newspapers brought the refugees' story to those in uninvaded areas who otherwise would have been unaware of the magnitude of the problem and the extent of the suffering.

The editor of the Wilmington *Journal*, in 1863, called attention to the war's effects on various groups in the South and concluded, "The refugees are the greatest sufferers . . . and deservedly enlist . . . sympathy and admiration." He ranked in second place "the women who supported themselves and [their] families," many of whom were also refugees. The editor believed that "farmers, merchants, mechanics and brokers [were] . . . doing better than before the war." Although the accuracy of this generalization might be questioned, the writer's sympathy for the displaced people is evident. His purpose in editorializing on this subject was to urge that the profiteers be "taxed more heavily for the benefit of the unfortunates." [1]

Although the refugees were never given the consideration tendered the soldiers, in the spring of 1864, the Columbia *Guardian* called for the founding of an organization similar to those created to assist the servicemen. This suggestion attracted the attention of other newspapers, among them the Charleston *Mercury*, Columbia *South Carolinian*, Athens *Southern Banner*, and Galveston *News* in Houston, which reprinted the editorial. The editor of the *South Carolinian* noted that if people failed to recognize their responsibility to the refugees they would be guilty of a "crime" which, if permitted "to spread to any great extent," would compel the writer to conclude 'the nation had lost all capacity to appreciate its duty." But lost also would be "all title to the sympathies of the world and all rights to the protection of God." He thought that the lack of a refugee relief program was a "horrible exhibition of selfishness," and only because he feared "violating some of the proprieties of journalism" did he restrain himself from expressing "half the indignation" he felt.[2] This diatribe came in the third spring of the war when, as yet, nothing more than erratic, disorganized relief had been provided the displaced people.

Commenting on the *Guardian*'s proposal, the editor of the *Southern*

Banner not only supported the idea but added, "There is no doubt . . . that there is suffering, and the refugees are the principle sufferers." He noted also that the "families of soldiers are wisely and amply provided for by the State Legislature, but . . . no legislation nor concerted action of committees has been had for men who have been deprived of their homes and stript [*sic*] of their whole fortunes." He attributed this lack of policy to the "silent and uncomplaining manner in which these people have borne their privations," and to so many of them being from well-educated, affluent, proud classes that "the world does not know how much they bear." He called on Georgians to formulate "some practical measures for their relief" which would be "more efficient and less repulsive than . . . individual aid which may in their eyes assume the appearance of charity." [3]

Excepting the spasmodic assistance of both armies, very little was done by either government to help the refugees until the United States Congress established the Freedman's Bureau in March, 1865. This agency did assist white refugees to return to their homes or place of employment and it fed and rendered other aid to them, but it was primarily concerned with Negroes and Unionists, as were the various Federal agencies established earlier.[4] However, Congress made no appropriation to the Bureau until July, 1866, and in the meantime income from abandoned lands dwindled. Therefore, it did not aid displaced Southern sympathizers during the war, and those within Confederate lines throughout the conflict got only sporadic aid from the Confederate Army, local organizations, a few organized groups, and interested civilians. The Confederate Congress evidenced almost no interest in the homeless civilians, but this body rarely enacted laws which might have remedied the people's daily problems. Political, military, and diplomatic issues consumed the legislators' time and attention, and about the only interest shown in the refugees related to whether or not they should be conscripted.

Except in a few instances when the political leaders could not ignore the refugees, they expressed little interest in them. President Davis was especially indifferent to their plight although he did occasionally mention them, but he gave no indication of thinking that they were a problem worthy of consideration by the Confederate government. Typical of his disinterest was his attitude toward the Atlanta exiles. These people had arrived in Macon only a few days before Davis unexpectedly appeared in the city, and on the evening of his arrival a meeting was scheduled to discuss "a means of relief" for the displaced Atlantans. The President was invited to address the meeting and make suggestions as to how the problem could be handled, but when he came before the group he devoted most of his speech to the need for additional troops and in closing, he merely expressed the hope that "the refugees and the exiles would be well provided for." To the great disappointment of his audience, he only "alluded to the object for which the meeting had assembled." [5] This was typical of his other statements relating to displaced Southern sympathizers but it was also typical of the degree of interest evidenced by many other citizens.

Laws designed to aid refugees originated primarily with the state legislatures, and this can be attributed, in part, to the States' Rights philosophy which maintained that such matters were the prerogative and responsibility of the state and not of the Confederate government. State officials were also closer to the problems of the citizens and it was to these men that the people most often directed their requests and complaints. Yet even the state leaders were exceedingly slow to recognize the problem, and legislatures procrastinated in enacting relief legislation applicable to refugees. Most state aid early in the war came from funds established by law to assist other groups which in many instances could be interpreted to include refugees. However, most displaced people were ineligible for state aid during the first two years of the war. It was 1863 or later before most states made any specific provision for them.

All Southern states enacted laws providing assistance for the indigent families of soldiers, and the laws in South Carolina, Alabama, Texas, Tennessee, Arkansas, North Carolina, and Mississippi were so worded that they could apply to families driven from the county in which they had registered.[6] Virginia, Georgia, Florida, and Louisiana had to amend their original laws or enact new ones to take care of the displaced families of soldiers. Georgia provided that the refugees would be issued certificates which they could take into another county of the state and which were to be honored by the proper officials in that county. In 1864, Georgia enacted a separate law providing for any refugees whether or not they were families of soldiers.[7] Florida was one of the first states to provide relief for servicemen's families, but it was not until 1863 that provision was made for those who left their home county because "of invasion." [8] It was also in 1863 that Louisiana legislated in behalf of indigent refugees from "the occupied parishes," whether or not they had relatives in the service.[9] Excepting the laws of Georgia and Louisiana, those in the other states were applicable only to the displaced, indigent families of soldiers, or in some cases, their widows and orphans, or disabled servicemen.

Legislation in several states provided for the relief of certain groups of refugees. South Carolina, for example, appropriated money for the "transient poor" in several cities. From 1861 through 1863, an annual appropriation of $7,000 was made to the Charleston City Council for this purpose and in 1864, it was increased to $10,000.[10] This represented only a fraction of the amount expended for "the transient poor" in Charleston; it was reported to the General Assembly in 1863 that during that year the city had spent $27,574.84 in addition to the state appropriation. Charleston had also expended $79,605.64 on other indigent people, many of whom were refugees.[11]

During the last two years of the war the Georgia legislature passed several laws which benefited refugees. "Because of enemy depredations, drouth and early frost" in the state's sixteen northern counties, the legislature provided in 1863 for the distribution of 93,000 bushels of corn to those in need. The indigent families of soldiers would be given their allotment after which the remainder would be distributed first to other destitute persons and then to those who would pay the transportation cost. Four months later, in a called session, the legislature noted that many of these northern counties had been overrun by the enemy since the passage of the original acts, and for this reason any of their citizens who had fled to other counties would be "entitled to the benefit of the acts." [12] In November, 1863, the Georgia Assembly voted a tax levy on the citizens of Chatham County, the income to be used "to pay house rent for indigent families of soldiers, not to exceed $8.33 a month." [13] While this law does not specifically include refugees, it is safe to assume that those who were indigent and related to Confederate soldiers benefited from its provisions.

The most ambitious refugee project approved by the Georgia General Assembly was the Fosterville settlement established for the Atlanta exiles in Terrell County. It was already in existence when the legislature convened in November, 1864, and Governor Brown sought the body's approval and requested that "proper provision be made by law to supply those who are destitute, with shelter and the necessities of life till they can provide for themselves." [14] On March 11, 1865, Quartermaster General Ira Foster was authorized "to continue to provide for maintenance of said exiles, or such of them as are unable by their labor to support themselves, and their families for the balance of the present year." Foster was authorized to draw on funds allotted his department and required to keep a list of all persons so aided, his records to be submitted to the governor who would report at the next meeting of the General Assembly.[15]

The Louisiana lawmakers were especially "refugee-conscious" and included the displaced people in various aid programs. In June, 1863, the legislature appropriated $300,000 for the relief of destitute individuals "expelled by the Federal authorities of New Orleans." This is especially significant because other states made no provision for their displaced citizens who crossed state lines. The law specified that any of the impoverished New Orleans exiles were eligible for this assistance except men of conscription age, and the governor was authorized "to appoint one or more commissioners to proceed to Mobile and such other places as may be necessary, for the purpose of distributing . . . as much of said appropriation as may be necessary . . . not exceeding $50 to each individual." In the preface to the act the legislators expressed heartfelt sympathy for the "unfortunate citizens" who had been exiled, "deprived . . . of their property," and landed "destitute on the Shores of the States of the Confederacy." [16]

Several states appropriated money to be used in the removal of noncombatants from endangered areas. During the Peninsular Campaign, the Virginia General Assembly allotted $200,000 to aid in the removal and "temporary maintenance of such persons as may . . . be unable to withdraw from the effects of . . . bombardment." A proviso was added, however, that this money could be used only if "notice is given by the proper authorities for the removal of such persons." [17] South Carolina provided free "refugee tickets" to indigent Charlestonians when General Beauregard was trying to remove the residents from the city in 1863. All of the money appropriated for this purpose was not used, however, and $5,000 was withdrawn and used to purchase cotton cards and spinning wheels for any of the 4,500 indigent evacuees who needed them to make cloth.[18] Georgia also appropriated $300,000 for the removal of "indigent white noncombattants [*sic*] . . . from any part of the State threatened with invasion or attack," but this money could be used only if military authorities ordered a mass evacuation.[19] Alabama made a similar provision for removing "helpless women and children" from Mobile.[20] Only in Georgia did the law apply to any area within the state; in all other cases the funds were to be used in the evacuation of a specific community. The majority of refugees had no assistance when they chose to flee and were entirely dependent on themselves unless they had assistance from the armies.

State legislatures authorized certain business and financial groups to change their place of residence when this was necessary to protect their assets. Banks and insurance companies were most often included in these laws, the first of which was enacted in Virginia and related specifically to banks. Typical of the laws in other states, it placed the responsibility for the removal on the president and directors of the institution and gave them the privilege of conducting business in their temporary quarters. However, when the home area was free from danger the banks must return, and under no conditions were they to be moved out of Virginia. These same conditions applied to insurance companies which were sometimes, as in the case of Florida, provided for in the same law as the banks, and in other cases, as in Virginia, in separate statutes.[21]

Provision was also made for the removal of courts, court records, state and county offices, and archives. In the case of county courts and offices the laws required that they remain in the county if possible and if not, they must remain in the state. The Mississippi law, however, allowed county officials to go "to the most convenient place of safety." [22] Before the war it had been legal for the Georgia Supreme Court to sit only in Atlanta, Milledgeville, or Macon, but in 1864 the General Assembly took note of the situation and provided that the Court might "move to such places in the State" as it may "deem best for the interest of the people." [23] Other states enacted similar laws which approved the removal of government offices, but in Alabama the county official entrusted with the removal "of any records, papers or books" was to make "the best arrangements and provision he can for their preservation." [24] In Arkansas the legislature specifically granted the governor the right to remove the state government out of the state "in case the enemy overruns the whole State, . . . and when the danger is removed to immediately cause the same to be reconvened in the State Capital, wherever it may be." It was at this time, September, 1864, in Washington near the Louisiana and Texas lines, and it looked as though it might be pushed into either of these states. However, the act drew such protests from the citizens that it was repealed.[25] Ironically the Louisiana legislature belatedly approved the removal of the capital from Baton Rouge to Opelousas and then to Shreveport after it was temporarily located in Opelousas. It appropriated $5,000 to be used in the removal of state records should it again be necessary.[26]

Other groups were provided for in state laws, including executors, administrators, curators, guardians, trustees, and holders of mortgaged properties, who were granted permission to remove their properties and papers to places of safety. The Florida law itemized possessions which might be legally moved when an area was endangered, including "all negroes, mules, horses, cattle and other perishable property." [27] The Louisiana General Assembly legislated on the right of the people to remove their personal property out of the state in February, 1865, but by this time hundreds had already done so.[28] In the same month the Louisiana legislators tried to solve the problem of the lack of food and fodder by providing for the cultivation of abandoned farms and plantations. The governor was to appoint "one or more Syndics in each parish to take charge and work" the abandoned properties of "enemy aliens" and to confiscate all "mules, horses and implements of husbandry found thereon." Lands belonging to loyal Confederates and having unsupervised slaves on the premises were to be worked in order to produce supplies and at the same time protect the property until the owners returned.[29]

In all Confederate states laws were passed to exempt refugees and others from a part or all of their property taxes. Since most of these related to land, slaves, and other property within Federal lines, the refugees stood to benefit from the legislation. However, when the property was under Federal jurisdiction the state governments could not collect the taxes from citizens staying at home. The intent of these laws was to cancel the levies until the area was freed from enemy control. South Carolina enacted the first tax-exemption law in December, 1861, extending it thereafter for each year of the war, and by 1863 other states had adopted similar measures. The Georgia law of 1863 made specific mention of refugees who were to be exempt of all taxes on their abandoned property except "a nominal tax of one cent per acre." Later legislation suspended all tax collection in "overrun areas . . . until a reasonable time after it was freed of the enemy," and only a month before the war's end the Georgia General Assembly provided for the refunding of all taxes paid in 1864 on "property destroyed or rendered valueless by the enemy or casualty of war." [30]

Alabama suspended tax collection for one year at a time and Louisiana enacted similar laws which were applicable everywhere in the state and not merely in overrun areas, excepting "licenses on trades, professions and occupations." [31] In January, 1863, the Louisiana General Assembly also suspended collection of municipal taxes in occupied cities "during the present war and six months thereafter." [32] There is a certain pathos in this legislation which implies that the legislatures simply accepted that which could not be remedied at the time, yet they were trying to offer immediate relief to those whose properties lay in occupied areas and were working on the assumption that when the enemy was driven out, the returning refugees would not be burdened with a backlog of unpaid taxes. They did not foresee the South's defeat, the confiscation of abandoned property, and other complicating factors resulting from the Confederacy's losing the war.

Other laws were enacted to protect the property of refugees by preventing foreclosures, sale of land for back taxes, and impressment. An 1861 Texas statute suspended "all laws for the collection of debts and liabilities on bonds, promissary notes, bills of exchange, and contracts for payment of money until January 1, 1864," and this was later amended to extend for twelve months after peace or until otherwise provided by law.[33] Laws in other states generally included the same provisions. Because the people protested against state and Confederate impressment policies, legislatures sometimes petitioned that refugees be exempt. The Georgia General Assembly, in 1862, resolved:

Whereas, there are several persons, refugees from the coast of this State, . . . who have had a portion of their slaves seized and carried off . . . ; and whereas, said persons have purchased lands in the interior, . . . for the future support of their families; and whereas, the slaves of such persons are now subject to impressment for public defense, . . . Resolved That the Governor be requested to relieve said citizens from such impressment of their slaves.[34]

In an effort to protect against impressment the property of refugees and of those bringing produce to market, an Alabama law specifically forbade the impressment of "wagons, teams of mules or horses and negroes . . . except on the plantation or residence of the owner."[35]

In July, 1864, the Washington (Arkansas) *Telegraph* called attention to the lack of legislation providing for the probating of wills of those who had left home to avoid the enemy, and the editor urged the General Assembly to study the matter which was of "grave importance and demands immediate legislative action." He noted also that "the evils are already felt, and several hardships have occurred." The following fall, the legislature authorized any probate court in the state to issue "Letters of Administration" upon the estates of deceased persons when such estates and properties were located anywhere in the state of Arkansas.[36]

Among the laws which could affect refugees were those relating to lost baggage. One such enactment was that of the Mississippi General Assembly which made railroads responsible for all freight and baggage consigned to them, notwithstanding "any obligation which may be entered into between the railroads and other parties."[37] Another was a Georgia law of March, 1865, which "compelled keepers of Inns, Hotels and other houses of public entertainment to give receipts or checks for the baggage of their guests when requested to do so." Failure to comply carried a fine of "not more than $500."[38]

All state legislatures passed laws and resolutions and governors issued proclamations in behalf of displaced citizens. They were intended as concessions to these people but some either complicated the situation or were of slight consequence. Legislation giving the refugees the right to vote in counties other than those in which they had previously lived ostensibly favored this group, but the process was usually so complicated that it is doubtful the laws favored the potential voters. A Virginia law gave the refugees the right to vote "in any election [in which] they would be entitled to vote in the county or corporation of their domicil [*sic*]" but they could cast their ballot only at the county courthouse and not in the precinct polling places.[39] This provision incensed a Lynchburg editor who said that he hoped the refugees would go to the polls but he doubted that many would if they lived some distance from the county seat.[40]

Individual displaced people figured in the business of the state legislatures. The 1861 session of the Texas General Assembly jointly resolved that the wives of General Sterling Price and Captain Dave Bouldin be welcomed to the state. Both were refugees, "having sought safety in Texas, from the horrors of war now raging in Missouri." Mrs. Price was welcomed "out of respect to her and admiration for her gallant husband, for the brilliant victories he has achieved at the head of the army of Missouri, in defense of the southern cause. . . ." Because Mrs. Bouldin was accredited with carrying "the news of the position and designs of the Federal troops, when [they were] about to attack General Price," it was resolved that she be tendered the "sincere thanks" of the Texans.[41] This cordial gesture came early in the war when there were as yet few displaced people moving into the state, but after hundreds flocked to Texas the practice was abandoned.

The combination of all state laws relating in any way to refugees scarcely affected the majority of them. Those aiding indigent families of Confederate soldiers either did not include refugees or were so late in doing so that thousands were denied the assistance to which they were entitled. Because most laws included provisions which complicated procedures or restricted benefits, they were more helpful in theory than in practice. Relief measures were almost always late in coming and there is little indication that legislators looked ahead to provide for possible future displacements. The lag can be partially explained by the fact that lawmakers could legislate only when the bodies were in session and in the intervening months much could and did happen which no one had predicted. The timidity of state legislatures to plan ahead and formulate practical policies also can be explained by their hoping and expecting a turn in the war which would send the people home. The refugee problem confused the legislators as it did the armies. It was first ignored and then treated with inadequate palliatives, but it was never solved by legislative bodies.

Most assistance to refugees came from sources other than the states, but the legislatures did at times combine efforts with others to provide for specific groups of displaced people. In each year of the war there was a spectacular mass displacement which aroused great public sympathy and was ardently supported by the press. The first to attract widespread interest was the Charleston fire in December, 1861. Although not a direct result of the war, it merits brief mention because it did contribute to the homeless population and it also serves as an example of Southern generosity early in the war. Later displacements involving hundreds or thousands of people brought fewer and fewer contributions, not because Southerners were any less sympathetic but because they were less able to support later drives as generously as this first one. No other displaced group received as much attention as the Charleston fire victims. The South Carolina, Virginia, Georgia, and Louisiana legislatures and even the Confederate Congress appropriated money for their relief. When Virginia forwarded $50,000 to Charleston the editor of the Richmond *Dispatch* expressed sympathy for the "sufferers" but doubted the right of the General Assembly to contribute to groups "in a distant State." He thought it more in the line of duty to assist the refugees from Hampton "who were willing to apply the torch to their own houses and destroy all they possessed for the advancement of the glorious cause." [42] Georgia appropriated $100,000, Louisiana $25,000, and South Carolina lagged behind both Virginia and Georgia with an appropriation of only $30,000, and the Confederate Congress appropriated $250,000 for the fire sufferers. Never was another displacement to command so much from so many legislative bodies.

The press emotionally described the horrors of the fire and the Charleston *Mercury* estimated its damage at between four and eight million dollars. It told of the "hundreds of poor, bewildered families" who were driven from their homes "destitute of even their scanty effects." [43] The *Courier* was no less dramatic in its description and both papers led a crusade to raise funds for the homeless people. Thousands of dollars were contributed by individuals, churches, fraternal organizations, cities, and other groups. Within a month after the disaster a total of $181,660.84 in addition to legislative appropriations had been contributed, and this does not include gifts of provisions or services such as that of the railroads which conveyed donations to the city free of charge.[44]

In the second winter of the war the largest mass displacement was that of the Fredericksburg citizens, and the appeals for assistance again met with a generous response but less was contributed than the year before. Newspapers publicized the suffering of the displaced people and none did more than the Lynchburg *Daily Republican* which, on December 4, called attention to the hundreds "crowded in the country, . . . camping out in the fields, and living on such scanty and precarious subsistence as is at hand." From this time through the spring of 1863, the paper continued to support the relief drive.[45] All of the Richmond newspapers joined in the appeal for donations and on Christmas the *Dispatch* called on the citizens not to forget the needy refugees who would have no holiday without public contributions. He asked what better "Christmas gift" could be placed "on the altar of Almighty God, what better thanks offering for His great deliverance . . . at this same Fredericksburg, and by which we ourselves . . . have been saved from being homeless." [46] On this Christmas all churches in the city accepted contributions for the Fredericksburg refugees.

For several months after the evacuation of Fredericksburg donations of money and provisions continued to arrive in Richmond. By mid-December, the Richmond City Council had raised $9,360, Danville had sent $760, and in early January General John B. Hood's Division contributed $9,063.[47] On March 12, 1863, the editor of the *Examiner* reported on his trip to Fredericksburg and reminded his readers that hundreds of its displaced citizens were as yet camping out and living in congested quarters, unable to get back to their homes. He met once-affluent women who were trudging back along the roads which were "one mass of mud," and he saw indigent refugees "everywhere" in the area, living in "cabins and shanties" and entirely dependent on charity. He reported that the funds contributed for the people's relief were almost depleted, and at least one-fourth of the 6,000 "despoiled population" was destitute. Emphasizing "the urgency and the occasion of the suffering," he called for contributions from "every

Southern community." This appeal brought gifts from Virginians and citizens of other states whose donations were acknowledged in the paper.

The *Examiner* received communications from groups and individuals who had provisions to give the Fredericksburg refugees but who could not transport them to Richmond. On March 31, the paper carried a letter from a North Carolinian who reported that the Enfield citizens had collected food and clothing valued at several thousand dollars, but the railroads refused to convey the products to the sufferers. He indignantly wrote, "No one, save Jew or speculator, can get transportation on the roads . . . to Richmond," and he asked the editor if anyone in the city could arrange for transportation. It is presumed that no one volunteered, for on April 21, the *Examiner* quoted a traveler as saying that people as far away as Louisiana wanted to send provisions to the Fredericksburg people but could not obtain rail service. The irate editor noted that he had received similar complaints and had been helpless to remedy the situation. "Why is it," he asked "that the railroads are prostituted to the liquor smugglers and speculators in giving transportation to barrels of whiskey and bales of goods, when supplies tendered our Government and the poor . . . are refused . . . and bread kept from the mouths of impoverished refugees." He asked his readers to "walk the streets of Richmond and see the piles of boxes on the side walks; . . . take up a paper and read about the thousands of barrels of whiskey 'just received' and then think that the railroads cannot be induced to take even so much as a basket of provisions to the suffering families driven from their homes."

The late spring and summer of 1863 witnessed General Banks's banishment of the New Orleans people, and this group naturally aroused the pity of Southerners. The New Orleans *Picayune*'s comments on the effects of this displacement were quoted in other Southern papers. The editor had watched the departure of the exiles whose "faith in the Confederacy could not be shaken by the power or softened by the clemency of the old Government," and he noted that "social and family ties have been rent asunder." Men and women who "had formerly luxuriated in wealth departed in poverty," and the writer could only draw this conclusion: "Strange are the changes— terrible the consequences produced by civil war." [48] The plight of the banished Louisianians inspired the formation of relief organizations in distant parts of the Confederacy. Charleston, whose situation was precarious at the time, had a meeting sponsored by the city's bankers on June 4, for the purpose of raising money for the indigent New

Orleans exiles. The bankers resolved to subscribe to a relief fund, to "receive contributions from the citizens" and to urge all other banks in the state to cooperate in the project.[49] The *Mercury* commended this action and stated that "no object could be presented which would more command the heartfelt sympathies of our whole people, . . . [for] the people of Louisiana have peculiar claims on South Carolina, and all who have staked themselves upon the independence of the South." The paper called on South Carolinians to assist the Louisiana refugees, for in so doing they would be "paying a debt" to those who had sacrificed so much for the Confederacy.[50]

An earlier refugee from New Orleans who was residing in Charleston gave $1,000 to the fund, the City Council contributed $10,000, and in addition to these donations, a total of $3,446 had been raised by June 30. Gifts continued to arrive at the Charleston offices and during the first two weeks in August $1,221 were contributed but after that time money only trickled in and finally ceased to arrive.[51] Richmond also organized in behalf of the Louisianians with a Louisiana native, Judah P. Benjamin, leading the movement. As a result of a meeting held on June 2, a committee of seven persons was appointed to determine how money could be raised "to aid the exiles." It was agreed that this same committee would receive all contributions and forward them to the committee in Mobile which had been organized to relieve "the distress of the exiles." [52]

The Richmond editors were less enthusiastic about the cause of the New Orleans refugees than were the Charleston papers, but they had spent most of their energy on those from Fredericksburg and that battle was not yet won. The press did comment on the brutality of Banks's order but the pleas for assistance were not generally convincing. The *Sentinel* described the "barbarous manner" in which "ladies were ordered to leave their homes on a few hours notice . . . allowed to take . . . only sixty pounds" of luggage and only a hundred dollars. In desperation the editor asked, "What are we to do with these exiles?" All he could suggest were generalities, "receive them kindly, . . . fling open the doors and divide cheer with them, . . . receive them warmly and generously . . . [and] warn Lincoln . . . [of] retaliation." [53] These words may have encouraged some readers to make contributions to the relief fund, but no constructive program was proposed by the press. The list of Richmond donors to the relief committee show several contributions of $1,000 or more, but most are much smaller and few in number. The Lynchburg press showed a much greater interest in the exiles than that in Richmond and it urged that all who could do so contribute to their relief. One editor noted, however, that the people's banishment might be a blessing in disguise, for by removing "all true Southern sympathizers" from the city the Confederates need not hesitate to bombard New Orleans and recapture it.[54] Another Lynchburg editor spoke of the Virginians' and Louisianians' "common cause" and urged all Southerners "to rally around" and aid the displaced people. He reported that fund-raising drives for the New Orleans refugees had been organized in Lynchburg, Petersburg, Danville, Clarksville, and Mecklenburg County, as well as in Richmond.[55]

So many of the indigent New Orleans exiles remained in Mobile that they created problems for themselves and their host city. A group of the displaced leaders organized the Louisiana Exile Relief Committee in the city and set about trying to raise funds and render services to the refugees. Thomas Murray was the head of the committee and well trained for the task. He had served as the president of the New Orleans Free Market, an organization to aid families of soldiers, until he was arrested under orders of General Butler. Now free from prison and an exile in Mobile he chose to assist his displaced neighbors. One of the greatest services rendered by his committee was bringing together scattered, displaced families. The Committee was a clearing house for all Louisianians who wanted to find relatives and friends or get messages to them. Typical of the newspaper announcements was that published by the committee in the October 7, 1863 issue of the *Daily Advertiser and Register*:

I am desirous of hearing from the following list of persons, exiles from New Orleans, it being to their advantage to communicate their address and post office as early as possible. Direct to me, Louisiana Exile Relief Committee of Mobile.

> Mrs. Conners, whose husband was taken prisoner on the blockading
>   steamer, *Planter*
> Mrs. Caulkins or Culkins
> Mrs. Morrison
> Mrs. Warren
> Mrs. Shean
> Mrs. or Miss Du Hurst

(Signed) Thomas Murray

These announcements were transmitted to other newspapers as the committee made an earnest effort to locate individuals and communicate vital information to them.

In 1864, it was the Atlanta exiles who commanded the attention of Southerners, most of whom were sympathetic to their plight but too hard-pressed to render much assistance. Because of the congestion in the contracting Confederacy, the scarcity of provisions, inadequacy of transportation, and lack of money and commodities, less could be done for these refugees than had been done for earlier ones. Virginians who had heretofore supported relief programs were confronted with Grant's forces, and the Richmond papers were seeking aid for its citizens displaced by the Wilderness Campaign and battles elsewhere in the state. These homeless people were arriving by the hundreds in Richmond, as one editor noted, with only the clothes they wore and "without a meal's victuals." He described their overcrowded accommodations and told of one small house furnishing lodging for twenty-four refugees who had no provisions or means of getting them. This was the situation in Richmond on the eve of the Battle of Atlanta, and it had not improved three months later after Sherman had exiled the residents.[56] Judith McGuire's expression of sympathy for the Atlantans was all she had to offer, "May the good Lord have mercy upon them, and have them in His Holy Keeping!" [57] Others, like Mrs. McGuire, could do nothing more than pray for refugees in this last year of the war.

Even the usually relief-conscious Charleston press could muster little strength for the cause of the Atlanta exiles although it did express sympathy for them. The *Mercury* carried a weak appeal on September 27, the purpose of which was to "prompt a spirit of charity toward the exiles on the part of those who have the means." No longer were the South Carolinians being told that they were traitors to the Confederacy when they failed to contribute to worthy causes, for the resources from which donations came were rapidly diminishing and the South Carolinians were bracing themselves for Sherman's next move. Because of the general condition of the Confederacy, the Atlanta exiles were primarily dependent on their Georgia neighbors to assist them. Newspapers called on the citizens to aid them and the *Intelligencer* reminded its readers that the refugee problem had "come home with appalling and dreadful weight" to the people of Georgia. They must therefore "extend to the distressed the charities and kindness that Christianity demands." [58]

The Georgia cities into which the earlier voluntary refugees and later banished citizenry had gone appealed for assistance from the residents and those in other areas. The meeting held in Macon for the exiles brought pledges of $40,000 and plans to receive other contributions for "the destitute families." Other communities were "earnestly invited to cooperate" with Macon by offering the exiles "places of shelter, and contributions to supply their necessities." [59] Augusta had been receiving refugees from distant points and from invaded areas of Georgia throughout the war, and the coming of the Atlantans created additional problems for the city. Before Sherman's exile order Mayor Robert H. May had arranged for the homeless people to tent on the Augusta race track and parade grounds and use the adjacent buildings for shelter. A local relief committee was organized to assist displaced people from north Georgia before the Battle of Atlanta began, and benefit performances were being given during the summer of 1864 to raise money for those already in Augusta before the exiles arrived. Editors supported these performances, and one told of a citizen who bought fifty tickets for a concert, at five dollars a ticket, and destroyed "forty-four on the spot." He urged others to "go forth and do likewise." [60]

When the Atlantans were banished in September, Augusta's problems were as serious as Macon's and had been building up for a longer period. Newspapers reminded the Augustans of the new crop of refugees "which the fortunes of war have thrown . . . into . . . the city," and urged that they be treated "with all the generosity and consideration" due them. The residents were reminded how hospitably Atlanta had received displaced people throughout the conflict, and others must now "lay aside their selfishness and avarice" to help them in their hour of need. One man was so impressed by these words that he forwarded $200 to the editor to be used for the "relief of the Atlanta exiles." [61] With the approach of winter, housing presented a major problem in the city, for many of the refugees were living in "hovels, tents, cars and other such domiciles." The press pleaded with both Georgians and South Carolinians to take the unfortunates into their homes and reminded the citizens that these people were not renegades but most were people "of cultivation and taste . . . who would adorn any circle of society." Because they did not have money to buy property and there was nothing but hovels available to them they must stay in these undesirable places until those with spare rooms were willing to give them board and lodging "on equitable terms." He urged those with space to "hunt up some homeless refugee of congenial taste and character" and take him into their homes.[62] Editors were no longer talking of giving free of charge that which was now so scarce.

The Savannah people who left home in late 1864 and early 1865 moved into various Georgia and South Carolina communities, but a large percentage of the 200 transported out of the city by Sherman went to Charleston. Only a half-hearted attempt was made to aid this group, for the Charlestonians were expecting Sherman to march into their city next and many were leaving when the Georgians arrived. Although Charleston had cordially received refugees from coastal areas throughout the war and local newspapers had urged the citizens to support relief measures, there was no enthusiasm shown for assisting this group. The *Courier* offices were headquarters for the fund to aid them, and the paper called on Charlestonians for contributions and accommodations, but the usual pressures and emotional appeals were lacking.

When hundreds of Columbians fled from their homes as the Federals approached, they had to shift for themselves. Although newspapers in the state asked that these refugees be kindly received by those in the uninvaded areas, the editors seem to have been too dumbfounded and weary to have been convincing. The Yorkville *Enquirer* was as persuasive as any when it called on the people "to heed well the promptings of generosity under these circumstances, [for] if ever a people deserved sympathy, it is those who come as peniless [*sic*] exiles from luxurious homes. . . . Let sympathy, for once, have its will." Like those elsewhere, the editor did not ask charity but only that they be sold the necessities at fair prices.[63] The displacement of South Carolinians in early 1865 prompted a resident of the Pickens District to offer the use of his "large landed estate and . . . all materials on it" to refugees who had the endorsement of "the State, or the cities of Charleston or Columbia," and who could provide shelter for themselves as well as "all implements of husbandry." [64] Had the offer been extended earlier he might have had a great many applications, but coming as it did in February, 1865, few refugees could meet his requirements.

The South Carolina refugees, like those from Atlanta, were primarily dependent on their neighbors for assistance. All expressions of sympathy and appeals in their behalf did not originate in South Carolina, however, and the benevolent Mayor Robert H. May called on the Augusta residents to help this group as they had others. "With sorrowful heart," he announced, "I am again impelled to appeal to you for the relief of the destitute, homeless and suffering inhabitants of our sister city of Columbia. . . . We are now beginning to understand the awful condition to which these, our stricken brethren have been reduced by the ravages of war. . . ." [65] His proclamation reveals the sadness, weariness and helplessness Southerners felt by 1865.

Although the drives for funds to aid large groups of refugees were spectacular, there were thousands of individuals who were generous, thoughtful, and courteous to the displaced people. The kindness of most of these was never publicized, but some of the recipients mentioned the donors and gifts in their records and newspapers occasionally reported those who evidenced a special interest in the homeless people. A Georgia editor told of a man who planted a part of his farm in grain which was sold only to refugees on credit and at below market prices. The farmer assured the purchasers that he did not expect payment until "they returned to their home after the war," and even then he would charge no interest.[66] A South Carolina planter sold corn "at bare cost of production to *bona fide* refugees" in Columbia, and those having no means of transporting it into the city could purchase it from a local minister to whom it was delivered. The planter required that the displaced people prove their need, pledge that the corn would not be used by Negroes, and swear that they had never engaged in speculation.[67] Manufacturers of cloth sometimes set aside a part of their stock for refugees who were given tickets permitting them to purchase material. A lady in Augusta told of getting a "refugee ticket" which entitled her to purchase cloth at $1.10 a yard, but she was irritated by the red tape involved. She first had to prove she was a displaced person before the ticket would be issued and she had to stand in line for an hour in "a dirty shop . . . with a dozen or so greasy women and men, and take in return what the man gave." She did not seem very appreciative for the favor accorded her.[68]

Unpublicized at the time was an exceptionally generous gift of George Trenholm. When General Beauregard was trying to remove the Charlestonians out of the city in 1863, the children in the local orphanage had nowhere to go. Trenholm purchased a building previously used as a female academy in Orangeburg and arranged for the children to live there.[69] The move was made quietly, and not until the building burned in November, 1864, was his original gift widely publicized. At the time of the fire there were 260 youngsters in the orphanage, and with their displacement came a call for contributions to be used in relocating them.[70]

Wherever Louisianians went they always evidenced great interest in others from their state and did more than any other group to provide for them. Those in Richmond combined efforts and money to convert a hotel into a home for soldiers and transient refugees from Louisiana. Room and board were furnished "at little or no cost," but to insure a steady income a few Louisiana refugees were permitted to live there for extended periods. The reading room was supplied with newspapers from the home state and the club was an "intelligence office" for displaced Louisianians who were requested to send their names and addresses to the manager so that their friends might know where they were located. Contributions were sought and received by the management of the establishment. Newspaper editors in other states were intrigued by the project and suggested that others emulate the Louisianians.[71] Although wayside homes for soldiers became fairly common during the war, the refugees were seldom accorded the privilege of staying in them.

Senator Williamson Oldham told of a friend of his, a refugee from Tennessee, who purchased a hotel in Newnan, Georgia, for the sole purpose of giving his family and friends a home. Travelers coming into the village often mistook it for a commercial establishment and asked for rooms which the owner readily supplied. Not until the guests tried to pay for their accommodations did they realize that the building was now a private home—the owner refused to accept payment for the lodging. Oldham noted that "they seemed unable to comprehend the fact and were unable to account for the hospitality."[72] Judge Garnett Andrews, a Georgia Unionist, was just as hospitable to refugees who sought shelter in his home. His daughter said that he ran "a free hotel" and welcomed "everybody as long as there . . . [was] a square foot under his roof." Although the family was inconvenienced by the overflow of guests, his daughter enjoyed making "new friendships every day."[73]

Despite the highly publicized fund drives for groups of refugees, the contributions of money and provisions from thousands of individuals and organizations, and the support of the press, the majority of refugees never benefited from gifts other than those bestowed on them personally by individuals with whom they came in contact. This type of aid was at best uncertain; most displaced persons received no regular assistance from any source. What was usually given them was in the form of charity, which they resented, and token gifts which were insufficient to their needs. No satisfactory broad program was devised to care for the displaced people nor were employment agencies organized to help them find jobs. Those who were in a mass displacement could not wander away from the crowd if they expected to benefit from the funds collected to aid them, and for this reason many of the indigent remained where they had first gone and contributed to problems of the community. Refugees who moved out of their native state could not hope to collect relief payments appropriated by the state legislatures, and as previously noted, when they moved from one county to another within the state some went months or years without assistance. Only the Confederate government was in a position to establish an efficient relief program for refugees, and it did nothing about the problem.

Although the displaced people were never adequately cared for, they received less as the war continued. The contributions diminished appreciably from the time of the Charleston fire in 1861 to the flight of the South Carolinians in 1865, and a study of the number of donors and the amounts given to the relief programs reveals the gradual economic collapse of the Confederacy. Yet, as the donations decreased, the number of refugees increased and the gap between available aid and the needy people widened. During the last year of the struggle nearly all of the refugees were in dire circumstances, especially those who had moved many times in the four years. A Georgian wrote Mrs. Howell Cobb in February, 1865, that she had a friend who had made twelve moves during the war.[74] This was an extreme case, but many had been uprooted four or more times in the period. Most who had money had Confederate currency which had depreciated to such a point that Southerners were increasingly reluctant to accept it. Before the end of the war the people might as well have done as Mrs. McGuire's family did: put Confederate bills and bonds in "a Confederate envelope, seal it up, and endorse it, 'In memory of our beloved Confederacy.'"[75] Most Southern people were impoverished when the war ended, but the refugees were not only impoverished, they were miles from their homes. They were then, as they had been for varying periods during the conflict, "the greatest sufferers."

... *such a scene*
should be painted

After the refugees recovered from the first shock of knowing that the war had ended in a Confederate defeat, the thought uppermost in their mind was to go home. But the majority were compelled to delay their journey because of circumstances beyond their control. In many cases, of course, they lacked funds for the trip, having only Confederate currency or none at all. Public transportation was disrupted, and owners of private conveyances and dray animals were reluctant to rent or sell them or to transport passengers for any distance. Because of the scarcity and abnormal demand for all means of transportation, travelers could expect at any time to lose their vehicles, horses, or mules, to anyone powerful enough to appropriate them. The unsettled, lawless conditions in the South made women hesitate to start for home when there was no man in the party, and many awaited the return of their menfolk before leaving their place of refuge. The multifamily caravan of refugees so often seen during the war was rarely in evidence after the conflict when most people traveled alone or with their own family. Women and children also delayed their departure if the husband insisted on going home first to check on the situation, plant a crop, open his business, or get things in order before sending for his family. Displaced farmers, among them a great many Louisianians in Texas, who had already planted a crop before the end of the war were reluctant to leave until it had been harvested. But a major delaying factor was the bewilderment, depression, and lethargy which overcame the refugees when they realized that their sacrifices had been in vain. They did not know what to do or where to turn, and it was months before some of them could collect their thoughts sufficiently to make plans.

As previously noted, many displaced people returned to their homes before the end of the war, even when it meant living under Federal rule. They grew weary of retreating with the Confederate forces, and after a brief taste of refugee life, thousands concluded that it was to their best interest to let the armies do the moving while they returned to their own firesides as spectators. All who went home during the war did not have to live in close contact with the Federals, and those who had fled in the face of an enemy invasion which did not materialize often returned as soon as the immediate danger had passed. When they had been uprooted once by a false alarm, they were more reluctant to move the second time, and some Southerners came and went or remained at home through all the threats and bombardments. This was true of hundreds of Charlestonians, many of whom left in 1861–62 and returned just in time to be requested to move again. A native of the city who was also stationed there wrote his brother in the summer of 1862 that "a considerable number of families have returned . . . how many I do not know, but several ladies came down on the train with me. . . ." [1]

Typical of many Charlestonians, and of some from other communities, was the woman who left the city in 1862, taking the family's furniture and other transportable properties to her refuge in the interior. Her husband remained in Charleston and, in the spring of 1863, was so confident that the danger had passed that he wrote her to come home and bring their possessions with her. This she did, but six weeks later General Beauregard requested the removal of all noncombatants and her husband again sent her away, this time with only her clothes. She slipped back into Charleston in late summer, but after two weeks was again asked to leave. From this time until the end of the war her husband forbade her to return, but she once went to Orangeburg hoping that if she got that close to Charleston he would let her come home. She reminded him many times that she would rather endure the bombardment in her own home than live anywhere else, but after the summer of 1863 Charleston was "off limits" to her. [2]

A South Carolina widow who had left her plantation early in the war returned in 1864 and wanted more than anything to remain at home. She noted that it was "so much more refined & . . . bears the evidence of a better sort of existence" than those she had known in Greenville and Augusta. She was willing to risk all dangers because she felt "more right" on her plantation "than anywhere else," but

Sherman's troops were expected momentarily and friends urged her to leave. She reluctantly acquiesced and this time went to a sister's house in Athens, Georgia. Her property was declared abandoned, then confiscated, and turned over to the Freedmen's Bureau; she was unable to return to her home until December, 1865, when her friends interceded and got the plantation restored. However, the nine months following the war were miserable, uncertain ones and as agonizing as any she had known during her displacement.[3]

Refugees were so anxious to return home that they often followed the Confederates when they invaded areas that had been previously lost. When General Longstreet's forces marched into east Tennessee in 1863, hundreds of displaced citizens from the region traveled in their wake.[4] And there were other homeless Tennesseans who watched and waited to see if the Confederates would hold the area before leaving their refuge. One of these was a woman who was temporarily residing in Iredell County, North Carolina. When she heard of Longstreet's invasion she packed her baggage and kept herself in readiness to return to her Tennessee farm. Like so many others, she was confident that at any time she would be able to go home and yet be within Confederate lines.[5] This hope and confidence of hundreds of refugees, whenever they heard of a raid or counterattack by the Confederates, doomed them to disappointment. It was late in the war before most people realized that they must choose between displacement or living under Federal rule.

When Vicksburg was first endangered in 1862, many of its citizens left and then returned a few months later. Referring to this group, a local editor reported, "Our city is beginning to exhibit signs of . . . life again. The people are flocking back to their homes, stores are being opened, and the pulsations of business have gained a fresh impetus. . . ." [6] After Vicksburg fell, many of the refugees came back to the city or to their plantations, and in November, 1863, a friend wrote Jefferson Davis that planters had returned because "they have been . . . disgusted with what they call extortion and inhospitality." He said that others who had not yet returned were planning to do so, and all were making "preparations . . . to raise cotton and open trade with the enemy along the river." He reported that "from 20 miles below the mouth of the Arkansas River to Memphis, this state of affairs already exists." [7] The economic benefits derived from going home drew thousands back long before the end of the war.

It was not an unusual sight to see the refugees going home even as the war was being fought. Some had experienced only a brief displacement but others had been away for a longer period. Many frightened Memphis citizens fled the city before the appearance of the Federals and some of these returned within a few days "to secure their property and collect their rents." [8] After the First Battle of Manassas the displaced farmers drifted back "to take possession of their houses," and by fall they were "cultivating their fields and repairing the damage." [9] After the Confederates recaptured Galveston many of its citizens returned and were determined to remain at home regardless of what the future held. Mrs. William Pitt Ballenger pleaded with her husband to permit her to go back to Galveston, as many of her friends were doing, but her teasing, cajolery, and tears failed to move him, and she retained her refugee status until the end of the war.[10]

A similar movement was going on in other areas. It was reported that 2,300 of 2,500 refugees from St. Augustine, Florida "had returned to their homes and . . . resumed" their normal activities within a few weeks after the city's capture.[11] The percentage of returning citizens seems so high that the accuracy of this statement must be questioned, but it was not unusual for the majority of those leaving to return. As previously noted, many residents fled to some nearby refuge in search of safety and returned after the battle regardless of its outcome. Because fear motivated the flight of so many civilians, thousands fled when they supposed the enemy approached, and such was the case in Macon after Atlanta fell. As soon as they realized that Sherman had another goal in mind, most came home. An officer's wife wrote her husband a few weeks after the scare that "Macon begins to look again as it did before the excitement of the Yankee advance . . . ; the citizens have nearly all returned and the country people are bringing in provisions to sell." [12] As Sherman's troops were marching toward Savannah, an Augusta newspaperman told of "refugees from Upper Georgia and Tennessee" who were going home, and he reasoned that they might as well go back to those areas which "are as safe as any portion of the Confederacy." [13]

This movement of the people back and forth was confusing for all concerned but especially for the armies. These returning refugees were largely responsible for Federal officials' requiring the oath of all who entered their lines and the pledge that they would not cross them again for the duration of the war. This movement increased appreciably after the summer of 1863, but most of the returning refugees were from the poorer classes who could not provide for themselves within Confederate lines and who realized that they had done nothing which would make them vulnerable to Federal abuse. For the sake of themselves and their families they were going back to their farms, jobs, and friends. If necessary, they would take the oath in order to end their exile, for this group was often angry with themselves and with others who had created the hysteria and panic which had set them adrift in the first place.

Although the roads leading home were traveled by many refugees throughout the war, thousands were still displaced in April, 1865. To most of these people the end of the war meant going home. As an Arkansas editor noted, "Probably no other portion of the whole American people will be more overjoyed at the return of peace than those embraced under the head of refugees." He believed they welcomed the war's end even more than the soldiers because "they had been cast about from place to place . . . until the hope has died within them and they have been ready to despair." Once back home they could experience "joys not known in a refugee camp," and the writer hoped they would "offer prayers of thanks to God" for permitting them to return and begin life anew. He assured them that they would be welcome and urged them to come home immediately if they were "planning to return at all," for if they did they could still "raise at least half crops for next year," and possibly save their property from confiscation. In his opinion, there was "no excuse for staying away." [14]

In his last address to the people of Louisiana, Governor Henry Watkins Allen urged, "Refugees return to your homes, repair, improve, plant. Go to work with hearty good will." [15] This appeal was circulated over the state and in nearby areas. The Texas newspapers transmitted his message to his displaced constituents in the state, and it was heart-warming for refugees to know that they had not been forgotten. People who left their homes during the war suffered psychologically from their actions as they worried about what their friends and neighbors thought of their having fled in the face of danger. Most refugees did not have regular contact with their home communities after they were overrun by the enemy, and hearing nothing from those who had remained they imagined that they were forgotten or condemned. Their imaginations worked overtime as they brooded and feared rejection and censure. The displaced people were desperately in need of reassurances when the war ended, and the hand of friendship extended them by newspapers and officials was both consoling and gratifying.

A Louisiana planter in Texas wrote a friend that he was "anxious to return home," for he would rather be there than anywhere "the sun now shines on," but he had no illusions about the future. He predicted great trouble ahead for the Southern people, but he would rather endure it in his own home "surrounded by a people who would at least sympathize with us in our common troubles." Although anxious to return to Louisiana, he had to remain in Texas until he could harvest his corn crop, but no sooner had this been done than he began to doubt and fear the policies of President Andrew Johnson. He wrote friends that his return now depended on whether or not he was "admonished by some . . . bull of Andy Johnson's programe [*sic*]," and if that did not delay his family's coming home, there was nothing else "to keep them in Texas." [16] He had learned, as had others, that the policy of patient, watchful waiting had its merits.

When Mrs. Meriwether heard of Lee's surrender she was "stunned" as were others who "discussed the news in whispers," incredulous that it could be true although "in their hearts" they knew it was. She immediately contacted her husband to find out whether he preferred that she remain in Tuscaloosa until he could join them or that she immediately take the boys home to Memphis. He urged her to go home as soon as it could be arranged, for as a Confederate officer he might be delayed for months or years. Mrs. Meriwether and the children left for Memphis shortly thereafter, riding in the same buggy drawn by the same mule that had taken them out of the city two and one-half years earlier. Her chief concern was for the beast Adrienne, who was "so weak and thin." Should the animal die on the road she did not know what they would do. It would be tragic indeed to be "left on the roadside with a dead mule," for chances were slim that she would find a replacement, and Mrs. Meriwether was very devoted and grateful to Adrienne. Despite anxious moments along the way, the mule performed its assignment faithfully and was still in harness when the refugees arrived in Memphis.

The Meriwethers left Tuscaloosa with a bushel of boiled potatoes and "a supply of cornbread," but they hoped to supplement this scanty diet with food purchased along the way. After trying without success to buy eggs and other commodities, the refugees were riding through northern Mississippi when Mrs. Meriwether smelled bacon cooking for the first time "in nearly a year." She followed the aroma to a Negro cabin where she asked the colored woman if she might buy some bacon and eggs. The woman called to her daughter to "bile" a dozen eggs, fry some bacon and make "a batch ob hoe cakes" for the travelers to take with them. Mrs. Meriwether was surprised when told that the price of the food was only five dollars, but she was shocked, as well she might have been, when the Negro insisted that it be in Confederate bills because she didn't "know 'nuthin about Yankee money.'" Mrs. Meriwether gave her ten dollars in the currency she requested and rode away with the provisions. The only other time that the family broke their potato and corn bread diet was when they stopped with the big-boned, tobacco-chewing Peppercorn women with whom they had stayed on their flight out of Memphis. Their background and way of life were different from Mrs. Meriwether's, yet they enjoyed seeing each other again, and after the war Mrs. Meriwether sent them gifts and had at least one letter from Sukey Peppercorn.

When the Meriwethers arrived in Memphis their home was occupied by a cheerful Irish couple who offered to move immediately, but Mrs. Meriwether preferred that they remain until her husband returned. She had not been sure that the home was still hers, but her friends had paid the taxes and there was no question of ownership. She sat at the gate a few moments and mused, "Such a scene, typical of thousands of others . . . should be painted by a great artist and entitled 'The Refugee's Return.'" Comparing herself to Homer's Ulysses, she noted that her odyssey had been "marred by many ills," and she believed hers had been the "more pitiful" of the two. Yet her homecoming was far more pleasant than that of many other displaced people, for she had her home, and friends had collected her furniture and personal possessions immediately following her banishment and had held them until her return. Even her finest china and family heirlooms had been safeguarded during her absence. She had reason enough to be thankful for her good fortune.[17]

Joseph Davis also heard of Lee's surrender in Tuscaloosa, but he and his granddaughter, Mary Elizabeth Mitchell, did not leave until September, 1865. The young lady explained that their late departure was due to their dejection, bewilderment, and shock, and for a time there seemed to be nothing to do but "sit at home." Then criticizing her choice of words she wrote, "What mockery to call this home. We are poor refugees. How suggestive that word refugee is to my poor heart, of sorrows past, present anxieties and future misery." Through the long trouble-filled summer they brooded in Tuscaloosa, and when they left, it was in "a carriage drawn by mules" with their baggage in "a wagon drawn by oxen." However, the latter conveyance was not overloaded on the return trip because the refugees were "not troubled to bring much back." Joseph Davis had less to draw him from his refuge than did Elizabeth Meriwether, for his plantation had been confiscated and his palatial home burned. He was one of the displaced people who never went home again. After pausing briefly in Jackson and visiting in New Orleans, he went to Vicksburg where he took rooms in a hotel. Davis was ruined financially and depressed about his brother's fate, and his granddaughter was also in low spirits. The only happy event in her life was her father's return from his displacement in Texas, but arriving at his Louisiana plantation he found his home in ashes and had to live in slave quarters while his family stayed with relatives. His daughter lamented, "This homeless existence is worse than refugeeing, for then we had excitement attendant to war, and the hope of a glorious future to sustain us. Now the present is dreary and comfortless, we can but mourn our dear lost cause, and sicken at the remembrance of the sea of blood shed in vain." [18]

Miss Mitchell was not alone in feeling a greater dejection immediately after the war than she had experienced during the conflict. The people's displacement at first contained an element of adventure when they were enthusiastic and confident of victory, but by 1865 they were tired of running and struggling, crushed in spirit and disillusioned, bitter and bankrupt. As they jogged or plodded their way home, they saw about them the ruins of war and wondered if this same desolation and destruction would greet them when they turned in their own gate. Those who started their trip back happy to be going home were soon depressed by the scenes along the road.

A young South Carolinian who was a refugee in central North Carolina, as she said, "forty miles from anywhere," experienced much the same depression as did Miss Mitchell. She had not, however, been displaced as long, for she was sent out of Columbia only a few days before the Federals arrived and yet, when she heard that the war was over her first thought was, "I must go home." She had found it "comparatively easy to endure the separation from dear ones when the excitement of suspense or continual action kept the mind at fever-heat," but now that peace and defeat had come, her "poor heart fled like a frightened bird to its nest." Yet the two hundred miles to Columbia could not be flown, and "railroads were destroyed, horses and mules . . . had been seized by friends and foes; vehicles of all sorts were appropriated or in a state of utter dilapidation." She had no choice but to delay her trip until midsummer when she got a ride to Greensboro in "a dilapidated buggy" drawn by a "spavined mule." Despite the poor transportation, the forty miles that took her away from her refuge were "the shortest . . . on record." She traveled by train from Greensboro to within three miles of Winnsboro, South Carolina, beyond which the tracks to Columbia were destroyed. She rode to Winnsboro in a wagon "drawn by a very spare horse and a very small mule," and from that point to Columbia "in an old fashioned stage-coach, revived by the necessities of the case." The roads were in a dreadful state of disrepair and the countryside was dotted with burned homes, lonely chimneys, and destroyed fences. Gloom was everywhere, and rumors of marauders kept the passengers in a state of tension, but through the ordeal she remembered she was going home, and the thought helped her endure the unhappy aspects of her journey.[19]

Jorantha Semmes remained in Alabama until the fall of 1865 when she traveled with her husband's cousins to their home in Canton, Mississippi. After being mustered out of the army, Major Semmes went to Memphis to get "a few months start" before sending for his family.[20] It was around the first of January, 1866, before Mrs. Semmes and the children returned to the city which was to be her home for the remainder of her life. Living to the ripe old age of ninety-eight, she watched from the sidelines as the united country fought the Spanish-American and First World Wars. Although it must be only a supposition, the chances are that she compared these conflicts with the one she had known in the 1860's and gave thanks that neither she nor her loved ones had to endure the life of a refugee.

April, 1865, found John and Judith McGuire, like hundreds of other refugees, still in Richmond, unable to leave when the officials and their families fled from the city. The couple had no money, no home, and no job. All they could do was await further developments, and for three depressing weeks after the occupation they remained in Richmond. The streets were patrolled by Union soldiers, a large part of the city lay in ruins, and the future seemed hopelessly dark, yet Mrs. McGuire continued her daily visits to the hospital and regularly attended church services, but these activities and quiet visits with friends were her only diversions. When she talked with her displaced friends they invariably asked each other, "When and where are you going?" Most of them had no income, money, or transportation, and a great many had nowhere to go. Those who had invitations from relatives were reluctant to accept them because everyone faced grave economic problems which were only compounded when there were additional mouths to feed. A lady told Mrs. McGuire that she had been invited to "visit" her cousins but hesitated to go because she could not remain indefinitely with "ruined relatives," and when the time came to leave, she would again be confronted with the question of where to go. Mrs. McGuire was in the same situation for she and her husband had an invitation from her brother who lived in Hanover County, but eventually they must "look around for some other place, in which to build up a home. . . ." It would not be easy at their age to start over again.[21]

When Emma Mordecai spent the day of April 18 in Richmond she noted how difficult it was for the departing refugees to say goodbye to those with whom they had shared the war years, and she commented, "It was a sad, sad parting for all." [22] It was also on April 18 that Judith McGuire wrote that she and her husband were "striving to get out of the city." Three days later the trains were again operating and the Federals were issuing free tickets to the indigent who wished to leave, but the McGuires had no money for incidental expenses until an old friend insisted that they take half of what he had, which was "twenty-five or thirty dollars." They reluctantly accepted a gift of $10, received their transportation tickets and boarded the train which took them to Mrs. McGuire's brother's home. He met them at the station with a wagon, his only conveyance, and drove them to his once beautiful estate which was now in such a state of disrepair that Mrs. McGuire was appalled by the sight of it. She was more depressed than at any time during the war, but reverting to her philosophy that she was happiest when helping others, Judith McGuire was soon tutoring her young niece. For financial reasons the child's governess had been dismissed, but her aunt assumed the duties cheerfully, happy that she could in this way partially repay her brother's hospitality.[23]

William Gale's family remained in Asheville until he came for them, and Mrs. Gale spent the weeks immediately following the war getting the children "presentable" to travel. She repatched their threadbare garments but there was no money for shoes, so the youngsters had to travel barefoot. As soon as Gale arrived he was assigned the task of finding transportation for the family and finally located two men who agreed to drive them to Greeneville, Tennessee, in their wagons, but only after they had received "a good round sum." The family's conveyance was a "dilapidated express wagon . . . without paint . . . [and] *with broken springs* [and] *no seats*." A cloth was "stretched over the top to keep out the rain and the wheels were loose and wobbled fearfully." The horses "were perfect skeletons & one *very* lame." However, the Gales worried more about traveling through the mountains than about the wagons and horses, for lawless men were at large throughout the area. Mrs. Gale noted that the trip was indeed "a perilous one, as no party . . . unless under guard of soldiers, had gone over the mountains unscathed, and in many instances [were] murdered." Despite their misgivings and fears, the family was ready to leave Asheville by early summer, 1865.

It was difficult for Mrs. Gale to part with her Asheville friends, and she later recalled, "It was impossible to break from it all without real sadness and genuine regret." As the family rode out of town, friends along the way bade them farewell and some brought food and simple gifts as tokens of their affection. Sad to be leaving, afraid of what lay ahead, but excited to be going home, the Gales spent three days and two nights traveling from Asheville to Greeneville. They carried their food with them and slept on pallets both nights. Because they feared an attack, Gale walked the distance, rifle in hand, guarding the party. The first night was spent in Marshall, twenty miles from Asheville, and Mrs. Gale lay awake all night listening to the pistols which were "fired incessantly, amid curses & fearful oaths of an intoxicated crowd." She was especially nervous because they were camping on the property of a "southern sympathizer" in the middle of Unionist country. They planned to spend the second night with old friends, but when they arrived at the once "lovely mountain home" they found the house "a shell . . . [and] not a human about the place." It was getting dark and the family decided to camp on the property, and the next night they stayed with friends near Greeneville and slept in "real beds."

From Greeneville they traveled by boxcar to Chattanooga, and their companions were "several . . . very polite" Federal soldiers who entertained the children with stories of the war. Weighted down with an odd assortment of baggage, the family was entering a hotel in Chattanooga when the children's pet bantam rooster escaped from its cage and ran down the street amid the screams of the owners. Two Federal soldiers standing nearby took up the chase and it was some time before they caught and returned the creature to its cage. The following morning, the Gales were assigned places in a boxcar going to Nashville, but when Katherine Gale arrived at the station the military guard insisted that a lady merited better accommodations, and ignoring the protests of the conductor who shouted that he "had his orders," the family was given seats in a passenger car. Arriving in Nashville with "barely enough money to pay omnibus fare," the refugees went to a hotel where Gale knew the manager who would credit them with a night's lodging. The next morning they went to

Gale's parents' home on the outskirts of town and found the house filled with refugees who were staying there en route to their homes. The Gales were at home for Nashville was to be the family's postwar headquarters.[24]

It was six months after the war's end before Kate Stone's family started their trek back to Louisiana and faced an "appalling" future without "money . . . credit, heavily in debt and [with] an over-flowed place." The last reference was to "Brokenburn" which had been plagued with floods after the levees were cut in the war, and it was this problem that later caused the Stones to move to Mississippi, but in 1865 their destination was their Louisiana plantation. Kate was looking forward to the privacy she would have at "Brokenburn," for she was weary of living in "such crowded quarters" as she had endured during her displacement. On their return trip the family camped along the way, and although they "had every appliance for camping," Kate was no more enthusiastic about out-of-door living than she had been earlier.

The most enjoyable part of the trip for Kate was seeing old friends, and once they crossed into Louisiana she saw a great many, some of whom had only recently returned from their displacement. The Stones stayed with a family in Minden who had also spent the war years in Tyler, and Kate was happy that their lovely home and its contents were undamaged. The returning refugees also stopped to see the Wadleys near Monroe. Kate was anticipating close contact with Sarah in the years ahead, but when they arrived the family was packing to leave for Georgia where they were to make their new home. Kate sadly noted that the distance between Georgia and Louisiana was too great to permit their seeing each other often, and she regretted having to tell them goodbye. It was also on this trip home that Kate saw her "Prince Charming" of Tyler days, now plain "Mr. Holmes," and in Kate's eyes still "handsome and beautifully dressed." Disappointed to learn that he had "been spending a wild summer and fall," she could not bring herself to accept his proposal even though he assured her that marriage would change him for the better. At the time, Kate thought that there was "little hope for him," but as previously noted, she later changed her mind.

The two days spent in getting through Tensas Swamp were the worst part of the Stone's trip, and midway through the ordeal their conveyance broke down and the family had to ride "muleback" for the remainder of the trip. Kate's spirits had been sinking since she had heard of Sarah Wadley's leaving and had broken up with Holmes, but she was even more depressed when she arrived at her once beautiful home, which "did not seem the same place" she had left three years earlier. It was terribly defaced, their furniture and heirlooms were gone, and the "gardens, orchards and fences had been . . . mostly swept away." The area was so deathly quiet that Kate wondered if the gaiety of Tyler had not "spoiled . . . [them] for plantation living." Kate determined to be cheerful despite her misfortunes but it was easier said than done, and in the weeks following her return she was more dejected than she had been at any time during the war and "did not want to see anybody." From November, 1865, until September, 1867, she made no entries in her journal, and when she again wrote she explained her long silence as the result of a difficult period of readjustment. It had been a time "of hard endeavor to raise a crop [and] reconstruct the place with . . . hired labor," as the Stones battled "high water and cotton worms." The austerity, sadness, and confusion of these years were far more difficult for Kate than her displacement had been.[25]

The John B. Grimballs were typical of many affluent families who were financially ruined by the war. Their property near Charleston had suffered enemy depredations and was seized as abandoned; therefore, 1865 found the Grimballs impoverished and still living in Spartanburg. Soon after the war ended Grimball went to Charleston to try to regain his lost property and straighten out his financial affairs, but Mrs. Grimball had to stay behind in their refuge. Her postwar letters to friends and relatives indicate that for many years after the conflict the only source of income she and her husband had was that from her late father's estate in New York. The couple's daughter, Elizabeth, who had taken a position in a girls' school, continued to teach until 1867 when she married an attorney in Union.[26]

Among the Confederate officials who left Richmond before the flight of Jefferson Davis and his cabinet was Senator Williamson Oldham of Texas, and his account of the trip home vividly describes travel difficulties confronting most refugees in the spring of 1865. His journey took him into all of the eleven Confederate states excepting Tennessee and Florida, and he had ample opportunity to observe the disrupted transportation, devastation, and depression everywhere in the South and to meet and converse with returning refugees. It took three months for him to make the trip from Richmond to Washington, Texas, and being an impatient man, he was often frustrated, irritated, and angered by the delays and obstacles that beset him.

Oldham's journey by train to Chester, South Carolina, was uneventful, and arriving in the village and finding no railroad to Newberry, he approached a Confederate quartermaster who had an ambulance and wagon and asked for one of the conveyances, explaining that he was a Confederate Senator. He was told that both vehicles were being held for Louisiana Senator Thomas J. Semmes and his family who were expected momentarily, and so angry was Oldham at hearing this that he was "very much inclined to wring . . . the neck" of the quartermaster but doubted that it would "expedite matters." When asked why the Semmes family should have two conveyances when he had none, Oldham was told that Semmes had "done . . . favors" for the officer who was now doing one for him, but he suggested that the Texan could probably get a seat in the wagon if he would await Semmes's arrival. Having no choice in the matter, he waited for three days and became increasingly angry, for he said that the delay cost him thousands in gold and made him "30 or 40 days later" in getting home. When the Louisianians arrived, Oldham was told he could ride in the wagon as far as Newberry. The two nights spent in "palatial homes" which were untouched by the war made him even more disgruntled, for both were spent on the floor and he was fed in neither. Oldham concluded, "In those districts of the country over which the Yankees had swept, . . . no soldier or citizen in public service was ever denied a meal or night's lodging . . . if within the power of the citizen to furnish it. It was alone in those districts and sections never visited by the enemy, that this selfish, inhospitable spirit manifested itself."

Oldham traveled from Newberry to Washington, Georgia, in a mule-drawn wagon, and on to Covington by train, but from that point to Atlanta the tracks were destroyed so he had to spend the night in Covington. He went to the local hotel, confident that as a Confederate Senator he would have no trouble getting accommodations, but the establishment was "crowded to overflowing with refugees" so he had to sleep in the hall. The next morning he and a family of refugees located a man who was willing to take them to Atlanta in his wagon, and once in the city he was hospitably received by a friend who had lost "everything except his home." Oldham walked about the town and noted that many refugees were returning to their "desolated homes" and others were living in "any spot that afforded the least shelter." Some of the "returned fugitives" had covered the "roofless walls of their homes with canvass," and hundreds were living in boxcars or caves. These tragic scenes depressed Oldham who welcomed the opportunity to move on to Newnan where he stayed with his old friend, Congressman Arthur St. Clair Colyar of Tennessee. Colyar's displaced family had lived in the village through most of the war, and it was while the Texan was in Newnan that he heard of the disrupted rail service in Alabama and the presence of large numbers of Federals in the state. He then realized that his route would have to be changed and his journey would be hazardous.

Oldham traveled by train from Newnan to LaGrange where he got space in a Confederate Mining and Nitre Bureau wagon to Oxford, Alabama. Here he visited with Jabez L. M. Curry and then continued his journey to within eight miles of Marion where he heard that the Federals were questioning all travelers coming into the town. Not wanting to be interrogated, he followed a circuitous route to Demopolis, where he stopped at the home of Congressman Francis Strother Lyon, after which he zig-zagged his way out of Alabama, spent eight days in Mississippi, crossed the river at Vicksburg, cut across southeastern Arkansas, and proceeded to Shreveport. From this point he went to Marshall, Texas, then to Houston and by boat up the Brazos River to Washington. He was weary, depressed, disgusted, and intended to travel no more, but a few months later he joined other Confederate officials in flight to Mexico, where he wrote his memoirs before going to Canada. He returned to Texas where he died in 1868 without ever having received a pardon from the Federal government.[27]

Oldham's travel experiences were in some ways similar and in others dissimilar to those of most refugees. He had a greater number of friends along the route than many of the displaced people and advantages they did not have in commanding places in government vehicles, but he was also more vulnerable to harsh treatment from the Federals if captured. Therefore, he had to travel many miles out of the way to avoid meeting the enemy. He had sufficient funds for the trip, which most refugees did not have, but he also carried greater responsibilities than the average citizen. Because he had been a Confederate official he was shocked and angered when refused the accommodations and respect that he thought he merited, but by 1865 most refugees expected nothing and were, therefore, not surprised to encounter rudeness and hostility. Oldham's account of his trip clearly indicates that he resented strangers' being unimpressed by his importance, and he found it more difficult to ride in a wagon, walk, sleep on the floor, and miss meals than did the displaced people who took such things for granted. He was compelled to share with the plain people the ordeals of travel in a wartorn, defeated South.

Of all those who watched the flight of the Confederate leaders, none gave a more delightful description than Eliza Frances Andrews who had a grandstand seat for the pageant taking place in her hometown of Washington, Georgia. As previously noted, the war's end brought many prominent figures to the village and to her father's home, for despite Garnett Andrews' being a Unionist, he played host to many ardent Confederates. His daughter watched them come, heard them talk of going to Mexico or Brazil, and commented, "If all go who say they are going . . . , we shall have a nation made up of women, Negroes and Yankees." Among the eleventh hour refugees who visited in the Andrews home were General Arnold Elzey and his staff and Burton Harrison, official escort for Mrs. Jefferson Davis who stayed elsewhere in the town. Senator Louis T. Wigfall bobbed in and out of town when, after leaving the first time, he had his mules stolen a short distance from the village and had to return. Also coming through Washington were Jefferson Davis, Postmaster General John Reagan, Secretary of Navy Stephen Mallory, General and Mrs. John Gordon, and others. Eliza Frances Andrews accurately described the situation when she noted, "The town is full of celebrities, and many poor fugitives, whose necks are in danger. . . ." [28]

A great many impoverished refugees could not get home and some of them sought assistance from state officials. Typical of letters received by leaders was that written to Governor Isaac Murphy of Arkansas by an indigent, bewildered, uneducated mountain woman who was only twenty-five miles from her home. She had lost her husband during the war, had a large family of small children, and wrote Murphy, ". . . my children has not had one mouthfull to eat in fore dais . . . i am livin twenty five miles of home and i have tride all means that were to git home and becaus i have no monney folks will not hep me." [29] Many others were in the same predicament, and even those who were better-educated and once wealthy sometimes found that without "monney" they need not expect "hep."

Some displaced people settled in new areas after the war and one of these was the peripatetic banker, J. G. M. Ramsey, who after leaving Augusta proceeded to Charlotte where he joined his wife and daughter. Poor transportation had handicapped him many times during the war, but never had he experienced the difficulties he knew in 1865 when he could no longer "call on government wagons." Owners of vehicles and animals refused to sell, rent, or even take them on the roads because, as Ramsey explained, travelers and Confederate soldiers either appropriated them or "jumped on them in large enough numbers to damage them." Ramsey's transportation problem was also due to his moving in the opposite direction from that of most travelers, and he had less opportunity to ride with others. On his trip from Augusta to Charlotte he walked while a Negro carried his trunk, and rode in a buggy, carriage, and on a railroad flatcar. When his train reached Rock Hill, South Carolina, twenty-six miles south of Charlotte, he wanted to visit with his son who was living with friends in the country, but finding no way of getting there he proceeded to the home of a friend in Charlotte. He had great difficulty finding his family, for he did not know with whom they were staying, but after questioning everyone he met he finally located them. The future looked hopeless, for the Ramsey's Tennessee home was burned and their combined finances amounted to seventeen dollars in silver and twenty-five dollars in gold. Ramsey was sixty-eight, his wife was sixty-four, and it would not be easy for them to begin anew; but they purchased a farm near Charlotte which they named "Exiles Retreat," and despite their poverty they entertained other refugees who were having difficulty getting home.[30]

Among the refugees who never returned to their prewar home was Sarah Morgan who remained in New Orleans until her brother Jimmy came for her and their mother in 1866. He took them to his recently acquired plantation in South Carolina, and when economic reverses caused him to lose the property, the family moved to Charleston where Sarah married the prominent, fiery editor, Francis W. Dawson. After fifteen years of marriage, Dawson was killed in 1889, but Sarah remained in Charleston for ten more years before going to France where she died in 1909. Nor did Cornelia McDonald ever return to her home in Winchester, although she did visit in the village. For eight years after the war she remained in Lexington, working hard but getting deeper in debt. She continued teaching and boarded college students, but she could not provide for her family and pay her ever-mounting financial obligations. In 1873, she was persuaded to join her sons in Louisville, Kentucky, and there she died the same year as Sarah Morgan Dawson. Mrs. McDonald had made many friends as a refugee and after going to Louisville she was delighted to find several living in the city, among them Henrietta Johnston, daughter of Albert Sidney Johnston, who had been a refugee in Lexington.[31]

Most refugees left their wartime home with mixed feelings about the place and its people. As an Augusta editor watched hundreds leave the city, he was reminded that their "deprivations" had been "great," but he hoped that they "would carry with them some pleasant recollections of . . . [the] section, which would cement the ties of good fellowship in the future." He urged the departing refugees to remember the kind, generous, sympathetic people who had come to their assistance and to forget, if they could, the selfishness and greed displayed by a few in the community.[32] A great many who wrote after the war indicate that they did remember the happy and amusing incidents of those troubled years, as they wrote with greater detachment than had been possible at the time. Many refugees made lifelong friends during their displacement and, in time, became nostalgic about the community in which they had lived. They did "carry with them pleasant recollections," as the Augusta editor had hoped they would.

Several questions may be raised regarding the refugees, and one is whether or not they suffered more than civilians who stayed at home. Generally speaking, they did. The plight of those who refused to flee cannot be ignored and should not be minimized, but their worst hours and days were those immediately following an invasion and occupation, when they were most afraid and were most apt to be subjected to harsh treatment, insults, or indignities. As the enemy moved on or brought even a stern rule to the community, those who had remained usually accustomed themselves to the unhappy situation. If they quietly and peacefully pursued their normal activities they were often permitted to stay at home and provide for themselves amid familiar surroundings. But those who ran from the enemy usually had to keep running if they were to stay out of his clutches, and this hopping from place to place was demoralizing and expensive for both the refugees and the communities into which they went. As they crowded into congested areas, scarcities developed, followed by speculation and inflation. Everyone was affected, but the people who stayed in their own homes escaped paying the exorbitant rents charged refugees for crowded, unhealthy quarters. The cost of displacement was greater than that of living at home, for the people had to pay travel expenses, increasingly high rents, and usually, higher prices for provisions. They also risked losing both the possessions they carried with them and those they left behind, and their daily struggle for survival and gradual impoverishment in strange communities contributed to their lowering morale. Before the war ended most refugees had all the problems of citizens who stayed at home and none of the advantages.

Another question relates to whether or not the voluntary exiles regretted their decision to join the refugee ranks. If they did they did not specifically say so; a very few implied that they had erred. They very often gave evidence of being homesick and expressed a desire for the war to end so that they could go home, but those who stayed away throughout the conflict rarely gave serious thought to returning before peace was restored. To the contrary, they left the impression that displacement was the only choice they had, and those who wrote during and after the war took for granted that theirs was a patriotic act. Although most Southerners who left their homes voluntarily did so for personal reasons, they believed that they were acting in the best interests of the Confederacy and argued that all loyal citizens should stay together within Confederate lines. They rationalized their actions in this way after they had fled, but thousands did not think at all as they were making the decision. They did not think of the ultimate effect of their flight on themselves, their families, their property, or the Confederacy. They simply did what they preferred to do at the moment.

Two groups of displaced people viewed the matter in a different light from the voluntary exiles who stayed away until the end of the war. One was composed of those who fled and then returned home before the cessation of hostilities; their actions make obvious their recognition of an earlier mistake and they proceeded to correct it. The second group consisted of those who were banished by Federal authorities and who carried to their graves a deep-seated resentment for the officer responsible. Mrs. Meriwether, writing fifty-four years after the war, admitted her hatred for General Sherman who made her an exile, and this feeling was transmitted to her son. Although the voluntary refugees also blamed the enemy for their displacement, the decision had been theirs. Whether they stayed at home or fled, there were risks involved, but once they left they justified their actions.

A final question might be raised as to whether or not the South and the refugees themselves would have benefited had those with a choice in the matter stayed at home. This is difficult to answer because it lies largely in the realm of supposition and no one can say what might have happened in individual cases. Again generally speaking, it seems safe to assume that many military and civilian problems would have been minimized if not averted. As previously noted, the refugees did complicate life for themselves and others in innumerable ways and contributed to the breakdown of homefront morale, yet had the battle lines separated them from their men in the service this, too, would have created a morale problem at home and in camp. It would not have been pleasant living within Federal lines, but the people's chances would have been better for getting provisions, protecting property, and being near others who could assist them in time of need. They could have been spared the indifference and hostility they often encountered in strange communities and the risks involved in wartime travel. Had the civilians not fled, their postwar problems and those of the South would have been fewer in number, for peace would have found them at home and most would have been in possession of their property. There would have been some destruction and damage, but even so, it would have been easier to pick up the pieces and begin anew had they never left home. In the last six months of the war newspapermen were overwhelmingly of the opinion that displacement had been a mistake and they pleaded with the people to run no more.

The Civil War, like all others, converted a home-loving people into refugees. Southern civilians were shocked to discover that this was a war in which they were directly and personally involved, and they reacted in a perfectly natural human fashion. They often acted before they thought, for they were psychologically unprepared for a war on their doorsteps and they had little or no guidance in making decisions. Leaders seemed disinterested in their problem unless it in some way touched the military situation, therefore the civilians did what seemed best at the moment. However, the Southern people were also undisciplined to the demands and responsibilities placed on them by a war of invasion, and most of them did not understand that they must restrict or sacrifice many of their usual liberties and privileges, whether or not they wanted to do so. From Fort Sumter to Appomattox, the civilians tended to do what they preferred to do in so far as they could. If they chose to travel, they traveled; and if they wanted to settle in already congested communities, they did so. Their records indicate that they ignored others as they made their own decisions. Tens of thousands of unprepared, unguided, and undisciplined Southerners voluntarily displaced themselves and floundered around the contracting Confederacy for months and years, but they paid a high price for the privilege.

Notes

Chapter I

1 Judith Brockenbrough McGuire, *Diary of a Southern Refugee During the War* (New York, 1867), 1–20. Hereinafter cited as *Diary*.
2 Douglas Southall Freeman, *R. E. Lee: A Biography* (New York, 1934), I, 510. See also Katharine M. Jones (ed.), *Heroines in Dixie*, 26–27.
3 John Avery Benbury to Harriet Ryan Benbury, July 26, 1861, Benbury-Haywood Papers, Southern Historical Collection, University of North Carolina.

Chapter II

1 *Confederate Union* (Milledgeville), May 26, 1863.
2 Mrs. Thomas Taylor *et al.*, *South Carolina Women in the Confederacy* (Columbia, 1907), I, 219.
3 *Rockingham Register and Advertiser* (Harrisonburg), May 15, 1863.
4 Charleston *Daily Mercury*, September 7, 1861, March 19, 1862.
5 Mrs. George (Madeline Saunders) L'Engle to her brother-in-law, Edward L'Engle, March 18, 1862, Edward M. L'Engle Papers, Southern Historical Collection, University of North Carolina.
6 Diary of William Pitt Ballenger (Typescript in Eugene C. Barker Collection, University of Texas).
7 Emma E. Holmes Diary (Typescript in Southern Historical Collection, University of North Carolina).
8 John Berkeley Grimball Diaries (MSS in Southern Historical Collection, University of North Carolina).
9 Mrs. John (Annie Maney) Schon to her sister, Mrs. John (Bettie Maney) Kimberly, March 10, 1862, John Kimberly Papers, Southern Historical Collection, University of North Carolina.
10 Charleston *Daily Mercury*, March 3, 1862.
11 Mary Long to Mrs. Jeremy Francis Gilmer, May 20, 1862, Jeremy F. Gilmer Papers, Southern Historical Collection, University of North Carolina.
12 Diary of Samuel Andrew Agnew (MS in Southern Historical Collection, University of North Carolina).
13 Leonidas Polk to his wife, Frances Deveraux Polk, February 15, 16, 1862,

Leonidas Polk Papers, Southern Historical Collection, University of North Carolina.

14 John Avery Benbury to his wife, Harriet Ryan Benbury, January 22, 1862, Benbury-Haywood Papers.

15 Jeremy Francis Gilmer to his wife, Louisa Alexander Gilmer, February 22, 27, March 2, 3, 4, 6, 1862, Gilmer Papers.

16 Louisa Alexander Gilmer to her husband, Jeremy Francis Gilmer, March 5, 1862, *ibid.*

17 Charles Woodward Hutson Reminiscences (MS in Southern Historical Collection, University of North Carolina).

18 Katherine Polk Gale, "Recollections of Life in the Southern Confederacy, 1861–1865," Gale-Polk Papers, Southern Historical Collection, University of North Carolina.

19 Fanny Page Hume Diary (MS in Southern Historical Collection, University of North Carolina).

20 Papers of Mrs. W. K. Bachman (South Caroliniana Library, University of South Carolina).

21 J. G. M. Ramsey Autobiographical and Genealogical Notes, James Gettys McGready Ramsey Papers (Southern Historical Collection, University of North Carolina).

22 Charleston *Daily Courier*, February 18, 1863.

23 Louis A. Bringier to Stella Turead Bringier, April 23, 1864, Louis Amede Bringier Family Papers, Department of Archives and Manuscripts, Louisiana State University.

24 Sarah Morgan Dawson, *A Confederate Girl's Diary*, ed. James I. Robertson, Jr. (Indiana, 1960), 342–87.

25 *The War of Rebellion: A Compilation of the Official Records of the Union and Confederate Armies* (Washington, 1880–1901), Series I, Vol. XXII, 446. Hereinafter cited as *Official Records*. All references are to Series I unless otherwise stated.

26 John H. Chrisman Reminiscences, 1854–1865 (MS in Eugene C. Barker Collection, University of Texas); *Official Records*, V, 917.

27 New Orleans *Daily Crescent*, February 27, 1862.

28 *Official Records*, XV, 125.

29 *Ibid.*, XIV, 716.

30 Joseph Eggleston Johnston to Louis Trezevant Wigfall, March 6, 1864; Halsey Wigfall to Louise Wigfall, April 19, 1864, Louis Trezevant Wigfall Papers, microfilm in Eugene C. Barker Collection, University of Texas; and Joseph Eggleston Johnston to William Whann Mackall, December 31, 1864, January 26, 1865, William Whann Mackall Papers, Southern Historical Collection, University of North Carolina.

31 Petersburg *Daily Express*, October 14, 1862.

32 *Southern Banner* (Athens), July 13, 1864.

33 Rabun Lee Brantley, *Georgia Journalism in the Civil War Period* (Nashville, 1929), 47.

34 *Confederate Union* (Milledgeville), July 19, December 13, 1864.

35 Charleston *Daily Courier*, December 27, 1864.

36 *Ibid.*, January 4, 1865.

37 *Official Records*, VIII, 577–78.

38 Clara E. Soloman Diary, 1861–1862 (Typescript in Department of Archives and Manuscripts, Louisiana State University).

39 Mrs. Aaron V. Brown to John Gibson Parkhurst, January 27, 1865, John Gibson Parkhurst Papers, Manuscript Division, Duke University.

40 Mrs. Aaron V. Brown to Mrs. John Gibson Parkhurst, March 25, 1865, *ibid.*

41 Benedict Joseph Semmes to Jorantha Semmes, April 2, 1862, Benedict Joseph

Semmes Papers, Southern Historical Collection, University of North Carolina.

42   Jorantha Semmes to Benedict Joseph Semmes, June 3, 1862, *ibid.*

Chapter III

1   Wilmington *Journal*, March 26, 1863.
2   J. G. M. Ramsey Autobiographical and Genealogical Notes, Ramsey Papers.
3   Mrs. Richard Burwell to Edmund Burwell, September 24, 1864, Burwell Papers, Southern Historical Collection, University of North Carolina.
4   McGuire, *Diary*, 66.
5   *Ibid.*, 233.
6   Mary Boykin Chesnut, *A Diary From Dixie* (Boston, 1950), 519–20.
7   Mary Elizabeth Mitchell Book, 1838–1870 (MS in Southern Historical Collection, University of North Carolina).
8   Katherine Polk Gale, "Recollections of Life in the Southern Confederacy, 1861–1865," Gale-Polk Papers.
9   Elizabeth Avery Meriwether Recollections, 1824–1916 (Microfilm in Southern Historical Collection, University of North Carolina).
10 See letters of Jorantha and Benedict Joseph Semmes, Benedict Joseph Semmes Papers.
11 Frank E. Vandiver, *Mighty Stonewall* (New York, 1957), 418–19.
12 Mrs. Edmund Kirby Smith to Mrs. Joseph Lee Smith, September 22, 1863, Edmund Kirby Smith Papers, Southern Historical Collection, University of North Carolina.
13 Charles L. Pettigrew to William S. Pettigrew, August 22, 1864, Pettigrew Family Papers, Southern Historical Collection, University of North Carolina.
14 Alfred Jackson Hanna, *Flight into Oblivion* (Richmond, 1938), *passim.* See also Rembert W. Patrick, *The Fall of Richmond* (Baton Rouge, 1960), 3–40; J. H. Averill, "The Evacuation of the City of Richmond," *Southern Historical Society Papers*, XXXV (1897), 268.
15 Anna Holmes Trenholm Diary, April–June, 1865 (Typescript in Southern Historical Collection, University of North Carolina).
16 Josiah Gorgas Journal, 1857–1864 (Microfilm, Southern Historical Collection, University of North Carolina).
17 Williamson Simpson Oldham, "Last Days of the Confederacy" (Typescript, Eugene C. Barker Collection, University of Texas).
18 Cornelia Peake McDonald, *A Diary With Reminiscences of the War and Refugee Life in the Shenandoah Valley, 1860–1865* (Nashville, 1934), 207–208. Hereinafter cited as *Diary*.
19 Richmond *Enquirer*, July 20, 1864.
20 Josiah Gorgas Journal, 1857–1864.
21 Richmond *Enquirer*, April 29, 1864, quoting the Petersburg *Daily Express*, n. d.
22 *Daily South Carolinian* (Columbia), May 1, 1864.
23 Henry C. Lay to Mrs. Lay, January 30, 1865, Bishop Henry C. Lay Papers, Southern Historical Collection, University of North Carolina.
24 *Confederate Union* (Milledgeville), September 1, 1863, quoting Chattanooga *Rebel*, n. d.; Mary Boykin Chesnut, *A Diary From Dixie*, 434–35.
25 Robert McGill Loughbridge to David C. Williams, n. d., David C. Williams Papers, Eno Collection, Arkansas History Commission, Department of Archives and History.

26 Richmond *Enquirer*, December 22, 1863.
27 *Texas State Gazette* (Austin), July 13, 1863.
28 Julia LeGrand to Mrs. William H. Branch, February 10, 1864, William H. Branch Papers, Southern Historical Collection, University of North Carolina.
29 Charleston *Daily Courier*, September 13, 1864.
30 Joseph LeConte Journal (MS in South Caroliniana Library, University of South Carolina).
31 *Ibid.*
32 Daniel Walker Hollis, *University of South Carolina* (Columbia, 1951), I, 227.
33 For discussion of the refugee newspapers see chap. ix.
34 *Southern Confederacy* (Atlanta), July 10, 1864. See also A. A. Hoehling, *Last Train From Atlanta* (New York, 1958), 72.
35 William E. Woodruff to J. M. Jebbals, December 29, 1865, William E. Woodruff Papers, Arkansas History Commission, Department of Archives and History; Washington (Arkansas) *Telegraph*, March 16, 1864.
36 James Dunwoody Brownson DeBow to Charles Gayarre, June 22, November 29, 1862, Gayarre Papers, Grace King Collection, Department of Archives and Manuscripts, Louisiana State University.
37 Richmond *Examiner*, March 25, 1865, quoting the New York *Herald*, n. d.
38 John Cheesborough to Mrs. Cheesborough, June 6, 1862, John Cheesborough Papers, Southern Historical Collection, University of North Carolina.
39 John Berkeley Grimball Diaries.
40 Mary Louise DuBrutz Reston Memoirs (MS in Southern Historical Collection, University of North Carolina).
41 J. G. M. Ramsey Autobiographical and Genealogical Notes, Ramsey Papers.
42 *Ibid.*; Sue Ramsey Alexander, "Women in the War," *ibid.*
43 Edward Porter Alexander to Mrs. Alexander, June 11, 1861, E. P. Alexander Papers, Southern Historical Collection, University of North Carolina.
44 Catherine Cooper Hopley, *Life in the South: from the Commencement of the War* . . . (London, 1863), I, 366–67.
45 Richmond *Whig*, August 29, 1862.
46 Lynchburg *Republican*, August 25, 1862.
47 Richmond *Daily Examiner*, January 4, 1864.
48 Phoebe Yates Pember to Mrs. Jeremy Francis Gilmer, February 19, 1864, Phoebe Yates Pember Papers, Southern Historical Collection, University of North Carolina.
49 George B. Kain to Phoebe Yates Pember, September 14, 1864, Pember Papers.
50 Mrs. Basil Wilson Duke to Mrs. Henrietta Morgan, January 29, 1864, Duke-Morgan Papers, Southern Historical Collection, University of North Carolina.
51 Jeremy Francis Gilmer to Mrs. Gilmer, September 28, 1862, Gilmer Papers.
52 Elodie Todd to Nathaniel Henry Rhodes Dawson, November 9, 1861, December 28, 1861, Nathaniel Henry Rhodes Dawson Papers, Southern Historical Collection, University of North Carolina.
53 George Cadman to Esther Cadman, November 5, 1863, George Cadman Papers, Southern Historical Collection, University of North Carolina.
54 *Harper's Weekly*, September 19, 1863; May 14, November 5, 1864.
55 *Tri-Weekly Gazette* (Austin), October 12, 1863.
56 Eliza Frances Andrews, *The War-Time Journal of a Georgia Girl* (New York, 1908), 133. Hereinafter cited as *Journal.*

Chapter IV

1 Sarah L. Wadley Diary (MS in Southern Historical Collection, University of North Carolina).

2 Katherine Polk Gale, "Recollections of Life in the Southern Confederacy," Gale-Polk Papers.
3 Jorantha Semmes to Benedict Joseph Semmes, January 19, 1865, Semmes Papers.
4 Hume Diary.
5 Emma Wray to unidentified "Dear Friend," January 24, 1865, Barrow Papers, microfilm, Southern Historical Collection, University of North Carolina.
6 John Q. Anderson (ed.), *Brokenburn: The Journal of Kate Stone, 1861–1868* (Baton Rouge, 1955), 191. Hereinafter cited as *Brokenburn*.
7 Mrs. W. D. Chadwick, "Civil War Days in Huntsville" (Huntsville *Times*, n. d., Southern Historical Collection, University of North Carolina).
8 Leeland Hathaway Recollections (Microfilm in Southern Historical Collection, University of North Carolina).
9 Galveston *Tri-Weekly News*, August 10, 1864. Although retaining its name for most of the war years, the newspaper was published in Houston.
10 Joseph LeConte Journal.
11 Thomas H. Weightman to John Moore, March 23, 1864, David Weeks Family Papers, The Weeks-Hall Memorial Collection, Department of Archives and Manuscripts, Louisiana State University.
12 Daniel Huger Smith, *et al.* (eds.), *Mason Smith Family Letters* (Columbia, 1950), 195–96.
13 Phoebe Yates Pember, *A Southern Woman's Story* (Jackson, 1959), 168–69.
14 Jorantha Semmes to Benedict Joseph Semmes, October 3, 1862, Semmes Papers.
15 McDonald, *Diary*, 182.
16 Fannie A. Beers, *Memories: A Record of Personal Experience and Adventure During Four Years of War* (Philadelphia, 1888), 140. Hereinafter cited as *Memories*.
17 McDonald, *Diary*, 178.
18 John Q. Anderson (ed.), *Brokenburn*, 194.
19 Jorantha Semmes to Benedict Joseph Semmes, August 28, 1863, Semmes Papers.
20 *Gulf City Home Journal* (Mobile), May 25, 1863.
21 Myrta Lockett Avary, *Dixie After the War* (New York, 1906), 10.
22 Andrews, *Journal*, 165.
23 Matthew Page Andrews (ed.), *The Women of the South in War-Times* (Baltimore, 1920), 247–50.
24 Clara Eno, "Reminisences of the War Between the States" (MS in Eno Collection, Arkansas History Commission, Department of Archives and History).
25 Daniel Huger Smith, *et al.* (eds.), *Mason Smith Family Letters*, 170.
26 Charleston *Daily Courier*, December 29, 1863.
27 McGuire, *Diary*, 220.
28 Meriwether Recollections.
29 Jorantha Semmes to Benedict Joseph Semmes, September 11, 1863, Semmes Papers.
30 Mary Webster Loughborough, *My Cave Life in Vicksburg* (New York, 1864), 28.
31 Katherine Polk Gale, "Recollections of Life in the Southern Confederacy," Gale-Polk Papers.
32 John Townsend Trowbridge, *A Picture of the Desolated States and the Work of Restoration* (Hartford, 1868), 554.
33 Joseph LeConte Journal.
34 Sally Elmore Taylor Memoir (MS in Southern Historical Collection, University of North Carolina).
35 Chesnut, *Diary*, 485.

36 Houston *Tri-Weekly Telegraph,* June 6, 1862.
37 Andrews, *Journal,* 150.
38 Susan Dabney Smedes, *Memorials of a Southern Planter* (Baltimore, 1887), 221.
39 Mary A. H. Gay, *Life in Dixie During the War* (Atlanta, 1894), 85.
40 J. G. M. Ramsey Autobiographical and Genealogical Notes, Ramsey Papers.
41 Lafayette McLaws to Mrs. McLaws, November 22, 1862, General Lafayette McLaws Papers, Southern Historical Collection, University of North Carolina.
42 Mrs. Basil Wilson Duke to Mrs. Henrietta Morgan, January 29, 1864, Duke-Morgan Papers.
43 Mrs. D. Giraud Wright, *A Southern Girl in '61: The War-Time Memories of a Confederate Senator's Daughter* (New York, 1905), 179–80. Hereinafter cited as *A Southern Girl in '61.*
44 Katherine Polk Gale, "Recollections of Life in the Southern Confederacy," Gale-Polk Papers.
45 Frances Fearn, *Diary of a Refugee* (New York, 1910), 15.
46 McDonald, *Diary,* 187–88.
47 Louise C. Sheppard Recollections (Microfilm in Southern Historical Collection, University of North Carolina).
48 Sally Elmore Taylor Memoir.
49 Josiah Gorgas Journal, 1864–1876 (MS in Southern Historical Collection, University of North Carolina).
50 New Orleans *Daily Crescent,* March 1, 1862.
51 Chadwick, "Civil War Days in Huntsville," Huntsville *Times,* n. d.
52 Meriwether Recollections.
53 Mrs. Basil Wilson Duke to Mrs. Henrietta Morgan, January 29, 1864, Duke-Morgan Papers.
54 John Q. Anderson (ed.), *Brokenburn,* 170, 199.
55 Joseph LeConte Journal.
56 John Q. Anderson (ed.), *Brokenburn,* 221–25.
57 Wadley Diary, MS.
58 Annie Laurie Broidrick, "A Recollection of Thirty Years Ago" (MS in Southern Historical Collection, University of North Carolina).
59 Henry C. Lay to Mrs. Lay, January 12, 1863, Bishop Henry C. Lay Papers.
60 Mitchell Book.
61 John Q. Anderson (ed.), *Brokenburn,* 192.
62 Joseph LeConte Journal.
63 Clara Eno, "Reminiscences of the War Between the States," Eno Collection.
64 Sheppard Recollections.
65 Galveston *Tri-Weekly News,* August 19, 1863.
66 Wadley Diary.
67 McGuire, *Diary,* 172.
68 Charleston *Daily Mercury,* March, 1862, quoting the Gainesville *Cotton States,* n. d.
69 McDonald, *Diary,* 180.
70 August Conrad, *The Destruction of Columbia, S. C.* (Roanoke, 1902), 27.
71 Sheppard Recollections.
72 T. U. Taylor, "Swamp Fox of the Sulphur or Life and Times of Cullen Montgomery Baker" (Typescript in Eugene C. Barker Collection, University of Texas). *Flake's Daily Bulletin* (Galveston), December 15, 1868, referred to Baker as "an outlaw" and stated, "Few characters are more notorious." The authorities of Texas and Arkansas were looking for him in 1868. He was killed in January, 1869.
73 Wadley Diary.

74 Meriwether Recollections.
75 Diary of Samuel Andrew Agnew.
76 John Q. Anderson (ed.), *Brokenburn*, 221.
77 Hume Diary.
78 Jorantha Semmes to Benedict Joseph Semmes, August 28, 1863, Semmes Papers.

Chapter v

1 McGuire, *Diary*, 20.
2 Matthew Page Andrews to Anna Robinson, May 7, 1861, Charles Wesley Andrews Papers, Manuscript Division, Duke University.
3 Charleston *Daily Mercury*, November 8, 1862.
4 Willis F. Jones to Mrs. Basil Wilson Duke, December 28, 1863, Duke-Morgan Papers.
5 Julian C. Ruffin to Lottie Ruffin, April 29, 1862, Meade-Ruffin Papers, Southern Historical Collection, University of North Carolina.
6 John Avery Benbury to Harriet Ryan Benbury, May 7, 1862, Benbury-Haywood Papers.
7 Augusta *Daily Chronicle and Sentinel*, July 7, 1864.
8 Atlanta *Intelligencer*, July 8, 1864.
9 *Confederate Union* (Milledgeville), February 23, 1864.
10 Louise Wigfall to Mrs. Louis T. Wigfall, May 12, 1862, Wigfall Papers.
11 Lafayette McLaws to Emily McLaws, February 2, May 9, 1863, McLaws Papers.
12 Unidentified writer to her mother, January 20, 1863, William Slade Papers, Manuscript Division, Duke University.
13 James Earl Bradley Diary (MS in James Earl Bradley Papers, Department of Archives and Manuscripts, Louisiana State University).
14 Edgeville *Advertiser*, December 4, 1861.
15 Mrs. Martha Williams to unidentified person, October 2, 1864, Hulda Briant Letters, Manuscript Division, Duke University.
16 *Tri-Weekly Carolinian* (Columbia), November 17, 1863.
17 Galveston *Tri-Weekly News* (Houston), May 25, 1863.
18 Fitzgerald Ross, *A Visit to the Cities and Camps of the Confederate States* (Edinburgh, 1865), 102–103. Hereinafter cited as *Cities and Camps;* Walter Lord (ed.), *The Fremantle Diary* . . . (Boston, 1954), 164; McGuire, *Diary*, 88; Charleston *Daily Courier*, February 5, 1863.
19 Emma Mordecai Diary, 1864–1865 (MS in Southern Historical Collection, University of North Carolina).
20 Richmond *Daily Whig*, April 30, 1863.
21 Richmond *Daily Examiner*, July 25, 1864.
22 McGuire, *Diary*, 175, 206.
23 Mrs. Roger Atkinson Pryor, *My Day: Reminiscences of a Long Life* (New York, 1908), 194. Hereinafter cited as *My Day*.
24 Edward Porter Alexander to Adam Leopold Alexander, March 7, 1862, E. P. Alexander Papers.
25 *Official Records*, XXI, 557.
26 Charleston *Daily Courier*, January 29, 1862.
27 Edward Porter Alexander to Bettie Mason Alexander, April 6, 1862, E. P. Alexander Papers.
28 Lavinia Dabney to Robert Lewis Dabney, May 22, 1862, Charles William Dabney Papers, Southern Historical Collection, University of North Carolina.

29 Ross, *Cities and Camps*, 23; *Official Records*, XXVII, 352.
30 Mrs. —— Brodnax to John P. Brodnax, May 2, 1862, John G. Brodnax Papers, Manuscript Division, Duke University.
31 Betty Herndon Maury Diary (MS in Manuscript Division, Library of Congress).
32 James Ryder Randall to Kate S. Hammond, October 6, 1863, Randall Letters, Southern Historical Collection, University of North Carolina.
33 Mannie Pipkin to her mother, March 30, 1865, P. D. Gold Papers, Southern Historical Collection, University of North Carolina.
34 John Avery Benbury to Harriet Ryan Benbury, February 21, 1862, Benbury-Haywood Papers.
35 Mrs. P. C. Calder to William Calder, May 23, June 3, October 29, 1862, William Calder Papers, Southern Historical Collection, University of North Carolina.
36 William Calder to Mrs. P. C. Calder, December 28, 1862; Mrs. P. C. Calder to Robert Calder, March 30, 1862, *ibid.*
37 William Dorsey Pender to Mrs. Pender, July 29, 1862, William Dorsey Pender Papers, Southern Historical Collection, University of North Carolina.
38 Mrs. John Kimberly to Mrs. John Schon, November 18, 1861, June 8, 1862, Kimberly Papers.
39 Louise Wigfall to Mrs. Louis T. Wigfall, May 12, May 19, 1862, Wigfall Papers.
40 J. G. M. Ramsey Autobiographical and Genealogical Notes, Ramsey Papers.
41 Richmond *Daily Dispatch*, July 14, 1862; Wright, *A Southern Girl in '61*, p. 229.
42 E. H. Harpin to Caroline Patterson, February 23, 1864, Lindsay Patterson Papers, Southern Historical Collection, University of North Carolina.
43 Chesnut, *A Diary From Dixie*, 478–506.
44 Henry C. Lay to Mrs. Lay, January 30, January 31, 1865, Bishop Henry C. Lay Papers.
45 Columbia *Phoenix*, April 8, 1865.
46 Diary of Captain J. J. Westcoat (Typescript in Manuscript Division, Duke University).
47 Charleston *Daily Courier*, June 12, 1863.
48 Sumter *Tri-Weekly Watchman*, May 30, 1862.
49 Holmes Diary.
50 Richmond *Daily Whig*, March 24, 1865.
51 Charlotte R. Holmes (ed.), *The Burckmeyer Letters, 1863–1865* (Columbia, 1926), 232.
52 Chesnut, *Diary*, 256, 441–42.
53 Edgeville *Advertiser*, December 4, 1861.
54 Charlotte R. Holmes (ed.), *The Burckmeyer Letters, 1863–1865*, p. 446.
55 Charleston *Daily Courier*, December 7, 1862.
56 Grimball Diaries.
57 William Ferguson Calcock Autobiography (Microfilm in Southern Historical Collection, University of North Carolina).
58 J. G. M. Ramsey Autobiographical and Genealogical Notes, Ramsey Papers.
59 Elizabeth Wiggins to her mother, June 12, 1864, Elizabeth S. Wiggins Letters, Manuscript Division, Duke University.
60 Macon *Telegraph*, July 21, September 16, 1864.
61 G. Fain to Hulda Briant, March 14, 1862, Briant Letters.
62 *Confederate Union* (Milledgeville), July 19, 1864.
63 Augustus Longstreet Hull, *Annals of Athens, Georgia, 1801–1904* (Athens, 1906), 260–61.
64 Augusta *Chronicle and Sentinel*, January 17, 21, 1865.

65 Robert Franklin Bunting, correspondent to the Houston *Tri-Weekly Tele-graph*, July 21, 1863, February 27, 1864, Robert Franklin Bunting Letters, Eugene C. Barker Collection, University of Texas.
66 Caroline Phillips Myers Memoirs, Phillips-Myers Papers, Southern Historical Collection, University of North Carolina.
67 Reminiscences of Philip Phillips, *ibid.*
68 Columbus *Enquirer*, June 16, 1863.
69 *Official Records*, XXVI, 817.
70 Mrs. John Claudius L'Engle to Edward L'Engle, March 6, April 4, 1862, L'Engle Papers.
71 Charleston *Daily Courier*, April 14, 1862.
72 Richard Barksdale Harwell (ed.), *Kate: The Journal of a Confederate Nurse* (Baton Rouge, 1959), 89, 243, 261.
73 Montgomery *Daily Advertiser*, February 14, 1864.
74 Mobile *Daily Register*, May 24, 1863.
75 Lord (ed.), *The Fremantle Diary*, 105.
76 *Official Records*, XXVI, 112.
77 *Gulf City Home Journal* (Mobile), September 12, 1863.
78 Elodie Todd Dawson to N. H. R. Dawson, August 21, 1863, Nathaniel Henry Rhodes Dawson Papers.
79 Jorantha Semmes to Benedict Joseph Semmes, November 15, 1862, Semmes Papers.
80 Harwell (ed.), *Kate*, 141.
81 Sheppard Recollections.
82 C. W. Anderson, "After the Fall of Fort Donelson," *Confederate Veteran*, IV, 289–90.
83 *Arkansas True Democrat* (Little Rock), November 7, 1861.
84 Henry C. Lay to Mrs. Lay, January 11, 1863, Bishop Henry C. Lay Papers.
85 Henry C. Millery to Mrs. William Woodson King, July 20, 1863, William Woodson King Papers, Grace King Collection, Department of Archives and Manuscripts, Louisiana State University.
86 Charleston *Daily Courier*, August 18, 1864.
87 James Earl Bradley Diary, Bradley Papers; Sarah Johnston Estes Diary (Microfilm in Southern Historical Collection, University of North Carolina).
88 Joseph Lancaster Brent to Mrs. Louis A. Bringier, April 29, 1864, Bringier Papers.
89 John F. Leigh to John O. Moore, November 30, 1863, July 15, 1864, Weeks Family Papers.
90 *Tri-Weekly Gazette* (Austin), October 9, 1863, quoting the Marshall *Republican*, n. d.
91 Sheppard Recollections.
92 John Q. Anderson (ed.), *Brokenburn*, 232.
93 Lord (ed.), *The Fremantle Diary*, 51; Houston *Tri-Weekly Telegraph*, January 23, 1862.
94 Fayetteville *Observer*, February 9, 1865, quoting the Lynchburg *Daily Republican*, n. d.

Chapter VI

1 Holmes Diary.
2 Meta Morris Grimball Journal (MS in Southern Historical Collection, University of North Carolina).
3 McGuire, *Diary, passim.*
4 Richmond *Daily Whig*, April 30, 1863.

5 McDonald, *Diary*, 178–95.
6 Fearn, *Diary of a Refugee*, 44–58.
7 Jorantha Semmes to Benedict Joseph Semmes, September 20, October 11, 27, November 2, 1863, Semmes Papers.
8 Katherine Polk Gale, "Recollections of Life in the Southern Confederacy," Gale-Polk Papers.
9 Maggie Weeks to John Moore, January 25, 1865, Weeks Family Papers.
10 Holmes Diary.
11 Lafayette McLaws to Emily McLaws, April 12, 1863, McLaws Papers.
12 McGuire, *Diary*, 173.
13 Richmond *Daily Whig*, April 30, 1863.
14 Francis W. Dawson, *Our Women in the War* (Charleston, 1887), 16.
15 McGuire, *Diary*, 301.
16 Mrs. P. C. Calder to Robert Calder, May 25, 1863, Calder Papers.
17 Grimball Journal.
18 Charleston *Daily Courier*, May 14, 1862.
19 Fearn, *Diary of a Refugee*, 19–21.
20 Clara Minor Lynn Papers, Manuscript Division, Confederate Museum, Richmond; McGuire, *Diary*, 172.
21 Pryor, *My Day*, 201.
22 George Washington Cable (ed.), "A Woman's Diary of the Siege of Vicksburg," *The Century Illustrated Monthly Magazine*, XXX (1885), 772.
23 Mrs. Frances Bernard Goolrick, "Suffering in Fredericksburg," *Southern Historical Society Papers*, XXXVII (1909), 357.
24 Chapman J. Milling, "Ilium in Flames," *Confederate Veteran*, XXVI, 182.
25 Robertson (ed.), *A Confederate Girl's Diary*, 128–34.
26 Mrs. R. W. Meade to Mrs. Julian Ruffin, July 11, 1864, Meade-Ruffin Papers.
27 Lilly Logan Morrill (ed.), *My Confederate Girlhood: The Memoirs of Kate Virginia Cox Logan* (Richmond, 1932), 61–62.
28 *Official Records*, XXXV, 64.
29 Augusta *Chronicle and Sentinel*, July 21, 1864.
30 Macon *Confederacy*, September 28, 1864; Atlanta *Intelligencer*, September 23, 1864.
31 Loulie Gilmer to Jeremy Francis Gilmer, September 28, 1863, Gilmer Papers.
32 Parthenia Antoinette Hague, *A Blockaded Family: Life in Southern Alabama During the Civil War* (Boston, 1888), 148.
33 Macon *Confederacy*, September 24, 1864; Sumter *Republican* (Americus), October 1, 15, 1864.
34 Augusta *Chronicle and Sentinel*, September 25, 29, 1864; *Confederate Union* (Milledgeville), October 4, 1864.
35 *Confederate Union* (Milledgeville), November 8, 1864.
36 Beers, *Memories*, 166.
37 *Daily Southern Chronicle* (Knoxville), July 29, 1863.
38 Broidrick, "A Recollection of Thirty Years Ago."
39 Loughborough, *My Cave Life in Vicksburg*, 17, 61–62, 96–97, 114.
40 David Dodge, "Cave Dwellers of the Confederacy," *Atlantic Monthly*, LXVIII (1891), 516–17.
41 Trowbridge, *A Picture of the Desolated States and the Work of Restoration*, 357.
42 Mobile *Daily Advertiser and Register*, December 13, 1863.
43 Daniel Huger Smith, *et al.* (eds.), *Mason Smith Family Letters*, 196.
44 Katherine Polk Gale, "Recollections of Life in the Southern Confederacy," Gale-Polk Papers.
45 Grimball Journal.
46 *Ibid.*

47 Jorantha Semmes to Benedict Joseph Semmes, September 20, 1863, Semmes Papers.
48 Katherine Polk Gale, "Recollections of Life in the Southern Confederacy," Gale-Polk Papers.
49 Mobile *Daily Advertiser and Register,* November 1, 1863.
50 Daniel Huger Smith, *et al.* (eds.), *Mason Smith Family Letters,* 57.
51 Mrs. John Schon to Mrs. John Kimberly, May 27, 1862, Kimberly Papers.
52 Augustine T. Smythe to Mrs. Thomas Smythe, October 19, 1863, Augustine T. Smythe Papers (Typescript in Southern Historical Collection, University of North Carolina).
53 Mrs. Leonidas Polk to Mrs. William Gale, December 17, 1863, Gale-Polk Papers.
54 Daniel Huger Smith, *et al.* (eds.), *Mason Smith Family Letters,* 17.
55 Charleston *Daily Courier,* June 24, 1862.
56 Pryor, *My Day,* 238.
57 Katherine Polk Gale, "Recollections of Life in the Southern Confederacy," Gale-Polk Papers.
58 T. T. Wiatt to William Patterson Smith, November 27, 1864, William Patterson Smith Papers, Manuscript Division, Duke University.
59 Goolrick, "Suffering in Fredericksburg," 358–59.

Chapter VII

1 Jorantha Semmes to Benedict Joseph Semmes, September 20, 1863, Semmes Papers.
2 Benedict Joseph Semmes to Jorantha, August 18, October 10, 1863, *ibid.*
3 Jorantha Semmes to Benedict Joseph Semmes, October 21, 1863, *ibid.*
4 Jorantha Semmes to Benedict Joseph Semmes, November 2, 1863, *ibid.*
5 Benedict Joseph Semmes to Jorantha Semmes, July 13, 1864, *ibid.*
6 Mrs. John Schon to Mrs. John Kimberly, October 18, 1863, March 19, 1864, Kimberly Papers.
7 Mrs. George L'Engle to Edward M. L'Engle, August 14, 1863, L'Engle Papers.
8 J. C. L'Engle to Edward M. L'Engle, April 1, 1864, *ibid.*
9 Diary of William Pitt Ballenger.
10 Theodore Honour to Mrs. Honour, April 6, September 23, 1863, Theodore A. Honour Papers, South Caroliniana Library, University of South Carolina.
11 Mrs. Theodore Honour to Theodore Honour, September 25, 1863, *ibid.*
12 Sidney Harding Diaries (MSS in Department of Archives and Manuscripts, Louisiana State University).
13 William Calder to Mrs. P. C. Calder, December 17, 1862, Calder Papers.
14 Mrs. P. C. Calder to Robert Calder, May 14, 1863, *ibid.*
15 Mrs. John Claudius L'Engle to Edward L'Engle, April 14, 1862, L'Engle Papers.
16 Edward Porter Alexander to Mae Alexander, January 21, 1862, E. P. Alexander Papers.
17 Jestin C. Hampton to Thomas B. Hampton, March 18, 1864, April 3, 1864, July 10, 1864, Thomas B. Hampton Papers, Eugene C. Barker Collection, University of Texas.
18 Grimball Journal.
19 John F. Leigh to John Moore, March 7, 1865, Weeks Family Papers.
20 Mrs. Richard Pugh to Richard Pugh, December 18, 1862, Richard Pugh Papers, Department of Archives and Manuscripts, Louisiana State University.
21 Mitchell Book.

22   Grimball Journal.
23   Katherine Polk Gale, "Recollections of Life in the Southern Confederacy," Gale-Polk Papers.
24   McDonald, *Diary,* 195.
25   Maggie S. Weeks to John Moore, January 25, 1865, Weeks Family Papers.
26   Harding Diaries.
27   Elodie Todd to N. H. R. Dawson, January 12, 1862, February 2, 1862, November 2, 1861, Dawson Papers.
28   Louis M. DeSaussure Plantation Record (MS in Southern Historical Collection, University of North Carolina).
29   Harding Diaries.
30   Katherine Polk Gale, "Recollections of Life in the Southern Confederacy," Gale-Polk Papers
31   Mrs. Richard Pugh to Richard Pugh, November 9, 1862, December 12, 1862, Pugh Papers.
32   Mrs. John Schon to Mr. and Mrs. Thomas Maney, June 4, 1862, Kimberly Papers.
33   Mrs. John Schon to Mrs. John Kimberly, May 31, 1862, *ibid.*
34   Edward R. Thomas to J. B. Smith, September 14, 1862, Joseph Belknap Smith Papers, Manuscript Division, Duke University.
35   Ruth A. Hairston to Bettie Hairston, January 25, 1863, Hairston-Wilson Papers, Southern Historical Collection, University of North Carolina.
36   Wadley Diary.
37   Hutson Reminiscences.
38   McDonald, *Diary,* 235–36.
39   Meriwether Recollections.
40   Benjamin D. Lay to Mrs. Elizabeth Eggleston, May 22, 1863, Eggleston-Roach Papers, Department of Archives and Manuscripts, Louisiana State University.
41   Chadwick, "Civil War Days in Huntsville," Huntsville *Times,* n. d.
42   Mrs. H. H. Simons, "The Burning of Columbia" (MS in Mrs. H. H. Simons Papers, South Caroliniana Library, University of South Carolina).
43   Benedict Joseph Semmes to Jorantha Semmes, October 10, 1863, Semmes Papers.
44   Jorantha Semmes to Benedict Joseph Semmes, October 21, 1863, *ibid.*
45   John Q. Anderson (ed.), *Brokenburn.* 249–51.
46   Mrs. Rawley Sivley to Jane Sivley, February 26, 1864, Jane Sivley Letters, Southern Historical Collection, University of North Carolina.
47   *Southern Confederacy* (Atlanta), June 1, 1864; Sumter *Watchman,* June 8, 1864. See also, Charles H. Smith, *Bill Arp, So Called: A Side Show of the Southern Side of the War* (New York, 1866), 84–92. Hereinafter cited as *Bill Arp, So Called.*
48   Sumter *Daily Republican* (Americus), September 24, 1864, quoting Augusta *Register,* n. d.; Charles H. Smith, *Bill Arp, So Called,* 97–103.
49   Sumter *Daily Republican* (Americus), July 1, 1864, quoting *Southern Confederacy,* n. d.; Charles H. Smith, *Bill Arp, So Called,* 103–109.
50   Mrs. Campbell Bryce, *The Personal Experiences of Mrs. Campbell Bryce During the Burning of Columbia, South Carolina . . .* (Philadelphia, 1899), 35–36.
51   Grace B. Elmore Diary (MS in Southern Historical Collection, University of North Carolina).
52   John Q. Anderson (ed.), *Brokenburn,* 233, 249, 311, 336–38, 358–59, 361–63.
53   Edgefield *Advertiser,* November 30, 1864.
54   Chesnut, *Diary,* 488, 495.
55   *Ibid.,* 484–500.

56 Meriwether Recollections.
57 John Q. Anderson, *Brokenburn*, 233–34.
58 Harriet Warren's Reminiscences (MS in private possession of Mrs. Mary Vardell Fraser Harrell, Spartanburg, South Carolina).

Chapter VIII

1 Daniel Huger Smith, *et al.* (eds.), *Mason Smith Family Letters*, 166.
2 John Q. Anderson (ed.), *Brokenburn*, 361.
3 Fearn, *Diary of a Refugee*, 22–23.
4 Henry Hunter Raymond to his mother, n. d., 1863, September 3, 9, 21, 29, 1863, October 5, 28, 1863, January 29, 1864, Henry Hunter Raymond Papers, South Caroliniana Library, University of South Carolina.
5 Augusta *Daily Chronicle and Sentinel*, January 20, 1864.
6 Sumter *Republican* (Americus), September 11, 1863, quoting Savannah *Republican*, n. d.
7 Taylor, *et. al.*, *South Carolina Women in the Confederacy*, I, 174–75.
8 Meriwether Recollections.
9 Taylor, *et al.*, *South Carolina Women in the Confederacy*, I, 207–208.
10 Richmond *Daily Examiner*, October 5, 6, 1863.
11 *Daily South Carolinian* (Columbia), December 3, 1864.
12 Fayetteville *Observer*, December 15, 1864. See also Charleston *Daily Courier*, December 9, 1864.
13 *Daily South Carolinian* (Columbia), December 16, 1864.
14 *Tri-Weekly South Carolinian*, August 12, 1863.
15 Mrs. Basil Wilson Duke to Mrs. Henrietta Morgan, January 29, 1864, Duke-Morgan Papers.
16 Louis A. Bringier to Mrs. Bringier, October 27, 1864, Bringier Family Papers.
17 Augusta *Daily Chronicle and Sentinel*, December 27, 1863, quoting the Richmond *Sentinel*, n. d.
18 Pryor, *My Day*, 187.
19 Meriwether Recollections.
20 Duncan Groner to Ella Calvert Groner, November 29, 1863, Virginius W. Groner Collection, Southern Historical Collection, University of North Carolina.
21 Elmore Diary.
22 D. S. Burwell to Edmund Burwell, October 6, 1863, Burwell Papers.
23 Mrs. R. Burwell to Edmund Burwell, February 16, 1865, *ibid.*
24 Arkansas *True Democrat* (Little Rock), November 7, 1861, March 13, 1862.
25 North Carolina *Standard* (Raleigh), January 13, 1863.
26 Wilmington *Journal*, March 26, 1863.
27 *Tri-Weekly Watchman* (Sumter), July 20, 1863.
28 Yorkville *Enquirer*, July 15, 1863. This is now York, South Carolina.
29 McDonald, *Diary*, 93.
30 J. G. M. Ramsey Autobiographical and Genealogical Notes, Ramsey Papers.
31 Holmes Diary.
32 Augustine T. Smythe to Louise McCord, January 12, 13, 1865, Augustine Thomas Smythe Letters.
33 Smedes, *Memorials of a Southern Planter*, 200.
34 Vicksburg *Daily Citizen*, February 19, 1863.
35 Wadley Diary.
36 Charleston *Daily Courier*, February 6, 1864.
37 "A Camden Girl as a Refugee in Texas" (Typescript in Arkansas History Commission, Little Rock).

38 *Southern Presbyterian*, January 12, 1865.
39 Katherine Polk Gale, "Recollections of Life in the Southern Confederacy," Gale-Polk Papers.
40 Meriwether Recollections.
41 —— Craig to Mrs. Elizabeth Eggleston, February 6, 1864, Roach-Eggleston Papers.
42 Louise Cunningham to Sarah Hamilton Yancey, August 27, 1864, Benjamin C. Yancey Papers, Southern Historical Collection, University of North Carolina.
43 Daniel Huger Smith, *et al.* (eds.), *Mason Smith Family Letters*, 29–30, 40.
44 Meriwether Recollections.
45 Charleston *Daily Courier*, April 16, 1862.
46 Holmes Diary.
47 Charleston *Daily Courier*, November 24, 1864.
48 *Daily Southern Guardian* (Columbia), September 15, 1863, quoting the *Confederate Baptist*, n. d.
49 Charleston *Daily Mercury*, November 21, 1861
50 Atlanta *Confederacy*, October 26, 1862.
51 North Carolina *Standard* (Raleigh), June 12, 1863; Lynchburg *Daily Republican*, June 13, 1863.
52 *Daily South Carolinian* (Columbia), December 11, 1864.
53 Vicksburg *Daily Whig*, July 1, 1862, July 11, 1862.
54 Winnsboro *Daily News*, February 15, 1865.
55 Houston *Daily Telegraph*, May 24, 1862; *Weekly State Gazette* (Austin), May 31, 1862.
56 Atlanta *Confederacy*, September 8, 1863; Charleston *Daily Courier*, September 11, 1863.
57 Sumter *Republican* (Americus), September 11, 1863.
58 Charleston *Daily Mercury*, April 15, 1862, quoting the Spartanburg *Express*, n. d.
59 *Southern Illustrated News* (Richmond), August 22, 1863.

Chapter IX

1 Charleston *Daily Courier*, September 8, 1863.
2 McGuire, *Diary*, 71, 205.
3 Harwell (ed.), *Kate*, 89, 260.
4 Andrews, *Journal*, 137.
5 McDonald, *Diary*, 246–47, 254.
6 Robertson (ed.), *A Confederate Girl's Diary*, 105, 435.
7 Grimball Diaries.
8 Reminiscences of Philip Phillips.
9 *Confederate Union* (Milledgeville), September 20, 1864.
10 *Southern Banner* (Athens), July 20, 1863, May 25, 1864.
11 Richmond *Daily Whig*, June 12, 1863, quoting the Atlanta *Appeal*, n. d.
12 *Ibid.*
13 *Natchez Daily Courier*, June 16, 1863, December 8, 1863.
14 *Daily South Carolinian* (Columbia), August 5, 1864; Richmond *Daily Dispatch*, August 17, 1864.
15 Columbus *Daily Enquirer*, September 24, 1864.
16 Brantley, *Georgia Journalism in the Civil War Period*, 101–102.
17 Wilmington *Journal*, July 20, 1864.
18 Ruth Ketring Nuermberger, *The Clays of Alabama: A Planter-Lawyer-Politician Family* (Lexington, 1958), 216–17.

19 *Tri-Weekly South Carolinian* (Columbia), July 16, 1864.
20 J. G. M. Ramsey Autobiographical and Genealogical Notes, Ramsey Papers.
21 Richmond *Daily Enquirer*, January 25, 1864.
22 William J. Bingham to General S. J. Patterson, December 11, 1863, January 8, 1864, Lindsay Patterson Papers.
23 Stephen Beauregard Weeks, "The University of North Carolina in the Civil War," *Southern Historical Society Papers*, XXIV (1896), 35. Also see Richmond *Enquirer*, December 31, 1864.
24 Natchez *Daily Courier*, October 20, 1863.
25 Arkansas *Patriot* (Little Rock), May 2, 1863.
26 J. G. M. Ramsey Autobiographical and Genealogical Notes, Ramsey Papers.
27 *Texas State Gazette* (Austin), August 20, 1862, October 1, 1862; Galveston *Tri-Weekly News* (Houston), September 4, 1862.
28 Charleston *Daily Courier*, October 25, 1862.
29 Vicksburg *Daily Whig*, January 7, 1862.
30 T. H. Weightman to John Moore, July 4, 1864, Weeks Family Papers.
31 McDonald, *Diary*, 235.
32 Anonymous Diary (in Manuscript Division, Duke University).
33 Macon *Daily Telegraph*, January 6, 1864.
34 McGuire, *Diary*, 174, 196, 238.
35 Mordecai Diary.
36 Louise Branch to Mrs. —— Hughes, February 12, 1862, Nicholson Papers, Southern Historical Collection, University of North Carolina.
37 McGuire, *Diary*, 96, 196–97, 238–39.
38 Jorantha Semmes to Benedict Joseph Semmes, January 23, 1865, Semmes Papers.
39 McGuire, *Diary*, 196.
40 *Ibid.*, 196, 205–206.
41 *Southern Illustrated News*, 1862–1864; Constance Cary Harrison, *Recollections Grave and Gay* (New York, 1911), 124–25.
42 Meriwether Recollections.
43 Columbus *Weekly Enquirer*, October 27, 1863.
44 Frank Webb to Thomas O. Moore, April 29, 1865, Thomas O. Moore Papers, Department of Archives and Manuscripts, Louisiana State University.
45 Lynchburg *Daily Virginian*, June 9, 1864.
46 Richmond *Daily Dispatch*, May 16, 1862.
47 Galveston *Tri-Weekly News* (Houston), March 27, 1862.
48 Natchez *Daily Courier*, June 16, 1863.
49 *Southern Confederacy* (Atlanta), August 15, 1862.
50 Jorantha Semmes to Benedict Joseph Semmes, June 13, 1863, Semmes Papers.
51 John Q. Anderson (ed.), *Brokenburn*, 320–21.
52 Chesnut, *Diary*, 121.
53 McGuire, *Diary*, 195.
54 McDonald, *Diary*, 248.
55 Fannie Beers, *Memories*, 211–17.
56 Grimball Journal.
57 Charleston *Daily Courier*, May 19, 1863.
58 *Ibid.*, March 24, 1862, April 2, 15, 24, 30, 1862.
59 Harrison, *Recollections Grave and Gay*, 94.
60 Harding Diaries.
61 McDonald, *Diary*, 198.
62 John Q. Anderson (ed.), *Brokenburn*, 321–22.
63 Stephen R. Mallory to Angela Mallory, August 31, 1862, Stephen R. Mallory Papers, University of North Carolina.
64 Richmond *Daily Examiner*, September 11, 1863.

65 Laura B. Comer Diaries (MSS in Southern Historical Collection, University of North Carolina).
66 Nuermberger, *The Clays of Alabama: A Planter-Lawyer-Politician Family*, 220.

Chapter x

1 Richmond *Daily Dispatch,* July 26, 1864.
2 Mrs. Basil Wilson Duke to Mrs. Henrietta Morgan, January 29, 1864, Duke-Morgan Papers.
3 McGuire, *Diary,* 328–29.
4 Mrs. Roger A. Pryor, *Reminiscences of Peace and War* (New York, 1908), 259, 327.
5 "A Trip to Dixie: Diary of Frances Woolfolk Wallace" (MS in Southern Historical Collection, University of North Carolina).
6 Reminiscences of Philip Phillips. See also Myers Memoirs.
7 Mrs. John Schon to Mrs. John Kimberly, March 13, 1863, Kimberly Papers.
8 Grimball Diaries.
9 John Q. Anderson (ed.), *Brokenburn,* 233, 255, 302 ff.
10 Harding Diaries.
11 Elodie Todd to N. H. R. Dawson, April 15, 1862, Dawson Papers.
12 Mrs. D. S. Burwell to "Ed" Burwell, October 6, 1863, Burwell Papers.
13 Elodie Todd to N. H. R. Dawson, January 5, 12, 17, 1862, February 1, 1862, Dawson Papers.
14 N. H. R. Dawson to Elodie Todd, November 12, 1861, *ibid.*
15 John Q. Anderson (ed.), *Brokenburn,* 320, 322, 328–32, 334, 336, 339, 341–48, 367.
16 *Ibid.,* 204.
17 Holmes Diary.
18 Louise Wigfall to Mrs. Louis T. Wigfall, July 11, 1864, Wigfall Papers.
19 Wright, *A Southern Girl in '61,* pp. 194–95.
20 Robertson (ed.), *A Confederate Girl's Diary,* 389–91.
21 Montgomery *Daily Advertiser and Register,* March 12, 1864.
22 O. V. Shearer, Jr., to Jane Sivley, March 10, 1864, Sivley Letters.
23 Willis R. Sivley to Jane Sivley, April 1, 1864, *ibid.*
24 Harding Diaries.
25 Holmes Diary.
26 Elodie Todd to N. H. R. Dawson, January 12, 1862, February 2, 1862, Dawson Papers.
27 Harding Diaries.
28 John Q. Anderson (ed.), *Brokenburn,* 233–39, 256, 270, 276, 280.
29 Harding Diaries.
30 Grimball Journal.
31 John Q. Anderson (ed.), *Brokenburn,* 225, 241.
32 *Ibid.,* 343.
33 Pryor, *My Day,* 187.
34 Williamson Simpson Oldham Memoirs (Typescript in Eugene C. Barker Collection, University of Texas).
35 Harding Diaries.
36 Daniel Huger Smith, *et al., Mason Smith Family Letters,* 1860–1868, 42.
37 Mary Elizabeth Massey, *Ersatz in the Confederacy* (Columbia, 1952), 77.
38 Harding Diaries.
39 Mrs. Charles L. Pettigrew to Charles L. Pettigrew, May 9, 1862, Pettigrew Family Papers.

40 Harding Diaries.
41 McGuire, *Diary*, 243–44.
42 *Ibid.*, 329.
43 Wright, *A Southern Girl in '61*, p. 119.
44 McGuire, *Diary*, 341.
45 Katherine Polk Gale, "Recollections of Life in the Southern Confederacy," Gale-Polk Papers.
46 Jorantha Semmes to Benedict Joseph Semmes, March 31, 1864, Semmes Papers.
47 Katherine M. Jones (ed.), *Heroines in Dixie* (Indianapolis, 1955), 246–47.
48 Katherine Polk Gale, "Recollections of Life in the Southern Confederacy," Gale-Polk Papers.
49 Jorantha Semmes to Benedict Joseph Semmes, December 25, 1863, Semmes Papers.
50 Meriwether Recollections.
51 John Q. Anderson (ed.), *Brokenburn*, 268–69.
52 Robertson (ed.), *A Confederate Girl's Diary*, 306–307.
53 Richmond *Daily Dispatch*, December 28, 1863.
54 Charleston *Daily Courier*, December 25, 1863.
55 McGuire, *Diary*, 323.
56 Grimball Journal.
57 Charleston *Daily Mercury*, September 24, 1863.
58 Grace King, *Memories of a Southern Woman of Letters* (New York, 1932), 9.
59 Reminiscences of Philip Phillips.
60 Edward Owen Guerrant Papers, Southern Historical Collection, University of North Carolina.
61 N. H. R. Dawson to Elodie Todd, March 15, 18, 21, 24, 1862, Dawson Papers.
62 John Q. Anderson (ed.), *Brokenburn*, 240.
63 *Ibid.*, 321.

Chapter XI

1 *Official Records*, XIII, 606, 616.
2 Kate Mason Rowland and Mrs. Morris L. Croxall (eds.), *The Journal of Julia LeGrand* (Richmond, 1911), 95–96.
3 *Official Records*, XVII, Pt. 2, pp. 88, 98–99.
4 *Ibid.*, 114, 240, 280, 860. See also, William Tecumseh Sherman, *Memoirs of General William T. Sherman* (Bloomington, Ind., 1957), I, 268. Hereinafter cited as *Memoirs.*
5 *Official Records*, XVII, Pt. 2, pp. 156, 169–71; William T. Sherman, *Memoirs,* I, 271–73; Meriwether Recollections.
6 *Official Records*, III, 133.
7 *Ibid.*, XX, Pt. 2, p. 82.
8 *Ibid.*, XXIV, Pt. 3, pp. 154, 206.
9 *Ibid.*, XXX, Pt. 3, p. 223.
10 *Ibid.*
11 *Ibid.*, XXXVII, Pt. 2, p. 378.
12 Jefferson Davis Bragg, *Louisiana in the Confederacy* (Baton Rouge, 1941), 136.
13 *Official Records*, XV, 576–77; Bragg, *Louisiana in the Confederacy*, 135, 136.
14 Rowland and Croxall (eds.), *The Journal of Julia LeGrand*, 281–82.
15 *Ibid.*, 70–71, 95.
16 *Harper's Weekly*, June 6, 1863.
17 Mrs. John Schon to Mrs. John Kimberly, May 25, September 4, 1863, April 10, 1864, Kimberly Papers.

18 *Official Records*, XVIII, 204, 664–65.
19 *Ibid.*, XXXIV, Pt. 4, p. 9.
20 *Ibid.*, XVI, Pt. 1, pp. 1009–10.
21 Sherman, *Memoirs*, II, 234.
22 *Official Records*, XXXVIII, Pt. 5, pp. 73, 76–77, 92, 104.
23 *Ibid.*, 794; Sherman *Memoirs*, II, 111.
24 *Official Records*, XXXVIII, Pt. 5, pp. 822, 837–38.
25 *Ibid.*, XXXIX, Pt. 2, p. 481.
26 *Sumter Republican* (Americus), September 24, 1864.
27 Macon *Telegraph*, September 9, 1864; Columbus *Daily Enquirer*, September 28, 1864; Charleston *Daily Courier*, September 20, 1864.
28 Henry C. Lay, "Two Months within the Lines," Bishop Henry C. Lay Papers.
29 Papers of Mrs. H. H. Simons; Sherman, *Memoirs*, II, 185–86.
30 Sherman, *Memoirs*, II, 187. A man leaving Columbia a week after the fire told a friend in York, South Carolina, that General Sherman left not only 500 head of cattle but also "1200 bushels of grain and some salt" to be distributed among the poor of the city. Yorkville *Enquirer*, March 9, 1865.
31 *Official Records*, XXX, Pt. 3, p. 402.
32 *Ibid.*, X, Pt. 1, p. 912.
33 *Ibid.*, VIII, 577–78.
34 *Ibid.*, LXIII, 1277, 1279–80.
35 Diary of William Pitt Ballenger.
36 Galveston *Tri-Weekly News* (Houston), December 21, 1864.
37 *Official Records*, VI, 22–23.
38 Charleston *Daily Courier*, February 24, April 6, 1863.
39 *Official Records*, VI, 22–23.
40 Sheppard Recollections.
41 *Official Records*, XXIII, Pt. 2, p. 847.
42 *Ibid.*, XXXIX, Pt. 2, p. 794.
43 *Ibid.*, XXIV, Pt. 4, p. 291.
44 *Ibid.*, XI, Pt. 1. pp. 268–70, Pt. 3, pp. 67, 71, 334–35; V, 52, 341–46.
45 *Ibid.*, XIV, 675.
46 Richmond *Daily Examiner*, June 6, 1863.
47 *Official Records*, XXII, Pt. 2, p. 601.
48 *Ibid.*, XXXIV, Pt. 3, p. 404.
49 *Ibid.*, XX, Pt. 2, pp. 391–92.
50 *Ibid.*, VIII, 405–407, 431–32.
51 Jeremy Francis Gilmer to Mrs. Gilmer, December 14, 22, 1861, Gilmer Papers.
52 *Official Records*, XIII, 691, 693, 736, 791–92, 806.
53 *Ibid.*, XXII, Pt. 2, pp. 825–26, XXX, Pt. 3, p. 506, XXXI, Pt. 3, pp. 58, 477–78.
54 *Ibid.*, XX, Pt. 2, pp. 391–92.
55 *Ibid.*, XLIII, Pt. 3, p. 987.
56 *Ibid.*, XVI, Pt. 1, pp. 785–86.
57 *Ibid.*, XL, Pt. 3, p. 355.
58 *Ibid.*, XIII, 467–68.
59 *Ibid.*, XXII, 456–57.
60 McDonald, *Diary*, 151–56.
61 *Ibid.*, 167–68.
62 *Official Records*, XLI, Pt. 4, p. 753.
63 *Ibid.*, XI, Pt. 3, pp. 568–69.
64 *Ibid.*, II, 844.
65 *Ibid.*, XVI, Pt. 2, p. 493.
66 *Ibid.*, XVI, Pt. 2, p. 368, XXXI, Pt. 1, p. 679.
67 *Ibid.*, III, 98.

Chapter XII

1 *Official Records*, VIII, 577–78.
2 *Ibid.*, VIII, 70.
3 *Ibid.*, II, 196.
4 *Ibid.*, VI, 200–201.
5 Richmond *Daily Inquirer*, June 25, 1861.
6 *Official Records*, IV, 571–72.
7 *Ibid.*, 567–68.
8 Richmond *Daily Dispatch*, August 12, 14, 1861.
9 Richmond *Daily Enquirer*, January 23, 1862.
10 Wilmington *Daily Journal*, February 12, 27, 1862; Memphis *Daily Appeal*, February 16, 1862.
11 Richmond *Daily Examiner*, May 23, 1862.
12 *Daily Mississippian* (Jackson), March 5, 1862.
13 Richmond *Daily Enquirer*, January 30, 1862.
14 Sherman, *Memoirs*, II, 185–86.
15 *Daily Mississippian* (Jackson), April 3, 1862, quoting the Huntsville *Democrat*, n. d.
16 New Orleans *Bee*, March 8, 1862.
17 New Orleans *Delta*, March 9, 1862; Memphis *Daily Appeal*, March 12, 1862.
18 *North Carolina Daily Standard* (Raleigh), February 26, 1862.
19 Robertson (ed.), *A Confederate Girl's Diary*, 176.
20 Jorantha Semmes to Benedict Joseph Semmes, June 3, 1862, Semmes Papers.
21 Memphis *Avalanche*, March 6, 1862; Galveston *Tri-Weekly News* (Houston), March 15, 1862.
22 Charleston *Daily Courier*, March 17, 1862.
23 *Official Records*, XXVI, Pt. 2, p. 268.
24 *Ibid.*, 268–69.
25 *Ibid.*, 581, XXII, Pt. 2, p. 1071.
26 *Ibid.*, XXXIV, Pt. 2, p. 318.
27 Mrs. R. L. Dixon to Henry St. John Dixon, April 30, 1864, Henry St. John Dixon Papers, Southern Historical Collection, University of North Carolina.
28 *Official Records*, III, 701.
29 Bunting Letters. Bunting wrote these letters to various newspapers in Texas. The first, dated November 9, 1861, was published in the San Antonio *Herald*, November 30, 1861. The other was dated November 13, 1861, but no place of publication was given.
30 Charleston *Daily Courier*, October 14, 1863.
31 *Official Records*, V, 998–99.
32 Charleston *Daily Courier*, August 22, 1862.
33 *Official Records*, IV, 554, 559.
34 Charleston *Daily Courier*, March 2, 1862, quoting the Chicago *Tribune*, n. d.
35 Augusta *Chronicle and Sentinel*, August 4, 1864, quoting St. Louis *Republican*, n. d.
36 Louis M. Starr, *The Bohemian Brigade: Civil War Newsmen in Action* (New York, 1954), 170.
37 *Official Records*, VI, 5–6.
38 *Ibid.*, IX, 200.
39 John Q. Anderson (ed.), *Brokenburn*, 197, 203.
40 *Official Records*, XXIII, Pt. 1, p. 246.
41 Wadley Diary.
42 *Official Records*, V, 543.
43 J. G. M. Ramsey Autobiographical and Genealogical Notes, Ramsey Papers.

44 Meriwether Recollections.
45 Robertson (ed.), *A Confederate Girl's Diary*, 175–76, 194–202.
46 Diary of William Pitt Ballenger.
47 *Official Records*, XIV, 126; *Ibid.*, XV, 628–29.
48 Charleston *Daily Courier*, December 30, 1863, quoting the Gainesville (Florida) *Cotton States*, n. d.
49 *Official Report Relative to the Conduct of the Federal Troops in Western Louisiana, During the Invasion of 1863 and 1864* (Shreveport, 1865), 38–40.
50 Galveston *Tri-Weekly News* (Houston), October 30, December 14, 1863.
51 *Arkansas State Gazette* (Little Rock), January 24, 1863, quoting Chicago *Journal*, n. d.

Chapter XIII

1 Wilmington *Journal*, August 27, 1863.
2 Columbia *Tri-Weekly South Carolinian*, April 19, 1864; Charleston *Daily Mercury*, March 18, 1864; Galveston *Tri-Weekly News* (Houston), April 11, 1864; *Southern Banner* (Athens), April 20, 1864.
3 *Southern Banner* (Athens), April 20, 1864.
4 George R. Bentley, *A History of the Freedmen's Bureau* (Philadelphia, 1955), 76–77, 140–42.
5 *Confederate Union* (Milledgeville), October 4, 1864, quoting the *Macon Telegraph*, n. d.
6 *Acts of the General Assembly of South Carolina*, December 21, 1861, pp. 13–14, December 18, 1862, pp. 119–21, December 17, 1863, pp. 164–67, December 23, 1864, pp. 205–11; *Acts of the State of Mississippi*, December 16, 1861, pp. 53–55, January 11, 1863, pp. 68–72, December 2, 1863, pp. 113–22, April 4, 1864, p. 34; *Acts of the General Assembly of Alabama*, November 11, 1861, pp. 4–8, November 12, 1862, pp. 26–29, August 31, 1863, pp. 16–17, December 8, 1863, pp. 81–82; *General Laws of the State of Texas*, March 5, 1863, p. 13, March 6, 1863, pp. 20, 22, 29–30, December 15, 1863, pp. 21–22; *Public Acts of the General Assembly of the State of Tennessee*, March 19, 1862, p. 6, February 11, 1862, pp. 57–60; *Public and Private Laws of the State of North Carolina*, February 10, 1863, pp. 63–64, December 14, 1863, pp. 26–27, May 28, 1864, pp. 16–18; *Acts Passed by the General Assembly of Arkansas*, December 1, 1862, p. 74.
7 *Acts of the General Assembly of the State of Georgia*, December 14, 1862, p. 23, November 18, 1864, p. 8, March 11, 1865, pp. 63–65.
8 *Acts and Resolutions Adopted by the General Assembly of Florida*, December 2, 1861, pp. 12–13, December 5, 1862, pp. 19–23, December 2, 1863, pp. 38–41, December 4, 1864, pp. 30–31.
9 *Acts of the State of Louisiana*, January 3, 1863, pp. 35–36, January 4, 1864, pp. 15–16, January 23, 1865, pp. 3–4.
10 *Acts of the General Assembly of South Carolina*, December 21, 1861, p. 8, February 6, 1863, p. 84, December 23, 1864, p. 203.
11 *Reports and Resolutions of the General Assembly of South Carolina*, December 4, 1863, pp. 334–35.
12 *Acts of the General Assembly of the State of Georgia*, November 18, 1863, pp. 66–68, March 17, 1864, pp. 159–60.
13 *Ibid.*, November 18, 1863, pp. 97–98.
14 *Confederate Union* (Milledgeville). November 8, 1864.
15 *Acts of the General Assembly of the State of Georgia*, March 11, 1865, pp. 81–82.
16 *Acts of the State of Louisiana*, June 18, 1863, pp. 18–19.

17 *Acts of the General Assembly of Virginia,* May 15, 1862, p. 14.
18 *Reports and Resolutions of the General Assembly of South Carolina,* December 17, 1863, p. 300.
19 *Acts of the General Assembly of the State of Georgia,* December 13, 1862, p. 15.
20 *Acts of the General Assembly of Alabama,* November 17, 1862, pp. 201–202.
21 *Acts of the General Assembly of Virginia,* June 24, 1861, pp. 54–55, May 14, 1862, p. 14; *Acts of the General Assembly of Alabama,* November 7, 1862, pp. 103–105. See also, *Acts of the General Assembly of Georgia,* November 22, 1861, p 24; *Acts and Resolutions Adopted by the General Assembly of Florida,* December 7, 1861, pp. 14–15; *Public Acts of the General Assembly of Tennessee,* March 15, 1862, pp. 55–56; *Laws of the General Assembly of Texas,* February 11, 1863, p. 70.
22 *Acts of the State of Mississippi,* December 31, 1862, p. 90, December 9, 1863, pp. 148–49.
23 *Acts of the General Assembly of Georgia,* November 18, 1864, pp. 16–17.
24 *Acts of the General Assembly of Alabama,* November 26, 1862, pp. 74–75.
25 *Acts Passed by the General Assembly of Arkansas,* September 28, 1864, p. 1; Washington (Arkansas) *Telegraph,* November 30, 1864.
26 *Acts of the State of Louisiana,* January 3, 1863, p. 30, June 20, 1863, p. 33.
27 *Acts and Resolutions Adopted by the General Assembly of Florida,* November 25, 1862, p. 9.
28 *Acts of the State of Louisiana,* February 3, 1865, p. 21.
29 *Ibid.,* February 4, 1865, pp. 34, 38–39.
30 *Acts of the General Assembly of Georgia,* November 30, 1863, p. 82, November 18, 1864, p. 34, March 3, 1865, pp. 71–72.
31 *Acts of the State of Louisiana,* January 23, 1862, p. 79, January 3, 1863, p. 20, February 9, 1864, pp. 21–22.
32 *Ibid.,* January 3, 1863, pp. 15–16.
33 *General Laws of the State of Texas,* December 6, 1861, pp. 5–6, December 2, 1863, pp. 5–6.
34 *Acts of the General Assembly of Georgia,* December 10, 1862, p. 112.
35 *Acts of the General Assembly of Alabama,* December 9, 1862, p. 42.
36 Washington (Arkansas) *Telegraph,* July 27, 1864, October 2, 1864.
37 *Acts of the State of Mississippi,* December 9, 1863, pp. 146–47.
38 *Acts of the General Assembly of Georgia,* March 9, 1865, pp. 61–62.
39 *Acts of the General Assembly of the State of Virginia,* March 26, 1863.
40 Lynchburg *Daily Virginian,* May 27, 1863.
41 *General Laws of the State of Texas,* November 27, 1861, p. 55.
42 Richmond *Daily Dispatch,* January 9, 1862.
43 Charleston *Daily Mercury,* December 12, 1861, December 14, 1861.
44 Charleston *Daily Courier,* December 12, 13, 14, 18, 1861, January 14, 1862.
45 Lynchburg *Daily Republican,* February 9, 1863.
46 Richmond *Daily Enquirer,* December 10, 1862, December 12, 1863.
47 Richmond *Daily Dispatch,* January 9, 1863.
48 New Orleans *Daily Picayune,* May 17, 1863.
49 Charleston *Daily Mercury,* June 5, 1863; Charleston *Daily Courier,* June 5, 1863.
50 Charleston *Daily Mercury,* June 5, 1863.
51 Charleston *Daily Courier,* June 22, July 1, August 17, 1863.
52 Richmond *Daily Whig,* June 2, 1863, June 4, 1863.
53 Richmond *Daily Sentinel,* June 1, 1863.
54 Lynchburg *Daily Republican,* May 21, 1863.
55 Lynchburg *Daily Virginian,* June 8, 1863.
56 Richmond *Daily Dispatch,* June 14, 15, 16, 1864.

57 McGuire, *Diary,* 309.
58 Atlanta *Intelligencer* (Macon), September 23, 1864.
59 Macon *Telegraph,* September 24, 1864.
60 Augusta *Chronicle and Sentinel,* July 21, 24, 27, 1864.
61 *Ibid.,* September 23, 1864, October 1, 1864.
62 *Ibid.,* October 28, 1864.
63 Yorkville *Enquirer,* March 16, 1865.
64 Charleston *Daily Courier,* Ferbuary 11, 1865, quoting the Columbia *Daily Guardian,* n. d.
65 Augusta *Chronicle and Sentinel,* February 28, 1865.
66 *Southern Banner* (Athens), April 20, 1864.
67 *Tri-Weekly South Carolinian* (Columbia), May 19, 1864.
68 Daniel Huger Smith, *et al.* (eds.), *Mason Smith Family Letters,* 82–83.
69 Holmes Diary.
70 Charleston *Daily Courier,* November 18, 1864, December 8, 1864.
71 *Tri-Weekly South Carolinian* (Columbia), October 19, 1864.
72 Oldham Memoirs.
73 Andrews, *Journal,* 196.
74 Mrs. Lenora Clayton to Mrs Howell Cobb, February 3, 1865, Cobb Papers, University of Georgia.
75 McGuire, *Diary,* 360.

Chapter XIV

1 Theodore Honour to Patrick Honour, July 18, 1862, Honour Papers. The Charleston *Courier,* February 28, 1863, reported that large numbers of the citizens who had left their homes the preceding year had returned and "broken circles are again united."
2 Theodore Honour to Mrs. Honour, April 30, 1863, May 1, 1863, August 21, 1863, August 28, October 24, November 25, December 19, 1863, Honour Papers.
3 Daniel Huger Smith, *et al.* (eds.), *Mason Smith Family Letters,* 150, 254.
4 J. G. M. Ramsey Autobiographical and Genealogical Notes, Ramsey Papers.
5 Richmond *Daily Examiner,* September 24, 1863. The writer of the letter was apparently a friend of the editor and the letter was addressed to him.
6 Charleston *Daily Mercury,* August 18, 1862, quoting the Vicksburg *Whig,* n. d.; Natchez *Daily Courier,* August 13, 1862.
7 *Official Records,* XXXI, Pt. 3, pp. 690–91.
8 *Ibid.,* XXXII, Pt. 3, p. 634.
9 Richmond *Daily Dispatch,* September 11, 1861.
10 Diary of William Pitt Ballenger.
11 Charleston *Daily Courier,* April 9, 1862.
12 Annie Anderson to Clifford Anderson, December 5, 1864, Clifford Anderson Papers, Southern Historical Collection, University of North Carolina.
13 *Daily South Carolinian* (Columbia), December 11, 1864, quoting the Augusta *Chronicle and Sentinel,* n. d.
14 *Arkansas State Gazette* (Little Rock), May 13, 1865.
15 Last Address of Governor Henry Watkins Allen, June 2, 1865, Moore Papers. The Clarksville *Standard,* July 15, 1865.
16 John F. Leigh to John Moore, April 25, 1865, June 13, 1865, Weeks Family Papers.
17 Meriwether Recollections.
18 Mitchell Book.
19 Clara D. MacLean, "Return of a Refugee," *Southern Historical Society Papers,* XIII (1885), 502–15.

20 Jorantha Semmes to General John A. Dix, August 2, 1865, Semmes Papers.
21 McGuire, *Diary,* 357–58.
22 Mordecai Diary.
23 McGuire, *Diary,* 358–60.
24 Katherine Polk Gale, "Recollections of Life in the Southern Confederacy," Gale-Polk Papers.
25 John Q. Anderson (ed.), *Brokenburn,* 362–70.
26 Grimball Diaries; Grimball Journal. See also Mrs. Grimball's postwar letters in the same collection.
27 Oldham, "Last Days of the Confederacy."
28 Andrews, *Journal,* 184, 198.
29 Mrs. Mary E. Davis to Isaac Murphey, March 10, 1865, Luther C. Gulley Collection, Arkansas History Commission, Little Rock.
30 J. G. M. Ramsey Autobiographical and Genealogical Notes, Ramsey Papers.
31 McDonald, *Diary,* 7–9.
32 Augusta *Chronicle and Sentinel,* January 9, 1865.

Bibliography

I

PRIMARY

A. MANUSCRIPTS

"A Camden Girl as a Refugee in Texas." Typescript in Manuscript Division, Arkansas History Commission.

Samuel Andrew Agnew Diary. Southern Historical Collection, University of North Carolina.

James Lusk Alcorn Papers. Southern Historical Collection, University of North Carolina.

Edward Porter Alexander Papers. Southern Historical Collection, University of North Carolina.

Clifford Anderson Papers. Southern Historical Collection, University of North Carolina.

Charles Wesley Andrews Papers. Manuscript Division, Duke University.

Anonymous Diary. Manuscript Division, Duke University.

Mrs. W. K. Bachman Papers. South Caroliniana Library, University of South Carolina.

Diary of James H. Baker. Eugene C. Barker Collection, University of Texas.

George Johnson Baldwin Papers. Southern Historical Collection, University of North Carolina.

Diary of William Pitt Ballenger. Typescript in Eugene C. Barker Collection, University of Texas.

Barrow Papers. Microfilm in Southern Historical Collection, University of North Carolina.

Benbury-Haywood Papers. Southern Historical Collection, University of North Carolina.

James Earl Bradley Papers. Department of Archives and Manuscripts, Louisiana State University.

Rosella Kenner Brent Recollections. Typescript in Department of Archives and Manuscripts, Louisiana State University.

Theodore Washington Brevard Papers. Southern Historical Collection, University of North Carolina.

Hulda A. (Fain) Briant Letters. Manuscript Division, Duke University.

Louis Amede Bringier Papers. Department of Archives and Manuscripts, Louisiana State University.

John G. Brodnax Papers. Manuscript Division, Duke University.

Annie Laurie Broidrick, "A Recollection of Thirty Years Ago." Southern Historical Collection, University of North Carolina.

Letters of Robert Franklin Bunting. Eugene C. Barker Collection, University of Texas.

Burwell Papers. Southern Historical Collection, University of North Carolina.

Thomas Butler and Family Papers. Department of Archives and Manuscripts, Louisiana State University.

George Cadman Papers. Southern Historical Collection, University of North Carolina.

William Ferguson Calcock Autobiography. Southern Historical Collection, University of North Carolina.

William Calder Papers. Southern Historical Collection, University of North Carolina.

Diary of Kate S. Carney. Southern Historical Collection, University of North Carolina.

John Cheesborough Papers. Southern Historical Collection, University of North Carolina.

John H. Chrisman Reminiscences. Eugene C. Barker Collection, University of Texas.

Clement Claiborne Clay Papers. Manuscript Division, Duke University.

Cobb Family Papers. Division of Special Collection, University of Georgia.

Elizabeth Collier Diary. Southern Historical Collection, University of North Carolina.

Laura B. Comer Diaries. Southern Historical Collection, University of North Carolina.

John Couper (and Family) Papers. Microfilm in Southern Historical Collection, University of North Carolina.

Charles William Dabney Papers. Southern Historical Collection, University of North Carolina.

Nathaniel Henry Rhodes Dawson Papers. Southern Historical Collection, University of North Carolina.

Louis M. DeSaussure Plantation Record. Southern Historical Collection, University of North Carolina.

Henry St. John Dixon Papers. Southern Historical Collection, University of North Carolina.

Donnell Papers. Southern Historical Collection, University of North Carolina.

Duke-Morgan Papers. Southern Historical Collection, University of North Carolina.

Eggleston-Roach Papers. Department of Archives and Manuscripts, Louisiana State University.

Grace B. Elmore Diary. Southern Historical Collection, University of North Carolina.

Clara Eno Collection. Manuscript Division, Arkansas History Commission.

Sarah Johnston (Mrs. Bedford Mitchell) Estes Diary. Microfilm in John Johnston Papers, Southern Historical Collection, University of North Carolina.

Gale-Polk Papers. Southern Historical Collection, University of North Carolina.

Charles E. A. Gayarre Papers. Grace King Collection, Department of Archives and Manuscripts, Louisiana State University.

Jeremy F. Gilmer Papers. Southern Historical Collection, University of North Carolina.

P. D. Gold Papers. Southern Historical Collection, University of North Carolina.

Josiah Gorgas Journal, 1857–1864. Microfilm in Southern Historical Collection, University of North Carolina.

Josiah Gorgas Journal, 1864–1878. Southern Historical Collection, University of North Carolina.

John Berkeley Grimball Diaries. Southern Historical Collection, University of North Carolina.

Meta Morris Grimball Journal. Southern Historical Collection, University of North Carolina.

Virginius W. Groner Collection. Southern Historical Collection, University of North Carolina.

Edward Owings Guerrant Papers. Southern Historical Collection, University of North Carolina.

Luther C. Gulley Collection. Manuscript Division, Arkansas History Commission.

Hairston-Wilson Papers. Southern Historical Collection, University of North Carolina.

Letters of Mrs. Jestin Collins Hampton. Typescript in Manuscript Division, University of Texas.

Letters of Thomas B. Hampton. Typescript in Manuscript Division, University of Texas.

Sidney Harding Diaries. Department of Archives and Manuscripts, Louisiana State University.

Leeland Hathaway Recollections. Microfilm in Southern Historical Collection, University of North Carolina.

Emma E. Holmes Diary. Typescript in Southern Historical Collection, University of North Carolina.

Theophilus Hunter Holmes Papers. Manuscript Division, Duke University.

Theodore A. Honour Papers. South Caroliniana Library, University of South Carolina.

Fanny Page Hume Diary. Southern Historical Collection, University of North Carolina.

Charles Woodward Hutson Reminiscences. Southern Historical Collection, University of North Carolina.

John Kimberly Papers. Southern Historical Collection, University of North Carolina.

Grace King Papers. Microfilm in Southern Historical Collection, University of North Carolina.

Diary of William King. Southern Historical Collection, University of North Carolina.

William Woodson King Papers. Grace King Collection, Department of Archives and Manuscripts, Louisiana State University.

Bishop Henry C. Lay Papers. Southern Historical Collection, University of North Carolina.

Journal of Emma Frances LeConte. Southern Historical Collection, University of North Carolina.

Joseph LeConte Journal of Three Months Personal Experience During the Last Days of the Confederacy. South Caroliniana Library, University of South Carolina.

Edward M. L'Engle Papers. Southern Historical Collection, University of North Carolina.

Clara Minor Lynn Papers. Manuscript Division, Confederate Museum, Richmond.

William Whann Mackall Papers. Southern Historical Collection, University of North Carolina.

General Lafayette McLaws Papers. Southern Historical Collection, University of North Carolina.

Stephen R. Mallory Papers. Microfilm in Southern Historical Collection, University of North Carolina.

Betty Herndon Maury Diary. Manuscript Division, Library of Congress.

Meade-Ruffin Papers. Southern Historical Collection, University of North Carolina.

Elizabeth Avery Meriwether Recollections. Microfilm in Southern Historical Collection, University of North Carolina.

Mary Elizabeth Mitchell Book. Southern Historical Collection, University of North Carolina.

Harriet Ellen Moore Diary. Microfilm in Southern Historical Collection, University of North Carolina.

Thomas O. Moore Papers. Department of Archives and Manuscripts, Louisiana State University.

Emma Mordecai Diary. Southern Historical Collection, University of North Carolina.

Matilda Lamb Morton, "Memories of the War Between the States." Southern Historical Collection, University of North Carolina.

Nicholson Papers. Southern Historical Collection, University of North Carolina.

Williamson Simpson Oldham, "Last Days of the Confederacy." Typescript in Eugene C. Barker Collection, University of Texas.

Williamson Simpson Oldham Memoirs. Typescript in Eugene C. Barker Collection, University of Texas.

John Gibson Parkhurst Papers. Manuscript Division, Duke University.

Lindsay Patterson Papers. Southern Historical Collection, University of North Carolina.

Samuel Finley Patterson Papers. Manuscript Division, Duke University.

Phoebe Yates Pember Papers. Southern Historical Collection, University of North Carolina.

William Dorsey Pender Papers. Southern Historical Collection, University of North Carolina.

Pettigrew Family Papers. Southern Historical Collection, University of North Carolina.

Phillips-Myers Papers. Southern Historical Collection, University of North Carolina.

Leonidas Polk Papers. Microfilm in Southern Historical Collection, University of North Carolina.

Richard Pugh Papers. Department of Archives and Manuscripts, Louisiana State University.

Rabb Family Papers. Photostats in Manuscript Division, University of Texas.

James Gettys McGready Ramsey Papers. Southern Historical Collection, University of North Carolina.

Randall Letters. Southern Historical Collection, University of North Carolina.

Henry Hunter Raymond Papers. South Caroliniana Library, University of South Carolina.

Marie Louise DuBrutz Reston Memoirs. Southern Historical Collection, University of North Carolina.

Roach-Eggleston Papers. Southern Historical Collection, University of North Carolina.

Edmund Ruffin Papers. Southern Historical Collection, University of North Carolina.

Ellen Buchanan Screven Reminiscences. Division of Special Collection, University of Georgia.

Benedict Joseph Semmes Papers. Southern Historical Collection, University of North Carolina.

Louise C. Sheppard Recollections. Microfilm in Southern Historical Collection, University of North Carolina.

Mrs. H. H. Simons, "The Burning of Columbia." Mrs. H. H. Simons Papers, South Caroliniana Library, University of South Carolina.

Diary of Lizzie Hatcher Simons. Typescript in Eugene C. Barker Collection, University of Texas.

Jane Sivley Letters. Southern Historical Collection, University of North Carolina.

William Slade Papers. Manuscript Division, Duke University.

Edmund Kirby Smith Papers. Southern Historical Collection, University of North Carolina.

Joseph Belknap Smith Papers. Manuscript Division, Duke University.

William Patterson Smith Papers. Manuscript Division, Duke University.

Augustine Thomas Smythe Letters. Typescript in Southern Historical Collection, University of North Carolina.

Clara E. Soloman Diary. Department of Archives and Manuscripts, Louisiana State University

Cornelia Phillips Spencer Letters. Southern Historical Collection, University of North Carolina.

Sally Elmore Taylor. Southern Historical Collection, University of North Carolina.

T. U. Taylor, "Swamp Fox of the Sulphur or the Life and Times of Cullen Montgomery Baker." Manuscript Division, University of Texas.

Anna Holmes Trenholm Diary. Typescript in Southern Historical Collection, University of North Carolina.

Sarah L. Wadley Diary. Southern Historical Collection, University of North Carolina.

Harriet Warren's Reminiscences. In the possession of Mary Vardell Fraser Harrell, Spartanburg, South Carolina.

Diary of Frances Woolfolk Wallace. Southern Historical Collection, University of North Carolina.

David Weeks Family Papers. Weeks Hall Memorial Collection, Department of Archives and Manuscripts, Louisiana State University.

Artha Brailaford Wescoat Diary. Manuscript Division, Duke University.

Diary of Captain Joseph Julius Westcoat. Typescript in Manuscript Division, Duke University

William J. Whatley Correspondence. Eugene C. Barker Collection, University of Texas.

Louis Trezevant Wigfall Papers. Microfilm in Eugene C. Barker Collection, University of Texas.

Elizabeth S. Wiggins Letters. Manuscript Division, Duke University.

William E. Woodruff Papers. Manuscript Division, Arkansas Historical Commission.

Benjamin C. Yancey Papers. Southern Historical Collection, University of North Carolina.

B. Published diaries, letters, memoirs, reminiscences

Anderson, C. W., "After the Fall of Fort Donelson," *Confederate Veteran,* IV (1896).

Anderson, John Q. (ed.), *Brokenburn: The Journal of Kate Stone, 1861–1868.* Baton Rouge: Louisiana State University Press, 1955.

Andrews, Eliza Frances, *The War-Time Journal of a Georgia Girl.* New York: D. Appleton and Company, 1908.

Avary, Myrta Lockett, *Dixie After the War.* New York: Doubleday, Page and Company, 1906.

Avary, Myrta Lockett (ed.), *A Virginia Girl in the Civil War.* New York: D. Appleton and Company, 1903.

Averill, J. H., "The Evacuation of Richmond," *Southern Historical Society Papers,* XXV (1897).

Beers, Mrs. Fannie A., *Memories: A Record of Personal Experience and Adventure During the Four Years of War.* Philadelphia: J. B. Lippincott Company, 1888.

Borcke, Johann Heinrick Heros von, *Memoirs of the Confederate War for Independence.* 2 vols. New York: Peter Smith, 1938.

Bryce, Mrs. Campbell, *The Personal Experiences of Mrs. Campbell Bryce During the Burning of Columbia, South Carolina by General W. T. Sherman's Army, February 17, 1865.* Philadelphia: J. B. Lippincott Company, 1899.

Burge, Dolly Lunt, *A Woman's Wartime Journal: An Account of the Passage Over A Georgia Plantation of Sherman's Army on the March to the Sea.* New York: The Century Company, 1918

Cable, George Washington (ed.), "A Woman's Diary of the Siege of Vicksburg," *The Century Illustrated Monthly Magazine,* XXX (1885).

Chadwick, Mrs. W. D., "Civil War Days in Huntsville, Alabama," Huntsville *Times* (Special Supplement) n.d., Southern Historical Collection, University of North Carolina.

Chesnut, Mary Boykin, *Diary From Dixie.* Boston: Houghton Mifflin Company, 1950.

Childs, Arney Robinson (ed.), *The Private Journal of Henry William Ravenel.* Columbia: University of South Carolina Press, 1947.

Clay-Clopton, Mrs. Virginia, *A Belle of the Fifties.* New York: Doubleday, Page and Company, 1905.

Cockrell, Monroe F. (ed.), *Civil War Letters of Colonel George W. Guess.* Chicago: Privately printed, 1946.

Conrad, August, *The Destruction of Columbia, South Carolina.* Roanoke: The Stone Printing and Manufacturing Company, 1902.

Davis, Varina Howell (Mrs. Jefferson), *Jefferson Davis: A Memoir.* 2 vols. New York: Bedford Company, 1905.

Dawson, Sarah Morgan, *A Confederate Girl's Diary,* ed. James I. Robertson, Jr. Bloomington: Indiana University Press, 1960.

Easterby, James Harold (ed.), *The South Carolina Rice Plantation as Revealed in the Papers of Robert F. W. Allston.* Chicago: University of Chicago Press, 1945.

Fearn, Frances, *Diary of a Refugee.* New York: Moffat, Yard and Company, 1910.

Fontaine, Mrs. Felix G. de, "Old Confederacy Days," *Confederate Veteran,* IV (1896).

Gay, Mary A. H., *Life in Dixie During the War.* Atlanta: The Foote and Davies Company, 1894.

Goodnight, Mrs. T. H., "War Recollections," *The Virginia Magazine of History and Biography,* XLIII (1935).

Goolrick, Mrs. Frances Bernard, "Suffering in Fredericksburg," *Southern Historical Society Papers,* XXXVII (1909).

Graydon, Mrs. Sterling (ed.), "Journal of Artha Brailaford Wescoat, 1863, 1864," *The South Carolina Historical Magazine,* LV (1954).

Hague, Parthenia Antoinette, *A Blockaded Family: Life in Southern Alabama During the Civil War.* Boston: Houghton Mifflin Company, 1888.

Harrison, Constance Cary (Mrs. Burton), *Recollections Grave and Gay.* New York: Charles Scribner's Sons, 1911.

Harrison, Constance Cary (Mrs. Burton), "A Virginia Girl in the First Year of the War," *The Century Illustrated Magazine,* XXX (1885).

Hart, William Octave, "A Boy's Recollection of the War," *Publications of the Mississippi Historical Society*, XII (1912).

Harwell, Richard Barksdale (ed.), *Kate: The Journal of a Confederate Nurse*. Baton Rouge: Louisiana State University Press, 1959.

Holmes, Charlotte R. (ed.), *The Burckmyer Letters, March 1863—June 1865*. Columbia: The State Company, 1926.

Hopley, Catherine Cooper, *Life in the South: from the Commencement of the War.* . . . 2 vols. London: Chapman and Hall, 1863.

Jackson, Mary Anna (Mrs. Thomas Jonathan), *Memoirs of Stonewall Jackson*. Louisville: The Prentiss Press, 1895.

Jervey, Susan R., and Ravenel, Charlotte St. John, *Two Diaries From Middle St. John's, Berkeley, South Carolina*. Charleston: St. John's Hunting Club, 1921.

Jones, John Beauchamp, *A Rebel War-Clerk's Diary*. 2 vols. New York: Old Hickory Bookshop, 1935.

Jones, Katharine M. (ed.), *Heroines in Dixie*. Indianapolis: The Bobbs-Merrill Company, 1955.

King, Grace, *Memories of a Southern Woman of Letters*. New York: The Macmillan Company, 1932.

Lord, Walter (ed.), *The Fremantle Diary: Being the Journal of Lieutenant Colonel James Arthur Lyon Fremantle, Coldstream Guards, on his Three Months in the Southern States*. Boston: Little, Brown and Company, 1954.

Loughborough, Mary Webster, *My Cave Life In Vicksburg*. New York: D. Appleton and Company, 1864.

MacLean, Mrs. Clara Dargan, "Return of a Refugee," *Southern Historical Society Papers*, XIII (1885).

McDonald, Cornelia Peake, *A Diary With Reminiscences of the War and Refugee Life in the Shenandoah Valley*. Nashville: Cullom and Ghertner, 1934.

McGuire, Judith Brockenbrough, *Diary of a Southern Refugee During the War*. New York: E. J. Hale and Son, 1867.

Milling, Chapman, "Ilium in Flames," *Confederate Veteran*, XXXVI (1928)

Morrill, Lily Logan (ed.), *My Confederate Girlhood: The Memoirs of Kate Virginia Cox Logan*. Richmond: Garrett and Massie, 1932.

Pearson, Elizabeth Ware (ed.), *Letters From Port Royal Written at the Time of the Civil War*. Boston: W. B. Clark Company, 1906.

Pember, Phoebe Yates, *A Southern Woman's Story*. Jackson: McCowat-Mercer Press, 1959.

Pringle, Elizabeth Waties Allston, *Chronicles of Chicora Wood*. New York: Charles Scribner's Sons, 1922.

Pryor, Mrs. Roger Atkinson, *My Day: Reminiscences of a Long Life*. New York: The Macmillan Company, 1908.

Pryor, Mrs. Roger Atkinson, *Reminiscences of Peace and War*. New York: The Macmillan Company, 1904.

Putnam, Sallie A., *Richmond During the War: Four Years of Personal Observations*. New York: G. W. Carlton and Company, 1867.

Ross, Fitzgerald, *A Visit to the Cities and Camps of the Confederate States*. Edinburgh: William Blackwood and Sons, 1865.

Rowland, Kate Mason, and Croxall, Mrs. Morris (eds.), *The Journal of Julia LeGrand, New Orleans, 1862–63.* Richmond: Everett Waddey Company, 1911.

Saint-Amand, *A Balcony in Charleston.* Richmond: Garrett and Massie, 1941.

Sherman, William Tecumseh, *Memoirs of General William T. Sherman.* 2 vols. Bloomington: Indiana University Press, 1957.

Smedes, Susan Dabney, *Memorials of a Southern Planter.* Baltimore: Cushings and Bailey, 1887.

Smith, Charles H., *Bill Arp, So Called: A Side Show of the Southern Side of the War.* New York: Metropolitan Record Office, 1866.

Smith, Daniel E. Huger, *et al.* (eds.), *Mason Smith Family Letters.* Columbia: University of South Carolina Press, 1950.

Sosnowski, Sophia, "The Burning of Columbia: A Thrilling, a Faithful and Graphic Description of a National Crime," *The Georgia Historical Quarterly*, VIII (1924).

Taylor, Mrs. Thomas, *et al.*, *South Carolina Women in the Confederacy.* 2 vols. Columbia: The State Company, 1903, 1907.

Wright, Mrs. D. Giraud, *A Southern Girl in '61: The War-Time Memories of a Confederate Senator's Daughter.* New York: Doubleday, Page and Company, 1905.

C. Collected Sources, Journals, and Public Documents

1. *General*

Freeman, Douglas Southall (ed.), *A Calendar of Confederate State Papers.* Richmond: The Confederate Museum, 1908.

Matthews, James M. (ed.), *The Statutes at Large of the Confederate States of America.* Richmond: R. M. Smith, Printer to Congress, 1862–64.

Moore, Frank (ed.), *The Rebellion Record: A Diary of American Events with Documents, Narratives, Illustrations, Incidents, Poetry, Etc.* 11 vols. New York: G. P. Putnam, 1862–68.

Ramsdell, Charles William (ed.), *Laws and Joint Resolutions of the Last Session of Confederate Congress Together with Secret Acts of Previous Congress.* Durham: Duke University Press, 1941.

Richardson, James Daniel (ed.), *A Compilation of the Messages and Papers of the Confederacy.* 2 vols. Nashville: United States Publishing Company, 1905.

Journal of the Congress of the Confederate States, 1861–1865. 7 vols. Washington: Government Printing Office, 1904–1905.

The War of Rebellion: A Compilation of the Official Records of the Union and Confederate Armies. 130 vols. Washington: Government Printing Office, 1880–1902.

2. *State*

Acts of the General Assembly of Alabama.
Acts Passed by the General Assembly of Arkansas.

Acts and Resolutions Adopted by the General Assembly of Florida.
Acts of the General Assembly of the State of Georgia.
Acts of the State of Louisiana.
Acts of the State of Mississippi.
Ordinances of the Convention of the State of North Carolina.
Public Laws of the State of North Carolina.
Private Laws of the State of North Carolina.
Acts of the General Assembly of the State of South Carolina.
Public Acts of the General Assembly of the State of Tennessee.
General Laws of the State of Texas.
Acts of the General Assembly of the State of Virginia.
Official Report Relative to the Conduct of Federal Troops in Western Louisiana, During the Invasions of 1863 and 1864. Shreveport: News Printing Establishment, 1865.

D. NEWSPAPERS

Arkansas Patriot, Little Rock.
Arkansas State Gazette, Little Rock.
Arkansas True Democrat, Little Rock.
Athens *Post,* Athens, Tennessee.
Atlanta *Intelligencer,* Atlanta and Macon.
Banner of Peace, Nashville.
Belleville *Countryman,* Belleville, Texas.
Brownlow's Weekly Whig, Knoxville.
Camden *Confederate,* Camden, South Carolina.
Charleston *Daily Courier,* Charleston.
Charleston *Mercury,* Charleston.
Chattanooga *Daily Rebel,* Chattanooga, Atlanta.
Columbia *Phoenix,* Columbia.
Confederate Union, Milledgeville.
Daily Bulletin, Charlotte.
Daily Chronicle and Sentinel, Augusta.
Daily Express, Petersburg.
Daily Journal, Wilmington.
Daily Register, Knoxville, Atlanta.
Daily Republican, Lynchburg.
Daily South Carolinian, Columbia.
Daily Southern Chronicle, Knoxville.
Daily Southern Crisis, Jackson, Mississippi.
Daily Southern Guardian, Columbia.
Daily Mississippian, Jackson, Meridian, Selma.
Daily Picayune, New Orleans.
Daily True Delta, New Orleans.
Dallas *Weekly Herald,* Dallas.
Des Arc *Semi-Weekly Citizen,* Des Arc, Arkansas.
Eastern Clarion, Paulding, Mississippi.
Edgefield *Advertiser,* Edgefield, South Carolina.
Fayetteville *Observer,* Fayetteville, North Carolina.

Floridian and Journal, Tallahassee.
Fort Smith *New Era*, Fort Smith, Arkansas.
Galveston *Tri-Weekly News*, Houston.
Greensborough *Patriot*, Greensboro, North Carolina.
Gulf City Home Journal, Mobile.
Hillsborough *Recorder*, Hillsboro, North Carolina.
Houston *Daily Telegraph*, Houston.
Houston *Tri-Weekly Telegraph*, Houston.
Jackson *Daily News*, Jackson, Mississippi.
Lancaster *Ledger*, Lancaster, South Carolina.
Lynchburg *Daily Virginian*, Lynchburg.
Macon *Daily Telegraph*, Macon, Georgia.
Macon *Tri-Weekly Telegraph*, Macon, Georgia.
Memphis *Appeal*, Memphis, Atlanta.
Memphis *Avalanche*, Memphis.
Memphis *Daily Argus*, Memphis.
Mobile *Daily Advertiser and Register*, Mobile.
Mobile *Daily Register*, Mobile.
Mobile *Evening News*, Mobile.
Montgomery *Daily Advertiser*, Montgomery.
Natchez *Courier*, Natchez.
New Orleans *Bee*, New Orleans.
New Orleans *Daily Crescent*, New Orleans.
New York *Herald*, New York.
North Carolina Semi-Weekly Standard, Raleigh.
North Carolina Weekly Standard, Raleigh.
Opelousas *Courier*, Opelousas, Louisiana.
Republican Banner, Nashville.
Richmond *Daily Dispatch*, Richmond.
Richmond *Daily Enquirer*, Richmond.
Richmond *Daily Examiner*, Richmond.
Richmond *Sentinel*, Richmond.
Richmond *Whig*, Richmond.
Rockingham Register and Advertiser, Harrisonburg, Virginia.
Savannah *Daily Republican*, Savannah.
Southern Banner, Athens, Georgia.
Southern Confederacy, Atlanta, Macon.
Southern Presbyterian, Columbia, Augusta.
Southwestern, Shreveport.
Standard, Clarksville, Texas.
Sumter Republican, Americus, Georgia.
Texas State Gazette, Austin.
Tri-Weekly Watchman, Sumter, South Carolina.
Tri-Weekly Carolinian, Columbia.
Tri-Weekly Gazette, Austin.
Tyler Reporter, Tyler.
Vicksburg *Daily Whig*, Vicksburg.
Weekly Enquirer, Columbus, Georgia.
Weekly Mississippian, Jackson.

Weekly Reporter, Lynchburg.
Western Democrat, Charlotte.
Washington *Telegraph*, Washington, Arkansas.
Winnsboro *Daily News*, Winnsboro, South Carolina.
Yorkville *Enquirer*, York, South Carolina.

E. Contemporary magazines and journals

Harper's Weekly, New York.
Magnolia Weekly, Richmond.
Southern Illustrated News, Richmond.
The Mercury, Raleigh.

II

SECONDARY

Andrews, Matthew Page (ed.), *The Women of the South in War Times*. Baltimore: The Norman Remington Company, 1920.
Bentley, George R., *A History of the Freedmen's Bureau*. Philadelphia: University of Pennsylvania, 1955.
Bettersworth, John K., *Confederate Mississippi: The People and Policies of a Cotton State in Wartime*. Baton Rouge: Louisiana State University Press, 1943.
Bill, Alfred Hoyt, *The Beleaguered City: Richmond 1861–1865*. New York: Alfred A. Knopf, 1946.
Bragg, Jefferson Davis, *Louisiana in the Confederacy*. Baton Rouge: Louisiana State Univerity Press, 1941.
Brantley, Rabun Lee, *Georgia Journalism of the Civil War Period*. Nashville: George Peabody College for Teachers, 1929.
Brockett, Louis Pierpont, and Vaughan, Mary, *Women's Work in the Civil War: A Record of Heroism, Patriotism and Patience*. Philadelphia: Zeigler, McCurdy and Company, 1867.
Bruce, Philip Alexander, *History of the University of Virginia*. 3 vols. New York: The MacMillan Company, 1921.
Bryan, Thomas Conn, *Confederate Georgia*. Athens: University of Georgia Press, 1953.
Coulter, E. Merton, *College Life in the Old South*. New York: The Macmillan Company, 1928.
Cunningham, Horace H., *Doctors in Gray*. Baton Rouge: Louisiana State University Press, 1958.
Coulter, E. Merton, *The Confederate States of America, 1861–1865*. Baton Rouge: Louisiana State University Press, 1950.
Dawson, Francis Warrington, *Our Women in the War*. Charleston: Walker, Evans and Cogwell, 1887.
DeLeon, Thomas Cooper, *Belles, Beaux and Brains of the 60's*. New York: G. W. Dillingham Company, 1909.
DeLeon, Thomas Cooper, *Four Years in Rebel Capitals: An Inside View of Life in the Southern Confederacy, From Birth to Death: From*

Original Notes, Collected in the Years 1861–1865. Mobile: Gossip Printing Company, 1892.

Dodge, David (pseud. of O. W. Blacknall), "The Cave-Dwellers of the Confederacy," *Atlantic Monthly*, LXVIII (1891).

Donald, David, "The Confederate as a Fighting Man," *The Journal of Southern History*, XXV (1959).

Donald, David (ed.), *Why the North Won the Civil War.* Baton Rouge: Louisiana State University Press, 1960.

Easterby, James Harold, *A History of the College of Charleston.* New York: Charles Scribner's Sons, 1935.

Fisher, Clyde O., "The Relief of Soldiers' Families in North Carolina during the Civil War," *South Atlantic Quarterly*, XVI (1917).

Fletcher, John Gould, *Arkansas.* Chapel Hill: University of North Carolina, 1947.

Freeman, Douglas Southall, *R. E. Lee: A Biography.* 4 vols. New York: Charles Scribner's Sons, 1934.

Govan, Gilbert E. and Livingood, James W., *The Chattanooga Country, 1504–1951.* New York: Dutton Company, 1952.

Hanna, Alfred Jackson, *Flight Into Oblivion.* Richmond: Johnson Publishing Company, 1938.

Hoehling, A. A., *Last Train From Atlanta.* New York: Thomas Yoseloff, 1958.

Hollis, Daniel Walker, *University of South Carolina.* 2 vols. Columbia: University of South Carolina Press, 1951.

Hull, Augustus Longstreet, *Annals of Athens, Georgia, 1801–1901.* Athens: Banner Office, 1906.

Massey, Mary Elizabeth, *Ersatz in the Confederacy.* Columbia: University of South Carolina Press, 1952.

Nuermberger, Ruth Ketring, *The Clays of Alabama: A Planter-Lawyer-Politician Family.* Lexington: University of Kentucky Press, 1958.

Parks, Joseph Howard, *General Edmund Kirby Smith, C. S. A.* Baton Rouge: Louisiana State University Press, 1954.

Patrick, Rembert W., *The Fall of Richmond.* Baton Rouge: Louisiana State University Press, 1960.

Ramsdell, Charles William, *Behind the Lines in the Southern Confederacy.* Baton Rouge, Louisiana State University Press, 1944.

Sellers, Charles Grier (ed.), *The Southerner as American.* Chapel Hill: University of North Carolina Press, 1960.

Simkins, Francis Butler and Patton, James Welch, *The Women of the Confederacy.* Richmond: Garrett and Massie, 1936.

Starr, Louis M., *Bohemian Brigade: Civil War Newsmen in Action.* New York: Alfred A. Knopf, 1954.

Tate, Allen, *Stonewall Jackson, the Good Soldier.* New York: Minton, Balch and Company, 1928.

Trowbridge, John Townsend, *A Picture of the Desolated States and the Work of Restoration.* Hartford: L. Stebbins, 1868.

Vandiver, Frank E., *Mighty Stonewall.* New York: McGraw-Hill Book Company, 1957.

Vickery, Dorothy Scovil, *Hollins College, 1842–1942.* Hollins College: 1942.

Walker, Peter F., *Vicksburg: A People at War, 1860–1865.* Chapel Hill: University of North Carolina Press, 1960.

Weeks, Stephen Beauregard, "The University of North Carolina in the Civil War," *Southern Historical Society Papers,* XXIV (1896).

White, Joseph F. "Social Conditions in the South During the War Between the States," *Confederate Veteran,* XXX (1922).

Wiley, Bell Irvin, *Southern Negroes, 1861–1865.* New York: Rhinehart and Company, 1953.

Wiley, Bell Irvin, *The Plain People of the Confederacy.* Baton Rouge: Louisiana State University Press, 1944.

Zornow, William F., "Aid for the Indigent Families of Soldiers in Virginia, 1861–1865," *Virginia Magazine of History and Biography,* LXIX (1958).

Zornow, William F., "State Aid for Indigent Soldiers and their Families in Florida, 1861–1865," *Florida Historical Quarterly,* XXXIV (1956).

Zornow, William F., "State Aid for the Indigent Soldiers and their Families in Louisiana, 1861–1865," *Louisiana Historical Quarterly,* XXXIX (1956).

Index

DATE DUE

NOV 30 '76			
AP 3 '78			
DEC 5 '83			
DE 1 '88			